westerns

Previously published in the AFI Film Readers Series
edited by Charles Wolfe and Edward Branigan

westerns

films

through

history

edited by
janet walker

routledge

new york and london

Published in 2001 by
Routledge
29 West 35th Street
New York, NY 10001

Published in Great Britain by
Routledge
11 New Fetter Lane
London EC4P 4EE

Routledge is an imprint of the Taylor & Francis Group.

Library of Congress Cataloging-in-Publication Data

Westerns: films through history / Janet Walker, editor.
   p.   cm.
  Includes bibliographical references and index.
  ISBN 0–415–92423–5 — 0–415–92424–3 (pbk.)
    1. Western films—United States—History and criticism.
  I. Walker, Janet, 1955–   II. Series.

PN1995.9.W4 W44 2001
791.43'6278—dc21   00–051708

10 9 8 7 6 5 4 3 2 1

Printed in the United States of America on acid-free paper.

contents

part three. film history: widening horizons

part four. history through narrative

acknowledgments

An AFI Film Reader on the western has been a recurring dream of the wonderful editors of this series, Edward Branigan and Charles Wolfe, and I am honored to have been invited to imagine a way of realizing it. I could not have done so without the generous help of many people. Thanks are due to Chuck and Edward in their series editor hats and as brilliant commentators on my own contributions to the book. Their knowledge of the western and western history and their willingness to share it is boundless. Of course, the book wouldn't exist at all without the contributors, and I owe them a great debt for all the solitary and collaborative work it takes to make a volume. Special thanks are due to K. Kalinak whose intellectual acuity and generosity were ever evident during this process, who edited the editor, and whose longstanding friendship is a source of happiness.

I can't help but take a historical view of acknowledgments, which means mentioning the inspiration of Janey (*The Western Films of John Ford*) Place, my first film teacher, who was very influential indeed. Thanks also to my colleague Anna Brusutti, whose lectures to beginning film students I think of whenever I see Charles Bronson's eyes in close-up; I appreciate her many insights into the western and the extended loan of her copy of *Spaghetti Westerns*. I would also like to thank Robert Burgoyne for encouragement and support, and for the energizing, progressive conversation about history, heritage, and *Thunderheart* that took place from Greenfield Village, Michigan, to Santa Barbara to Chicago. For able research assistance I would like to thank the highly competent film cognoscenti, Lauren Edwards and Jennifer Baumgartner. Jennifer continued to assist me even after graduating and becoming a professional archivist, and I am grateful for her skill, her generosity, and the great cover still she found. For editorial assistance I thank Cynthia McCreery for her way with texts, fictional and otherwise, and Juan Monroy for his digital dexterity. I am also grateful to the National Endowment for the Humanities for a summer stipend that aided the writing of my own contribution, and to Constance Penley, chair of Film Studies at the University of California, Santa Barbara, who enabled me to arrange my teaching schedule to accommodate the work on this volume. Thanks are due to Bill Germano at Routledge for his ethusiasm and faith that the volume would appear, to the hard-working and efficient Damian Treffs, and to wonderful production editor Julie Ho.

A student in a film history course I conducted traveled to the UCLA Film and Television Archives to view a print of the early sound western *In Old Arizona*; listening carefully to the now scratchy soundtrack, the student was stunned to hear a familiar musical theme, a tune his grandfather had whistled for as long as he could remember. I would like to thank that former student, now turned film editor, Aram Nigoghossian, for his perceptions about how the past returns in westerns. Also I would like to thank the students of "The Western: 'Cowboys' and 'Indians,'" for joining the expedition into territory that was for some familiar but for others unfamiliar, either because movie westerns at the end of the century are fewer and farther between or because I insisted that one could love westerns and still approach them from a feminist and antiracist perspective. I am afraid I might forget one of you if I try to name you, but our conversations and your papers remain in my memory; thank you all for what you taught me. By name I would like to thank the film studies graduates who served as readers for the course and contributed their lively opinions and their judicious comments: Jamie Gluck, Lisa Brende, and, once again, Cynthia McCreery.

Finally, thanks are due to Steve Nelson, who brought *Signs and Meaning* and *Horizons West* to our marriage, and who is always willing to rent another western when nothing else appeals; and to Ariel Nelson, who encouraged my tendency to see westerns historically as well as mythologically, saying "you're right, Mom, if they were just myths they'd have gods and imaginary creatures and all that." Thank you both for constancy and joy.

introduction

westerns through history

janet walker

The insight that "the western is history" is everywhere and nowhere. In "The Evolution of the Western" (1955), André Bazin declared that "the western is rooted in the history of the American nation."[1] Jim Kitses was even bolder in 1969, and it is from him that I borrow the untamed metaphor of my first sentence,[2] but I could just as well have borrowed it from one of Richard Slotkin's chapter headings in *Gunfighter Nation* (1992), "The Western is American History."[3] Absent from these latter two examples is Bazin's notion of the western's organic rootedness. The western does not "spring from," nor "grow out of" history. No sense of boundaries nor of separate entities is couched. The western *is* history.

three paths in a conceptual topography

Discussions of the western, from any perspective, generally begin with the acknowledgment that it is a historical genre by virtue of its constituent films being set in the past, and in particular, overwhelmingly, between the end of the Civil War and the "closing of the frontier" in 1890.[4] And sources that develop discussions of the western *as historical* tend to pursue its historicity down one of several paths. First, it is often emphasized that the industrial production of motion picture westerns dates back far enough to have a history that dovetailed with that of frontier settlement. In other words, early westerns may be seen to have a discernible documentary quality, a certain authenticity springing from their ability to use still extant western settings and to employ genuine westerners as actors, directors, writers, and consultants. Richard Schickel and Thomas Schatz refer to this sense of actuality in their descriptions of early westerns. Schickel writes:

> In those pre-metropolitan days [Los Angeles] was, moreover, in spirit a real western town, the last railhead on the Santa Fe line. Ranching was still one of California's major industries, and Los Angeles was always full of genuine cowboys who had driven their herds to market there or had simply come to town to spend their pay. Raoul Walsh, a director who had been a cowhand in his youth, would recall that one of his first movie jobs was rounding up stray cowboys after the saloons closed, helping them on their horses and, before dawn, leading them across the hills to Western locations in the San Fernando Valley.[5]

In Schatz's terms:

> As cultural and historical documents, the earlier silent Westerns differ from the later Westerns. In fact these earlier films have a unique and somewhat paradoxical position: Although they were made on the virtual threshold of the Modern Age, they also came at a time when westward expansion was winding down [but was still going on]. . . . (In fact, *The Great Train Robbery* related events that had occurred only a few years previously and as such was something of a turn-of-the-century gangster film.) But eventually, the cumulative effects of Western storytelling in the face of contemporary civilization's steady encroachment served to subordinate the genre's *historical function* to its mythical one.[6]

A second path in the "western *is* history" topography leads out from the perception that the western is not historical by virtue of the period in which it is set (because, as everyone knows, westerns have a tendency to be inauthentic with regard to period and person), but by virtue of the period in which a given film was produced. *The Searchers* is, as Brian Henderson and Peter Lehman have argued, as much about America in 1956 as it is about Texas in 1868: "The conventions of the western allowed [director John] Ford to displace present-day racial tensions into the past and onto another race."[7] Or, recall Robert Sklar's contribution to the anthology *American History/American Film* in which he discusses the Howard Hawks western *Red River*. The film, Sklar wrote, "is not only about capitalism; its form and its destiny were also *the products of* capitalism, specifically of the changing economic structure of the Hollywood film industry in the postwar years."[8] Stanley Corkin follows suit in his article on postwar westerns (*Red River* and *My Darling Clementine*) and the Cold War, published in what is, as I write this, the most recent issue of *Cinema Journal*.[9] Probably the most complex treatment of this avowedly redoubled western historicity is that of Richard Slotkin. The full title of the aforementioned chapter is "The Western is History, 1939–1941," for there Slotkin makes the case that westerns of those years are very much engaged with contemporaneous sociopolitical currents, presented with reference to a mythic past wherein the more current dilemmas are seen to originate. Films of the turn of the decade were a response to "a widely felt need for a renewal of that sense of progressive and patriotic optimism."[10]

Third, there has been intense interest in the veracity of a given western's rendering of historical personages and events (in the "biopic" and the "event pic") and also of western settings (in the fictional film set against a western backdrop). In fact, such comparative studies of films and their historical contexts make up what is likely the most prolific and still growing area of comment and publication on the film western.[11] But this is not to say that all writers employ the same theoretical framework, be it implicit or explicit, for conceptualizing the film/reality relationship. A great many authors are satisfied merely to disabuse the public of film-induced misimpressions that what they see on the screen corresponds directly to what really happened. For example, Buck Rainey's half-page introduction to his 1998 publication of *Western Gunslingers in Fact and on Film* indicates that "[t]here are still many folks who honestly believe that Jesse James was a modern day Robin Hood, that Wyatt Earp was a staunch upholder of law and order and that Wild Bill Hickok was the greatest gunslinger the West produced. Generally speaking, they base these beliefs on what they have learned from film and novels. . . . This book allows the reader to compare film characters with their real life counterparts."[12]

Yet, other authors are concerned with both the ideological ramifications of the departures from fact *and* the ideological ramifications of the will to accuracy itself as shared by scholars and quality filmmakers alike. For example, Ward Churchill's provocative review of *Black Robe* (1991) shows the disingenuousness of the production's drastic measures in the name of accuracy (paying $37,000 to transport cedar bark for use in building Huron huts; fashioning digging implements out of moose shoulder bones) by contrasting it with other ways in which the film's historiography is grievously biased. The film depicts the Iroquois people in 1634 New France (now Quebec), enjoying acts of cruelty that extend to the remorseless execution of an Algonquin child, even though anthropological evidence suggests that in reality Iroquois clan mothers controlled village life and would likely have adopted and raised a child held captive.[13] Thus, in Churchill's view, the film's pretentions to historical authenticity are highly selective and, as such, part of the film's strongly racist import. Of course, I vastly prefer the theoretical sophistication of Churchill's orientation to the naïveté of Rainey's approach, but it's likely that Rainey's work is the more representative of western film criticism and modes of reception at large.

My cartographic metaphor serves to delineate the routes of western film historiography, but it must be qualified to allow that the historian can be, and often is, in two places at once. Slotkin, for example, while emphasizing the currency of films for audiences of the early 1940s (the second path), reflects as well on their relationship to the real subjects they represent (the third path), including Dodge City, Kansas, the Civil War, George Armstrong Custer, and Jesse James. All told, the insight that the western is history would seem to pervade and perhaps even to dominate the critical literature on the western.

But I would like to suggest something to the contrary. A close examination of the major writings on the western genre reveals a marked *disinclination* to give substantive attention to the western as historical. Genre approaches to the western deliberately eschew the suggestion that westerns are genuinely historical, concentrating instead on narrative and structure: "The fact is," writes Schatz, "that Hollywood's version of the Old West has as little to do with agriculture—although it has much to do with rural values—as it does with history."[14] This ahistoricity is often attributed to the changing nature of the films themselves. As exemplified by Schatz's passage, the genre's historical function is seen as having become subordinated to its mythical one. According to this line of reasoning, if it was appropriate for George N. Fenin and William K. Everson in *The Western* (1962) and Kevin Brownlow in his long section in *The War the West and the Wilderness* (1978) to give prominent attention to the western as historical, that is because they wrote about silent westerns. Later westerns did not share the genre's coevality with events in western history.

Observe in addition the clear statement that it is present-day America as much as, if not more than, America's past that is the subject of the mature western. As Schatz notes, "efforts to document the historical West on film steadily gave way to the impulse to exploit the past *as a means of examining the values and attitudes of contemporary America*."[15] Here the Old West is viewed as apt subject matter that supports the wider sociological function of the western.

Perhaps Kitses's statement that "the western is history" is not metaphoric but rather metonymic; that is to say that from a certain perspective, the historical dimensions of the western (its milieu and mores) seem to represent the whole. From another perspective, however, one of greater distance, this dimension recedes from view, as Kitses claims that "Ford is not the western; nor is the western history. For if we stand back from the western, we are less aware of historical (or representational) elements than of form and *archetype*."[16] In genre criticism, the historical setting and themes that are so conspicuous initially as to suggest that they are the western's most salient feature are not as important, finally, as the operations of genre and authorship that require attention to "form and archetype."

Although informed by historical consciousness (Schatz went on to write the well-known studio history *The Genius of the System*[17]), Kitses's book and Schatz's substantial chapter on the western epitomize—and indeed help to constitute—the genre approach to the western. They do not purport in the final analysis to be historical studies, but rather formal analyses of the narrative and iconographic patterns of genre film. It is, however, that very slide—from taking seriously the historical function of the western to seeing that function as antiquated in the genre (and in genre criticism), usurped by formal and ideological issues—that I wish to point to as being characteristic of literature on the western.

What is most surprising is that avowedly historical approaches share with the genre-based approach this disinclination to investigate the historical aspects of the genre. Even the best historical scholarship on film evinces a tendency to separate the historiographic impetus of the western film, perceived as being merely felicitous or "nominal,"[18] from its contemporaneous context of production, perceived as being significant—but not necessarily historical. *The BFI Companion to the Western,* an intelligent, invaluable guide (and a historical one at that, with its longest section devoted to "A Cultural and Historical Dictionary" of actual western people, events, places, and themes), begins with a disclaimer about the genre's historicity: "The Western's narrative structure and motifs are seen to derive less from any real world than from the economic and artistic imperatives of Hollywood, each film finding its plausibility and terms of reference in the audience's previous experience of the genre."[19] In the thought that the western's intrinsic material "derive[s] less from any real world" and more from "the economic and artistic imperative of Hollywood," the historical specificity of the generic material, be it relevant to past or present contexts, is lost; for such imperatives must govern the representational patterns of American cinema as a whole.

Even Richard Slotkin's magisterial trilogy on myths of the American frontier evinces a tendency (and granted, as with *The BFI Companion to the Western,* it is one tendency among others, but a significant one I believe) to receive the western-as-myth as being set apart from history. That is, the film western (as with other cultural forms) is *not historical in and of itself;* it *draws on* historical material. But while history is argumentative and discursive, westerns give *narrative form* to ideological beliefs and values. As Slotkin writes, "myths are stories drawn from [but not discursive renditions of] a society's history."[20] This is a division emphasized by the cover blurb for Slotkin's *Gunfighter Nation,* which identifies the book as a work of "literary *and* history scholarship [emphasis mine]," thus dividing the two.

The Crowded Prairie: American National Identity in the Hollywood Western, by historian Michael Coyne, makes a similar distinction between western films and historiographic function. As a historian, Coyne is critical of the "mythic approach" (represented by John Cawelti's *The Six-Gun Mystique*), "the auteurist aproach" (which saw the analysis of films by directors including Howard Hawks, Anthony Mann, Budd Boetticher, Raoul Walsh, and others), and "the structuralist approach" (as represented by Will Wright's *Sixguns and Society,* and, again, by Cawelti) for what Coyne regards as their insufficient attention to the historical context of western film production. The "political/allegorical approach" as represented by Philip French in *Westerns,* John Lenihan in *Showdown,* and once again by Wright, seems more to Coyne's liking and he locates his own "in-depth appraisal of the crucial relationship between era and artifict" within it.[21] However, in setting out what he sees as the four main approaches that have been adopted with regard to the film western, the text/context distinction between westerns and history is preserved. Westerns may "interact with history," Coyne affirms, but the western, as the "ideologically seductive" and "quintessentially American" melodrama, *is not history.*

The third path down which the thought that the western is history is pursued—that of prolific accuracy/inaccuracy deliberations—is similarly subject to mudslides. If film studio publicity departments touted the authenticity of their output (which they did), and if the films themselves would begin quite often with a statement to the effect that "what you are about to see is a true story" (which they did), then film scholarship would define itself in and through the task of illuminating the dramatic license taken by western films. For example, the format of *Past Imperfect: History According to the Movies* is to include with each chapter a page layout organized around the headings "History" and "Hollywood." In the "History" section we are given the facts of the matter: a capsule summary of Custer's career for *They Died with Their Boots On*; a photograph of the real Fort Apache for the Fort's filmic namesake; and so on with Wyatt Earp, Davy Crockett, and the other subjects of the westerns included in the book. The "Hollywood" section provides mainly film production history: how many Academy Award nominations *The Alamo* received, Darryl Zanuck's editorial interference in *My Darling Clementine.* In this way the nonhistorical nature of westerns is emphasized. Westerns get their facts wrong and they encompass a large imaginative component, therefore, they are not historical. . .but rather, again, mythological.

There is, however, an advantage to be gained from scholarship that has well established the dramatic license that westerns inevitably take and disabused readers of the western film's historical conceit. Now, largely because of these developments and the dangers to which they've alerted us, it is possible to study the relationship to the real that absolutely does inform the Hollywood western. "The considerable extent to which the

Western frequently . . . asserts its basis in history hasn't been adequately considered," writes Corey Creekmur in his contribution to this volume. His chapter, along with this volume as a whole, is an attempt to begin to rectify that lack. Yes, westerns take dramatic license; but it is also true that westerns take *historical license.*

I indicated above that one tendency in Slotkin's work is to separate the mythological function of the narrative western from the discursive or argumentative function of history writing. In fact, Slotkin's conceptual framework is larger and more suggestive, and I think that ultimately the troubling separation of myth and history in his book resolves itself into a useful, if inexplicit, distinction between the two rather than creating an absolute opposition. The trajectory traced in *Gunfighter Nation* is chronological, concentrating on the changes that myths and genres undergo over time as they are affected by "historical contingency."[22] The book is a cultural history; and the western genre, therefore, in literature and film is a mythological "activity and process" through which people formulate, grapple with, and revise the "problems that arise in the course of historical experience,"[23] with historical experience taken to be fundamental to the content and patterns of cultural products including films. There is a historiographic element to mythological discourse. And the reverse may be true as well for Slotkin. There many be a mythographic component to history writing. "A culture has its heritage of 'lore," writes Slotkin, which is "preserved for use by lore-masters, story-tellers, *or historians.*"[24]

dramatic license/historical license

We need to take seriously the profound and multifaceted historical and historiographic functions of the film western; they are the subject of this volume. Historical interpretation is a feature of the film western as well as of western history, and western history, like the western film, is constituted through narrative and ideological patterns. This is not to suggest that the West and the western be conflated. Moreover, I do believe in the utility of the distinction between nonfictional and fictional modes of representation; but when history is conceived to take various narrative forms (as does the western) and the western is conceived to take various argumentative modes (as does written history), one needs to look carefully to untangle and highlight the different reading protocols adopted in the two forms of representation. The rejection of the western's historicity on the basis of its dramatic license is specious; and falsity is not a grounds for dismissal, since fictions are not simply false nor nonfictions simply true.

In studying the historical nature of westerns it is useful to make reference to contemporary film-studies literature on the historical film. Both George Custen's industrial analysis of Hollywood biopics and Robert Burgoyne's study of the historical film of the 1980s and 1990s take seriously the historical function of the films they analyze,[25] and neither author falls prey to the historical mystification of the films under study. Custen refers to biopics' "obvious distortions ranging from the minor to the outright camp," and Burgoyne to such films' "somewhat glancing relationship to the historical record."[26] Nor does either author neglect the contributions the films make to the evolving national imaginary in the present. Indeed, for Custen the very definition of the biopic "shifts anew with each generation" so that "[t]racing a code for the biopic is an exercise in reconstructing a shifting public notion of fame,"[27] and Burgoyne's book is thoroughly involved with how the films in and implied by his corpus reconstruct American mythologies of nation for the contemporary audience. Yet while they confront head on the very issues that have led many scholars of the western away from the western *as* history, these authors continue to assert the centrality of the historical dimension of the films they study. As Burgoyne eloquently asserts, "What I try to stress . . . is the way *the cinematic rewriting of history* currently unfolding articulates a *counternarrative* of nation."[28]

Custen and Burgoyne both allow—indeed insist—that history and narrative are capable of interpenetration and that there is such a thing as historical narrative. Directly influenced by the work of Hayden White, both film historians emphasize the validity of the insight at the basis of his work (which insight White attributes to Paul Valéry, Martin Heidegger, Claude Lévi-Strauss, Jean-Paul Sartre, and Michel Foucault): namely, that history is always reconstructive and generally fictive. Of course White's work is part of a larger analytical tradition that includes the work of E. H. Carr, J. H. Hexter, Paul Veyne, Peter Novick, Dominick LaCapra, and Michel de Certeau, and that is attuned to "the rhetoric of history," to "the tropes, arguments, and other devices of language used to write history and to persuade audiences."[29] White's particular contribution has been to study "the 'artistic' elements of a 'realistic' historiography,"[30] or the historical permutations of the premise that "the historical monograph is no less 'shaped' or constructed than the historical film or historical novel."[31] And from the opposite vantage point he assumes (and elaborates when necessary) that realist narrative can have a historical component. "There is no reason," White writes in the context of a discussion of historical novels and films, specifically *The Return of Martin Guerre*, "why a filmed representation of historical events should not be as analytical and realistic as any written account."[32] The salient distinction for White is not between history and narrative, nor even between fiction and nonfiction, but rather between "historiography"— written history—and "historiophoty"—"the representation of history and our thought about it in visual images and filmic discourse."[33]

This rhetoric-of-history approach, and Hayden White's corresponding ideas about history and narrative, are quite well known in film studies and in film historiography,[34] but are incorporated only sporadically into studies of the western.[35] That must change, I submit, if we are to understand—and because it is crucial to understand—the historical vicissitudes of the film western. To reverse the terms and concentrate on studies of historical films that incorporate westerns, George Custen's study does include some western titles and Robert Burgoyne's book contains a chapter on *Thunderheart*, but neither book is designed to handle westerns as a group (see Corey Creekmur's chapter for more discussion of this point with regard to Custen's book). In fact, I would suggest that it's precisely because the films are regarded in these studies mainly as historical films and only secondarily as generic westerns that their hospitability to historiographic practice is recognized.

The restraint in genre criticism against recognizing the historical aspects of the western has an ancillary effect: the deflection of attention away from nonwhite characters and their real-world counterparts. Although Native Americans are major characters in about one-fifth of all westerns, minor characters in many more, and the enemy of record in still others, the dominant story form involves the mythic cowboy hero and the mythic function of the community as an oasis of civilization in the wilderness. In westerns, as we have learned, the cowboy is the breakaway rider of Manifest Destiny; he is not part of the settlement pack, but clears the way for western expansion and for the pioneers to whom, as the films have it, we owe "our" heritage.

Genre criticism has actually taken cognizance of the biases of the western, acknowledging the concomitant (non)representation of Native American worldviews. However, genre criticism has been better at recognizing such biases, of which it is critical, than at initiating any critical practice that can supercede them. "The Anglo-Saxon focus may indeed have been central to the ideological power of the Western and its nostalgic appeal," wrote Douglas Pye in his introduction to *The Book of Westerns,* coedited with Ian Cameron.[36] Or, as Edward Buscombe explains, "The Western as a genre has traditionally celebrated the myth of taming the frontier 'wilderness.' As such it has been able to see the Indian only as the unknown 'other,' part of those forces which threaten the onward march of Euro-American civilization and technological progress . . . [C]onsequently, the portrayal of Native Americans could scarcely but be unsympathetic, Eurocentric and degrading." [37] As Pye sees it, "Women and Indians are key terms in the generic equation, as it were, but with their representation largely constrained by their roles in a symbolic drama dominated by the fantasies of White men."[38] If we stay within the story realm given by the western text it is difficult indeed (but not impossible, as I've tried to show in my own contribution to this volume) to discern, against the grain of the text, a "symbolic drama" at least informed by the fantasies of Indians. This is why genre study, as a text-dependent form of analysis, gives so little play to Indians whose stories are "lost," as Tag Gallagher has written.[39]

Genre criticism wants to have it both ways when it comes to myth and history in the western: westerns are said to be mythic with respect

9

to the portrayal of Indians. John Ford's Indian characters are "mythic apparitions" and "icons of savage violent beauty dread," in Gallagher's words;[40] therefore, since *everybody knows* that those are not "real Indians" up there on the screen, nobody should be offended by their negative portrayal. But then shouldn't the same thing hold when it comes to the white characters? If Indians qua Indians can't be represented in a mythic system, how can whites qua whites be represented? To accept Gallagher's terms for the moment, I would say that the stories of settlers are also lost—in an inflated narrative of defensive self-satisfaction. Genre criticism, however, tends to renege on protestations that westerns are mythic in the assumption that white stories, unlike Indian stories, *can* be told in westerns. Genre criticism has a tendency to recapitulate the bias it pretends only to reveal. It allows historical interpretation presented in narrative form to parade as mere myth.

If we accept that westerns do have a historical function, one could assert that Indian stories were never really lost. The films are as much *about* Indians (even where the latter are represented by their non-appearance as a structuring absence) as they are *about* settlers. It's just that the stories are told from the colonists' perspective—from the perspective of celebration rather than boundless grief at the "taming of the frontier 'wilderness.'" My point is that history and myth are related and textual. If this weren't so, then the western corpus could include a narrative turn in which Europeans are repulsed, pushed back across the sea, or in which they decide to withdraw once they see how their diseases are killing Native Americans. But these possibilities seem ludicrous because *that's not the way it actually happened.* The western is a profoundly historical genre.

As such, the western is a genre that repays a historical approach to its analysis. And when we go outside the text for our points of reference in reading westerns, alternatives begin to present themselves. Yes, it's true that white perspectives also dominate historical accounts of the frontier era, but the plentiful existing primary documents and the appearance of more and more counterhistories in the subfield known as New Western History provide the cultural historian of the western with new bases for analysis.[41] Some such counterhistories have begun to press the argument that somewhere between nine million and twenty million Native Americans were living in North America at the time of Columbus's landing here.[42] Ward Churchill states unequivocally that the American holocaust "was and remains unparalleled, both in terms of its magnitude and the degree to which its goals were met, and in terms of the extent to which its ferocity was sustained over time by not one but several participating agencies."[43] Knowledge of this history can aid film analysis in identifying the nature of "lost stories," in finding what is there residually, and in comprehending a new form of western being made in the late 1980s and '90s, a form that includes stories of Native American heritage such as *Powwow Highway* (Jonathan Wacks, 1989), *Thunderheart* (Michael

Apted, 1992), *Smoke Signals* (Chris Eyre, 1998), and *Backroads* (Shirley Cheechoo, 2000). These films feature contemporary Native-American protagonists, but they are still very much about the past: about how tribal values may or may not figure in the lives of present-day Native Americans; and about the consequences in the present of a history of conquest, genocide, and survival.

The chapters in this book are deeply concerned with this counterhistorical function of the western. It is no coincidence that all of the authors represented in the book have elected to contribute writing on films and issues that prioritize perspectives outside the white-dominated mainstream. For example, a significant section of Alexandra Keller's chapter considers a film (*Posse*) by a black director (Mario Van Peebles) portraying black characters, and Peter Bloom has written about the Algerian redubbing of a French "camembert" western. The chapter by Melinda Szaloky, "A Tale N/nobody Can Tell: The Return of a Repressed Western History in Jim Jarmusch's *Dead Man,*" and chapters by Claudia Gorbman and myself, discuss Indians as nobodies and somebodies. Tomás Sandoval's chapter investigates the counterhistorical possibilities in *Lone Star*—a film about everybody: blacks, whites, Indians, and Mexicans.

That histories as well as westerns must absolutely be received in their fully rhetorical dimensionality as constructed texts struck me recently when I attended the exhibit on Buffalo Bill's Wild West at the Gene Autry Museum in Los Angeles. I had just read Kevin Brownlow's account of William "Buffalo Bill" Cody's involvement in events preceding and following the massacre at Wounded Knee in December of 1890, including the execution of Sitting Bull one week prior to the massacre:

The general commanding the troops was Nelson Appleton Miles, a veteran of the Civil War, who had defeated the Kiowas, the Comanches, and the Cheyennes.... As the government had been alarmed by the Ghost Dancers, so the Sioux took fright at the troops. They evacuated the reservation and fled to the Bad Lands, where they were joined by a thousand more tribesmen. Sitting Bull had returned from exile in Canada, and General Miles decided to isolate him in case he tried to seize command of the Sioux. Miles asked Cody, on the staff of the governor of Nebraska and recently returned from a highly successful tour of Europe with the Wild West, to talk to his former trouper [Sitting Bull had appeared with Buffalo Bill's Wild West in 1885]. Cody agreed, but he could not resist an all-night drinking session with cavalry officers. Next day President Benjamin Harrison, alerted by the local Indian agent, canceled Cody's mission. The agent sent a detachment of Indian police; Sitting Bull refused to submit and was killed. His white horse, given him by Cody, was trained to kneel at the sound of gunfire. As the Indian police shot Sitting Bull, the horse knelt—a source of wonder in Indian oral history.[44]

Here the tragic ironies are multiplied. The defensive actions of the Sioux were misunderstood. Cody just missed an opportunity to intervene. Sitting Bull was shot by fellow Sioux. Sitting Bull's horse mistook reality for stage play.

Imagine my surprise at the museum exhibit's very different treatment of these events. To give its visitors some historical background, the printed commentary mounted on the museum's walls describes the death of Sitting Bull and the Wounded Knee massacre. But then, as we move from that panel to the next, we read that "Buffalo Bill's Wild West had been touring Europe at that time and had set up its winter quarters. It was not certain that the Indians, who had returned to the USA, would be permitted to rejoin the show, so Cody and his business partner Nate Salsbury decided to incorporate a new element into their performance, one 'that would embody the whole subject of horsemanship.'" This is rather confusing. Where were the winter quarters set up? Were they in Europe or America? When did the Indians return? Was it before or after the massacre at Wounded Knee? The main elision, however, is that of the presence of Cody in the military camp at the time of Sitting Bull's death. The passage suggests, without stating it, that he was nowhere around, perhaps even as far away as Europe. Yet the exhibit also includes a painted poster that depicts General Miles and William Cody at Pine Ridge in January of 1891 and bears the label "Viewing Hostile Indian Camp."

My guess is that the exhibit's curators sought to downplay Cody's indirect involvement in Sitting Bull's death in case such a reference might cast a pall over the commemorative aspects of the exhibit or undermine the illusion of Cody's powers—powers that justify him as the subject of an exhibit in the first place—by suggesting that Cody couldn't save his "former trouper."

The point is that written history, be it found in books or on the walls of museums, is not necessarily less selective or interpretive than the history presented in film westerns. For another example, consider the statistics provided here with regard to the genocide of Native Americans. Informed readers of the aforementioned passage may have been skeptical about the figures quoted, perhaps finding them inflated. The Smithsonian Institution had asserted until recently that not more than one million people lived north of Mexico prior to the arrival of Columbus. Lately, however, they have upped their estimate to two million, indicating that the earlier estimate was in error. But in a long impeccably researched chapter with more than six hundred footnotes, Ward Churchill surveys military, government, newspaper, scholarly, and epidemiological documents and literatures to show that work based on archival records indicates a preinvasion population that scholars have begun to approximate at fifteen million.[45] Obviously, the death of 90 percent of two million people is harrowing enough. But to say that nearly fifteen million died, and to argue as Churchill does that they were *exterminated* (since we accept that Jews who died in concentration camps of disease were exterminated as surely as their compatriots who died in gas chambers), is to place a very different interpretation on the history of hemispheric holocaust.

History, then, may be said to take dramatic license just as films take historical license. There are valuable insights to be gained in studying the two in concert, as is the goal of this volume concisely put.

westerns and histories

The relationship between westerns and histories has various facets that are intrinsic to the subject matter and capable of serving as heuristic categories. We can study westerns in their variety and as they have developed through(out) history and film history from the silent era to the present. Or we can regard westerns as histories on film, interpreting past events alongside written histories from which they may draw. We can even see some westerns as fulfilling a historiographic function by evincing a self-consciousness about the history writing process at the same time that they share in it. Through the lens of history, we come to realize that westerns incorporate, elide, embellish, mythologize, allegorize, erase, duplicate, and rethink past events that are themselves—as history—fragmented, fuzzy, and striated with fantasy constructions. The relation between the western and the history of the West must be more complex than an "is."

To complicate matters, these categories for engaging in the study of westerns are not discrete. This is largely because westerns themselves fall into different subcategories with varying relationships to the past-as-thematic-material, and varying formulations of the fictive material that bears the historical along. Some, but not all, westerns are biopics or event pics, which means that some but not all are what film scholars generally mean by historical films.[46] These particular westerns lend themselves to analysis as histories because their relationship to the real past is avowed and detailed in their treatment of historical personages and events and not just landscape and historical sweep. And in fact there have been several articles (fewer in number than we may have thought) that have measured individual biopics and biopic cycles against historical record while keeping in mind the aesthetic specificity of historiophoty and not falling into simplistic comparisons between film and "reality."[47] Other westerns are "merely" set in the past making no reference to actual historical events and personages. These have not generally been discussed as historical films. And yet, as Creekmur indicates in chapter 6 of this volume, "While most film genres, including the most fantastic, often make some claims upon historical reality, the Western appears unique in its regular, perhaps even inherent, reference to a geographically and historically delimited time and space."

How can we begin to account for the subcategories of the western genre's characteristic "reference to a historically delineated time and

13

space?" In "Traces of the Past: From Historicity to Film," Philip Rosen used the nineteenth-century debate in architecture between restorationists and preservationists to begin a taxonomy of historical filmmaking practice.[48] Whereas the restorationist's urge (epitomized by Eugene-Emmanuel Viollet-le-Duc) is to return a historical building to its original style even if it means razing subsequent, even centuries-old additions that are viewed as inauthentic, the preservationist (represented by William Morris or John Ruskin) is "willing to subordinate organic order to the disordering work of time.[49] Applied to film—like architecture a medium where there is "an iconicized trace—a mechanical presentation of sights and sounds from the past"—the restorationist/preservationist dialectic is echoed most simply in the documentary/fiction dyad. Whereas documentaries are concerned with providing a real relation to the past, fiction films are later versions, products of their own time as well as of past time. Extrapolating from Rosen's argument to the western, one achieves the ability to distinguish between more or less highly interpretive, embellished, stylized, or add-on histories of the west on film.

I see westerns arrayed along a continuum, at the right end of which are found the mainly fictional westerns and at the left end of which are found the mainly "biopictional." Wholly fictional films (but I doubt such an animal exists; all films, including science-fiction films, refer to the relationships of an inhabited world and so make reference to our own) would be off the scale to the right; wholly documentary films (or at least our imagined conception of them, since I'm *sure* such a thing does not exist) would be off the scale to the left. *The Searchers* would crowd the right end of the continnum; Ethan Edwards and his quest are made up, but Texas 1868 and the Civil War, from which Edwards is supposed to have just returned, are real. *The Life of Buffalo Bill* (Thomas Edison, 1912) would crowd the left end; William Frederick Cody plays himself in part of the film, and the exploits he recalls are based on historical occurrence, but sheer imagination and the fictional trappings of reenactment also play a signficant role just as they did in Buffalo Bill's traveling Wild West exhibition. In this volume, the chapters by Corey Creekmur and Joy Kasson contain explicit discussions of these matters and they, along with the chapter by William Simon and Louise Spence, grapple with the historically interpretive features of Buffalo Bill vehicles as a case study of the historical function of the western biopic.

In the middle of the continuum we find films such as *Thunderheart* and *Powwow Highway* that are fictional in the main but also figure past historical incident as resurgent material with which the films' characters must deal. In *Thunderheart* a modern-day FBI agent (played by Val Kilmer) has several visions including a vision of himself "running with the elders" at Wounded Knee. In *Powwow Highway* the main character (played by Gary Farmer) has a vision of Cheyenne Indians led by Dull Knife escaping from Fort Robinson. Moreover, instead of being contemporary to the time they were made, both films are actually set in the 1970s. Thus, they are also at pains to reference real events and cultural practices of that decade. Matters are more complicated still: *Powwow Highway* and *Thunderheart* hark back to even earlier 1970s events, with both films making reference to the Vietnam War; *Thunderheart* also brings in the 1975 firefight at the Pine Ridge Reservation and the 1973 occupation of the Wounded Knee monument.

The continuum, however, could use a third dimension, for all stretches of the line support the potential for a film, however balanced between fictive and historical elements, to function also as a "historiographic metafiction." Coined by Linda Hutcheon in her book *The Poetics of Postmodernism*, this phrase is adopted by William Simon and Louise Spence (in chapter 4, here) to describe how Robert Altman's *Buffalo Bill and the Indians, or Sitting Bull's History Lesson* "self-consciously suggest[s] the discursive nature of all reference"—including, I would emphasize, historical reference. One might say the same about Altman's other anti-western *McCabe and Mrs. Miller*. Although the film is fiction, it nonetheless points up gritty realities that were a feature of actual life on the frontier and it highlights, by contrast, the prettification engaged in by classical westerns. Self-consciousness about historical representation characterizes many westerns because—no matter how attuned a twentieth-century film is to the ideologies of the nineteenth century—the time lapse creates the potential for metahistorical reflection. In analyzing an individual Altman film as historiographically metafictional, Simon and Spence thus offer an analysis with wider applicability to the genre as a whole.

What, then, are we to make of this melange of history, fiction, and historiographic metafiction that characterizes the western genre while figuring in individual films and film groupings in seemingly endless combination? Although boundaries between heuristic categories are blurred, I submit that there are distinct affinities among types of westerns and types of perspectives on the western. It is these affinities that govern the section divisions of this book.

In chapter 1, "Generic Subversion as Counterhistory: Mario Van Peebles's *Posse*," Alexandra Keller proposes that 1990s postmodern westerns are unique in that they "show a marked preoccupation not only with their own generic value as westerns, but also with the discourse of history itself, and their relation to it." Left to my own devices I would hang onto the possibility that a rogue postmodern western could be found in any decade and I suspect that Simon and Spence would disagree with Keller's claim that *Buffalo Bill and the Indians, or Sitting Bull's History Lesson* (1976) falls short of "full-blown postmodernism." But these are fascinating questions and Keller has met the challenge of explaining, finally, what our intuitions have told us: that the "90s postmodern western" is a coherent category whose coherence relies on the way its constituent films are skeptical of official history and "foreground the difference between history and the past." She argues that if the western "has always been a revisionist genre it has not, until relatively recently, wanted to announce itself as such." Her essay specifies such distinctions in wonderful detail and with reference to a number of key films including *Walker* and *Dances with Wolves*. It then brings these ideas to bear on a close analysis of *Posse*. Part 1 of this volume was therefore established to follow Keller's lead (and her chapter leads off), and it features three essays on the postmodern 1990s western as the self-consciously historiographic western par excellence.

In her essay, "A Tale N/nobody Can Tell: The Return of a Repressed Western History in Jim Jarmusch's *Dead Man*," Melinda Szaloky poses the question of whether revisionist westerns can "remember differently" the frontier history they have been "forced to forget" as we have become more enlightened about racial inequities and national statism. Can the "scattered remnants of the frontier myth" reappear as history, or are they merely countermyth? This is the same litmus test of the postmodern western posed by Keller and, by those standards, Szaloky's close reading of *Dead Man* would indicate that it is indeed a postmodern text. Drawing on the work of Michel de Certeau and of Sigmund Freud, Szaloky suggests that history writing necessarily involves a process of selection *and erasure,* and that traumatic events that have been erased/repressed from mainstream histories do have the potential to return in revisionist westerns. This they do in *Dead Man,* she argues, particularly through the character of N/nobody, whose captivity by whites and abduction overseas reverses the captivity narrative trope of the western, and whose points of view and dreams upon his return are manifestations of the "return of the white man's repressed other." The representations of death and violence in the western, and their frequent poeticization, Szaloky argues, are exposed in *Dead Man* as being linked to the "Westerner's quest for origins" and identity. *Dead Man* renders these dilemmas differently by posing them in relation to "Nobody's desire to return the white man to the land of his fathers." The perspectives of the other, Szaloky argues, suppressed in life and repressed in films and histories, return in the postmodern strategies of *Dead Man.*

In chapter 3, Tomás Sandoval refers to ideas in Hayden White's famous essay "The Burden of History" to bring out *Lone Star*'s initiative with regard to the weight of historical occurrence.[50] Not only does the film suggest alternate remembrances of things past (revisionism foregrounded), it also suggests that past occurrences may be taken up— or not—in the present and future of human endeavor. The film, in his reading of it, suggests that historical subjects need not also be *subjugated* to past events: "blood only means what you let it," quotes Sandoval. And he demonstrates how this "belief in human agency" is particularly crucial for those groups whose blood was let in a past that included inequality, slavery, and conquest in the face of democracy.

I have indicated above that "Cowboy Wonderland, History and Myth: 'It Ain't All That Different than Real Life,'" by William Simon and

janet walker

Louise Spence provides a detailed analysis of a single film, Altman's *Buffalo Bill and the Indians, or Sitting Bull's History Lesson*, as a self-conscious work of historiography. On this basis the essay fits in well with the three essays in part 1, and I could have placed it there and let you as readers figure out whether the film's revisionist characteristics are different than or the same as those of the more recent 1990s films. But the essay also belongs with the two other chapters on Buffalo Bill westerns, and, in the absence of a graphic (hypertextual?) means to place the essay in two places at once, I have elected to include it as the first essay in part 2.

Each of the three chapters in this section uses Buffalo Bill—the historical personage *and* fictionalized persona—to investigate issues of biography, authenticity, representation, and history. "No single character summarizes the transformation of the historical reality of the American frontier into commercial entertainment as fully as William F. 'Buffalo Bill' Cody," writes Corey Creekmur. It was Cody who "made familiar throughout the United States, Canada, and Europe" the "most memorable scenes and incidents [that] had been part of the popular imagination for a quarter-century," writes Joy Kasson. He did it by being not only a scout in the "Indian Wars" but a showman as well. One is almost sympathetic to the hyperbole of the Buffalo Bill exhibit at the Gene Autry Museum, which tags Cody the "most famous person living" at the time. With its 600 men, 500 horses, 11-acre mobile showground, and 23,000 yards of tent canvas, Buffalo Bill's Wild West company needed 52 train cars to travel. And travel they did, on the European tour of 1895, for example, to 131 sites in 190 days, covering 9,000 miles. The German Army was ordered to study the operation.

The chapters in this section approach the Buffalo Bill phenomenon from various angles. Simon and Spence are interested in Altman's film critique of Buffalo Bill mythology, and they discuss the use of Paul Newman in the title role and the film's numerous inventive metafictional devices. But the teeth of that critique—the pointed result of the film's ample allusions to the mechanic of storytelling—chew on *Sitting Bull's History Lesson,* the film's subtitular indication that "the story of the American West is less a tale of civilization, progress, heroic action and triumph than oppression, displacement, exclusion, and defeat." It is no coincidence, Simon and Spence point out, that the Altman film is set "between 1885 (when Sitting Bull joined Buffalo Bill's Wild West) and 1890 (when Sitting Bull was killed at Standing Rock)." The chapter ends with an intriguing discussion of the film's inclusion of the Wild West's inclusion of two rather different Last Stand scenes. The first shows Custer being vanquished, but in the second sequence Newman plays Buffalo Bill playing Custer, who vanquishes Sitting Bull played by Will Sampson playing William Halsey playing Sitting Bull. The first sequence is a "comic travesty," write Simon and Spence, the second a "postmodern parody."

While Altman confined himself to Buffalo Bill's Wild West, Kasson informs us that Cody directed much more. He was the subject of numerous films, as Kasson and Creekmur both point out, and in addition was the driving force behind an ambitious undertaking discussed by Kasson: the filming of the Indian Wars, including the Battle of Wounded Knee by involving the actual participants.

As an American studies scholar, Joy Kasson fleshes out her characterization of Cody and his endeavors through an astute reading of diverse documents from archives including the Yale Collection of American Literature, the Buffalo Bill Historical Center in Cody, Wyoming, and the Library of Congress. Here the reminiscences of Cody's business partner Nate Salsbury are analyzed in light of the grand claims of the Wild West's program notes and other promotional materials. Apparently Salsbury himself saw the contradictions in the Buffalo Bill persona that Altman, and Simon and Spence, develop. According to Kasson's research findings, Salsbury wrote, "There were two of him to me. One the true Cody as he has always been from his birth, and the other was a commercial proposition that I discovered when I [!] invented the Wild West."

Indian War Pictures overreached Cody's masterful use of artifice, for with that project he "diminished the element of fictionality and heightened the claims to authenticity." There were difficulties, however, and the film ended up disrupting "the delicate balance between role-playing and memory" that he had been able to maintain with the Wild West. A contributing factor must have been the disturbing subject matter itself. Cody had never before staged the massacre at Wounded Knee, during which 146 Indians including women and children were killed by the Seventh Cavalry, and the attempt to do so failed to draw in an audience. The death of Sitting Bull also figured into *Indian War Pictures*, Kasson explains.

Moving in this section from an essay focused on one film to an essay focused on Cody productions we arrive at chapter 6, "Buffalo Bill (Himself)," by Corey Creekmur. He, like Kasson, is interested in Edison's *The Life of Buffalo Bill* as a film within which "reality and artifice" do battle: as I mentioned above, Cody plays himself in the framing story. But where Kasson moves on from *The Life of Buffalo Bill* to analyze Cody's subsequent attempt with *Indian War Pictures* to make what contemporary critics might call "docudrama" or documentary reenactment, Creekmur's essay moves from *The Life of Buffalo Bill*, with its elements of "actuality," to *Buffalo Bill* (William Wellman, 1944) as a standard biopic.

In keeping with the other contributions in this section, Creekmur's goal is to examine these individual films not only to understand their particular combination of dramatization and reportage, but as part of a larger project: to investigate "a consistent blurring between the western and the biopic that hasn't been directly investigated."

Part 3 of the volume is given over to new essays on the history of the western. This is not to say that other essays in the volume do not pertain to film history. Kasson's and Creekmur's essays might be categorized as being a mix of social and aesthetic film history with further reflections on how the two necessarily entwine in western film history. And even the four essays on single films set their analyses within the historical context of the genre's propensity to become more and more self-conscious. The three chapters in this third part of the volume, however, examine successive westerns in the context of diverse research materials ranging from minstrel song sheets (Kathryn Kalinak) to field recordings of American Indian tribal music (Claudia Gorbman) to journalism in the colonies of French North Africa (Peter Bloom).

Listening to the car radio a few days ago, I heard an interview with composer-guitarist Bill Frisell talking about new developments in his musical interests. He had always been most interested in the newest, coolest thing, he said. But now he's older, more secure, and more willing to explore musical forms that he would have rejected previously as unhip. What was the particular musical form in question? American popular song. That's what he now finds crucial to his development as an American musician. Those of us who have grown up in the United States can hum and probably muster lyric fragments of "Oh! Susanna," "Camptown Races," "Dixie," and others. These songs represent our heritage. They were sung in mining camps, on western trails, and in film westerns, by soldiers, explorers, and cowboys. They are authentic western music, or so we thought. Kathryn Kalinak's chapter "How the West Was Sung" teaches us that there's much more to know (surprises perhaps) about the history of such songs, and about their plentiful incorporation into film westerns, both silent and sound. Their use in western film narrative, Kalinak argues, redoubles the film work to affirm American community through the exclusion of African Americans, Native Americans, and the problems of racism. And yet, since the songs themselves cannot always sustain the totalizing white supremacy of their overt meanings, and certain songs are explicitly about the tragedies of slavery, their adoption by films can sometimes bring up racial issues, including antiracist perspectives.

Focused on composer Stephen Foster but ranging far wider, Kalinak's essay is the definitive word on the music of the frontier as used in western films, from James Cruz's silent *The Covered Wagon* to John Ford's Civil War westerns, *The Horse Soldiers* and *Sergeant Rutledge*. It also suggests how knowing the "archaeology," as she puts it, of these songs expands the corpus of films we must study to understand the western. Until now, who realized the importance of the 1939 Vitaphone short *Royal Rodeo*, or heard the strain of abolitionism in *The Telegraph Trail*? Through their songs, these films figure the "racial turmoil" that has "always been at the center of American identity."

Where one film music scholar, Kathryn Kalinak, explores the racial content of frontier songs, another, Claudia Gorbman, discusses the role of the film score in "determining the spectator's reception of the other." "How," Gorbman asks, "does music inflect the nature and degree of the

19

Indian's otherness?" Technical, but made accessible to film scholars with much less musical knowledge than Gorbman, the essay "Drums Along the L.A. River: Scoring the Indian," begins by identifying "musical clichés" such as "tom-tom" drumming that have cued the presentation of Indians on screen. She confirms our suspicion that these musical stereotypes "bear little relation to authentic Indian music," but their history, as described, is fascinating. Moreover, art composers of the turn of the century did appropriate Indian music, known from ethnographers' transcriptions and field recordings, and their use of it raises issues of accessibility and translation that are of particular relevance to the musical scene today where "commercial interests pick and choose among the world's musicians and musical traditions in the insatiable search for new sounds to add to the global pop mix."

This is the framework for Gorbman's analysis of "Indian music" as it has developed over time from classical westerns (including *Stagecoach*, scored by Richard Hageman, John Liepold, W. Franke Harling, and Leo Shuken), to postwar liberal westerns (*Broken Arrow*, scored by Hugo Friedhofer), to 1970s westerns (*A Man Called Horse*, with its "faux ethnographic" score by Leonard Rosenman), to recent offerings (*Dances with Wolves*, scored by John Barry). The essay enlightens us as to the communication of "unheard" meanings.[51] For example, Gorbman's analysis of Friedhofer's score for *Broken Arrow* reveals how the liberalism of the film's story is undercut in various ways by the score in spite of—but yet in some respect *because* of—the film's use of diegetic Indian music in the form of the "actual music and dance of the Mountain Spirit from the girls' puberty ceremony of the White Mountain Apache." Apache chanting is also used in Ry Cooder's score for *Geronimo: An American Legend*, but this time to rather different effect—one that seems to link the promise of earlier appropriations to an American counterhistory of loss.

In chapter 9, Peter Bloom takes us not only "Beyond the Western Frontier," to quote the essay's main title, but beyond national boundaries as well. Recent years have seen a proliferation of new work by established scholars on political economies and cultures under globalization. And the importance of new media technologies to these configurations is not lost on these scholars, among them Néstor Canclini, Fredric Jameson and Masao Miyoshi, Saskia Sasson, and Zillah Eisenstein.[52] But these very important accounts of the processes of globalization risk becoming, in a word, *global*. It's extremely difficult to paint a picture as meaningful close-up as it is from afar.

Peter Bloom's essay does just that, however. His study of "an evolving process of reception and reappropriation of the Western film genre in France and the French colonies," is much needed, pioneering work that rewards the desire for more detail. Bloom begins with an industrial analysis of the international reach and popularity of the American western in the interwar period. He follows this trajectory to France and then to Algeria, Morocco, and French Indochina, where "junk prints" were shown in film caravans as well as first- and second-run movie theaters. Then, turning to contemporaneous sources, including French journalism in the colonies, he suggests how the adventures of "Bronco Billy" Anderson, William S. Hart, Tom Mix, Art Acord, and the other western stars might have been received at a distance from the context that gave birth to them. This entails an understanding of the Algerian political context and a close description of the films' themes, both of which Bloom provides. The western, with its "good badman" hero, was subject, Bloom shows, to local translation, and even allegorization, by its avid spectators.

This was the context for the development of a form of spectatorship involving parody and cultural translation. And it was the context for the Algerian redubbing (*Dynamite "Moh,"* 1966) of a French "camembert" western (*Dynamite Jack*, 1961) that was itself a parody of the American westerns with which the European and African screens had been flooded. "*Dynamite 'Moh,'*" writes Bloom, suggests that "the subversion of dominant meanings is an ongoing, dynamic process, nearly simultaneous with the reception of the speech act itself"—and it is profoundly historical.

Cathy Caruth, whom I quote in the volume's concluding chapter, has written that "to be traumatized is precisely to be possessed by an image or event."[53] Alone in part 4, my own essay makes the claim that, even when they do not explicitly reference outside events—or perhaps *because* they do not—some westerns allude to the violent history of American settlement through narrative retrospection and stylistic antirealism. Such westerns— and there is a surprisingly large number of them—are *internally* historical. Evoking the past through flashbacks, ellipses, and indeterminate signifiers—images that hold characters and audiences captive—these "traumatic westerns" mark an obsessive return to troubling memories that refuse to dis-/resolve. The form of the films themselves is traumatized, as are the worthy spectators inscribed by their texts.

The essay studies two patterns that lend themselves to traumatic representation: the narrative of captivity and the narrative of familial succession. *The Searchers* provides the main example of the first, while *Pursued, Once Upon a Time in the West,* and *Lone Star,* exemplify the second pattern. These films are part of a prominent subgroup of westerns "in which past events of catastrophic nature are represented so as to challenge both the realist representational strategies of a genre that often trades on historical authenticity and the ideological precepts of the myth of Manifest Destiny."

With only a few exceptions, the essays presented here were written expressly for this volume. They all share the aim to consider the "western through history." In a footnote in his introduction to *The Western Reader*, Jim Kitses reports that he was "critiqued [after the publication of *Horizons West* in 1969] for arguing that 'first of all the Western is America History.'"[54] Writing in 1998 he declares, "I remain unrepentant."[55] I applaud that statement, and in fact would like to see it freed of its status as an apologia. Likewise, in their introduction to *Back in the Saddle*

Again, Edward Buscombe and Roberta E. Pearson state that "the collection ends where it began, with history. . . . History . . . is at the heart of the genre."[56] The present volume begins, ends, and is shot through with historical considerations that have formed the western genre and its reception, for it is the western's status as a historical phenomenon, a body of films multifariously bound up with the incarnate fortunes of North America and the United States, that seems to me its most salient and enduring aspect.

notes

I would like to extend my thanks to Edward Branigan, Chuck Wolfe, and K. Kalinak for spending their precious time and prodigious talents reading and commenting on this essay.

1. André Bazin, "Evolution of the Western" (1955), reprinted in *The Western Reader,* ed. Jim Kitses and Gregg Rickman (New York: Limelight Editions, 1998), 49. Originally published in English in *What Is Cinema?* vol. 2, trans. and ed. Hugh Gray (Berkeley and Los Angeles: University of California Press, 1967).
2. Jim Kitses, *Horizons West* (Bloomington: Indiana University Press, 1969), 8.
3. Richard Slotkin, *Gunfighter Nation: The Myth of the Frontier in Twentieth-Century America* (New York: HarperCollins, 1992), chapter 9, "The Western Is American History, 1939–1941," 278.
4. Sources generally cite as the epitaph for the "old frontier" Frederick Jackson Turner's address, "The Significance of the Frontier in American History," delivered at a meeting of the American Historical Association in Chicago, July 12, 1893, during the World's Columbian Exposition. It is reprinted in *The Frontier in American History* (Tucson: The University of Arizona Press, 1986).
5. Richard Schickel, foreword to *The BFI Companion to the Western,* ed. Edward Buscombe (London: The British Film Institute, 1988/New York, Da Capo Press paperback edition), 10.
6. Thomas Schatz, *Hollywood Genres* (New York: Random House, 1981), 46; emphasis and bracketed text added.
7. Peter Lehman, "Texas 1968/American 1956: *The Searchers,*" in *Close Viewings: An Anthology of New Film Criticism,* ed. Peter Lehman (Talahassee: Florida State University Press, 1990), 411. See also "*The Searchers*: An American Dilemma,"in *Movies and Methods: An Anthology*, vol. 2, ed. Bill Nichols (Berkeley and Los Angeles: University of California Press, 1985), 429–49.
8. Robert Sklar, "Empire to the West: *Red River*" in *American History/American Film: Interpreting the Hollywood Image,* ed. John E. O'Connor and Martin A. Jackson (New York: Ungar, 1987), 170; emphasis added.
9. Stanley Corkin, "Cowboys and Free Markets: Post–World War II Westerns and the U.S. Hegemony," *Cinema Journal* 39, no. 3 (2000): 66–91.
10. Slotkin, *Gunfighter Nation,* 279.
11. For some key examples see Ted Mico, John Miller-Monzon, and David Rubel, eds., and Mark C. Carnes, gen'l. ed., *Past Imperfect: History According to the Movies* (New York: Henry Holt, 1995); a significant number of the book's chapters are on various westerns (see chapters by James Axtell, Richard White, Anthony F. C. Wallace, Marshall De Bruhl, Sean Wilentz, Alvin M. Josephy Jr., and John Mack Faragher), which attests to the importance of the western to considerations of films in the historical context.) See also Jon Tuska, *The Filming of the West* (Garden City, NY: Doubleday, 1976), especially "Frontier Legends," parts 1 and 2; Jon Tuska, *The American West in Film: Critical Approaches to the Western* (Westport, Conn.: Greenwood Press, 1985),

janet walker

especially part 3, "Frontier Legends"; and Buck Rainey, *The Western Gunslingers in Fact and on Film: Hollywood's Famous Lawmen and Outlaws* (Jefferson, N.C.: McFarland, 1998).

12. Rainey, *Gunslingers*, 1.

13. Ward Churchill, "And They Did It Like Dogs in the Dirt," *Z Magazine*, December 1992, 20–24.

14. Schatz, *Hollywood Genres*, 47.

15. Ibid., 46; emphasis added.

16. Kitses, *Horizons*, 13, emphasis in the original.

17. Thomas Schatz, *The Genius of the System: Hollywood Filmmaking in the Studio Era* (New York: Pantheon, 1988).

18. Slotkin, *Gunfighter Nation*, 311.

19. Buscombe, *The BFI Companion*, 13.

20. Slotkin, *Gunfighter Nation*, 5.

21. Michael Coyne, *The Crowded Prairie: American National Identity in the Hollywood Western* (London and New York: I. B. Tauris, 1997), 13.

22. Slotkin, *Gunfighter Nation*, 8.

23. Ibid., 6.

24. Ibid., 7.

25. George F. Custen, *Bio/Pics: How Hollywood Constructed Public History* (New Brunswick, N.J.: Rutgers University Press, 1992); Robert Burgoyne, *Film Nation: Hollywood Looks at U.S. History* (Minneapolis: University of Minnesota Press, 1997).

26. Custen, *Bio/Pics*, 5; Burgoyne, *Film Nation*, 1.

27. Custen, *Bio/Pics*, 7.

28. Burgoyne, *Film Nation*, 11; emphasis added.

29. Allan Megill and Donald N. McCloskey, "The Rhetoric of History," in *The Rhetoric of the Human Sciences: Language and Argument in Scholarship and Public Affairs*, ed. John S. Nelson, Allan Megill, and Donald N. McCloskey (Madison: University of Wisconsin Press, 1988), 221. See also E. H. Carr, *What Is History?* (New York: Vintage, 1961), J. H. Hexter, "The Rhetoric of History," in *Doing History* (Bloomington: Indiana University Press, 1971), Paul Veyne, *Writing History: Essay on Epistemology*, trans. Mina Moore-Rinvolucri (Middletown, Conn.: Wesleyan University Press, 1984), Hayden White, *Metahistory: The Historical Imagination in Nineteenth-Century Europe* (Baltimore: Johns Hopkins University Press, 1973), Michel de Certeau, *The Writing of History*, trans. Tom Conley (New York: Columbia University Press, 1988), Dominick LaCapra, *Rethinking Intellectual History: Texts, Contexts, Language* (Ithaca, N.Y.: Cornell University Press, 1983), and Peter Novick, *That Noble Dream: The "Objectivity Question" and the American Historical Profession* (Cambridge: Cambridge University Press, 1988).

30. White, *Metahistory*, p. 3, n. 2.

31. Hayden White, "Historiography and Historiophoty," *The American Historical Review* 93, no. 5 (1988): 1195–96.

32. Ibid., 1196.

33. Ibid., 1193.

34. For a notable example see Vivian Sobchack, ed., *The Persistence of History: Cinema, Television, and the Modern Event* AFI Film Readers Series (New York: Routledge, 1996).

35. Roberta E. Pearson, in "Custer's Still the Hero: Textual Stability and Transformation," *Journal of Film and Video* 47, nos. 1–3 (1995): 82–97, does cite and incorporate the ideas of Hayden White.

36. Ian Cameron and Douglas Pye, eds., *The Book of Westerns* (New York: Continuum, 1996).

37. Buscombe, *The BFI Companion*, 156.

38. Douglas Pye, "Introduction: Criticism and the Western," in Cameron and Pye, eds., *The Book of Westerns,* 12.

39. Tag Gallagher, "Angels Gambol Where They Will: John Ford's Indians," *Film Comment,* September/October 1993, 70.

40. Ibid.

41. Works of New Western History include Patricia Nelson Limerick, *The Legacy of Conquest: The Unbroken Past of the American West* (New York: W. W. Norton, 1987), Richard White, *"It's Your Misfortune and None of My Own": A New History of the American West* (Norman: University of Oklahoma Press, 1991); Patricia Nelson Limerick, Clyde A. Milner II, and Charles E. Rankin, eds., *Trails: Toward a New Western History* (Lawrence, Kan.: The University of Kansas Press, 1991), and Forrest G. Robinson, ed., *The New Western History: The Territory Ahead,* (Tucson: University of Arizona Press, 1997).

42. See Ward Churchill, *A Little Matter of Genocide: Holocaust and Denial in the Americas 1492 to the Present* (San Francisco: City Lights, 1997), especially the chapter entitled "'Nits Make Lice': The Extermination of North American Indians, 1607–1996"; and Jared Diamond, *Guns, Germs and Steel* (New York: W. W. Norton, 1999), especially 210–12.

43. Churchill, *A Little Matter of Genocide,* 4.

44. Kevin Brownlow, *The War the West and the Wilderness* (New York: Alfred A. Knopf, 1979), 227.

45. Churchill, *A Little Matter of Genocide,* 129–37.

46. Robert Burgoyne's *Film Nation* is of further interest in this regard because his study of the "historical film" encompasses some films that employ a historical personage as a main character and some films that employ a fictional character as the protagonist.

47. For valuable historical work on the western see, for example, Steve Neale, "'The Story of Custer in Everything But Name?' Colonel Thursday and *Fort Apache,*" *Journal of Film and Video* 47, nos. 1–3 (1995): 26–32; and Roberta E. Pearson, "Twelve Custers, or, Video History," in *Back in the Saddle Again: New Essays on the Western,* ed. Edward Buscombe and Roberta E. Pearson (London: British Film Institute, 1998), 197–213.

48. Phil Rosen, "Traces of the Past: From Historicity to Film," in *Meanings in Texts and Actions: Questioning Paul Ricoeur ,* ed. David E. Klemm and William Schweiker (Charlottesville: University Press of Virginia, 1993), 67–89.

49. Ibid., 73.

50. Hayden White, "The Burden of History" (1966), in *Tropics of Discourse* (Baltimore: Johns Hopkins University Press, 1978).

51. Gorbman's analysis in this essay builds on ideas developed in her book *Unheard Melodies: Narrative Film Music* (London: British Film Institute, 1987).

52. Néstor Garcia Canclini, *Hybrid Cultures: Strategies for Entering and Leaving Modernity* (Minneapolis: University of Minnesota Press, 1995), Fredric Jameson and Masao Miyoshi, eds., *The Cultures of Globalization* (Durham, N.C.: Duke University Press, 1998), Saskia Sasson, *Globalization and Its Discontents* (New York: The New Press, 1998), Zillah Eisenstein, *Global Obscenities: Patriarchy, Capitalism, and the Lure of Cyberfantasy* (New York: New York University Press, 1998).

53. Cathy Caruth, introduction to her edited volume *Trauma: Explorations in Memory* (Baltimore: Johns Hopkins University Press, 1995), 4–5.

54. Jim Kitses, "Introduction: Post-modernism and The Western," in *The Western Reader,* 30, n. 4.

55. Ibid.

56. Edward Buscombe and Roberta E. Pearson, eds., introduction to *Back in the Saddle Again,* 6.

historical

metafiction:

the 1990s

western

part one

generic

subversion as

counterhistory

mario van peebles's *posse*

alexandra keller

Although all Westerns are concerned with history, no one goes to the
movies for a cynical history lesson. Audiences don't want history's
messy facts; they want its meaning.

—John Mack Faragher, "The Tale of Wyatt Earp," *Past Imperfect*

As historian Richard Slotkin has noted, the relation between myth and
genre is one of content and form.[1] Genres are formally familiar ways to
transmit certain widely held—sometimes widely contested—cultural
meanings, which coalesce as myths. The western genre as André Bazin's
"American film *par excellence*"[2] has also long been American myth *par
excellence*. Before 1980, a western could be "affirmative" like *My Darling
Clementine* (1946), *Red River* (1947), or *Shane* (1952), supporting ideas
of "regeneration through violence,"[3] the centrality of the individual, the
inevitability of progress, the pleasure and rightness of capitalism, the
necessity of force and law, the primacy of a community of men. Or it
could be "critical" like *High Noon* (1952), *Cheyenne Autumn* (1954), or

Little Big Man (1970), condemning violence, eschewing the one-dimensional hero for a more complex figure (even a "psycho"), denouncing the genocide of Native Americans. Either way, the films were sincere; there was little questioning of the necessity for the western itself.

In its 1990s resurgence, however, the western reemerged under distinctly different conditions, specifically those of postmodernism. Two significant marks of postmodernism are generic destabilization and the questioning of traditional myths and master narratives. That is, under postmodernism, the form-content relationship often can be radically altered. The crucial difference in the western's revitalization, then, is this: the western can no longer take its central position, or even its very existence, for granted. Almost every western made in the 1990s has to justify itself as a western.[4]

Any mention of postmodernism inevitably invites and incites anxiety about what, precisely, postmodernism is. There are two fundamental modes of analysis vis-à-vis the "P word," one critical of it and one celebratory, albeit in a cautionary fashion. The first tradition, initially articulated by sociologist Jürgen Habermas sees post-modernism as a willful renunciation of Enlightenment traditions, of which modernism was a progressive extension, and in the face of which postmodernism is a reactionary repudiation. Habermas sees postmodernism as *anti*modernism, a neoconservative *negation* of the modernist project that, as he sees it, was itself deeply suspicious and critical of dominant institutions and modes of expression. In a more rigidly Marxist mode, Fredric Jameson likewise criticizes postmodernism's refusal of universal representational codes in favor of nostalgic pastiche, "an alarming and pathological symptom of a society that has become incapable of dealing with time and history."[5] For its critics, then, postmodernism ironically signals at least one universality: the inability to think historically.

The second perspective, represented by Linda Hutcheon, Hayden White, and Charles Russell among others, notes the radical potential of postmodernism to renegotiate our relationships to long-standing master narratives and dominant ideologies. Against criticism from both neoconservatives like Hilton Kramer and neo-Marxists like Terry Eagleton that postmodernism is inherently apolitical, Hutcheon notes, "Postmodern art cannot but be political, at least in the sense that its representations—its images and stories—are anything but neutral, however 'aestheticized' they may appear to be in their parodic self-reflexivity. While the postmodern has no effective theory of agency that enables a move into political *action*, it does work to turn its inevitable ideological grounding into a site of de-naturalizing critique."[6] It hardly need be said, however, that when examining any individual postmodern trait, object, or event, these two "schools" of criticism tend to function far more on a continuum than as opposing modes of thought.

Once the western allegedly disappeared, a certain elegiac rhetoric pervaded criticism about it. The comprehensive first edition of *The BFI*

Companion to the Western proclaimed its task tenable in part because the western had passed into history as surely as had the West. As Richard Schickel wrote in that book's introduction, "[the western of the 1980s] always turns out to be either a conscious . . . or unconscious . . . parody, teaching us a surprising thing: that the western is (or was) a very fragile form. . . ."[7] In his review of that volume Peter Biskind noted, "It is ironic, but perhaps fitting, that a book like *The BFI Companion to the Western* becomes possible only when its subject is dying or dead, and thus a fit specimen for cultural archeologists."[8] Slotkin's own prognosis for the western was grim. "Westerns made since 1975 generally show a weakening sense of genre—a failure . . . to creat[e] . . . the *illusion of historicity* that is so central to the genre," he wrote. "To be sure, many of the ideological stances, mythical structures, and plot structures have reappeared in other film genres, for example, the police and the science fiction film. But this merely testifies to the continuity of the myth and ideology of American culture, not to the durability of genre. If Westerns do come back, it will be because someone has been able to duplicate John Ford's achievement of connecting the special language of the Western to a story and a set of images that—with absolute economy of form—will represent for us *our true place in history*."[9] The form of the western, then, rather than its content, was moribund. In other words, the demise of westerns had more to do with how the stories were told than what the stories were saying. But the diverse natures of 1990s westerns seem to say that the *how* and the *what* are not so discrete.

Slotkin's concern with "our true place in history" resonates profoundly in the newest crop of westerns, for even in their diversity, a significant number of recent westerns show a marked preoccupation not only with their own generic value as westerns, but also with the discourse of history itself, and their relation to it. A large number of the most recent westerns, including *Dances with Wolves* (1990), *Walker* (1987), *Wyatt Earp* (1994), *Tombstone* (1993), *Posse* (1993), *Wild Bill* (1995), and *Lone Star* (1996), foreground their concerns with history either through their narrative or aesthetic strategies, or both. In this essay I want to suggest that this concern with history, be it affirmative or critical of traditional notions of historical discourse, is one of the strongest characteristics of contemporary westerns, and that one of the clearest places to see this trait is in the lone western made in the 1990s from an African-American perspective, Mario Van Peebles's *Posse*.[10]

Posse can be situated toward the critically progressive end of a continuum of historically engaged westerns, all of which are revisionist in one way or another; this continuum's two polemical boundaries are Kevin Costner's *Dances with Wolves* and Alex Cox's far lesser known *Walker*. I want briefly to explain precisely how each of these westerns sets up its particular paradigm of history, and how that affects the film's claims to revisionism.

A caveat: westerns under postmodernism are probably more diverse in their approaches and agendas than they used to be, and it is crucial to remember that just because a western is made in the postmodern era it need not be a postmodern text any more than all art made after cubism is modern by default. *Walker* is the scathing biopic of American adventurer William Walker, his movement well beyond the geographical frontier of the United States, and his takeover of Nicaragua in the mid-nineteenth century. It is clearly not chronologically part of the onslaught of post–*Dances with Wolves* westerns, but it merits inclusion because it reminds us that, though *Dances with Wolves* (and subsequently *Unforgiven* [1992]) without a doubt encouraged the production of more westerns, its critical and financial success cannot singlehandedly be credited with revitalizing the genre any more than *Heaven's Gate* (1980) can be blamed for killing it off. There are risks in periodizing 1990s westerns strictly in terms of the numerical calendar. Just as American film of the 1970s is often considered to have started with the 1967 film *Bonnie and Clyde*, so we might consider that the first recognizably 1990s western, *Walker*, was actually made in 1987. Moreover, though its disappointing box office doesn't reflect it, *Walker*, shot in Nicaragua with the participation of the Sandinista government, was as highly anticipated as *Dances with Wolves*, and its production was thoroughly covered in American mainstream media, including the *New York Times* and *Newsweek*.

Taken as a pair, *Dances with Wolves* and *Walker* elucidate two limit cases of New Western Historicism, both seemingly liberal revisionist.[11] *Dances with Wolves* is a nostalgic revision, which uses traditional realist historical and narratological modes. *Walker* is a reflexive revision, which uses postmodern aesthetic tropes such as pastiche to construct a more discursive and ironic historical mode. To briefly bring us back to Slotkin's myth-genre distinction: *Dances with Wolves* plays on the familiarity of the western form (and Hollywood's traditional conceit that there is no distinction between form and content) to revise and critique the content of the western myth. But it does almost nothing to problematize the form of that myth. *Walker* starts from the more Brechtian assumptions that form and content have a frictive, unstable relationship, and that the proposal that their relationship is unproblematic is one of the most powerful rhetorical maneuvers of traditional westerns. The film therefore treats genre revision and myth revision as indivisible projects.

Postmodernism, marked as it is by blurred boundaries, including those between theory and practice, enables films to be made that are themselves acts of historiography as much as they are acts of (non)fictional narrative. For the western, especially, this is a radical shift from its own tradition. For at the same time as the western stakes its claims to authority in a discourse of historical specificity, accuracy of detail, and nostalgia, these very discourses simultaneously lay claim to a universalizing, transhistorical (perhaps even ahistorical) power, a totalizing approach to narrative rhetoric. Westerns have tended to engage in mythography far more frequently than historiography—and in the main they still do. But western mythology is set in a pseudohistorical framework that often camouflages its mythographic project. This is achieved through realist strategies of narration that conflate the historical and the discursive such that they "narrate past events in such a way that events seem to narrate themselves."[12] If westerns had no real relationship to historical discourse, they would hardly have the power they do. But the relationship is far more complex than the genre itself typically suggests.

Indeed, the easy conflation of history and myth in the western has given it an extraordinary ability to define American identity through a dual appeal to a framework of "fact" (the geospecifics of the West, the particular temporal framework) and "abstraction" (the concepts that are hung on this mise-en-scène, such as self-reliance, community, free enterprise, individualism and so on). Philip French has argued that "the one thing the Western is always about is America rewriting and reinterpreting her own past."[13] But if it has always been a revisionist genre it has not, until relatively recently, wanted to announce itself as such. The western's most traditional and austere forms of revision (e.g. *The Man Who Shot Liberty Valance* [1962], *Fort Apache* [1948]) have taken extremely localized and specific stories and proposed reinterpretation almost entirely within the hermeneutic framework presented by the film itself. These narratives close with an understanding that even if the official version of history is false, the notion of official history is a valuable one, and worth maintaining. Even now, such films as Lawrence Kasdan and Kevin Costner's *Wyatt Earp* reaffirm the necessity of myth over fact. At the end of *Wyatt Earp*, Wyatt (Costner) and Josie (Joanna Going), on a boat bound for Alaska, encounter a young man who tells the story of his uncle, whom Wyatt Earp saved in what appears to be a very dramatic way, true to the Earp legend. When Earp admits to Josie, "Some people say it didn't happen that way," she replies, "Never mind, Wyatt. It happened that way." This is the closing couplet of the film. The couple takes an active role in validating the myth. This "proactivity," to give it the nineties twist it warrants, is also an accurate reflection of the couple's postfrontier self-mythification.

Subsequent forms of revision, such as the cycle of Vietnam-influenced westerns in the 1970s, are counteractive, which is to say that in the process of debunking the standing mythohistory they seek to put a countermythohistory in its place (cf. *Little Big Man* [1970] and *Buffalo Bill and the Indians, or Sitting Bull's History Lesson* [1976]). The center of the genre was supplanted by the margin, but the margin then became the center. What marks the western genre's move into full-blown postmodernism, is a sense, in many of these films, that there is no center (though, as *Lone Star* suggests, this does not mean that there is no longer any place to which to be marginalized). This has the effect of looping the genre right back to its traditional maneuver of conflating myth and history but with a crucial difference: the aesthetic and narrative strategies employed, particularly intertextuality and pastiche, often highlight and

31

expose the potential artificiality of the distinction between history and mythology. That is, history is no less capable of ideological stupefaction than is mythology.

What postmodern historiography (and metacinematic historical narrative) does that previous forms of historiography and historical film narrative do not is distinguish and foreground the difference between history and the past. To put it another way, whereas Andreas Huyssen claims that postmodernism consigns historical discourse to "the dustbin of the obsolete episteme, arguing gleefully that history does not exist except as text,"[14] Linda Hutcheon (responding directly to Huyssen) proposes that postmodernism, "in arguing that *history* does not exist except as text . . . does not stupidly and 'gleefully' deny that the *past* existed, but only that its accessibility to us now is entirely conditioned by textuality."[15] Or, as Dominick LaCapra has it, "the past arrives in the form of texts and textualized remainders—memories, reports, published writings, archives, monuments, and so forth," so that we can only see the reality of the past in the gap between the text and the "fact" that it represents.[16]

This is even evident in the analysis of westerns that are liminally or protorevisionist, such as John Ford's *The Man Who Shot Liberty Valance*. Christian Delage has reread the famous split between fact and legend articulated by the newspaper editor ("This is the West, son. When the legend becomes fact, print the legend") not as a binary proposition between the truth and a lie, but instead as the space between an event and its narrative.[17] This gap—and the nature of that gap—is increasingly the subject of attention in westerns throughout the late 1960s and 1970s. But, in the western's apparent resurgence in the 1990s, the attention is marked by a recontextualization in an environment in which the textualization of the image and the imaging of text is the prevailing condition.[18] *Little Big Man* directly engaged the Vietnam War as its primary target of criticism. *Blazing Saddles* (1973) parodied aspects and criticized prejudices of the western genre as a whole. *The Outlaw Josey Wales* (1976) addressed the prior star persona of Clint Eastwood and sought to enlarge and (self-) critique it, and all of these films did so with some comprehension that they set themselves against a standing set of conventions in precisely that binary way the fact/legend opposition is typically understood to operate. Subsequent westerns, especially those made after the Reagan era, have assumed a stance of even greater irony in an effort to achieve critical distance. This shift in the understanding has a great deal to do with a shift in the way history is increasingly conceived in both academe and popular culture and society: contested, unstable, subject to change and revision.

We may therefore distinguish the historical sensibilities of *Walker* and *Dances with Wolves* in this way: *Walker* has a postmodern sense of history and historiography as always already textualized and interpreted (cf. Hutcheon and LaCapra), and *Dances with Wolves* has a realist sense of history, as expressed by Peter Gay, who writes, "The objects of the historian's inquiry are precisely that, objects, out there in a real and single past. Historical controversy in no way compromises their integrity. The tree in the woods of the past fell in only one way, no matter how fragmentary or contradictory the reports of its fall, no matter whether there are no historians, one historian or several contentious historians in its future to record and debate it."[19] Which is to say that, for a film like *Dances with Wolves*, there can be only one possible correct narrative for these events. A film like *Walker*, engaged as it is in critical postmodern historiography, not only makes clear that, though there may only be one set of real objects, they can be narrativized in any number of ways, and, as Hayden White puts it, "What we wish to call mythic narrative is under no obligation to keep the two orders of events, real and imaginary, distinct from one another. Narrative becomes a problem only when we wish to give real events the form of story. It is because real events do not offer themselves as stories that their narrativization is so difficult."[20]

The traditional sense of history to which *Dances with Wolves* adheres (through which the film presents its version of events as a definitive corrective), has typically been one of the fundamental markers of the western genre. As John Cawelti puts it, the rituals of and in the western are "means of affirming basic cultural values, resolving tension and establishing a sense of continuity between present and past."[21] What I want to propose as essential to the genre's turn toward the postmodern is a reformulation of Cawelti's astute summation. *Walker* as a postmodern western *interrogates* basic cultural values; it questions the very act of affirmation and establishes a critical sense of how any society draws continuities between the present and past.

In this sense, though Kevin Costner has certainly made a revisionist western in terms of *Dances with Wolves's* apparent content, it is in formal terms what we might call a *nostalgic* western. This is a category into which we might also put Clint Eastwood's influential and highly successful *Unforgiven*, though the latter film is more ambivalently nostalgic, and not necessarily because it intends to be.[22] This is not to say that either Eastwood or Costner wish to return to the "good old days" of racist hypocrisy—one can certainly argue that Eastwood's *The Outlaw Josey Wales* continues Ford's apologist project, which is eventually taken up by Costner in his own film. Rather, going back to Slotkin's myth/genre formulation, this paradigm of New Western filmmaking accepts the traditional western conceits and simply reverses them. This does not by default make *Dances with Wolves* a less potent critic than *Walker* of the worst of old western values (though to my mind it is). Nor does this make it a less legitimate instantiation of the qualities of New Westerns. It merely illustrates *Dances with Wolves's* investment in the kind of binary logic that predates postmodernism. We might even consider it a proto–Bill Clinton western: it presents its liberal credentials at the door, but as events really get cooking, we find it first drifting, then sprinting like mad, toward the center.

In fact, the nostalgia of *Dances with Wolves* is less for a real past than it is symptomatic of a desire to change the past itself—precisely the kind of nostalgic impulse that Fredric Jameson suggests is at the core of postmodern schizophrenia. If what the film remembers is more accurate than most classical western portrayals insofar as it acknowledges the series of betrayals effected by Anglos on Native Americans (particularly in an institutional context), it is nevertheless an attempt to recuperate the category of individual Anglos, particularly men. As *L.A. Weekly* film critic Helen Knode put it, "*Dances with Wolves* reworks the myth of the West into a fantasy of what might have happened if the white man weren't so ethnocentric and crude."[23] Roger Ebert concurred: "In a sense, *Dances with Wolves* is a sentimental fantasy, a 'what if' movie."[24] Elsewhere, Knode went further, implicitly connecting the rewriting of history to the character Dunbar's act of writing in his journals: "Lt. Dunbar rewrites the history of the West in a way that redeems the white man . . . archetypally true but not literally believable."[25] Even Costner himself seems at least somewhat aware of the dominance of nostalgia over revision in *Dances with Wolves*. As he remarked in one interview, the film was "a real experience of what the West may have been."[26] *Real experience; may have been:* the film's star-auteur seems on the face of it to be making claims for the film's historical discourse, but in fact Costner may be claiming no more than the real experience of a hypothetical.

Walker's historical concept, on the other hand, is invested in the idea that History is a master discourse, as is, in some sense, The Western (though not necessarily all individual westerns), and that this master status is very much in need of interrogation. This is emphasized by Alex Cox's use of pastiche. Jameson considers pastiche a regressive aesthetic maneuver—when parody, devoid of any sense of history, loses its critical teeth, we are left with the meaningless appropriation of previously used texts, or pieces of texts.[27] *Walker* is a convincing argument that pastiche itself has critical potential. (Van Peebles's *Posse*, directly influenced by *Walker*, employs the same strategy.) Simultaneous to William Walker's emphatic fall from heroic abolitionist to psychotic imperialist is an encroaching of the present tense (the 1980s) onto the past of the film (the 1850s). In classic postmodern pastiche, personal computers appear in Cornelius Vanderbilt's office, soldiers smoke Marlboros and drink Coca-Cola, the Nicaraguan aristocracy read *Newsweek* in their carriages, and finally, just as the town of Granada is going up in flames, the Marines land by helicopter to airlift all American citizens out of Nicaragua. As the end credits roll, a small television shows spliced-together news reports and Ronald Reagan's presidential press conferences, which compete with each other in revealing and denying that the United States is in any way involved in Nicaraguan affairs.

This image is not a finale but a coda wherein the appearance of the present is meant to illuminate the way that conventional historical models camouflage, rather than expose, the linear "inevitability" of

Manifest Destiny. It is a visual strategy consistent with sociologist Michael Rogin's assessment that during his administration Reagan "was replacing history by visionary myth."[28] It is against this visionary myth that Alex Cox speaks in *Walker*.

So *Dances with Wolves* wishes only to renovate the content of the western, and *Walker*, striving for metahistorical critique, attempts to problematize the ostensibly pat and naturalized relationship between the western's form and content. If these two films instantiate two extreme presentations of historical discourse, *Posse* lies somewhere in between, radical in its discursive impulses like *Walker*, but, like *Dances with Wolves*, far more accessible to a general public. Like *Dances with Wolves*, *Posse* is prone to certain simplistic strategies of reversal and replacement, seeming to slot in African Americans where Anglos traditionally appear in classical westerns. But *Posse* has a far more complex sociopolitical agenda than *Dances with Wolves*, one that reflects its intimate connection with *Walker*. For if *Walker*'s box office would seem to indicate that its influence did not extend into more mainstream cinema, *Posse* indicates that it most certainly did. Sy Richardson, who starred as Captain Hornsby in *Walker* (and appeared in every other film Cox had made up to that point) went on to cowrite *Posse* with Dario Scardapane, and some of the approach to historical discourse of Cox and screenwriter Rudy Wurlitzer (who also wrote *Pat Garrett and Billy the Kid* [directed by Sam Peckinpah, 1973]) is evident in this African-American western. The central conceits of *Walker*—that history is less about a chain of events than the construction of systems, that the past resonates deeply in the present, and that this is best illustrated both narratively and aesthetically by literally pushing representations of past and present together—exist in *Posse* in a set of codings that are simultaneously more mainstream Hollywood and also more specific to African-American popular culture.

Posse is an amalgamated history of Richardson's two grandfathers, an instantiation of what historian Robert Rosenstone calls a strategy of historical condensation.[29] As Richardson describes, "One of my grandfathers, the Reverend King David Lee was a minister with four churches in Georgia who wanted to form a township out of all of the congregations. My other grandfather fought in the Spanish Civil War and, although he didn't ride with Jesse James, his friends did. *Posse* is a combination of their stories."[30] Jesse Lee (Mario Van Peebles) and some of his company desert their Spanish Civil War unit when Lee discovers that his racist commander (Billy Zane), a very Walker-like Manifest Destiny addict, is sending his soldiers out to certain death not for ideological reasons but simply to procure a trunk of gold. Sneaking out of Cuba and into New Orleans, Lee, through a fairly standard series of western genre misadventures involving saloon girls, becomes an outlaw and forms a posse with his fellow soldiers and a pair of con artists, one black, one white. They head West to Freemanville, a utopian all-black settlement under threat both from without (the Ku Klux Klan) and from within (a devious businessman [Blair Underwood] behind a real estate scam). The group—Lee in particular—is pursued from all sides, including the reappearance of their commander.

The racial politics of *Posse* are extremely complex, and somewhat equivocal. On the one hand they seek to restore, perhaps even invent, a black vocabulary and speaking position in the larger lexicon of the western genre. In so doing, *Posse* is altogether explicit in its appropriation of contemporary African-American culture. Yet, as I shall discuss in more detail later, the culture it references is an urban one, an apparent historical and generic contradiction. On the other hand, the film seems to suggest that there is a certain virtue in color blindness, and it does this primarily through the film's one good white character, Little Jay (Stephen Baldwin).

Posse's history is a counterhistory, and in this sense it is a counter-western in the Last Western tradition of *Buffalo Bill and the Indians*, *McCabe and Mrs. Miller* (1971), and especially *Little Big Man*, a film it references explicitly by placing Woody Strode in the position of narrating from advanced age, a deep historical remove, and a place of critical irony, as did Dustin Hoffman's Jack Crabb. Strode's history lesson begins ahistorically, at least aesthetically, as he sits at his desk against a black background, out of space and time, abstracted and allegorical. It ends firmly rooted in the present, as we see a trio of reporters, two of whom are played by fellow black filmmakers Reggie and Warrington Hudlin, dressed in contemporary clothing and using a tape recorder (this too overtly references *Little Big Man*) and camera. *Posse*'s social project (in addition to the economic goals of all Hollywood products) attempts to set the record straight by reinscribing blacks in the history of the West.

But if *Posse* was an alternative and revisionist history of the American West, it was difficult to get American money to produce it. Strictly speaking, the $9 million budget came from a British production company, Working Title Films. It was subsequently distributed by Gramercy Pictures/PolyGram Filmed Entertainment. As Van Peebles recalls, "When I went to the studios, what'd they do? They laughed. 'Oh, a fried chicken Western.' 'Boyz N the Saddle.' 'Unfo'given.' They laughed me out of the studio."[31] At the same time, *Posse* also lays claim to an African-American prerogative to author and star in what had heretofore largely been the quintessential white genre. (Certainly for Mario Van Peebles this was a precedent set by his previous feature, *New Jack City*, which was largely read as an African-American treatment of the previously largely white gangster genre.)[32] In order to do this, the film must appeal to the history of the western, as well as to contemporary culture, especially the rap and hip-hop of black urban youth culture (which had by this time long become a far more transcultural powerhouse), as well as the longer standing and less economically powerful culture of black cinema itself.

The casting of Woody Strode, and the *Little Big Man*–like narrative conceit are the most immediate ways the film hails its own genre, as well as hints at what its larger historical project will be, though they are hardly the only gestures. But the film's casting strategies serve a twofold purpose: on the one hand, actors like Pam Grier, Nipsy Russell, Isaac Hayes, and Melvin Van Peebles situate the film *outside* the western tradition and inside other broader traditions of African-American cinema. But, just as Cox recalled the British punk ethos of the 1970s with former Clash band member Joe Strummer's soundtrack in *Walker*, Van Peebles situates *Posse's* historical agenda in the service of contemporary black subjects (and also addresses them) with his casting of both East and West Coast rappers (Tone Lōc, Big Daddy Kane). He also allies himself with a larger community of black filmmakers by casting Charles Lane and the Hudlin brothers. Screenwriter Sy Richardson also has a small part.

On its release it was received with mixed reviews, but almost all critics noted producer/star/director Mario Van Peebles's nearly encyclopedic reference to the prior history of westerns, in both auteurist and narrative terms. As Michael Wilmington wrote in the *Los Angeles Times, Posse* seemed to say to its audience, "'Think I can't do a Sergio Leone? A George Roy Hill? A Clint Eastwood? Watch *this*.'" *Posse* went "through virtually every Western structural motif and archetype they can think of: from Hunt-the-Man-Down to Cleaning-Up-the-Town, from holster-slapping six-gun duels to a climactic Gatling Gun holocaust that suggests *The Magnificent Seven* scrambled up with *The Wild Bunch* and *High Noon*."[33] For Wilmington this did not lead to a kind of Jamesonian schizophrenic incoherence in which rap was, if not randomly then certainly capriciously, laid down over the images of a period film; it simply made it as ambitious as (nearly) the only black western since *Buck and the Preacher* (1971) ought to be.[34]

For other critics *Posse's* appropriation of so many different elements from past westerns had a flattening effect. In the *San Francisco Chronicle* John Stanley wrote, "As wild, woolly and bloody as the work of Sam Peckinpah, as nihilistic and funky as the spaghetti Westerns of Sergio Leone, with a central character as grimly charismatic as Clint Eastwood and with occasional scenery out of a John Ford frontier saga, *Posse* could be subtitled 'The Hip Magnificent Seven Meet the Cool Young Guns.'"[35] What bothered Stanley most about the film was its "flippant '90s consciousness," especially when one character quotes Rodney King and asks "Can't we all get along?" (If Stanley found that cartoonish, I will eventually want to suggest that it is part of a larger strategy that forces two historical moments together in a single narrative.)

And the references are indeed dizzying. If Jonathan Kaplan's *Bad Girls* (1994) is an exceptionally unimaginative rip-off of a single film—Peckinpah's *The Wild Bunch* (1969)—Van Peebles's tactics are far more wide-ranging and better naturalized in the body of his film, and they make the contemporary elements he chooses to use stand out in even greater relief. His canted angles, extreme high and low angles, and extreme close-ups—especially when the screen is filled with shot and countershot of adversarial pairs of squinting eyes—are textbook Leone. His Cuban battle scenes and his male bonding at the watering hole are textbook Peckinpah. After being told by various subtitles that we are in "Cuba, 1989," then "New Orleans," we are finally told we are at the "Western Frontier," as a train screeches over the tracks and the camera. This shot cuts to the first traditionally western scene in the film—the posse riding over high plains with snow-capped mountains in the background—textbook Anthony Mann. Van Peebles leans toward quoting postclassical directors, but he acknowledges John Ford in pivotal scenes with frame-within-frame techniques.

Yet if Van Peebles did stretch to take into account as many elements of the western, and as many specific auteurist references as possible, it also points up just how anathema a Black Western remains, and how much a black filmmaker still has to prove what he knows about the genre in order to lay claim to it. For the authority of westerns to speak about American identity is founded on (among other things) a racialist discourse. If it is not always foregrounded that the subject of westerns is an Anglo-Saxon male—and that this is therefore what is meant by American identity—it is almost always taken for granted. And it is impossible to offer up such a subject without also displaying what that subject is *not*: female, non-Christian, nonwhite, and nonheterosexual. Richard Slotkin has pointed out that an essential component of most westerns is the articulation of racial difference almost immediately in the diegesis. This moment may be unimportant to the plot, but it is usually there. Even in narratives that seem to transpire entirely in a white world, the plot cannot move forward without some visible articulation of racial difference: in *My Darling Clementine*, Wyatt Earp's skills are proven through his disposal of the drunken Indian Charley; in *Ride the High Country* (1962) the initial conflict is introduced in a Chinese restaurant.[36] And these are films that seem to mark race through invisibility rather than visibility.

Richard Dyer has astutely asserted that in Hollywood, the concept of whiteness is as invisible as blackness is visible (and therefore both problematic and problematized). "White power secures its dominance by seeming not to be anything in particular," he writes. "This property of whiteness, to be everything and nothing, is the source of its representational power."[37] In some way identity politics has actually reenforced this sense of White as Universal Norm. As Dyer suggests, "Looking, with such passion and single-mindedness, at non-dominant groups, has had the effect of reproducing the sense of oddness, differentness, exceptionality of these groups, the feeling that they are departures from the norm. Meanwhile the norm has carried on as if it is the natural, inevitable, ordinary way of being human."[38] For the western and its stake in defining national identity, this was by extension, then, the natural, inevitable, ordinary way of being American. It was assumed that the hero would be white. (That the hero would be male is also assumed, and *Posse* has virtually nothing to say about that.) *Posse* not only offers a black hero, but also problematizes whiteness without making that the central focus of the diegesis. Heroism in *Posse*, and the individuality and subjectivity that it relies on, are not categories that have to be wrested from white society, but are proposed as just as intrinsic (or not) to black culture.

Posse's own project therefore hovers somewhere in between a nonracialist and a counterracialist discourse. (The counterracialism is already apparent in Van Peebles's work in *New Jack City*.) If John Ford's apology for racism arguably starts with *The Searchers* in 1956, it is continued with far less ambiguity in *Sergeant Rutledge* (1960), starring Woody Strode as a war hero wrongly accused of assaulting a white officer's wife. At issue, of course, remains the sacred trust of Western racialist discourse—the purity of a white woman, whom Rutledge is accused of raping. The film is as inflected with the courtroom drama genre as it is with the western, and is stylistically as close to film noir as Ford ever gets (and this in a color film). Narratively structured to alternate its present tense in the courtroom with a series of flashbacks largely consisting of frontier cavalry battles, *Sergeant Rutledge* plays with a Rashomonic structure to destabilize standing western traditions of white superiority. But the restitution of honor to Sergeant Rutledge is achieved at the expense of the Native Americans in the film, for it is they who are indeed responsible for the aggression that goes beyond that shown against Constance Towers and extends to the whole white frontier community, to whom Strode's Rutledge is an ancillary and ultimately servile presence. Ironically, this plays into a long tradition of the representation of Black Virilism in American cinema, a legacy even older than *The Birth of a Nation*, of depicting black men as profoundly threatening, especially insofar as they are portrayed to embody a sexual threat to white women (and therefore a threat to racial purity).[39] In order for Rutledge to be seen as nonthreatening—and proven so in a court of law—he must be desexualized and another equally threatening nonwhite identity must be asserted in his place—in this case the Native American. Though *Posse* certainly reverses the racial roles (the whites, especially but not exclusively in the form of the Ku Klux Klan, are the villains), not all whites are bad (Stephen Baldwin, part of the posse, provides the highly physical, utterly noncerebral comic relief traditionally left to an African-American character in white films), and not all blacks act heroically or even morally (e.g., the businessman Carter as capitalist tool).

Nevertheless, the film often seems unsure of how to say what it wants to say—and sometimes unsure of *what*, exactly, it wants to say about race other than that racism is, well, *bad*. On the one hand, Van Peebles reverses black and white roles, protagonist and antagonist: Jesse Lee, the hero, is black; his lover is biracial, African and Native American. The truly evil characters are all white, and one of them, a knife-wielding tracker, sports a long bleach-blond mohawk that simultaneously evokes the designated Native American villain nation, the Pawnee, and, with the two shot guns strapped to his back, the gang of marauders in the *Mad Max* films. The token differently raced member of the posse is white.

On the other hand, elsewhere in the diegesis Van Peebles seems to want to suggest that race makes absolutely no difference at all. He takes great pains to present what is a nearly abecedarian version of universal suffering under Anglo oppression, bringing together in one railroad construction scene former slaves, Chinese coolies, and Native Americans. In this he homogenizes the nature of the oppression, masking the cultural and historical specificity of the conditions in each case, which is an elision of history quite similar to that of which he and his film rightly accuse Hollywood and dominant white culture. In one of the more remarkable, and controversial, moments of the film, Little Jay (Stephen Baldwin) is dragged out of The Promised Land, a black saloon, by the white sheriff of the neighboring town (who tells him, "you kinda stick out in here") and beaten to death by the sheriff and his white thugs. During the beating, which clearly echoes the beating of truck driver Reginald Denny after the Rodney King verdict, the camera views him from overhead (how most of us first saw the Denny beating), and there is a graphic match of Little Jay's face with that of Jesse Lee's father King David Lee, who was beaten to death in a similar way by the same men. White on white violence, and the equivalence of a white martyred figure with a black one: *Posse*'s racial politics exceed the facile.

The intricacies of *Posse*'s racial cartography are echoed in the film's generic complexity. Despite Van Peebles's encyclopedic coverage of the western tradition, *Posse*'s generic hybridity was also noted in much of its prerelease press. Few articles ever spoke of it simply as a western, but would also designate it a comedy, an action film, a rap vehicle. It was highly anticipated as Van Peebles's follow up to his first feature, the extremely successful *New Jack City*. The hybridity was indivisible from its political project. Alex Cox's point in *Walker* was to tell the story of William Walker partly as a kind of retrieval historiography (he had been world famous in his day but was almost completely forgotten by the 1980s), and partly as a critique of Reagan's policies in Nicaragua by suggesting their roots in a longer tradition of Manifest Destiny. Van Peebles in some ways undertook an even more metacritical endeavor: in addition to drawing the connection between nineteenth and twentieth century racism, he used the suppressed history of blacks in the West to point up the suppressed present of blacks in mainstream American filmmaking.

In order to make the particular arguments about history Van Peebles does in *Posse*, he employs a form of postmodern pastiche that Jameson and other critics of postmodernism contend actually erases any historical consciousness, though it does so employing a logic more familiar to *Dances with Wolves* than *Walker*. The film opens with the iconic and highly evocative presence of Woody Strode—the most recognizable black actor in westerns since World War II, whose character name and relation to the story we are not given. Strode therefore assumes a mythic, allegorical status, playing himself as much as any actual character. The film closes with Strode revealing that he was a child who witnessed many of the events in the story, effecting a *Dances with Wolves*-like appeal to authenticity. Like Costner's film, then, *Posse* stakes some large measure of its authority on the value of the witness to—though perhaps not quite the participant in—history. It is the testimonial discourse of "I was there." The closing credits roll over both the famous opening of Sergio Leone's *Once Upon a Time in the West,* a discrete mininarrative unto itself featuring Woody Strode, and a much earlier series of black westerns that precede Strode's career, including *The Bronze Buckaroo* and *Harlem Rides the Range.* This strategy has the interesting effect of transforming the witness into an actant. Strode's character is a child who saw things happen. But the use of his past films, as well as other films that make up the prehistory of those films, adds an evidentiary gravity. "I was there" becomes something between "This happened to me" and "I did this." At its end, history in *Posse* oscillates between something that happens to people and something people make happen.

This is not the first time Van Peebles has used precisely this technique, one that requires the spectator to make extremely nimble generic and historical associations. In *New Jack City,* gangster Nino Brown (Wesley Snipes) stands screaming "top o' the world!" in front of a big screen television on which plays *Scarface.* During the course of the scene, the *Scarface* footage abruptly changes to scenes from *Sweet Sweetback's Baadasssss Song,* his father Melvin's breakthrough independent film of 1971. In this single gesture, which never disrupts the narrative flow, Van Peebles suggests that the equivalence of "gangsters" and urban "gangstas" is partially a construction that serves the dominant white culture far more than it serves the ultimately doomed gangsta himself. At the same time, he references what he considers to be black filmmaking's original gangsta, or perhaps more apt, guerrilla—his own father.

In *Posse*, these references, which come at the expense of a *Dances with Wolves*-style hermetically sealed authentic environment, are similarly forced into a historically critical pastiche, since the original soundtracks from all three sampled films have been replaced by a rap from (among others) Tone Lōc, who also plays Angel in the film. But this rupture of seamless historical recreation is not reserved only for the beginning and the end of the film. Rather, the present intrudes upon the past of the diegesis with regularity, and most consistently through the music. In New Orleans we hear a male quartet sing a cappella soul. In Freemanville a chanteuse romances one of the posse with the blues, and gospel in a style not innovated until the twenties is heard in many of Jesse Lee's flashbacks. Additionally, Van Peebles saves the markedly white sound of country and western, or stereotypically "cowboy" music, for the comical interludes at the watering hole.[40] Otherwise he prefers to stress the African aspect of this African-American western by using African-style percussion as the background music for most of the film.

41

Yet it is the spoken ruptures that are intended to snap the spectator back into the presence—to incite a bifocal vision in the viewer. The westerns of the late 1960s made us increasingly comfortable with western characters speaking in contemporary cadences and with a modern vocabulary, and *Posse* certainly hews to contemporary idioms. However, there are two particular moments that force the audience at least to consider the film as a political statement. At a moment when the townsfolk of Freemanville are debating whether or not to stand up to the crooked white sheriff, the character Papa Joe (who has already been beaten and arrested by the sheriff) shouts out, "No justice, no peace!" It is extremely significant, of course, that Papa Joe is played by Melvin Van Peebles. Later, during the final shoot-out (and with a decidedly more comic intent), Nipsey Russell, quoting Rodney King, shouts out to no one in particular, "Can't we all get along?"

Though he seems most comfortable taking genres that are traditionally white and treating them from an African-American perspective (rather than make films, as Spike Lee does, that are less generically marked), Mario Van Peebles (who seemed to sit for these exchanges with his father as often as not), speaks repeatedly in interviews of a fear of sequels, hearkening back to the serialization of blaxploitation films: "While we have the door open it is important that we diversify a little bit. It is important that we don't get trapped into the repetitive sequel business of the '70s—*Shaft Goes to 7-11* and *Superfly Comes Back Twice*."[41] Van Peebles largely attributed this relentless serialization to white financial control over black cinematic production: "If [*Posse*] fails, I know Hollywood will look at it and say, you should have stuck to *New Jack City Part 7*."[42]

Posse's counternarrative starts with its title. Rather than simply and ironically (since the heroes are the outlaws) signifying the group of law-abiding citizens who saddle up and chase down frontier criminals, the word reverts to the original meaning, which is simply, as the dictionary defines it, "A large group often with a common interest."[43] While still retaining all of its western overtones and authoritarian implications, the title speaks of the *re*appropriation of the word to the particular context of hip-hop culture, which *encircles* (rather than replacing or obliterating) its previous western connotation. Indeed, the complex oscillation in the title is indicative of the larger movement of the film itself. Like *Walker*, its diegesis starts *off* of U.S. soil (this time in Cuba rather than Mexico) and moves back through New Orleans before moving to the frontier—it moves north before it moves west. (New Orleans may be a historically accurate stopping point for both stories, but it is also one of the few genuine "melting pot" places of American culture, and it is this that enables the particular racial configuration that propels the diegesis.) Moreover, when the group of men is finally mythologized on a "wanted" poster, they are called, oxymoronically, "The Outlaw Posse."

Posse opens with an extraordinarily violent battle sequence that verges on the incoherent. In starting with violence rather than building up to it, the film aligns itself with the Vietnam-era westerns that, if they could not address the war directly, certainly addressed its violence graphically. By extension, *Posse*'s sense of its spectator's inevitably self-reflexive stance as a condition of postmodernity is evident in its view of the frontier, perhaps the sine qua non of any western. As Carter, the corrupt businessman, explains to Jesse Lee, "Ain't that black and white no more, Jesse. Soon the West is going to be settled, ain't goin' to be no more new frontier or frontiersmen. It's going to be about business, my friend, and businessmen." A pre–John F. Kennedy western would never have used a phrase like "no more new frontier." That said, however, *Posse* is a 1990s western with a 1960s upbringing, with Melvin Van Peebles as the film's paterfamilias, and a particularly utopian separatist (or at least highly selectively integrationist) view of the ideal frontier community.

Posse, or at least its star-director, makes a good counterargument for young audiences having lost the chance during the 1980s to learn how to watch westerns films the way previous generations of spectators had without interruption since *The Great Train Robbery*. So confident was Van Peebles that even young black urban audiences were fluent in the protocols that he deliberately employed a certain "shorthand" in character and plot development: "Everyone has seen 'Bonanza,' Leone, Eastwood, yeah, yeah. Nowadays they want you to cut to the chase. The kids, they already know what you're doing before you do it."[44] What seems implied in Van Peebles's assessment of the nature of that spectatorship is first of all that the lessons largely come from television. But perhaps more important, the lessons also come from the rapid-fire editing and narrative style of MTV, and it's that visual vocabulary that informs the film's style as much as the more baroque speed and movement of Leone and Peckinpah.

Although *Posse* is the only African-American western to have been made in the 1990s, it is in many ways consistent with one extremely important trend in the work of young black filmmakers. Paula Massood has noted a tendency of these filmmakers to move from making films set in an urban context to films that explicitly take place outside and beyond that context; as she writes, "The urban 'hood acts as a chronotopic motif within other genres (such as the western or the horror film) at the same time that the majority of young filmmakers who got their start with 'hood films (Van Peebles, John Singleton, Matty Rich, even the Hughes Brothers) went on to different genres and spatio-temporal locations."[45] After Making *Boyz N the Hood* and *Poetic Justice*, John Singleton turned his attention to *Rosewood*. Matty Rich followed *Straight Outta Brooklyn* with *The Inkwell*, set on Martha's Vineyard. Even Spike Lee ended *Clockers* with his central character heading West, to the desert, on an iron horse (even if it was Amtrak).

If for a dominant white culture the western has traditionally been a central site of affirmation, discussion, and contestation of American identity, *Posse* indicates that its spaces may also function as imaginary spaces—which is to say spaces for the imagination—of *African*-American identity. Indeed, at least as an imaginary space (for "The West," if it ever did exist, is certainly gone now), it is a mythic environment that offers resonant analogies for contemporary urban experience. As Intelligent Hoodlums says in "Posse Love," the rap that accompanies the closing credits, "Everyday is a new test/gettin' more and more like the Old Wild West."

If the typical western has excluded the black spectator less and less as the genre has moved beyond simple revisionism, it has rarely explicitly invited that spectator into the text. One mark of the genre's definitive shift toward metacriticism and self-conscious historiography is the increasing number of westerns that go out of their way to hail previously marginalized identities. In this *Posse*, though still unique in its focus on black subjectivity, is in fact clearly part of a larger group of westerns that define themselves not only generically but also in terms of identity politics. These include *The Ballad of Little Jo* (1993) and *Dead Man* (1996), as well as contemporary westerns like *Thunderheart* (1992) and *Lone Star* (1996). In all of these cases, myth, history and identity are proposed as deeply imbricated, complex and problematic categories, all of which can be worked through by appealing to, critiquing, and subverting the generic imaginary of the western and its conventions.

notes

1. Richard Slotkin, "Prologue to a Study of Myth and Genre in American Movies," *Prospects* 9 (1984): 407–32.
2. André Bazin, "The Western, or the American Film *par excellence*," in *What Is Cinema?* vol. 2, trans. Hugh Gray (Berkeley and Los Angeles: University of California Press, 1971), 140–48.
3. Richard Slotkin, *Regeneration through Violence: The Mythology of the American Frontier, 1600–1860* (Middletown, Conn.: Wesleyan University Press, 1973); see especially chapter 1.
4. The exception to this need for justification is, of course, the domestic westerns on television, which, since *Lonesome Dove* (1989) have enjoyed a resurgence as least as vigorous as that of big-screen westerns, but usually with significantly less self-reflexivity. Though *Lonesome Dove* was a national network miniseries, serious attention has yet to be paid to the influence of Ted Turner's two cable stations, Turner Network Television (TNT) and Turner Broadcasting System (TBS), which have turned out more westerns in the 1990s than anyone else.
5. Fredric Jameson, "Postmodernism and Consumer Society," in *The Anti-Aesthetic: Essays on Postmodern Culture*, ed. Hal Foster (Port Townsend, Wash.: Bay Press, 1983), 117.
6. Linda Hutcheon, *The Politics of Postmodernism* (New York: Routledge, 1989), 3.
7. Richard Schickel, introduction to *The BFI Companion to the Western*, ed. Edward Buscombe (New York: Atheneum, 1988), 11. See also Howard Hawks on the demise of the western in Joseph McBride, *Hawks on Hawks* (Berkeley and Los Angeles: University of California Press, 1982), especially 112–14.
8. Peter Biskind, "Book Review," *New York Times*, May 13, 1990, 14.
9. Slotkin, "Prologue," 430, emphasis added.

10. Though Barry Levinson's *Wild, Wild West* (1999) stars Will Smith, one of the most popular and powerful black stars in the United States, Smith's race, though periodically commented on in the diegesis, has almost nothing to do with either the plot or the film's proposed ideological content.

11. It is worth stressing that I am not concerned with the disparity between the historical facts of the frontier and the fiction of western movies. This oft-pronounced gap has been well described and critiqued in many places. Rather, I take factual discord for granted and ask *why* any film or group of films presents the version of the West that it does. See for instance, Gretchen Bataille and George P. Silet, eds., *The Pretend Indians: Images of Native Americans in the Movies* (Ames: Iowa State University Press, 1980); Ward Churchill, *Fantasies of the Master Race: Literature, Cinema, and the Colonization of American Indians*, ed. M. Annette Jaimes (Monroe, Me.: Common Courage Press, 1992), esp. "Fantasies of the Master Race: Categories of Stereotyping of American Indians in Film," 231–41; Richard Drinnon, *Facing West: The Metaphysics of Indian-Hating and Empire-Building* (New York: New American Library, 1980); Greg Garrett, "The American West and the American Western: Printing the Legend," *Journal of American Culture* 14, no. 2 (1991): 99–105; Henry Nash Smith, *Virgin Land: The American West As Symbol and Myth*, (Cambridge: Harvard University Press, 1950).

12. Hutcheon, *Politics*, 92.

13. Philip French, *Westerns* (London: Secker and Warburg, 1973), 24.

14. Andreas Huyssen, *After the Great Divide: Modernism, Mass Culture, Postmodernism* (Bloomington: Indiana University Press, 1986), 35.

15. Hutcheon, *Politics*, 16.

16. Dominick LaCapra, *History and Criticism* (Ithaca, N.Y.: Cornell University Press, 1985), 128.

17. Christian Delage, "John Ford and Michael Cimino," paper delivered at the Film/Culture/History Conference, Aberdeen University, August 1996.

18. For an explanation of both the pictorial turn which is one of the conditions of postmodernism and the "imagetext," an entity specific to late postmodernity, see W. J. T. Mitchell, *Picture Theory* (Chicago: University of Chicago Press, 1994).

19. Peter Gay, *Style in History* (New York: Basic Books, 1974), 210.

20. Hayden White, *The Content of the Form* (Baltimore: Johns Hopkins University Press, 1987), 4.

21. John Cawelti, *The Six-Gun Mystique* (Bowling Green, Ohio: Bowling Green State University Press, 1970), 32.

22. *Unforgiven* is in many ways a far less successful revisionist western than the older *Outlaw Josey Wales* largely because Clint Eastwood's star persona and status as icon of the individual's right to take matters into his own hands when the insititutions whose job that is fail him (cf. the entire *Dirty Harry* series), had by 1992 ossified into something practically nonnegotiable to the public. Though critics usually saw the antiviolence message in the film, audiences seem to have taken the final showdown as a straightforward instance of regeneration through violence, rather than the ironic commentary on it that Eastwood seems to have intended.

23. Helen Knode, film review, *L.A. Weekly*, November 9–15, 1990, 29; (*Dances with Wolves* clippings file, Margaret Herrick Library, Academy of Motion Picture Arts and Sciences, Los Angeles).

24. Roger Ebert, "A Unique Western: Epic 'Dances' Speaks to Dignity," *Chicago Sun-Times*, November 9, 1990.

25. Helen Knode, "A House with a View of the Moon," *L.A. Weekly*, November 23–29, 1990, 10.

26. Kevin Costner, quoted in Graham Fuller, "A Career at High Noon," *Elle*, September 1990, 164.

27. Fredric Jameson, "Postmodernism and Consumer Society." See also Jameson, *Postmodernism, or the Cultural Logic of Late Capitalism* (Durham, N.C.: Duke University Press, 1991), especially the chapter on film, "Nostalgia for the Present," 279–96.

28. Michael Rogin, *Ronald Reagan, the Movie and Other Episodes in Political Demonology* (Berkeley and Los Angeles: University of California Press, 1987), xvi.

29. Robert Rosenstone, "*Walker*: The Dramatic Film as (Postmodern) History," in *Visions of the Past: The Challenge of Film to Our Idea of History* (Cambridge, Mass.: Harvard University Press, 1996), 144.

30. Sy Richardson, quoted in Alex McGregor, "Cowboyz 'n' the Hood," *Time Out* (London), November 17, 1993, 18.

31. Mario Van Peebles, quoted in John Stanley, "Mario and Melvin Van Peebles Bring '90s Consciousness to 'Posse,'" *San Francisco Chronicle*, May 16, 1993, 22.

32. *New Jack City* was indeed a classic inversion of racial configurations, and though its trade was drugs rather than contraband booze à la *Little Caesar* (1930), it has far less to do with "gangsta" culture than films like Ernest Dickerson's *Juice* (1992), and its narrative codes are a significant remove from those aestheticized by gangsta rap.

33. Michael Wilmington, "'Posse': A New Take on the Old West," *Los Angeles Times*, May 14, 1993, F-1.

34. In fact, there were blaxploitation westerns subsequent to *Buck and the Preacher*, all of which starred ex-football star Fred Williamson: *The Legend of Nigger Charley*, and its sequel *The Soul of Nigger Charley* (1973), and *Boss Nigger* (1974); but their projects were not to engage or critique the prior white/Anglocentric historical discourse of westerns. As Jim Pine suggests, "the failure of blaxploitation Westerns to experiment with the conventions, and to go beyond adventure motifs undermines their ability to address the issues they evoke with genuine social critique." (Pine, entry on "Blacks," Buscombe, ed., *The BFI Companion to the Western*, 71).

35. Stanley, "Mario and Melvin Van Peebles," 22.

36. Conversation with Richard Slotkin, October 22, 1996.

37. Richard Dyer, "White," *Screen* 29, no. 4 (1988): 44–45.

38. Ibid., 44.

39. This may explain why Van Peebles makes near soft-core porn out of the obligatory sex scene between his character and Lana (Salli Richardson), his lover. This said, besides the fact that she also plays the traditional role of the school teacher (against tradition insofar as the school teacher tends to embody all that is virginal in westerns) there are two important details about Lana's character: first, she seems to be, from both physical appearance and dress, part Native American; and second, her father Papa Joe (Melvin Van Peebles) says about her, "she's my daughter but she's a woman first," acknowledging an independent female sexuality in a way few westerns do.

40. Van Peebles's reflexivity on the score of the cowboy mythology is more than musical. At one point while riding the range, one of the more "intellectual" characters complains, "Fuck this monotonous cowboy bullshit."

41. Mario Van Peebles, quoted in McGregor, "Cowboyz," 19.

42. Mario Van Peebles, quoted in Leo Banks, "We're Not in the 'Hood Anymore," *Los Angeles Times*, January 31, 1993, Calendar, 28.

43. "Posse," Merriam-Webster's Collegiate Dictionary, 10th ed. (Springfield, Mass.: Merriam-Webster, 1997), 909.

44. Mario Van Peebles, quoted in Stanley, "Mario and Melvin Van Peebles," 22.

45. Paula Massood, "Which Way the Promised Land: The Train Chronotope and Migration as a Primary Site," Ph.D. diss., Cinema Studies, New York University, 1997.

a tale N/nobody can tell

the return of a repressed

western history in

jim jarmusch's *dead man*

m e l i n d a   s z a l o k y

two

> Discourse about the past has the status of being the discourse of the dead.
>
> —Michel de Certeau, *The Writing of History*

In Jim Jarmusch's *Dead Man* (1995),[1] the character Bill Blake, an eastern "dude" misplaced in the Wild West, finds a gun under the pillow of a woman, Thel, who has taken him in for the night. "Watch it, it's loaded," she warns him as she takes the weapon from his hand. Blake looks stupefied, "Why do you have this?" The young woman replies with a wry smile, " 'cause this is America." Seconds later the film proves her caution justified as her ex-lover bursts into the room and, attempting to kill Blake, shoots her dead.

Before her untimely death (which connects her with other female characters in westerns who catch a bullet meant for the male hero) Thel is allowed one significant moment: she is the one who names the experience ("this is America") that Bill Blake has just begun to savor—life in the American West. More importantly, Thel's statement appears to call into question Blake's and, in general, the East's claim to Americanness. *This* is America (for better or for worse), Thel's twisted smile insinuates, and not the far-away East where people dress in checkered suits and flat hats and carry valises instead of firearms; the true America is being shaped here in the West through the law of the gun. Along with Richard Slotkin, J. Hoberman voices the same idea, writing that "in the national imagination America's real founding fathers are less those celebrated gentlemen who composed a nation in the genteel city of Philadelphia than 'the rogues, adventurers, and land boomers, the Indian fighters, missionaries, explorers, and hunters who killed and were killed until they had mastered the wilderness.'"[2]

Violence lies at the core of the western, the genre that America has long considered the quintessential manifestation of its national ethos. Stories and legends of westward "progression" have come to signify the history of American civilization as *progress*. The conflict between the code of morality of a modern western democracy—founded upon the dicta of the decalogue that sanctions the inviolability of life and property—and the proliferation, indeed veneration, of acts of violence in the western canon is resolved through the frontier myth, which posits the wilderness frontier as a "fatal environment" (to use Richard Slotkin's term). Because this wild nature (which includes the natives) resists the civilizing efforts of the enterprising brave it must be tamed and transformed *by force*. In this manner, the noble causes of progress and civilization provide an unassailable rationale for the western's exuberant violence legitimating American expansionism, first on the American continent and later abroad. (In other words, physical violence is naturalized through symbolic violence.[3]) In its golden age (the quarter-century following World War II), the Hollywood western, for example, promotes a hardy and resilient white male hero who is "licensed" to kill in the service of the Anglo-American values and interests that he represents, and who is often rewarded by emerging as the victor after a climactic shoot-out. Death (and erasure from the story), in turn, lies in ambush for the "bad guys": it is the punishment for failure, cowardice, incompetence, greed, overindulgence, miscegenation, or simply for belonging to a powerless "minority" group (e.g., Indians, women, Mexicans).[4]

In the wake of the wars fought in Korea and Vietnam, and as a result of social and cultural upheaval, and the strengthening of movements for civil liberties, the frontier myth as represented in the classic western became increasingly untenable as the great American epic. Revisionist film westerns emerged exposing the myth of "justified" killing by dealing out deadly blows for heroes and villains alike, strewing death throughout the rugged landscape. Many have argued that the genre, which, in Lee Clark Mitchell's words, degenerated into being "an empty arena for haphazard violation and death,"[5] itself has fallen prey to the Grim Reaper, verging on extinction.

The feeble comeback made by a reformed, politically correct, and environmentally conscious film western in the 1990s raises several questions concerning the future of the genre. In Jim Kitses's view, "films that in whole or part interrogate aspects of the genre such as its traditional representations of history and myth, heroism and violence, masculinity and minorities, can be seen now to make up the primary focus of the genre."[6] In other words, revisionism has become the rule. But can there be a true revival for a genre that has been forced to forget its past or, rather, to remember it anew? Is it at all possible to remember differently? If Roland Barthes is right in claiming that myth entails a drainage of history, what is left, may we ask, after the explosion of a myth? Is it history or is it simply countermyth that is yielded up from the scattered remnants of the frontier myth?

Jarmusch's *Dead Man* appears to be the ultimate revisionist/counter-western, a postmodern pastiche that seems to lay bare not only the traditional western genre's practices and devices but also new ones engendered by "traditional" revisionism. In this paper I will examine how Jarmusch's film simultaneously draws upon, exposes, and seeks to dismantle basic generic conventions of the western, its underlying mythology, as well as simplistic (i.e., countermythical) revisionist strategies in an attempt to tell a radically different story. It remains to be seen how successful such a venture might be given the overwhelming presence of myth in the tradition that chronicles the winning of the West. If indeed the western genre is based on the emptying out of history, what is there to be revised and rewritten into a new western history?

inventing the frontier

It is widely believed that the Myth of the Frontier constitutes the single most important frame of reference for America's self-understanding. The frontier myth alloys two major themes. On the one hand, it depicts the territory lying beyond the frontier as an abundant and unappropriated land that is simply there for the taking. On the other hand, it conceives of American history as a heroic and necessarily violent war against the Indians for possession of the land. Peculiarly, the myth appears to synthesize the two main traditional versions of Western history: one written by Frederick Jackson Turner and the other enacted by Buffalo Bill Cody in his "Wild West."[7] Turner, a prominent historian of his day, explained American development through "the existence of an area of free land, its continuous recession, and the advance of American settlement westward."[8] Buffalo Bill, a picturesque scout and showman,[9] in his turn, called the bullet "the pioneer of civilization" and staged scenes of heroic combat between whites and Indians, acknowledging in the process that the land had never been free. A curious blend of scholarship and popular culture (which may explain its versatility and long-standing popularity with establishment and populace alike), the frontier myth in its duality came to represent the essence of American history.

At this point we may ask, as does historian Richard White, how the particular versions of Turner and Buffalo Bill became the dominant and persistent representations of the West. White (who belongs to the "New Western Historians" propagating a revisionist, "anti-Turnerian," view of the frontier) believes that Turner and Buffalo Bill were successful because they "*erased* part of a larger, and more *confusing* and tangled, cultural story to deliver up a *clean*, dramatic, and compelling narrative."[10] In other words, they followed the classic gesture of the historian—as well as that of the mythmaker. (As we will see, these two functions are difficult to disentangle.) Historiography, Michel de Certeau reminds us, "promotes a selection between what can be *understood* and what must be *forgotten* in order to obtain the representation of a present intelligibility."[11] Facts in historiography speak of choices made by the historian and these choices point to a place, that is, to a certain political, cultural, and socioeconomic situation that determines whose point of view a history assumes. De Certeau emphasizes that "history" denotes both a scientific practice and a particular subject matter given that the "real" (i.e., the world of objects resisting symbolization) can be rendered meaningful "solely within the bounds of a discourse."[12] However, traditional bourgeois historiography works to efface this duality of practice and subject matter through relegating the actual origin of history, which is the historically situated and politically biased moment of research and writing, into an unfathomable and fuzzy past, the "depths of time."

The sly operation that posits history qua reality (by effacing the fact that history, a *story* of the past, is also a *discourse*, shaped and authorized by political interests of the *present*) is the work of ideology. In Barthes's view, ideology operates through myth, a metalanguage that projects the world as "a harmonious display of essences."[13] Doing away with dialectics and diversity, myth flattens, simplifies, and clarifies the world. It does not hide things; instead it "purifies them, it makes them innocent, it gives them a natural and eternal justification."[14] Myth creates a depoliticized and sanitized reality. Barthes's notion of myth as a purifier of the world is reminiscent of the historiographical operation as described by de Certeau. The multiplicity of experiences, points of view, and voices that constitute the social reality of a group at a given time and place need to be filtered and organized in order for a meaningful historical narrative to take (causal) shape. Forgetting, emptying out certain stories from the official history, is necessary for the sake of intelligibility. In this way, myth is not devoid of history, but, rather, of histories. Myth is history that suppresses, distorts, and masquerades as the "whole story."

The Myth of the Frontier is a case in point. As Richard White notes, Frederick Jackson Turner's dazzling master narrative of American progress and expansion (America's Manifest Destiny)—which skillfully deploys such widely circulating western icons as the log cabin, the covered wagon, and frontier farming—conveniently "forgets" to include in the nation's story the presence of an aboriginal population on the allegedly "free" land.[15] Buffalo Bill, in his turn, populates the frontier with Indians, who are portrayed as aggressors toward white Americans. Accommodating the dominant (white, Anglo-American) point of view, the myth here transforms conquerors into valiant defenders, victims of savage assailants. As Richard White acutely observes, "The great military icons of American westward expansion are not victories, they are defeats." Custer's Last Stand and the Alamo are the most conspicuous examples of this tendency.[16]

The power of Buffalo Bill's version of western history lay, naturally, in his claim that his "Wild West" show was based on lived experience—his own.[17] In fact, as Richard White notes, Buffalo Bill's enactments of "true" occurrences hopelessly intertwined "performance and history," with one constantly imitating the other.[18] Not only did Buffalo Bill appear as a "walking icon" of himself, that is of the frontiersman of the legend whom he claimed to personify, he also presented "actual Indians, who now inhabited their own representations." Through this "most complicated kind of mimesis," White insightfully explains, "Indians were *imitating imitations* of themselves. They reenacted *white versions* of events in which some of them had actually participated."[19] In other words, capitalizing on the reality effect of immediate witnessing, of "having been there," myth here converted actual Native Americans into embodiments of "the Indian," a cliché coined by whites. The significance of Buffalo Bill's idiosyncratic representation of the West can hardly be overestimated: many believe that our idea of the West (as propagated through countless western novels and films) has been shaped largely on the basis of *his* portrayal of cowboys and Indians.[20]

Although myth and history are inevitably confused in the historiography of the West, I must hasten to add that the infusion of myth into history is by no means a curious anomaly of this particular historiographical practice. As Richard Maltby correctly observes, "Legend becoming fact is a description of the process of history being written [in general]."[21] I have voiced a similar view by combining Barthes's notion of myth with de Certeau's anatomy of the historiographical operation. As I have argued, both Frederick Jackson Turner and Buffalo Bill Cody acted as historians through their selection of certain events as noteworthy (and the noteworthy, as Barthes has shown, is always an ideological elaboration[22]) accompanied by the erasure of other events that "did not fit."[23] Indeed, it is conceivable that because the actual history of the West was "negligible" (that is, not in the least "noteworthy"), as Lee Clark Mitchell claims, this history lent itself more easily to mythmaking. (Mitchell argues that actual conditions in the West were "marginal to the consciousness of most Americans" who viewed occurrences in the West as "pleasantly varied but inconsequential."[24])

How does this construction of Western history as a form of mythology affect the work of revisionism? Can a corrective, revisionist history of the West ever free itself from the legend? Richard Maltby does not believe so.

"The history of the West is," he claims, "in a sense a subgenre of the western, and revisionist history a subgenre of that."[25] According to this deterministic credo, revisionist histories are, to a great extent, destined to continue printing the legend that has become fact, following the lead of newspaper editor Scott in John Ford's *The Man Who Shot Liberty Valance*.[26] But should or could the history/myth of the West be subsumed in toto under the western genre? Richard Slotkin convincingly argues for the contrary when he identifies the Myth of the Frontier—"a body of literature, folklore, historiography and polemics produced over a period of three centuries"—as the source of the western. Moreover, he posits that by the early twentieth century, the frontier myth became "one of the central tropes of American ideology and cultural production" using the westward expansion as a metaphor for America's rapid rise to industrial world power.[27] Thus, the West as conceived through the frontier myth was always more than a region (and more than a limited period of time): it has been instrumental in creating a *national* iconography—which found its most widespread representation in the western.

Voicing a similar opinion, Lee Clark Mitchell asserts that the western has very little to do with an "actual West." Instead, "Westerns are always written from the East" and they answer to "anxieties about conditions from which people want to escape." In other words, the West as portrayed in westerns constitutes an exoticized and legendary staging of *the other* of the East.[28] The "frontier" then becomes a *psychic* margin that at once separates and joins culture and nature, the eastern self and its western other. East and West are more than geographical markers here: they function as metaphors for such binarisms as self/other, culture/nature, familiar/unknown, law/chaos. These oppositions are resolved through violence by a "frontier myth" that venerates the conquest of the unruly other and its assimilation to the fatherland. Mitchell borrows Henry Nash Smith's term to qualify the western genre as America's "objectified mass dream" and claims that the audience of the western always lacked (and still lacks) "a conviction that western history mattered."[29] What matters, instead, is the *belief* in the credibility of the brand of history propagated by the conventions of the genre. For Mitchell, the interpretation of historical facts is determined by "the conventions, clichés, and expectations established by legends that people believe."[30] This suggests that a revisionist western should relativize western conventions and clichés in order to question the constellation of beliefs that legitimates arbitrary (i.e., culturally determined) representations as historical facts. Since the western is American history, rather than simply western history, revisionist efforts are necessarily triggered by and will always reflect the changing social and political landscape of this country as a whole.

Similar to all historical narratives, the history of the West, written by the East, is based on the selection of what is meaningful and the effacement of what is deemed unnoteworthy, nonsensical, and/or threatening at a certain historical moment. However, since history is always anchored in what it has marginalized, omitted, or exorcised, these silences are essential structural constituents of each story told about the past and, thus, cannot be completely ignored. What has been left out will come back, Michel de Certeau claims, "on the edges of discourse, or in the rifts and crannies: 'resistances,' 'survivals,' or delays discreetly perturb the pretty order of a line of 'progress' or a system of interpretation."[31] Tracing the return of the repressed through attempting to articulate what has been declared unthinkable is a promising if highly exacting trajectory for a revisionist text to pursue. In what follows I will examine how Jim Jarmusch's *Dead Man* functions as an innovative revisionist western by highlighting and relativizing various taken-for-granted conventions and, through this, making way for the dreaded return of a history (of conquest and genocide masked as expansion and progress) forgotten, yet not dead: a history of the dead.

going west of everything

The story of *Dead Man*, similar to many westerns, is organized as a travelogue, a journey westward. Bill Blake (played by Johnny Depp), a young accountant from Cleveland, leaves his hometown and heads for Machine to take a job that he was offered in the Dickinson Metalworks. On arrival, Blake finds that his position has already been filled and—having been rudely dismissed by the proprietor, Mr. Dickinson—leaves the factory in desperation. Penniless and not knowing which way to turn, he drifts into the town bar where he meets Thel, a bargirl turned flowergirl, who invites him to stay the night. Unexpectedly, Thel's one-time beau, Charlie, appears and ends up shooting Thel (although the bullet was meant for Blake), upon which the bespectacled and horrified Blake takes several shots at Charlie and accidentally kills him. Badly hurt in the shoot-out, Blake escapes on Charlie's horse and is found by an Indian, Nobody (brilliantly portrayed by Gary Farmer), who takes him under his tutelage believing him to be the soul of the dead English poet William Blake. In the meantime, Charlie's father, the industrialist Mr. Dickinson, hires three killers to find his son's murderer and, perhaps more importantly, to recover the stolen horse. The hunt is on.

William Blake and Nobody roam the wilderness and from time to time come across white people who threaten their lives and whom they therefore kill. Gradually Blake sheds his civilized metropolitan ways and appearance and "goes native" as well as becomes a proficient killer. Meanwhile, the three bounty hunters are reduced in number as one of them, Cole Wilson, remorselessly kills (and eats) his two companions. He continues to pursue Blake and Nobody, who eventually abandon their horses and board a canoe for a trip down a river. They arrive at a village of Makah Indians, where William Blake is placed into a sea canoe and is set afloat on the ocean. In this way, as Nobody explains, he'll be taken back "where he came from and where all the spirits came from." Half-dead already and floating in his lonesome canoe, Blake looks back to the shore where Wilson, the bounty hunter, appears and shoots at him. Nobody and Wilson shoot each other and fall on the ground. The hunt is over, the journey continues.

Obviously, the plot flaunts many of the key ingredients of a western, including the enterprising young hero, the journey westward through diverse landscapes, the dichotomy of Metropolis and Frontier, the new settlement (Machine) with its bars, cowboys, and bargirls, as well as fatal shoot-outs, bounty hunters, a manhunt, Indians, trappers, and wilderness. In place are the conventional paraphernalia of "Indianness"—bearskins, feathers, arrows, teepees, face paint, and totem poles—while the gunmen are, properly, outfitted with horses, shiny guns, boots and spurs, Stetson hats, string ties, vests, and spangled shirts. And yet, as spectators we cannot help feeling that something is amiss when at the very beginning of the film we are shown several close-ups of the relentless piston of a locomotive. This grim opening shot is additionally underscored by the clanging sound of the moving mechanical parts of a steam locomotive, which provides a minimalist musical accompaniment to the images. Instead of grand vistas of vast and overpoweringly beautiful landscapes in Technicolor, the film opens with claustrophobic images in monochrome. Similarly, the sweeping music that has been associated with the western is reduced here to monotone. (Most of the music in *Dead Man* is provided by a single, psychedelic electric guitar that, somewhat reminiscent of Ennio Morricone's scores, hauntingly and unexpectedly punctuates certain images.) Although in the following sequence we catch a glimpse of majestic rocky mountains, vast open spaces, deserts with wild rock formations, and idyllic woods—all framed into widescreen format by the blinds of the train window—the landscapes seem to escape us as well as the protagonist whose point of view we are offered. High-contrast black-and-white cinematography bleaches out any inherent spectacle; the landscapes seem fleeting, foreign, and distant. Burnt out teepees and an abandoned, decrepit, covered wagon augur a sinister outcome for this journey—all the more so given the mythic significance attached to the covered wagon in the iconography of the West.

The widescreen framing of these archetypal western settings confined by the blinds of the train window suggests a generic self-awareness and, simultaneously, an ironic distancing from the western tradition of constructing mythic landscapes. Like a double entendre, irony allows the verso and recto of a meaning to simultaneously inhabit the same form. Curiously, a very similar gesture (that is, stating something and taking it back at the same time) is manifest in Jacques Derrida's concept of erasure, as Gregg Rickman notes in his insightful treatment of *Dead Man*. "The 'strange "being" of the sign' is that 'half of it is always "not there" and the other half always "not that."' A concept is but also simultaneously not,"

Rickman writes, paraphrasing Derrida's translator, Gayatri Spivak.[32] Rickman considers *Dead Man* "the filmic equivalent of an erased, lined out text" since it " 'erases,' inverts, and upends all the various western conventions."[33] However, as Rickman correctly notes, there is a paradox at work here: the erasure of western conventions could not happen without the film's firm rootedness in those selfsame conventions. In other words, a *re*visionist text always depends on a previous "vision" (or point of view) just like Derrida's erasure depends on what is being erased, and history, to be meaningful, depends on what has been "forgotten" or deleted. What makes *Dead Man* an unusual, and in my view highly effective, revisionist text is its acknowledgment of its ancestry and of the inseparability of history/legend in western historiography. Irony and erasure prove to be felicitous (and strikingly postmodern) textual strategies in *Dead Man* precisely because of the film's flamboyant display of the conventional paraphernalia (or, rather, regalia) of the genre. That such a flaunting of stereotypes does not erupt into parody is due to the pervasive sense of death that infuses the film with a grotesque and even morbid air. Jarmusch's West is the land of the dead.

The messenger of impending doom is the fireman of the train, whose shiny eyes irradiate knowledge of the netherworld from a face blackened with soot. He emphatically warns the protagonist, Bill Blake, that he "shouldn't trust no words written down on no piece of paper. Especially from no Dickinson out in the town of Machine." He reprimands Blake for leaving Cleveland and coming "all the way out here to hell" and adds, "You're just as likely to find your own grave." The ominous words are underscored by the "music" of gunshots as all of the passengers (who in this phase of the trip are mostly rugged-looking trappers clad in furs and skins) rush to the windows to shoot at buffalo. The reports of the guns punctuate the aimlessness of the killing: the trappers cannot retrieve— and neither do they need—the booty as the train speeds by. The West appears as a vast shooting gallery in which an entire animal species is destroyed to provide sport for thrill seekers.

The purposeless massacre of the buffalo by the passengers also incriminates the train, a conventional signifier of progress in western mythology. Indeed, the train figures here as an agency of regression. With a masterful gesture, the opening sequence of *Dead Man* shows the passengers of the train gradually shedding their eastern clothing and refinement and turning by stages into fur-clad, armed trappers with an almost semihuman semblance. The march away from civilization is further underscored by the eventual disappearance of all female passengers (given that women traditionally embody a civilizing force in the western) as the train traverses an increasingly abandoned landscape. Ingenuously, Jarmusch uses the train as a metaphor for one-half of the Turnerian tenet, namely that American progress started with a necessary regression to an earlier, primitive state of social development. The core of Turner's idea, the recapitulation of the stages of civilization, however, remains an empty promise, and is portrayed at best as a dubious enterprise throughout *Dead Man*. Here the train does not bring progress to the West—only a flustered Bill Blake, who has unwittingly embarked on a trip that takes him backward in time while nominally delivering him to his future.

The fireman's uncanny foreknowledge of the end of Blake's and the film's story ("Look out the window. And this is to remind you of when you were in the boat and . . . the water in your head was not dissimilar from the landscape.") infuses the film—if only retrospectively—with a sensation of déjà vu. Indeed, Blake's forthcoming floating toward the horizon in a sea canoe will serve as a subtle reminder of a previous (misty) voyage across the ocean, the one that brought the white man to the shores of America. That is, the journey portrayed in the film carries so far West that it approaches the forgotten East—the England of a repressed past, as well as of William Blake, Charles Dickens, and early industrial capitalism. (The "dark Satanic Mills," whose presence upon "England's green and pleasant land" is bemoaned by the poet Blake,[34] have found new "pastures" in the freshly "civilized" West—as illustrated by Machine.)

In order to invoke the return of what official histories have repressed, the film assumes a loose and episodic structure, with sequences reminiscent of the wakefulness of intermittent dreams. Frequent, extended blackouts punctuate the flow of images highlighting the narrative significance of structuring absences. Irreality becomes the norm as *Dead Man* sends its protagonist on a journey that finally (or early on?) takes him "west of everything," which, as Jane Tompkins explains, is a synonym for death.[35]

the machine experience

The young man who arrives at the town of Machine does not have the appearance of a western hero. Rather, attired in a foppish checkered suit and flat hat, he personifies the Eastern "dude." Obviously, he is utterly out of place in Machine. He seems to have slept through his intended destination and gotten off at the wrong station, an unsuspecting victim of involuntary time travel. According to Jane Tompkins, people "wearing suits and carrying valises" in a western "are doomed not because of anything anyone says about them but because of the mountains in the background and the desert underfoot which is continuous with the main street of the town."[36] Clearly, Tompkins evokes here the myth of the "fatal environment" that has justified much of western violence as well as drawn the shape of the true western hero in Social Darwinist terms. Through its choice of a peaceful, gentle, and inconspicuous scenery (the endless woods traversed by Blake and Nobody could be almost anywhere; only the redwood forest is evocative of the American West), *Dead Man* shows that the fatality of the environment should not be sought in nature but *elsewhere*.

Richard Slotkin argues that the fatal environment created by western myth can be escaped through "the demystifying of specific myths and of the mythmaking process itself."[37] *Dead Man* will reaffirm this idea but prove the optimism unwarranted. On the one hand the film exposes symbolic violence (that is, a mythic justification for *some* killings) through presenting *all* male characters (even Blake and Nobody) as perpetrators of violent acts with no redemptive value. On the other hand, it posits that the fatal environment is *inside* humans—as it is *human nature* placed in the liminal space of the frontier that erupts in the violent acts. (Inasmuch as this violence is in the service of the imperialist state, it will be legitimated through the symbolic power—and violence—of the writing of official history.) The pessimistic message of Jarmusch's film is that the only way to escape the myth that naturalizes human violence is through more death, the death of all involved in killing, the death of the West. The fact that it is the innocent who die first does not disprove *Dead Man*'s "necro" logic: through Bill Blake's journey the film portrays (in the spirit of the poet William Blake) the inevitable corruption of innocence by experience.[38]

As we have noted earlier, Bill Blake's arrival at Machine (the town ominously called "the end of the line" by the fireman) exudes an air of uneasiness. I believe that the sensation that Blake is in the wrong place is caused equally by *his* being there and by the fact that the *place* is wrong. A shot conveying Blake's point of view confirms that he is in "the Town of Machine, home of Dickinson Metalworks." The obligatory cacti, the conventional signifiers of western landscape, conveniently sprout from the ground next to the sign in order to dispel any doubts concerning the whereabouts of the place. However, as Edward Buscombe notes, the saguaro cactus often marks a constructed, and not a found, landscape, such as John Ford's Monument Valley.[39] In other words, the cactus comes to signify a mythic and not a geographic locale: the setting of the West of legend. Planting a cactus adjacent to the town sign, Jarmusch relies on and simultaneously subverts this convention through offering an irredeemably bleak image of a small but already industrialized frontier settlement that bears no resemblance to stylized settings of the mythic western narrative.

The main street of Machine, as it presents itself to Bill Blake's astonished look, is reminiscent of footage from a bleak cinema verité documentary: wooden shacks, a carriage transporting coffins, a tired and worn-looking woman with a baby carriage against a ramshackle wall, an undertaker's shop with more coffins, heaps of hides, skins, and animal skulls, a horse urinating, a pig wandering freely in the deep mud that covers the unpaved street, and a woman on her knees performing fellatio on a man who points a gun at Blake as he stares incredulously at the bizarre scenario. Towering at the far end of the street is the gray bulk of the Dickinson Metalworks, which appears as a materialization of Dickens's urban industrial nightmares (and, equally, of William Blake's hallucination of "dark Satanic Mills" violating a "green and pleasant land"). The office where Blake hoped to find employment has a decidedly Kafkaesque air, while Mr. Dickinson himself—played by Robert Mitchum almost as a parody of his earlier western personae—appears as the icon of a patriarch, surrounded by ostensible vestiges of his phallic power: his own larger-than-life portrait on the wall, a massive shotgun, an enormous cigar, stacks of money, and a ferocious-looking stuffed bear looming in the corner of his office. "The only job you're getting here is pushing up daisies from a pine box," he instructs Blake who, convinced by the argument of the gun (and the cigar) pointed at him, finds himself compelled to leave.

The only flowers that grow in the slush and mud of Machine are made of paper—by Thel who, like her flowers, is utterly out of place in this joyless and mechanical man's world that is fated to destroy her. Hers are the words that name the "Machine experience": "This is America" is her answer to Blake's quizzical look upon his discovery of a loaded revolver under her pillow. Thel's violent death, although in itself insignificant, marks a turning point in Blake's life: it triggers the killing of Dickinson's son—and, what appears to be more important to the bereaved father, the theft of one of his favorite horses—prompting Blake's hasty escape to the wilderness.

But does he really leave? Seriously wounded, he climbs out of Thel's window and falls down into the mud (followed by a basketful of Thel's white paper roses), where he remains. A shot from the mud beside the fallen paper roses can be construed as his point of view of the starry sky and a shooting star. Is this to intimate that his star has fallen and his life is at an end? Paradoxically, a man on horseback suddenly gallops by from behind the camera. If Blake is still prone in the mud, who is the rider? Is this the film's way of telling us that the rest of the story is the product of the dying Blake's imagination? Is it, as Nobody believes, Blake's spirit that now undertakes the journey through the wilderness in order to be returned to the place "where all the spirits come from and where all the spirits return"? And finally, since the opening sequence shows Blake falling asleep, could his, and Nobody's, entire journey simply be a dream that he had on the train en route to Machine?

In my view, the film does not offer a clear-cut answer to any of these questions. Instead, by featuring such ambiguous protagonists as a dying/dead/dreaming man and his shadowy doppelgänger, Nobody, *Dead Man* acquires a means well-suited to revisit representations of the past which, as Michel de Certeau reminds us, are fundamentally narratives of the dead. [40] In de Certeau's view, conflicts that the present cannot contain are relegated to the past and are declared dead. The act of writing history, he notes, claims to resuscitate the dead who, however, merely continue to pay with eternal silence for their vicarious existence since they can only speak their exploitation by the present. Resuscitating the dead is, in my view, what many revisionist westerns have striven to do in an attempt to voice stories (of Native and African Americans and of women) that were under- or misrepresented by traditional westerns. *Dead Man* chooses a more subtle solution: it acknowledges the impossibility of doing justice to forgotten/suppressed/falsified past experiences within the constraints of traditional linear narratives and within the domain of everyday normalcy. In order to circumvent this problem (like de Certeau, who seeks the "authentic" voice of the other among the "ravings" of mystics, lunatics, and writers of travelogues "ravaged" by the enchanting practices of aborigines[41]), Jarmusch exchanges the "indicative" for the "subjunctive" mode by developing his plot in the "gray zone" of liminality. It is against this setting of a dreamlike, hallucinatory, morbid, and fantastic netherworld, a world of mutually overlapping possibilities and oppositions, that *Dead Man* undertakes to trace what has been repressed about the white colonizer, and the Native American other.

he who speaks loud saying nothing

The Indian whose face appears to Blake's blurred and slowly clearing consciousness is fat and speaks fluent English. What the Indian's point of view reveals of Blake is a bleeding chest wound. The white man, weak and helpless, watches with benumbed eyes as the improbably corpulent Indian, after having unsuccessfully tried to pry the bullet out of his chest, proceeds to rummage through his coat pockets, reads, then impatiently throws away Mr. Dickinson's letter, and becomes angry when he finds that Blake has no tobacco. The Indian's address to Blake as "stupid, fucking white man" also sounds slightly out of character, that is, out of the "Indian-as-stock-character" as represented in westerns. The most frequent manifestations of this sterotype are the cunning and subhuman "red devil" and the "noble savage." More recently, the environmentally conscious "green" Indian has been added to the repertoire. ("Stereotypes of racial groups make no allowance for individuality," notes Hartmut Lutz.[42]) Jarmusch sets out to subvert this practice through his portrayal of Nobody as a loquacious and articulate human who swears, sings, prays, has a sex life, and possesses a life story that the film allows him to tell.

Nobody's story reveals that he is an outcast, rejected by his own people because of his mixed blood (his parents came from two different Indian tribes) and because he had been "contaminated" by European culture during a forced stay in England. As a child, he was kidnapped, caged, and shipped to Europe, where he familiarized himself with the language and culture of his captors. Hearing his improbable stories about experiences in foreign lands, his people called him a liar ("he who speaks loud saying nothing") and ostracized him. He became N/nobody in a world that attaches a stigma to interracial and cross-cultural experience.

Through Nobody's story, *Dead Man* foregrounds several significant yet underrepresented issues. First, it exposes the fact that racial and cultural intolerance is not confined to whites. Second, by positing a Native American as the (involuntary) hero of a captivity narrative, the film reshuffles the cast list of this genre, which conventionally features *white captives* and *Indian captors*. Similar to Buffalo Bill's stories of white self-defense in the face of Indian aggression, the traditional captivity narrative presents events removed from their larger historical context. Third, *Dead Man* shows through Nobody's travelogue that multiculturalism is not a late-twentieth-century phenomenon. Emphasizing the longtime commerce between cultures, the film invites the acknowledgment of the colonizers' cultural debt to the colonized. And finally, Nobody's story attempts to draw attention to the Indians as victims. The spectator may at first question the historical credibility of Nobody's flashback, which shows his capture by English soldiers, since English soldiers might or might not have roamed the coastal area of the present Washington state in the second half of the nineteenth century. However, if we assume that Nobody's recollections are the voices of a *collective memory* of Native Americans of their subjugation by white conquerors, then the historicity of the incident ceases to be an issue—all the more so given that the ruling version of the history of the period excludes the voices of Native Americans.

In order to escape the clutches of the stereotype of "the Indian," *Dead Man* sets out to create Nobody—by virtue of his mixed blood and his cross-cultural experience—as an Indian who is not one in the traditional sense. (As Edward Buscombe observes, Indians who "showed evidence of contact with whites . . . were no longer Indians" according to the creed of the ethnocentric, essentialist tradition.[43]) Through this "contaminated" Indian—whose ability to tell his own story in the white colonizer's language is credibly motivated by the plot—the film manages to diminish the "colonizing" effect of rendering otherness in terms of sameness (i.e., giving a voice to the other by merely putting familiar words in his or her mouth), a practice several well-meaning revisionist westerns are known to have explored. That the precautions taken by the film to portray a demythicized Indian ultimately result in a self-ironic and self-erasing N/nobody illustrates the near impossibility of eradicating this old and firmly established stereotype.

On the other hand, the irredeemable antagonism of the double entendre conveyed by the name (N/nobody) provides the film with an original strategy to highlight the absurdity of the frontier myth's treatment of Indians not as rational human subjects but as subhuman, animalistic (or, at times, noble) savages, objectified ingredients of the "fatal environment." In a pessimistic vein, *Dead Man* features a dying, dead, or dreaming Bill Blake as the only white man who allows N/nobody to become Nobody—that is, *somebody*, a human being with integrity and a distinctive voice. This intimates that the reverse of the cynical truism about good Indians is equally true: for an Indian, "the only good white man is a dead white man." However, in another twist, if we accept that Blake is already in some sense dead journeying through the West-as-underworld—an assumption supported by the image of Nobody, who, imitating the gesture of Charon ferrying the soul of the deceased across the Styx, transports William Blake's inert body down a river in a canoe—Nobody, again, is turned into nobody, a phantom accompanying a dead man. Thus, the Indian (both as an individual and as a group) is simultaneously there and not there, his existence affirmed and yet erased.

That N/nobody's authority and wisdom count for naught in the eyes of the white colonizer is poignantly illustrated through his humiliating treatment by the local store-keeper/Indian agent who, catching sight of an Indian entering his store, erupts in a tirade invoking the power of the "Lord Jesus Christ" to purge the earth from "heathens and philistines." "The vision of Christ that thou doest see is my vision's greatest enemy," N/nobody retorts, quoting (the poet) Blake. However, his cultivated reply falls on deaf ears: not only does the shopkeeper refuse to sell him tobacco, but he also crudely reminds Nobody of who he is (nobody) by offering him beads or blankets (which, as Nobody has previously informed Blake, are infected with the germs of a deadly disease).

N/nobody's intimate knowledge of the colonizer's language and culture is no antidote for his oppression. His speaking loudly will still say nothing so long as he is trying to dismantle, to paraphrase Audre Lorde, the master's house with the master's tools.[44] As Barthes teaches us, the oppressed "has only one language, that of his emancipation."[45] According to Barthes, "wherever man speaks in order to transform reality and no longer to preserve it as an image, whenever he links his language to the making of things, meta-language is referred to a language object, and myth is impossible."[46] Barthes argues that a woodcutter "speaks the tree," he does not speak *about* it; his language, therefore, is transitively linked to its object. "This is a political language: it represents nature for me only inasmuch as I am going to transform it, it is a language thanks to which I *act the 'object'*: the tree is not an image for me, it is simply the meaning of my action."[47]

Accordingly, the only language that promises to give N/nobody a distinctive voice is that of action and transformation, two things that in the western genre are most often equivalent to violence. *Dead Man* strikingly demonstrates this postulate in the sequence in which Bill Blake accosts three trappers in the woods. "I am with N/nobody," Blake truthfully yet deceptively tells the three men (evoking, as Gregg Rickman notes, the cunning of Ulysses, who introduces himself to the Cyclops as "Nobody"[48]). What turns nobody into Nobody (once again, *somebody*) is his killing of Big George, one of the trappers, who, through his death proves that *somebody* must have cut his throat. Violent action speaks where words are reduced to silence. This is the language that Nobody teaches Bill Blake when encouraging him to learn how to use a gun: "That weapon will replace your tongue. You will learn to speak from it. And your poetry will now be written with blood."

depoeticizing violence

There are few genres that would so unabashedly revel in a graphic depiction of violence as does the western. Richard Slotkin argues that "the irreducible core of the western story-line is to provide a rationalizing framework which will explain and perhaps justify a spectacular act of violence."[49] According to this rationale, the violent means becomes the end, the dénouement toward which the film narrative moves, whereas the rest of the narrative serves to justify this "meta-Machiavellian" move. Slotkin explains:

> [T]he act of violence became a natural focus for creative energy and the play of artistic and technical variation. Over time, this focus has tended to bring the act of violence forward as a scene good and necessary in and of itself: as a climax whose *aesthetic* necessity and power became an acceptable substitute for the moral and ideological plot-rationales that originally provided the scene's motivation and justification.[50]

In other words, as an ultimate justification of brutal killings, the western enlists style to create an aesthetic that makes palatable the spectacle of violence by an elaborate choreography that tends to substitute for ideas and argument. As the preeminent illusion of motion, the moving image with its life-like immediacy, depth, and flow is an ideal means for representing and glorifying the movement of force. When the traditional strategies of mythic western narratives (based on stereotyping and the pitting of symbolic opposites against each other according to a binary logic) were rendered obsolete (due to a changed political climate in the wake of the Vietnam War) a few filmmakers reconceived the genre in terms of highly aestheticized and carefully organized spectacles of apocalyptic violence. This trend of western revisionism is epitomized by Sam Peckinpah's "ballets of the bullet" which, as Paul Seydor claims, are based on the sensual beauty of the image when divorced from every evaluative context except that of the aesthetic.[51] Since the so-called pure form of the pleasurable spectacle offered by the "Vietnam westerns" defies all contextualization, including mythical contextualization, these films emerge as subtle mythmakers in the Barthesian sense; that is, "all that is left for one to do is to enjoy this beautiful object without wondering where it comes from."[52] When violence in itself is made to look pleasing, or cathartic, there is no need for its further explanation or legitimation.

Jim Jarmusch is no partisan of the above aesthetic. In spite of Nobody's comparison of poetry to the word of the gun, there is nothing poetic about the representation of violence in *Dead Man*. In this world people kill for a number of reasons, and their acts of violence always appear plain (almost trivial), matter of fact, and in no need of justification, or embellishment. Charlie Dickinson kills out of hurt pride,

Bill Blake kills to save his skin, Nobody kills to protect Blake, the bounty hunters and the marshals (are prepared to) kill for reward money. These people live the reality of the frontier, which is action, transformation, and destruction. Here violence is an everyday routine rather than a distinct event of heroic (or even political) proportions. *Dead Man* structures its narrative to follow exactly this pattern: it offers a string of loosely connected, almost anecdotal scenes, which are separated by lengthy blackouts and by the haunting, solitary, half-dissonant chords of the electric guitar. The casual, almost accidental connection of the scenes that make up the film is based on a principle of association and coordination rather than on a subordination of elements moving toward a climax or an argument driving to a conclusion. The film is suffused with an atmosphere of dreamlike drifting that works against any buildup of tension. Each killing is committed surprisingly quickly—several times by accident—and the camera never dwells on murder victims, killing techniques, or weapons. At times the camera even remains at a great distance from the (anti-)climatic killing. For example, the conventional final shoot-out is rendered in *Dead Man* through an extreme long shot, making the fighters barely visible.

The portrayal of the killings is never melodramatic; rather, these acts of extreme violence have a banal air. Bill Blake's haphazard shooting at Charlie Dickinson verges on burlesque, which, however, turns grotesque as Charlie unexpectedly dies pierced by a wayward bullet. Cole Wilson's remorseless and unmotivated killing of Johnny the Kid catches the spectator completely unawares (no dramatic buildup here) while the shooting of Conway Twill (Wilson's other companion) happens offscreen (or, rather, after the image has faded to black) with only the report of the gun marking the event. The single image that can qualify as destruction beautified is a shot of the profile of a marshal, now dead, framed in halo-like fashion by sticks of firewood and sagebrush. No act of iconoclasm could be more literal, and repulsive, than the bounty hunter Cole Wilson's foot crushing the skull until blood and brains spurt out of its nostrils. Wilson's snort "It looks like a goddamn religious icon" voices the whole film's attitude toward the veneration of beautified and sanctified violence. With Wilson's gesture Jarmusch remorselessly exposes what has been "aestheticized away" by the "ballet of the bullet": the utterly prosaic and immutable face of death.

63

the place where the sea meets the sky

Although the narrative of *Dead Man* consists of loosely connected and clearly separated episodes, organized horizontally rather than vertically, the story appears to move toward a definite end: William Blake must be returned to the land of the spirits from which he came and to which he belongs. "We must make sure that you pass back to the mirror at a place where the sea meets the sky," Nobody explains to Blake as he takes him on a river trip. As he paddles, the accompanying solo guitar score recalls the musical noises made by the locomotive in the first sequence of the film. Undoubtedly, the opening train journey is counterbalanced by the boat ride at the end in a symmetrical fashion. Another symmetry informs Blake's entries into Machine and the Makah village at the beginning and end of the film. Blake's point of view of the Indian village is comparable in its bleakness to the main street in Machine (also shown through Blake's eyes). Further parallels between the two locales are easily detected: an Indian woman with a child on her lap versus a white woman with a baby carriage, an abundance of animal skulls, antlers, and hides in both settlements, a large, totem-like structure towering at the far end of the Makah village versus the Dickinson Metalworks positioned in a similar fashion in Machine.

Clearly, the white and Native-American settlements mirror each other. Their near-isomorphic duplication brings together the beginning and end of the narrative converting the seemingly linear, forward-directed trajectory of the journey to a circularity or even stasis. The fireman's allusion in the opening sequence to the *memory* of Blake's forthcoming, final, canoe ride supports this circularity. Blake's journey delivers him nowhere in particular—that is, to his death in a featureless expanse where he becomes nobody. Nobody's journey, undertaken in order to exorcise the other (i.e., to send William Blake, a representative of the white Anglo-Saxon colonizers, back to where he came from), meets the same dead end. Ultimately, this circular or static journey epitomizes the western's quintessential, and doomed, aspiration: its endless (and endlessly futile) search for origins. The staple western tropes of the "frontier" and the "horizon" mark the fringes of the impenetrable "beyond" that this genre is obsessed with. "The western was . . . less a place than a movement," Ella Shohat and Robert Stam correctly observe.[53] However, in spite of the genre's elaborate efforts to represent this movement as the motor force of progress (in keeping with the spirit of the myth of the frontier) these narratives in fact tend to move along a circular orbit (following the setting sun) with no definite beginning and ending. In a symmetrical fashion, western heroes ride out from the fathomlessness of the horizon and ride off into the sunset. The westerner's quest for origins is inevitably linked with death, whereas his search for identity leads him to the equally enigmatic other. The end sequence of *Dead Man*, showing a dying/dead/dreaming Bill Blake as he floats off into a rainy sunset in the "mirror of the water" where the sea meets the sky is a pungent rendering of these dilemmas.

Although *Dead Man*'s protagonist is Bill Blake—through whose dreaming or dying subjectivity the story is told—it is Nobody's desire to return the white man to the land of his fathers that motivates and drives Blake's journey through the wilderness. I have already discussed certain aspects of the film's portrayal of Nobody as a rounded and active character. I believe that this discussion needs further elaboration. Let me, once again, turn to the curiously duplicated graphic motifs that abound in the film. A shot of burnt-out houses and an upturned canoe, showing Nobody's point of view from the river as he is ferrying Blake toward his final destination, appears to be the exact replica of one of Nobody's earlier flashbacks depicting, as he puts it, "sad things" that he saw on the way back to his people from his exile in England. What is the meaning of all this? How are Nobody's two trips connected? In Freud's view, recurring similarities often mark the return of something that has been repressed, whence their potential uncanniness.[54] According to this logic, the unexpected, eerie recurrence of an already-seen scene (that of a ruined settlement) in the film could be symptomatic of a repressed but resurging trauma.

The first time Nobody sees the burnt-out houses is on his way back to his people. This is also the first time he "travels" with the spirit of William Blake since Blake's poetry forms an integral part of the young Nobody's newly acquired knowledge of an "other" culture. This new, different Nobody is, however, rejected by his tribe, who consider him an inscrutable, threatening, and therefore to-be-repressed other, a N/nobody. Arguably, then, it is the trauma of his captivity (and, above all, the forced experience that resulted in his hybrid identity) that Nobody himself tries to repress. The futility of this enterprise is strikingly illustrated by Nobody's (second) chance encounter with William Blake's spirit and by his subsequent attempt to exorcise it from his (and his people's) memory by sending it back to Europe. Thus, eventually, the white man's psychedelic journey through the West to the Pacific Ocean and beyond obeys the long-silenced desire of his Native American other: the return of the colonizer to the land from which he had come. At the same time, Nobody as the Native American other has no substantial existence in the film but is, instead, a projection of Bill Blake's dreaming/hallucinating mind.

As Michel de Certeau's historiography demonstrates, psychoanalysis can be usefully applied to interrogate established and taken-for-granted narratives of the past. Dreams, Freud has asserted, allow us glimpses of the vast, inaccessible domain of mental contents and forces that have been banned from consciousness for the sake of "normalcy." History, in de Certeau's view, performs a similar censorship when it banishes certain instances of human reality to oblivion in an attempt to organize and make sense of the present. Through delving into the unconscious of history, its dreams, ravings, and hallucinations, the historian may be able to unearth suppressed and forgotten voices, truths, and experiences. Jarmusch's *Dead Man* follows a very similar path in its attempt to defamiliarize the myth of the West, which has been widely considered as the key to America's self-understanding. Fully aware of the power of representations to shape reality, Jarmusch sets out to deconstruct—through the distancing devices of irony and erasure—the conventions of the western, the genre that has long been instrumental in propagating and recreating America's (and the world's) belief in a certain blend of Western (and, thus, American) history.

melinda szaloky

To my mind, the most inventive revisionist strategy to be explored in the film is presenting the story of a white man's westward progression in the subjunctive, rather than the indicative, mode. The West, its stock characters, situations, and paraphernalia as popularized by the western, is viewed here through the distorting/distorted vision of a dying/dead/ dreaming protagonist. In this realm of the liminal, clearly-defined meanings lose their singularity as the intelligible metamorphizes into the imaginable allowing the unthinkable to take shape. It is through a portrayal of the West as a hallucinatory netherworld (reminiscent of the unconscious as conceived by psychoanalysis) that *Dead Man* seeks to recover untold, suppressed, and forgotten stories of the "winning" of the West.

In the alternative history that emerges here it is nearly impossible to separate the intermeshed voices, experiences, and even repressed traumatic memories of the Anglo-American Blake and the Native American Nobody. Each seems to dream the other. Indeed at times they are shown having joint points of view. Also, the film ingeniously brackets the white man's repressed other—that is, the Native American N/nobody who himself is haunted by his other, the white man of England/Cleveland—within a white man's dream/ hallucination creating multiple and embedded frames of reference in order to undermine and relativize established categories, hierarchies, and truths. The film portrays self and other as complementary rather than mutually exclusive entities and stresses the vital importance, and historical inevitability, of the intermingling of cultures. This said, *Dead Man* projects a distinctly pessimistic view of the possibilities of concord and understanding between races, suggesting that the different points of view and versions of history can only meet "where the sea meets the sky," in the unattainable infinity of the ever-receding horizon—the only place, presumably, that lies beyond physical and symbolic violence. In the end, the departing William Blake leaves death in his wake and an unanswered, disturbing question: is the future conceivable in terms other than as the unceasing return of the (mutually reflected) repressed of the dead?

notes

I would like to thank Janet Bergstrom, Edward Branigan, Stephen Mamber, Janet Walker, and Charles Wolfe for generously contributing many insightful comments to this paper. I am also grateful to my parents, Terézia and Pál, and my aunt Klára for making possible the writing of this essay by lovingly sharing with me the care of my infant son, Nicholas.

1. After this essay was completed and while it was in press, Jonathan Rosenbaum's recent book on *Dead Man* came to my attention. Space does not permit a detailed commentary on Rosenbaum's volume. However, I would like to mention that our arguments converge on several important issues (e.g., *Dead Man's* untraditional representation of Native Americans and of violence). Besides offering an insightful evaluation of the film, Rosenbaum's book provides detailed production information and engaging interviews with the filmmaker. See Jonathan Rosenbaum, *Dead Man* (London: BFI Publishing, 2000).

2. J. Hoberman, "How the West Was Lost," in *The Western Reader*, ed. Jim Kitses and Gregg Rickman (New York: Limelight Editions, 1998), 85.

3. I am using the phrase "symbolic violence" in Pierre Bourdieu's sense of "symbolic power." In Bourdieu, symbolic power is a misrecognized form of power. It is invisible and can only be exercised "with the complicity of those who do not want to know that they are subject to it." See Pierre Bourdieu, *Language and Symbolic Power*, ed. John B. Thompson, trans. Gino Raymond and Matthew Adamson (Oxford: Polity Press, 1991), 170.

4. The martyred hero's death—which happens often in westerns—does not result in the hero's erasure from the story but, as a rule, secures his accession to legend. This is the reason why I haven't included this case in my list of western victims.

5. Lee Clark Mitchell, *Westerns: Making the Man in Fiction and Film* (Chicago: University of Chicago Press, 1996), 228. Mitchell is specifically referring to Sergio Leone's West.

6. Jim Kitses, "Introduction: Post-modernism and The Western," in Kitses and Rickman, eds., *The Western Reader*, 19.

7. This pairing of Turner and Cody as the "two master narrators of American westering" has been suggested by both Richard White and Richard Slotkin. See Richard White, "Frederick Jackson Turner and Buffalo Bill," in *The Frontier in American Culture, An Exhibition at the Newberry Library, August 26, 1994–January 7, 1995*, ed. James R. Grossman (Berkeley and Los Angeles: University of California Press, 1994), 7, 9. See also Richard Slotkin, *Gunfighter Nation: The Myth of the Frontier in Twentieth-Century America* (New York: Atheneum, 1992), 55–59, 66–87.

8. The quote is from Turner and is used as an epigraph in James Grossman's introduction to *The Frontier in American Culture*, 1. Turner's seminal paper "The Significance of the Frontier in American History" was presented in 1893 in Chicago during the Columbian Exposition.

9. William Frederick Cody, better known as Buffalo Bill, launched his Wild West show in 1883 and it went on for thirty years with phenomenal success.

10. White, "Frederick Jackson Turner and Buffalo Bill," 11; emphasis added.

11. Michel de Certeau, *The Writing of History*, trans. Tom Conley (New York: Columbia University Press, 1988), 4; emphasis in the original.

12. Ibid., 21.

13. Roland Barthes, *Mythologies*, trans. Annette Lavers (New York: Hill and Wang, 1972), 142.

14. Ibid., 143.

15. White, "Frederick Jackson Turner and Buffalo Bill," 12.

16. Ibid., 27.

17. Barthes has shown that the "real" is supposed to be self-sufficient. The act of immediate witnessing, the documentary "having-been-there" of objects and things guarantees their reality in historical discourse, which treats its referent as completely external to discourse. See Roland Barthes, "The Reality Effect" and "The Discourse of History," in *The Rustle of Language*, trans. Richard Howard (New York: Hill and Wang, 1986), 146–47, and 138.

18. White, "Frederick Jackson Turner and Buffalo Bill," 29.

19. Ibid., 35; emphasis added.

20. Jane Tompkins argues that our conception of the appearance of Indians and cowboys is based on Buffalo Bill's presentation of these characters in his show. Because Buffalo Bill used only Sioux and other Plains tribes in his performances, westerns invariably portray feathered Indians on horseback (as was the practice of these tribes). The large Stetson hats worn by cowboys in films imitate the costume adopted by Buffalo Bill for his show and not the actual type of hat worn by early cowboys. See Jane Tompkins, *West of*

Everything: The Inner Life of Westerns (New York: Oxford University Press, 1992), 199–200.

21. Richard Maltby, "A Better Sense of History: John Ford and the Indians," in *The Book of Westerns*, ed. Ian Cameron and Douglas Pye (New York: Continuum, 1996), 38.

22. For Barthes, a fact can only be defined tautologically: supposedly what is "noted" issues from the "notable," however, the notable is only what is *being* noted. Historical discourse, as an ideological elaboration, is built on a paradox: although a fact exists only in and through language, "everything happens as if this linguistic existence were merely a pure and simple 'copy' of another existence, situated in an extra-structural field, the 'real.'" See Barthes, "The Discourse of History," 138.

23. Curiously, Richard White appears as an apologist of the historiographical operation represented by Turner and Buffalo Bill. He emphasizes the virtues of "this central imaginative narrative of the frontier" and the necessity of selectivity in the construction of historical narratives (leaving without comment why certain images "did not fit" in the story Turner and Buffalo Bill constructed of the past). See White, "Frederick Jackson Turner and Buffalo Bill," 55.

24. Mitchell, *Westerns,* 5–6.

25. Maltby, "A Better Sense," 39.

26. Editor Scott's famous comment "When the legend becomes fact, print the legend" in John Ford's *The Man Who Shot Liberty Valance* (1962) could stand as the motto for the western's brand of historiography.

27. Richard Slotkin, "Violence," in *The BFI Companion to the Western*, ed. Edward Buscombe (London: British Film Institute, 1988/New York: Da Capo Press paperback edition), 233.

28. De Certeau argues that history stages the *other* either through exoticism or criticism, and in the first case it assumes a legendary form. See de Certeau, *The Writing of History*, 85.

29. Mitchell, *Westerns*, 6.

30. Ibid., 21, 23.

31. De Certeau, *The Writing of History*, 4.

32. Gregg Rickman, "The Western under Erasure: *Dead Man,*" in Kitses and Rickman, eds., *The Western Reader,* 399.

33. Ibid.

34. William Blake, "Jerusalem." See, e.g., *A Book of English Poetry: Chaucer to Rosetti*, collected by G. B. Harrison (London: Penguin, 1950), 238.

35. Jane Tompkins borrows the phrase "west of everything" from Louis L'Amour, a popular writer of Western fiction. See Tompkins, *West of Everything*, 24.

36. Ibid., 74.

37. Richard Slotkin, *The Fatal Environment: The Myth of the Frontier in the Age of Industrialization 1800–1890* (New York: Atheneum, 1985), 20.

38. For a detailed discussion of the connections between William Blake's work and *Dead Man* see Gregg Rickman, "The Western under Erasure," 381–86.

39. Edward Buscombe, "Inventing Monument Valley: Nineteenth Century Landscape Photography and the Western Film," in Kitses and Rickman, eds., *The Western Reader*, 129.

40. As de Certeau observes, the construction of a history "is a labor of death and a labor against death" since a present intelligibility is always based on a breakage — one between past (other) and present (self). However, this breakage, or loss, is also denied through the privilege of the present to recapitulate (summarize, describe, judge) the past "as a form of knowledge." De Certeau, *The Writing of History*, 5.

41. See, for example, de Certeau, *The Writing of History*, chapters 5 and 6 (209–68).

42. Hartmut Lutz, "Indians/Native Americans," in Edward Buscombe, ed., *The BFI Companion*, 155.

43. Edward Buscombe, "Photographing the Indian," in *Back in the Saddle Again: New Essays on the Western*, eds., Edward Buscombe and Roberta E. Pearson (London: BFI Publishing, 1998), 35.

44. "The master's tools will never dismantle the master's house," states Audre Lorde in "The master's tools will never dismantle the master's house," in *Sister Outsider: Essays and Speeches* (Freedom, Calif.: The Crossing Press, 1984), 112.

45. Barthes, *Mythologies*, 149.

46. Ibid., 146.

47. Ibid., 145–46; emphasis in the original.

48. See Rickman, "The Western under Erasure," 396.

49. Richard Slotkin, "Violence," 233.

50. Ibid., 235.

51. Paul Seydor, *Peckinpah: The Western Films* (Urbana: University of Illinois Press, 1980), 128; emphasis added.

52. Barthes, *Mythologies*, 151.

53. Ella Shohat and Robert Stam, *Unthinking Eurocentrism: Multiculturalism and the Media* (London and New York: Routledge, 1994), 118. See also their subchapter, "The Western as Paradigm" (114–21), for an insightful critique of ideology and representational practices in western films.

54. Sigmund Freud, "The Uncanny," in *The Standard Edition of the Complete Psychological Works of Sigmund Freud*, vol. 17, ed. and trans. James Strachey (London: Hogarth Press, 1955), 249.

the burden

of history and

john sayles's

three   *lone star*

tomás f. sandoval, jr.

Pilar Cruz: Like your story's over?
Sam Deeds: I kind of feel that way, yeah.
Pilar: It isn't. Not by a long shot.

In an illuminating scene from John Sayles's film *Lone Star* (1996), Otis Payne (played by Sayles regular Ron Canada) accompanies his grandson (whom he has just recently met) through the Black Seminole Museum in the rear of his local bar. Otis is the most respected member of the small, black community in Frontera, Texas, a town on the U.S.-Mexican border where the struggle for power between Anglos and Mexicans eclipses the histories of all others. Within this contested landscape, Otis is proprietor of a bar that, along with a local church, are the only two institutions that cater specifically to the black community. It is a position that has earned him the honorary title "Mayor of Darktown," a reflection not only of his political significance to the ruling elite but also the respect and admiration he has earned from his own segregated community.

"The Big O'" is also a local historian, spending his free time uncovering and preserving the forgotten history of "his people" through the collection in his makeshift museum, which tells the story of runaway slaves escaping to the Florida Everglades and joining the ranks of Seminole Indians. It is the story of their mixed race descendants—two peoples made one—and their struggles against the forces of U.S. imperialism as some were forcibly migrated West while others resisted the process of Indian removal. In the museum are artistic representations of mixed-race heroes like John Horse—Juan Caballo in Spanish—who fought against removal for more than a decade before migrating across the border into Mexico and fighting in the armies of General Santa Ana. Their story eventually brought them to Texas where they became the Seminole Negro Indian Scouts and participated in the battles fought against "rednecks" and Indians alike as part of the U.S. Army. In present-day Frontera, an Army base is employer to a disproportionate number of the town's black community as well as a vital fixture of the general economy. Celebrating Black Seminole heroes of the past, the museum's artifacts tell the history that continues to live in the present through that base, Otis, and his grandson.

The young Chet Payne (Eddie Robinson) is learning this history—his own history—for the first time. Chet is an army brat, the son of the new commander who will oversee the local army base's shutdown. Otis and his own child, the boy's father, haven't spoken since Otis abandoned his wife and young son a generation earlier. A military transfer has now facilitated an unintentional family reunion as Chet seeks to learn of his familial past, his blood heritage. This visit in the museum is the first between grandson and grandfather, as it is between the young man and his more distant history. While his grandson is as much surprised as excited to learn he is part Seminole Indian, Otis is quick to check his grandson's enthusiasm in this newfound aspect of his heritage. Chet asks, "So I'm part Indian?" Otis cautions the young boy, "By blood you are. But blood only means what you let it." Chet responds by sharing the philosophy of his father: "From the day you're born you start from scratch."

The scene possesses lessons for the viewer on multiple levels, as well as on multiple topics. In today's United States, Otis Payne's statement is part of a distinct school of thought on race and ethnicity. In a nation founded concurrently on the ideals of equality and inequality, the institutions of democracy and slavery, and the processes of immigration and conquest, "blood" and the history behind it have always occupied multiple meanings. In the battleground of multiculturalism, groups that advocate the cultural assimilation of nonwhites into an acceptable and singular "American" culture operate from the implicit premise that people can choose how they access and reflect their heritage. In this respect, the "melting pot" is less an inevitability than a chosen path. On the opposite end of the political spectrum, groups advocating for the development of an ethnically conscious and proud politic share this belief in human agency when they rally people to draw upon their cultural heritage. Although sometimes more focused on the obligations one has to the past, nationalistic philosophies represent a conscious fluidity that relies on human analysis and decision. More commonly, those who operate within the vast region between assimilation and cultural nationalism support the notion that humans have the power to choose the manner in which they access their own histories but suggest a myriad of degrees to which they are, at the same time, beholden to the past in that process.

Of course, the mere expression of this philosophy does not mean that we are living in an age of freedom from the weight of the past. Even if blood only means what we let it, there is still the seemingly powerful inertia of history behind that blood telling us, and others, how and what we should let it mean. As most eventually learn, even if we will it, it isn't always possible to escape the burdens of history. Whether or not we—as a people—are coming closer to accepting a rhetoric of human power, the realities of contemporary daily life reveal pressures and tendencies seemingly much more potent than our mere will. Beyond the level of the individual, the inability of the United States to come to terms with the concept of race in its past (or even its present) is equally illustrative of the societal limits to surmounting that burden. Rather than reflecting a philosophy of human agency, the persistence of race and racism within the national discourse illustrates the belief that blood has concrete and inflexible meanings. From this perspective, our present can never be free from the past for it is the static, natural outgrowth of it.

A generation ago, Hayden White dealt with similar cultural processes within the modern, intellectual field in his essay "The Burden of History."[1] He lamented the growing sentiment that the discipline of history had outlived its usefulness and that it lingered in a nebulous area, incapable of dispelling the lure of that sentiment. The problem, as he saw it, arose from historians' adherence to Victorian forms that represented a "combination of *late-nineteenth-century* social science and *mid-nineteenth-century* art" (43). That potent combination bore the guilt for the rise in antihistoricist thought White traced throughout the twentieth century. The solution lay, at least in part, in refocusing the role of the historian to that shared by G. W. F. Hegel, Honoré de Balzac, and Alexis de Tocqueville, who "interpreted the burden of the historian as a moral charge to free men from the burden of history" (49). A history that served to teach society the responsibility and potential the individual possessed in "the fashioning of the common humanity of the future" is a history that "sensitized men to the *dynamic* elements in every achieved present, taught the inevitability of change, and thereby contributed to the release of that present to the past without ire or resentment" (49–50).

As White observed, the antihistoricist thought of the late nineteenth and early twentieth centuries arose out of the increasing realization that the (sometimes subconsciously) chosen forms the historian utilized in representing the past not only failed to represent the chaotic realities of everyday existence but also failed to depict the present as something more than the linear inevitability spewed forth by the past. The debilitating result for human society is the inability for the present to escape the specter of the past. Accordingly, when White called for the historian to "participate positively in the liberation of the present from the *burden of history*" (41), the prescription had the double meaning of advocating not only for a liberatory history for social consumption but also for a liberation of the field of history from the antiquated forms that plagued its current production.

In "reestablishing the dignity of historical studies" and creating that more lively form of historical discourse, the historian has first to recognize that her task is far more active than merely finding the story that the raw data of the past inherently possesses. Rather, it is the recognition that there is something quite different from historical fact and the creation of historiographic representations. More specifically, "all discourse *constitutes* the objects which it pretends only to describe realistically and to analyze objectively" (2). If the historian actively emplots the data for the purposes of telling the story, then the end result is merely "one way among many" (46).

Perhaps we can understand this a bit more casually: blood only means what we let it. Otis Payne's caveat to his grandson, as well as Chet's stating of his father's beliefs, suggests a more dynamic role for the place of history. Much in the same way that the Black Seminoles could eventually fight within both the U.S. and Mexican armies, and in both instances participate in wars against Native Americans, the young Chet Payne will have to decide for himself how to access his past in developing his identity. In explaining how the Payne ancestors could do such a thing as kill fellow indigenous peoples ("But they were Indians themselves"), Otis states, "They were in the army." In being part of those armies, and in choosing to fulfill their obligations to that unit rather than to any pan-ethnic one, these Black Seminoles did what all people must (and indeed seem to) do: decide which aspects of their past will live more actively in their present ethnic identities and then, what that will mean in the practices of daily life.

On the surface, *Lone Star* is the story of a man searching for the "truth" in a local town mystery and, in the process, discovering his own personal history. Into this main story, John Sayles weaves tales of other peoples' lives, all in some way also dealing with issues of history. Drawing from the problems that tear apart our own social fabric, as well as the demons that plague our individual mentalities, Sayles uses this mosaic of lives to better illustrate the role played by many complex levels of history. Metaphorically, the film develops the idea of borders (between Mexico and the United States, between father and child, between Anglo and Mexican, between truth and fiction) to deal with the nature of historiographic representation. In so doing, the film arrives at conclusions that exemplify the arguments of Hayden White and others while challenging the viewer to apply them without discrimination to subjects ranging from the choice of a school's textbook to the meanings of familial relations.

These conclusions are worth consideration for, in the manner White suggested, they speak to our own (post)modern condition. By doing more than simply echoing a simplistic notion of human agency, *Lone Star* offers insight into the ways in which human beings can exist beyond antiquated histories by choosing to exist within the present and focusing toward the creation of their future present(s). The film deals with the qualities of memory and myth that often appear seemingly insurmountable. In the end, knowledge of the past (or plainly, history) is only the first step in our liberation, as we as audience (or as subject? or historian?) are left to wonder whether this process of unburdening is overly optimistic. If blood (and history) only mean what we let it, then why have we always felt so compelled to act as if they derive their meanings from the past rather than from the present?

know thy history

"You live in a place, you should learn something about it."

—Cliff to fellow army man Mickey

Lone Star is a movie about literal and figurative borders. On the literal level this is presented through Sayles's choice of the Texas-Mexico border as his setting. Historically speaking, it is a site that represents contestation at every level—from the political to the cultural to the personal. Many of these aspects of the border are then cleverly replicated in Sayles's exploration of the relationships between people and their pasts. In discussing the concept Sayles says, "In a personal sense, a border is where you draw a line and say 'This is where I end and somebody else begins.'"[2] For the main protagonist of the tale, this process of definition is the overriding action of the film.

The main story revolves around Sheriff Sam Deeds (played by Chris Cooper). Sam is a man living in the shadow of his father, the well-respected (and dearly departed) Sheriff Buddy Deeds. Buddy (played in brief flashback appearances by Matthew McConaughey) was a man loved by the community of Frontera, Texas if only for the fact that the Sheriff he replaced, Charley Wade (wonderfully played by Kris Kristofferson), was the classic personification of evil. Charley was your typical murdering, bribe-taking, no-good law enforcing racist in a border town. Striking fear in the townspeople through the threat of harm (he could make a child lose control of his bladder with a mere wink), Sheriff Wade benefited from regular payments of cash from the local business community in exchange for security. With the reputation of having killed people in the past, the security most craved was to be free from Charley Wade.

Only a month after law officer Buddy Deeds came to town, and the very night he publicly called an end to the police state Sheriff Wade ran, the evil Wade mysteriously disappeared. Without ever saying as much, most people in Frontera assumed that Buddy played the lead role in Charley's disappearance. Because Charley was so evil, however, Buddy's guilt didn't matter to most people. The law under Buddy was endlessly more fair than it ever was under Charley. Sure, Buddy made certain that the town ran the way he wanted; he engaged in some electoral fraud here and again, and he sometimes abused the powers of the office he occupied for thirty years. (For example, he used prisoners as laborers to build a patio at his home.) Despite his minor infractions of the law, Buddy wasn't a flaming racist, he wasn't a megalomaniac, he didn't take bribes, and "nobody ever died under Buddy Deeds's watch." He wasn't a moral person in the least, but the town loved Buddy Deeds because he was not Charley Wade and, moreover, because he had freed them from Sheriff Wade's reign of terror. As Otis Payne remembered, "Buddy Deeds was my salvation."

Sam Deeds, an unlikely sheriff who was chosen for the job by the political machine of the town (which no doubt counted on the flexible law enforcement and name recognition of a "Buddy Jr."), has a different view of his father and, for that matter, justice. While no one in the town would ever speak ill of Buddy and almost everyone seems to celebrate the legend that he has become, Sam, his only son, doesn't think of him as fondly. To Sam, Buddy was a mean, immoral person who not only victimized the town and profaned justice, but also never understood his son. In addition, Buddy took away the one thing Sam ever held dear in his life when Buddy destroyed Sam's relationship with the boy's teenage lover, Pilar Cruz.

All of this is history as the movie begins. By the end of the film, however, the revelations about Sheriff Buddy Deeds and how his son feels about him are all challenged. As Sayles challenges the history of Buddy Deeds and Sam's feelings, the film reminds us that we operate in the present from our knowledge of the past and that, all too frequently, that knowledge is limited if not flawed. The public memory of Charley Wade is what initially established such a fond memory of Buddy Deeds. And the subsequent memory of Buddy Deeds, his public history, is a contested one. Of course, that doesn't mean that we shouldn't attempt to know the past. Rather, Sayles calls for us to seek "truth" in the past while always being conscious of the fact that it may escape us because of our human tendencies in the present.

In the opening of the film, two off-duty army officers are poking around in an abandoned shooting range. As one carefully studies and appreciates his surroundings, the other stumbles over the ground with his metal detector searching for stray bullets and relics. The ground they occupy has seen its share of history, as we learn when the metal detector picks up a tarnished sheriff's badge and, consequently, a skull. Sheriff

Sam Deeds is called out to the scene, and before too long and with the help of the coroner (with as much certainty as science can provide) surmises that the bones belong to the long lost body of Charley Wade. Accordingly, Sam sets out to solve the mystery of Charley Wade's murder. Not surprisingly, Sam's primary suspect is his father, Buddy Deeds. The past speaks to the present, but the past is, now, only a skeleton of its former self.

what can you know?

"We're not changing anything, we're just trying to present a more complete picture."

—Pilar Cruz, school teacher, to angry parents

The stage is set. Sam is searching for the "truth" of Charley Wade's murder, and in the process, trying to uncover the history that lies behind the legend that is his father. Sam is greatly preoccupied with the manner in which Buddy may have come to power in Rio County. For Sam, even the compounded evils of Charley Wade are no excuse for his father having shot him. Discovering such a truth about Buddy would only further the unflattering picture Sam already has of his father. Of course, Sam's research and eventual discoveries about Buddy are also revelations about himself. As the man who shares the name, the blood, and the badge of the main suspect, Sam's motivation is also to understand what and who he came from and, in a way, what and who he is today. He is in the process of "drawing a line," of creating a border between the past and the present.

The town of Frontera is also searching for its "true" self in the past. Frontera is a town where "nineteen out of twenty" people are Mexican and the rest are white or black. Of course the town's power structure rests (at least for the moment) in the hands of the white minority. The history behind this present situation is repeating itself, but this time the roles are reversed. Everyone in town knows that in the next elections, for the first time, the Mexican majority will assume its place in the city's government as they already have in the businesses, schools, and churches. And in several small but vivid scenes, we bear witness to the gradual Mexicanization of the Anglo power structure.

Situated right on the Mexican border, Frontera has been the site of many crossings, in both directions. Its sister town across the border—Piedras Negras—is as much a part of Frontera as its own residents. While there may be an imaginary line between the two, the people and cultures (and histories) are never constrained by that line. As a town in the state of Texas, Frontera has had, as Sam puts it, " a good deal of disagreements over the years." Currently, the town is a contested space, not only geographically, but also in the popular imagination of its residents. One of the earliest examples we see of this town's strife is in a community meeting about what version of the past will be taught in the school's textbooks. The town, then, is currently engaged in an all-out debate over history, over the story of how the imaginary lines came to be drawn, and over who deserves the privileged position of overseeing the story's telling.

Historians have had a hard time with "Truth" in the last century, to say the least. An onslaught of postmodern relativism, among other trends, has created a situation in which the "truth"—singular, certain, and finite—is perceived as unattainable. Even if we always adhere to "proper historical methods," we are never guaranteed that the history we produce will be any more accurate than that produced by some other historian using some other method in some other part of the world. The historiographic representation we create to understand the past is exactly that: a representation, a metaphor for what actually happened. Essentially, history has been relegated to the realm of perspective and to uncertainty.

It's a position of liberation for some. Hayden White's prescription for the field arrived at this realization as a positive step toward liberating present historiography from its past. Developing their discipline from flawed notions of what science and art ought to be, historians of the late nineteenth and twentieth centuries created neither good science nor good art. And the result had more profound consequences. As White posits, "The 'badness' of these hoary conceptions of science and art is contained above all in the outmoded conceptions of objectivity which characterize them" (43). The belief that facts are indisputable rather than "constructed by the kinds of questions the investigator asks" represent the crux of the problem. It limited the forms historians utilized in creating their stories as well as contributed to their belief that what they presented was an attainable reality, distinct and absolute.

White argues instead that historians inevitably employ metaphorical and artistic techniques, and "there is no such thing as a *single* correct view of any object under study but that there are *many* correct views, each requiring its own style of representation." He feels that "we should no longer naively expect that statements about a given epoch or complex of events in the past 'correspond' to some preexistent body of 'raw facts.' For we should recognize that *what constitutes the facts themselves* is the problem that the historian, like the artist, has tried to solve in the choice of the metaphor by which he orders his world, past, present, and future. We should ask only that the historian show some tact in the use of his governing metaphors..." (47). Thus, while objective truth is unattainable, and the historian is more like the artist or scientist who "exploits" a certain perspective with the data at his disposal, the chosen metaphor must remain useful and malleable. In some respects, however, this is a disconcerting trend. The problem lies in the ways that current theories may be used to escape all history. If all ways of conceiving, writing, and telling history are subjective interpretations (approaching but never reaching historical-objective fact), any one interpretation can always seem more or less valid than another. The inclination may be to disregard all views not in harmony with one's own or, even worse, to disregard all stories of the past.

White argued in fact that there are rules that still govern the historian's use of metaphors, "that he neither overburden them with data nor fail to use them to their limit; that he respect the logic implicit in the mode of discourse he has decided upon; and that, when his metaphor begins to show itself unable to accommodate certain kinds of data, he abandon that metaphor and seek another, richer, and more inclusive metaphor than that with which he began—in the same way that a scientist abandons a hypothesis when its use is exhausted" (47). There still is and must be a method and reason behind the writing and telling—if not the very understanding—of history. Optimistic prescriptions aside, we have to rely on some form of fact—some field of raw data—before we can draw conclusions about the past. But again, we still face the problem that one fact can be interpreted many different ways by as many different people. Take, for example, the situation with Texas. Is it a land created out of the courage and independence of a people who moved west? Or, is it a land created by a thieving people whose greed for slavery ushered in the brutal conquest of a land that did not belong to them? For the people of Frontera, each working from his or her own present and sense of the past, it is both, neither, and much more.

The local history teacher is leading a fight to offer the town's children a more complete picture of the history of Texas and of the Frontera community. The teacher is Pilar Cruz (played by Elizabeth Peña), Sam Deeds's old teenage sweetheart. While some believe that history should be told from the perspective of its noble winners, others want everyone to remember the motives behind the victories. Pilar seeks a consensus, fighting for a view that holds nothing back but rather understands the whole picture by depicting the complexity of the historical situation. That is not to say that Pilar is valorizing a specific history. Rather, in comprehending the relativism involved in history's understanding (i.e., the way that the present affects the past), Pilar stands in opposition to the "old" history, which tries to assert a singular "truth," and she advocates a multivocal history that still adequately incorporates the varied set of raw data.

The point is that while you can't know for certain which historical angle is correct, you can still have an impression of it that involves your present. The townsfolk are fighting over Frontera's history not because of what it says about the past but because of what it says about their present. Whites, Mexicans, and blacks in Frontera all cling to different images of the past, those that better suit their roles in, and understanding of, the social and political conditions of present-day Frontera. Pilar, the teacher of their children, tries to speak to all of them by showing how, in a matter of speaking, and relying on the facts, all their stories are true. But that truth isn't as absolute and singular as the "old" history.

Sam's search reveals the same tensions about truth and history. Sam is trying to understand the history behind this skeleton because it speaks to the here and now. The town is paying tribute to his father in the form of a bronze monument, as solid and unflinching as the "old" history. Through this monument, as well as in the popular imaginations of the townspeople, Buddy Deeds lives on in the present. Therefore, Sam is concerned with the impact of the history he may discover. If Buddy shot Charley, the truth the town believes in will prove to be far less solid than that bronze monument. In fact, the inclusion of this potentially new data (Buddy Deeds murdered Charley Wade) may destroy the metaphor through which the town understands the history of his father.

bet you wish you didn't know

"Imagine all that weight pressing down on you."

—Bunny, to her ex-husband Sam Deeds

The truth carries a price. Because history lives in the present and not in the past, revelations about past history always affect the present. That is another facet of the burden of history and, despite all the theorizing to the contrary, perhaps the most difficult to transcend. When it exists in the realm of historical fact and not historiographic interpretation, the burden of history is almost insurmountable. If Buddy shot Charley, we can understand the action in a variety of ways, but that will never change the fact that one took the life of another.

The love story that is part of *Lone Star* sheds further light on this predicament. The love Sam and Pilar felt for each other when they were children is rekindled when Sam comes back to town. Pilar and Sam never understood why his father and her mother were so vehemently opposed to their relationship in the first place. They assumed that it was all due to their parents' racist notions of the other's culture—a conservative effort on their part to protect the borders of social respectability. As Sam learns, however, the truth of the matter is far more complicated than that.

As Sam seeks to understand his father better, he learns things that, at first, make Buddy out to be an even worse person than Sam once thought. Buddy didn't take bribes, but he did use the instruments of his power for personal benefit. While the townsfolk seem to be more forgiving, Sam Deeds sees these perversions of duty as unforgivable acts. Another of these revelations is the discovery that Buddy Deeds had a longtime mistress. When Sam tries to discover who she was, he learns that most of the town knew of the relationship the whole time. His frustration continues until he learns the identity of the "other woman." It is Mercedes Cruz—Pilar's mother.

It takes Sam the rest of the film to piece together the whole story of

tomás f. sandoval, jr.

Mercedes's first husband, her relationship with Sam's father, and the truth about the shooting of Charley Wade. Eladio Cruz, Mercedes's husband, was killed by Sheriff Charley Wade. Eladio wasn't playing by Wade's rules when he refused to pay the sheriff a toll for "protection" while conducting his labor smuggling business. Eladio didn't respect the borders of Sheriff Wade's world and he paid the price. Sam thought Buddy Deeds always felt compassion for Mercedes Cruz because of how her husband was killed. Hence, he is not surprised to learn that Mercedes opened her restaurant with an amount of money equal to the city funds that disappeared with Charley Wade. But Eladio was killed a year before Buddy ever came to town. Even more surprisingly, Eladio was killed a year and a half before Mercedes gave birth to their daughter, Pilar. Anybody else starting to squirm?

Sam has been warned not to go poking around in the past because he might learn things he doesn't want to know. Now he knows why. Now he understands that Mercedes and his father were very much in love with each other and with their daughter. But, since the two young lovers—Pilar and Sam—were half-brother and half-sister, the two adults couldn't allow the romance to continue. This data also challenges the view Sam held of his father as a common, anti-Mexican fixture of the Anglo community. The issues raised by the film take a very individual turn now. If once we could have been happy with the manner in which "truth" and objectivity have been replaced by interpretation and relativism in history, our comfort level is quite different when history concerns something as certain and seemingly unchangeable as genetics. Rather than a constructed border that rests upon tradition and myth, Sam and Pilar seem separated by a border far more real than any other.

Otis Payne's words of caution to his grandson also suddenly become more complex with the issue of incest. If blood only means what we let it, then we can have some sort of control over the seemingly bronze-like facts of history. Perhaps there is simply a line to be drawn between certain types of facts and others—some you can move beyond and disregard, while others you are bound to forever. Tradition and history would dictate that, whether Sam and Pilar like it or not and regardless of the depth of their love, it cannot continue because of the reality of their blood.

Yet in strict adherence to his course of analysis, John Sayles, through *Lone Star*, disagrees. The film ultimately makes the judgment that the past is only what we let it mean in the present—absolutely. Rather than being passive actors who are victims of the past, the possibility that Sam and Pilar make the decision to continue their relationship (despite their histories) affirms the notion that history should be used to better understand our present and concretely build a better future. Instead of using the most interpretive facts of the past to lead us toward the argument of relative truth, John Sayles throws indisputable, objective facts at us and still leads us in the same direction.

Ultimately, while very conscious of the burden that history imposes on the present, the film is also very optimistic about the ability of people to choose creative strategies to unburden themselves from its weight. And, rather neatly, the film echoes the words of Hayden White, who writes that "history is not only a substantive burden imposed upon the present by the past in the form of outmoded institutions, ideas, and values, but also *the way of looking at the world* which gives to these outmoded forms their specious authority" (39).

liberated from the past

"Forget the Alamo."

—Pilar Cruz, to Sam Deeds

The film is careful to pay heed to White's described limits of metaphor construction. Sam's ex-wife is a perfect example of how selective myth construction can be hazardous. The two divorced awhile back because of her mental problems (she's a little bit "high strung"). Sam visits his ex-wife to search through his father's belongings. When we meet Bunny (Frances McDormand), we encounter a woman who is Texan in the biggest definition of the word. She loves football at the high school, college, and professional levels. Her favorite teams are all of the Texan persuasion. Dressed in her Dallas Cowboys jersey and Houston Oilers hat and surrounded by football memorabilia, she is a fanatic and becomes mentally unglued as she absorbs endless hours of scouting reports and watches tapes of old games. She revels in the sport that "real Texans" love most—a simulated battle occurring within a set of borders that creates allegiances and concrete, albeit temporary, communities.

However, she is also living beyond her history. Even though the Texan she portrays is as fictitious as the tooth fairy, she thrives in her fanatic masquerade because she is able to disregard the weight of "reality." In her awe of the football player who can bench press a huge amount of weight, we understand that she is a person who has made the choice to unburden herself and live in a created history. If history is subjective, if the facts can speak to people in thousands of different ways, then any history (adhering to some standards) is as valid as any other. Yet Bunny's past is pure myth, unable and unwilling to incorporate any form of data that reveals holes in its construction. She is accordingly presented as insane— a medicated flurry of emotions.

Lone Star suggests that history is something to be understood, whether or not the end result is something that we want to hear. In the end—if there can be an end—we are free (if not obligated) to choose whether or not we will live by that history. The truth, like the present (if not because of the present) is malleable. As White reminds us, "The contemporary historian has to establish the value of the study of the past, not as an end in itself, but as a way of providing perspectives on the present that

tomás f. sandoval, jr.

contribute to the solution of problems peculiar to our time"(41). Thus, once we have represented the raw data of the past using forms that stretch to maintain their internal consistencies and incorporate all the data in our field, we are still free to choose what those histories will mean to us in our construction of the future.

Returning to our main story, we get the most clear-cut example of this idea. As Sam probes deeper into the mystery before him, he finally learns who shot Charley Wade. In the final flashback of the film, we see Deputy Hollis Pogue shooting his superior, Sheriff Wade. He did it to defend his now longtime friend, Otis Payne. Hollis witnessed the shooting of Eladio Cruz, as well as a slew of other injustices committed by Sheriff Wade, and he wasn't going to allow Otis to be added to the count. The truth in this case is indisputable: Buddy Deeds did not shoot Charley Wade; Hollis Pogue did.

Yet Sam doesn't worry about exposing the "facts." Hollis (played in his older years by Clifton James) is the current mayor of Frontera. In all likelihood, he will be the last white mayor the town will have for quite awhile. He is also about to retire and live out the rest of his years in peace. With all that in mind, Sam decides never to let the "truth" out. Sam understands that history affects the living, not the dead. He also understands how it affects the memory of the past. To allow people to think that his father shot Charley Wade rather than know the raw truth that Hollis Pogue did is to make a conscious choice to not disturb the constructed, public stories of either Buddy or Hollis. Instead, as he concludes, "Buddy's a goddamn legend. He can handle it." And, after all, as Otis himself realizes, "people liked the story we told better than anything the truth might have been."

Once again we see how the film understands history. It is not a thing of the past but a created reality of the present. Sayles visually reminds us of this throughout the film as flashbacks occur without a fade away or a break in the action. For example, in the film's climactic revelation of the true murder of Charley Wade, the action goes directly, in one uncut shot, from the present-day bar of Otis Payne (where Sam is confronting Hollis and the owner with his theory of the crime) to the actual event of Charley's death, decades before. Sayles merely pans the camera across the room as the actors of the past reveal themselves as if they were standing beside the present actors all along. The viewer is reminded that the past is not a distant memory as much as a reality that almost shares space with our present. In the temporal space there are no borders. Sam doesn't feel the need to assure that the truth of who shot Charley Wade is known, because that history can still affect the living.

The final scene of the movie shows Pilar and Sam discussing what Sam has discovered about their relationship. They are parked in a now dilapidated drive-in movie theater. Sitting on the hood of his car, they both face a large and tattered, yet completely blank movie screen. Trying to make sense of "the rule" that forbids romantic love between them, Pilar tells Sam that she is unable to have children anymore, "if that's what the rule's about." She then asks, "So that's it? You're not going to want to be with me anymore?"

As Sam affectionately caresses her hand he answers her question. "If I met you for the first time today, I'd still want to be with you." In these final moments, they consider whether or not to "start from scratch" and forget "all that other stuff and all that history." Both must now decide how, if at all, the knowledge of their blood relation changes what they feel for each other. A choice in favor of a communal future, a choice to "forget the Alamo," would be an active choice to unburden themselves from history.

That does not mean, however, that John Sayles gives no value to history. In order to move beyond it, he argues, we must first know what it is. Luckily for the history profession, in order to live beyond the Alamo you have to know it in a way that affects your present. Second, by using seemingly objective events such as the shooting of Charley Wade and the kinship of Pilar and Sam to communicate an ideal of the relativity of history and truth, Sayles doesn't leave us in a world of uncertain knowledge. Rather, he appropriately destroys a world of borders. As Otis Payne, local historian, teaches Sam, "It's not like there's a line between the good people and the bad people. It is not like you're one or the other."

Lone Star teaches that there is no separation between the past and the present. The border that exists between them is only in our minds, for the past only exists in the present. Furthermore, there is no border between the objective and interpretive facts of the past; both only have power in the present insofar as we choose to utilize them for our own historical imaginations. History is something that can and should unite people in their common interests and needs. The citizens of Frontera, Texas are united by their common histories on their common landscape. Even though they may understand it differently and utilize it toward different ends, they are bound together through their present situation—a fragment of the past living and breathing in the present.

Our criteria for wading through the "truths" of the past should be based on our hopes for the future, on our ability to utilize those truths toward specific ends. The final illustrative scene of *Lone Star* finds Pilar and Sam staring at that blank screen. From one point of view, with the decision to continue or end their love affair still before them, their communal future is a wide, unexplored, and undetermined landscape, much like the empty screen. In her book *The Decolonial Imaginary*, Emma Pérez suggests another interpretation shared by some film critics. From this perspective, the final phrase uttered by Pilar to "forget the Alamo" is a liberatory choice of hope and love transcending "all that has come before, all that has been inherited only to damage daughters and sons who have fallen heir to a history of conquest, of colonialization, of hatred between brown and white."[3] As the mixed-race, female, decolonized character, Pilar makes the decision to "remake their story," one that the Anglo Sam, however postmodern a figure, is not in a position to make. With their decision made, they will have accepted the past and yet chosen to live beyond it. Whichever ending the audience interprets, the life Pilar and Sam will try to create with each other is providence not of the known, but the unknown.

I'm not saying that we should all go out and have sex with our siblings—and neither is John Sayles. But we should remember the lesson that both White and Sayles teach us—that is, that history is not, and should not be, a prison. Even the truths of the past can be overcome by creating in the present a new and future-oriented reality. The goal of both the historian and nonhistorian alike should always be to utilize the past while looking toward the future. And, even more important, White says it must also be "to confront heroically the dynamic and disruptive forces in contemporary life" (50). For it is within these complex and confusing spaces that history can best serve the individual. But if we always choose to live by the dictates of past, or if we can only understand it as linear inevitability that gave birth to our present, then we will never progress beyond its limitations.

notes

An earlier version of this essay appeared in the online zine *Bad Subjects: Political Education for Everyday Life* 28, October 1996. I want to thank their editorial staff for the opportunity to first tackle this topic. I am especially grateful to Charles Bertsch for the initial invitation as well as his helpful feedback and editorial skills.

1. Hayden White, "The Burden of History," in *Tropics of Discourse: Essays in Cultural Criticism* (Baltimore: Johns Hopkins University Press, 1978), 17–50. "The Burden of History" was originally published in *History and Theory* 5, no. 2 (1966). Hereafter, page numbers for White will be cited parenthetically in the text.
2. Dennis West and Joan M. West, "Borders and Boundaries: An Interview with John Sayles," *Cineaste* 22, no. 3 (1996), 14.
3. Emma Pérez, *The Decolonial Imaginary: Writing Chicanas into History* (Bloomington: Indiana University Press, 1999), 126.

historiophoty:

buffalo bill,

the indians,

and the

western biopic

cowboy

wonderland,

history

four
 # and myth

"it ain't all that

different

than real life"

william g. simon and louise spence

"If I wasn't real," said Alice—half laughing through her tears, it all seemed so ridiculous—"I shouldn't be able to cry."

"I hope you don't suppose those are *real* tears?" Tweedledum interrupted in a tone of great contempt.

—Lewis Carroll, *Through the Looking-Glass*

Buffalo Bill and the Indians, or Sitting Bull's History Lesson is Robert Altman's U.S. bicentennial film. Released on the fourth of July weekend, 1976, it examines the western as both national myth and commercial entertainment form; indeed, one might see the film's project as an exposé of the ideological functioning of the western, its white male hero, and the Native American over nearly one hundred years of American popular culture. The film stars Paul Newman in the role of William F. Cody, famous Indian scout and buffalo hunter who, at the time of the story, is co-owner and star of a part-rodeo, part-circus, part-melodrama traveling spectacle known as Buffalo Bill's Wild West. Seizing upon Buffalo Bill's Wild West as a crucial moment in the historical process through which the raw materials of history are transformed into the entertainment industries' myths, the film focuses on the disjunction between what it proposes as historical events and the representation of those events in the signs and symbols associated with our national culture, the language of national [be]longing.

Treating the Wild West show as a late nineteenth century prototype for the complex of popular entertainment forms that take their source from Western historical materials, *Buffalo Bill and the Indians* dramatizes the imaginative acts through which history is transfigured into the myths that bind our imagined community, the nation.[1] As such, the film carries out one of the central strategies that Richard Slotkin has since suggested for undermining the ideological power of western mythmaking: it demystifies the mythmaking process by rehistoricizing the mythic subject and detailing an account of the mythmaking enterprise.[2] Focusing on the processes through which the myth of the western hero has been constructed, the film employs irony to question the moral authority of the hero and the consequences for Native Americans.

Buffalo Bill and the Indians confronts us with the politics of history and historical representation and suggests that the story of the American West is less a tale of civilization, progress, heroic action, and triumph than oppression, displacement, exclusion, and defeat. The action of the film takes place between 1885 (when Sitting Bull joined Buffalo Bill's Wild West) and 1890 (when Sitting Bull was killed at Standing Rock). This was a time of crucial historical transition. The killing of Sitting Bull and the massacre at Wounded Knee shortly after signaled the end of the prolonged war of conquest to contain the Native American population. In 1890, the census reported that there were no longer any vast tracts of land remaining for American settlement,[3] and a few years later, at the 1893 Columbian Exposition, Frederick Jackson Turner proclaimed the close of "the frontier."[4] As Alan Trachtenberg has put it, the Exposition, celebrating the anniversary of Columbus's arrival in the Western Hemisphere, marked "not only four hundred years of 'progress' but also of destruction: the end not only of 'frontier' but independent native societies."[5] In the film, Buffalo Bill realizes that both the buffalo and the Indians on which his legend was based are vanishing.

While this first major phase of western history was coming to a close, Buffalo Bill's Wild West reached its highest popularity and influence. It set a pattern for the mythological portrayal of the western hero in literature, art, drama, film, television, and the modern theme park. In 1922 Eugene Manlove Rhodes, a New Mexico cowboy and writer of western tales, accused Cody's show of being responsible for the major misconceptions about cowboys and the West.[6] Contemporary historian Richard White argues the show "produced a master narrative of the West."[7] As a character in Altman's film asserts, they were out to "Cody-fy the world."

In Buffalo Bill's Wild West, the cowboy (actually still a hired hand on horseback) was part of a national morality play, sharpshooting, trick riding, and leaping from galloping horses to save numerous virgins riding in "the authentic Deadwood stage" from attacks by painted "savages." "The real" seems to have been an important part of the appeal of Buffalo Bill's Wild West, as audiences across America and Europe got to see real cowboys, real Indians, and the real celebrity, Buffalo Bill. An 1892 article in the *London Evening News and Post* exclaimed, "We hear a great deal about realism on the stage, where a working model of a Westend drawing room is hailed as a triumph of art, but the Buffalo Bill show is something more than realism—it is reality!"[8] The show's 1893 program contained the endorsement of Brick Pomeroy, a well-known midwestern journalist, calling the spectacle "a correct representation of life on the plains . . . brought to the East for the inspection and education of the public."[9] However, as Richard White points out, while talking about the "reality effect" of the Wild West, the Indians were often imitating imitations of themselves, reenacting "white versions of events in which some of them had actually participated."[10]

Buffalo Bill and the Indians, or Sitting Bull's History Lesson is concerned precisely with interrogating such effects of "the real." Self-consciously suggesting the discursive nature of all reference, the film is what Linda Hutcheon calls a "historiographic metafiction," a popular paradoxical manifestation of postmodernism.[11] It lays claim to historical events and personages, rewriting the past in order to open it up to current critique.[12]

Consider the film's opening sequence: before the first image is even seen, a cavalry bugle is heard. Then, as a second bugle calls, the film's first image shows an American flag being raised over a western fortress. As the camera tilts up with the flag to snow-covered mountains, the names of the film's backers (Dino De Laurentiis and David Susskind) are superimposed in lettering that imitates the heavily seriffed typescript and ornamental embellishments of nineteenth century theater programs. The wind howls in the background. The bugle calls, fortress, flag, mountains, and wind immediately invoke a familiar and highly conventionalized motif: the wilderness fort, poised at the edge of the frontier, maintained by the cavalry in the name of American nationhood.

While a third bugle call is heard and the camera pans left across the mountain vista, a playful title appears announcing "Robert Altman's Unique and Heroic Enterprise of Inimitable Lustre." Already a dissonance of discourses is suggested. The humorously self-conscious show business hype of this title is at odds with the traditional archetypal western view in the image. The title names the film's director and proclaims what we are about to see in hyperbolic and archaic language, resonant of the exaggeration of advertising promotion, indeed, wording that recalls Buffalo Bill's own posters.[13]

As the camera continues its traversal of the western horizon, another discourse is added. A male voice declaims a second account of what we are going to see: "Ladies and Gentlemen, you are about to experience not a show for entertainment," but "a revue of down-to-earth events that made the American frontier." Further increasing the level of dissonance, the voice-over makes claims for a serious historical project that seems at odds with language of the previous title. The familiar sideshow barker form of address itself contradicts the denial of the entertainment mode as well as the apparent seriousness of the narration's historical claim ("real events enacted by men and women of the American frontier").

As the voice-over continues, intoning the motifs of civilization and savagery, progress, and nationhood,[14] it seems to generate the images. Immediately after the voice extols the virtues of "anonymous settlers," the camera pulls back to reveal a frontier family working outside their cabin. Right after it refers to the settlers' need to survive the "savage instincts of man," a band of marauding Indians ride in, attacking the family and abducting a young, white woman.

While apparently proposing an authorial statement of the film's intent and conception, the voice itself lacks authority. It is an older man's raspy voice with a hint of hyperbole and a touch of rhyming oratory. The voice lacks the conviction necessary for its words to be taken as an authorial paratext. Its status also seems in competition with the film's public and ostensible "author," Robert Altman, just identified in the comic "show-biz" tone of the superimposed title. Soon after, the voice will in fact be specified as that of an old soldier, a crusty, habitual mythologizer, a role that definitely undermines his status as a reliable authorial voice.

On the soundtrack, over the shouting, neighing, and whooping of the Indian attack, a brass band begins to play a new upbeat theme redolent of circus music. The cast list rolls over the scene of the settlers and Indians, once again indulging in self-referential humor, billing the cast not by their character names, but by their functional identities in the Wild West (The Star, The Producer, The Publicist, The Legend Maker, etc.). The clash of two seemingly opposing impulses continues: the potential straightforwardness of the historical enactment is sharply attenuated by the interference of the self-referential humor of the music and the cast billing.

This attenuation is further extended as the cast list ends and an unidentified voice shouts "Cease the action!" This is followed almost immediately by a second unidentified voice commanding, "From the beginning, one, two, . . ." At this point, the action of the settlers and Indians does stop, suggesting that a rehearsal has been taking place. This is confirmed as the crew credits begin to roll and the camera slowly pulls back to show a wide view of an arena and behind-the-scenes activities. But is it a rehearsal for a Wild West show, or for a self-referential movie about the Wild West? The film's opening titles end on a new one, a diegetic one, a sign for Buffalo Bill's Wild West. The next scene begins in a crowded interior. A voice (later identified as that of writer Ned Buntline) speaks about finding a scrawny kid sleeping under a wagon, but as the camera slowly zooms in closer, we realize that this is not another voice-over narrator, but a man on screen telling how he created a legend: ". . . so I tell the kid, from now on your name is Buffalo Bill." The film cuts immediately to another man, the scraggly old soldier (whose voice is retroactively recognizable as the narrator of the settlers and Indians act) telling a story to a small group of Native American women and children, "I was so impressed that I nicknamed him Buffalo Bill."

Before we even see the central character of the film, two men claim to have "created" him, to have discovered and named him Buffalo Bill. The introduction of two initiating legends provokes us to question the veracity of both. Because both men claim to have been the originators, they call attention to the arbitrariness and instability of the legend-building process—and the notion of historical knowledge is radically problematized.

Before we actually see the movie star who plays Buffalo Bill, we hear several people speaking about him and see multiple representations of him. A cameo of Bill adorns the sign that identifies his show grounds. His nephew addresses a likeness of Bill painted on a canvas partition in the Wild West's headquarters. Margaret, Bill's mezzocontralto paramour, sings a salute to another portrait, the painting of Bill heroically mounted on a rearing white horse that dominates his private quarters; the camera remains on *his* image as Margaret leaves the frame. When we finally see the "real" Buffalo Bill, thirteen minutes into the film, it is only after he has been grandiously announced, "William F. Cody: Buffalo Bill . . . ," followed by another teaser (his portrait on a drum head being beaten by a mallet), and then he's one of several characters in an extreme long shot. This is hardly the way we expect to be introduced to a hero or a star.

Images of Buffalo Bill are everywhere in the Wild West, and he is often shown contemplating his image in portraits and mirrors as if to evaluate whether he measures up. At other times, he assumes the poses suggested by the idealized icons, heroically clasping his arm across his chest, with his hand on his shoulder, as he stares off into space. He seems to be taken in by his own legend, a consumer of his own image. During many of the behind-the-scenes activities (rehearsals, contract negotiations, photo sessions, new act planning, grooming, romantic entanglements, etc.), Bill "successfully" performs his heroic role. At other times, however, these poses and performances are in conflict with Bill's self-serving and less than honorable, brave, or accomplished behavior. For example, Bill objects to the two Native Americans, Sitting Bull and his interpreter William Halsey, standing next to Annie Oakley in a cast photo ("The fans won't like it . . ."). He suggests that the Indians be given slower horses; he is afraid of his lady friend's pet canary; and when he leads a group of men to track down Sitting Bull, he is unable to locate him. On stage and in many of his backstage activities, he is introduced in splendiferous terms, dressed in full "western" regalia, sometimes elaborately beaded with American flags. Other times, he is hungover, in his long johns, without his flowing blond Custer-style wig, juggling opera-singing lovers (one of whom he disappoints sexually), beset by accusations from his estranged wife, haggling over money and contracts, and dealing with demanding performers in an ill-tempered manner.

Bill is represented through numerous, often contrary modes: what people say about him, what people write about him, what he thinks and says about himself, publicists' blurbs, Wild West performances, paintings, mirror images, dreams, and hallucinations. By the film's end, Bill has been presented in so many ways that he himself no longer has a firm grasp on his own identity. And the film's spectator, as we shall see, is left to question the representational status and signification of many of the scenes.[15] The dissonance and disjunction between images and actions raise central questions about the relationships between reality and spectacle, identity and performance, history and mythology. In a perfectly Pirandellian moment, when called upon to perform an actual western piece of action, to go out into the wilderness and bring back the apparently escaped Indians, Bill rummages through his closet exclaiming, "Goddam it! Where's my *real* jacket?" This dynamic of competing discourses and calling into question of the very status of "the real" is the basic aesthetic method of *Buffalo Bill and the Indians*.

Paul Newman's performance as Buffalo Bill compounds the polyvalent image of the character. It also adds a critical dimension to his representation. Robert Altman, at a press conference and preview of the film held in New York City in May of 1976, said that he had wanted a movie star, not an actor, to play Buffalo Bill,[16] and in an interview during the editing of the film, explained that this was partially to secure backing, but also because "stardom is part of what we're talking about in *Buffalo Bill* ... a very conscious deflating of not only Buffalo Bill but Paul Newman, Movie Star."[17] Newman told the press that, symbolically, "Cody was the first star, someone who became a legend but couldn't live up to it"[18] and described his character as "a combination of Custer, Gable, Redford and me. In that order."[19] Newman acknowledged the tension he personally felt between himself and his screen image: "There's no way that what people see on celluloid has anything to do with me."[20]

In many ways, Newman's performance is built on this tension, this inscribed conjunction and disjunction between actor and role. Jean-Louis Comolli suggests that there is an inevitable "interference, even rivalry," in a historical film when a well-known performer plays a well-known historical figure.[21] There is a "double affirmation," an "improbable conjunction of two identities," and an "oscillating to-and-fro movement" in the spectator's experience of character as familiar historical personage and character as familiar movie actor.[22] In *Buffalo Bill and the Indians* this tension includes the spectator's prescient knowledge and prior interpretations of Buffalo Bill gained from other representations. It also includes what we know about the star who plays the historical person. The Buffalo Bill of dime novels, stage melodramas, and the Wild West show, the Buffalo Bill who impersonated himself in fifteen films and was represented in more than thirty others by assorted performers,[23] is now played by someone we know even better, Paul Newman, popular antihero (who not long ago was Billy the Kid, Rocky Graziano, Butch Cassidy, and Judge Roy Bean), a noted political activist, supporter of liberal and environmental causes.[24]

Newman, unlike a lesser-known actor, brings a constellation of intertextual cues to his role; a key one is his persona as an actor who is outside the Hollywood system, a self-proclaimed easterner who defines himself at a distance from the Hollywood apparatus. This allows him to play at being a star in this performance with a certain ironic detachment, an awareness of playing the role of someone playing a role. The film foregrounds the double affirmation and interference that Comolli attributes to any historical film by self-consciously frolicking with multiple superimpositions of stardom: Paul Newman, movie star, performing the role of William F. Cody, performing the star role of Buffalo Bill. Newman is at a sufficient distance from his character that he is able to inscribe an ironic dimension that is consistent with and central to the film's project. The hyperbolic self-consciousness of the performance helps to keep the audience aware of Buffalo Bill as a constructed image. It diffuses the character, making him *character* and *representation of character* simultaneously. In the casting of Buffalo Bill, Altman seems to have wanted this extra load of reference inscribed in the film experience. He seems to have calculated a viewing process that would be necessarily discursive. By choosing a twentieth-century celebrity to play a nineteenth-century celebrity, any strategies that attempt to evoke history weave a topography of potential schism.

The lack of synchrony between Paul Newman and Buffalo Bill, the appearance of players familiar from other Altman films (Geraldine Chaplin, Shelley Duvall, Bert Remsen), and the many references to "the real" all function to subvert the film's illusionism, drawing us away from the story toward the way it is being told. There is a certain irony in the film's carefully controlled colors reminiscent of nineteenth-century lithographs, the casting of a Native American (Frank Kaquitts), a tribal chief with a striking resemblance to photographs of the historical Chief Sitting Bull, the publicity material mimicking the rhetorical style and flourishes of period handbills, the sepia-toned portraits of the cast reminiscent of nineteenth-century tintypes, all evoking authenticity while at the same time the film undermines any fictional coherence and casts suspicion on the very possibility of "accuracy."[25] In *Buffalo Bill and the Indians*, a movie about fictive illusion, we are never able to become submerged in any fiction or any illusion. The film constantly questions what reality is by declaring its own artifice as well as its own confusion. When Sitting Bull arrives at the Wild West, Buffalo Bill assures him that he will like show business: "It ain't all that different than real life."

In Arthur Kopit's 1968 play *Indians* (which inspired Altman's film), in the middle of a performance for the president of the United States and the first lady and before he has a chance to rescue the virgin maiden from "torture, sacrifice and certain violations," Buffalo Bill feels obliged to explain to Wild Bill Hickok (who has begun to get highly humiliated impersonating himself) that they are really doing something quite ennobling: "Ya see, Bill, what you fail to understand is that I'm not being false to what I *was*. I'm simply *drawin'* on what I was . . . and raisin' it to a higher level. [*He takes a conscious pause.*] *Now.* On with the show!"[26] Both the movie and the play problematize the relation between spectacle and reality by provoking a dystopian sense of distance toward representation. Although both question the role western heroes have played in the values and aspirations of our national culture, the play is also a sardonic meditation on the possibility of progress and improvement, whereas the film is more concerned with illusion and disillusion.

The inclusion within the film's cast of characters of the historical figure, Ned Buntline, the pulp author who "discovered," developed, and promoted Buffalo Bill, serves as another means to highlight how provisional Buffalo Bill, as a character, really is. The gently aging Buntline, identified as The Legend Maker in the film's opening titles, plays the role of debunker, constantly reminding characters in the film and spectators in the movie theater of the fictional nature of Buffalo Bill: "No ordinary man would have had the foresight to take credit for acts of bravery and heroism that he couldn'ta done. And no ordinary man could realize what tremendous profits could be made by telling a pack of lies. . . . "

Buntline also illuminates some of the contradictions in Bill's status as show-business star and points out Bill's imperfections: his drinking, his lack of wilderness skills, and so on. As he holds court in the barroom, Ned's commentaries are frequently edited into the film so that they function as voice-overs, ironically framing Bill's performances both in the arena and with his admiring entourage. Buntline's dialogue plays against the heroic image of Bill that the Wild West strives to project, rehistoricizing the mythic subject, and undermining Bill's heroic posturing by reminding us how his image has been constructed and how that image, as Walter Benjamin has said of history, is "filled by the presence of the now" and serves the values and aspirations of our national culture.[27] This understanding is represented as a threat to the Wild West's functioning, and several of the characters voice concern that Buntline is on the premises.

Significantly, Buntline is given a privileged voice in the film. He is contemplative, distant, physically removed from and resistant to the show-biz ethos woven by the Wild West's illusion-making process. What he says tends to be confirmed by the ways in which Bill and the other characters behave. Consequently, the character can be understood as a spokesman for the film's authorial perspective, for its overall attitude toward the film's subjects.[28] As such, it provides one of several contra-dicting narrative points of view.

Buntline is played with quiet gravity by Burt Lancaster, who, as the film's only well-known star at the time other than Paul Newman, combines the pedigree of his long career in Hollywood as an action star, including numerous western roles, with the reflective intellectual persona that Luchino Visconti created for him in his middle and later years. In sharp contrast to the performance style of Buffalo Bill's show business acolytes, who are always skittering about and speaking in empty show-biz double talk ("In enlarging the show, we may have disimproved it."), Lancaster is given almost sculpturesque authority. He is almost always static and speaks with concern for the politics and poetics of his words. (Explaining why the army would be willing to transfer their captive, Sitting Bull, to the Wild West, for example, Buntline says, "They can't shoot him. Not till they get those Sioux treaties signed. So they put him in a Wild West show." He continues, "A rock ain't a rock once it becomes gravel.") He is specifically contrasted to rival dime novelist Prentiss Ingraham (played by the lesser-known actor Allan Nicholls) in his vocabulary, his physical stature, and his penetrating understanding of Buffalo Bill's enterprise. Toward the end of the film, just before the climactic scenes, Buntline and Bill meet in the bar and reflect on their time together ("The thrill of my life to have invented you!"). Lying, Bill assures him that he'd like to have him back with the show, "except that frankly, Nate can't stand the sight of you," and Buntline rides off onto the night as if to signify the passing of an era.

Buntline and the battery of other legend-making characters in the film (the old soldier, Bill's partner and producer, Nate Salsbury, Prentiss Ingraham, "The Publicist" Major Burke, Bill's adoring nephew, and William F. Cody himself) relate to a significant motif in many post–World War II westerns: the inscription within the film of the western mythmaking process itself, either by the inclusion of a journalist or novelist within the film's story (such as *The Left-Handed Gun* [Arthur Penn, 1958] and *The Shootist* [Don Siegel, 1976]) or by the self-conscious acknowledgment of popular culture's perpetuation of the falsification of historical accuracy (the "print the legend" motif in, for example, *Fort Apache* [John Ford, 1948] and *The Man Who Shot Liberty Valance* [Ford, 1962]). The presence of so many of these figures in *Buffalo Bill and the Indians* attests to the importance of mythmaking as a central subject of the film. Moreover, there is a significant oppositional dichotomy between these characters and Buntline. Whereas it is the job of the employees of the Wild West to enhance and bolster Buffalo Bill's image, Buntline exposes the circumstances and nature of their operation. The inclusion within the film of both mythmaking and its demystification suggest the degree to which disparate and contradictory proposals of fact, story, image, and the contestation of narrative authority are at the center of Altman's narrative method.

Of all the strategies the film deploys to interrogate and criticize the authority of Buffalo Bill as western hero, the strongest is his systematic comparison with Sitting Bull. This oppositional structure, the co-presence of two antagonistic narrative perspectives, the continuous "duel" between Sitting Bull and Buffalo Bill, is first posed by the film's two titles. *Buffalo Bill and the Indians* is the show-biz title designed for the theater marquee. It grabs the ticket buyer's attention by highlighting the film's famous hero, and, not coincidentally, reduces his antagonist to a racial category.[29] The film's alternative title, *Sitting Bull's History Lesson*, personalizes and individualizes the antagonist and associates him with the pedagogical, the teaching and learning of history, defined in the film as what really happened. Sitting Bull is essentialized as the real's unproblematic presence, the representative of the liberal humanist notion of "truth." Buffalo Bill's Wild West representations, and by extension our nation's popular memory of the West, are reciprocally defined as distortions, as molding "truth" to the interests of the mythmaking business and the ideology of nationhood. After Bill fires the chief for suggesting an act in which soldiers slaughter every man, woman, child, and dog in the village on Killdear Mountain, Annie Oakley informs Bill that Sitting Bull "wanted to show the truth to the people. Why can't you accept that, just once?" Bill replies angrily, "Because I have a better sense of history than that!"

The comparison of Buffalo Bill and Sitting Bull is elaborated on several levels. Sitting Bull, for instance, does not conform to the popular notion of the physical presence of a star persona; he is tiny and retiring in nature.[30] When he first arrives at the Wild West grounds, virtually the entire cast and crew (except Annie and Ned Buntline, who already know him) mistake his huge spokesman, William Halsey (who has the physical stature and bearing expected of a star), for the chief. Not only does Sitting Bull not conform to the appearance of a star ("Golly, it's the runt!"), but he refuses to perform the star act. While Bill wants him to reenact the Wild West's conception of his dramatic role in the Battle of the Little Bighorn, Sitting Bull insists instead on performing a modest horse act, "making the big grey dance," which the Wild West's audience initially jeers in disappointment but soon cheers for its grace and simplicity. This act is strikingly different from Buffalo Bill's heroic horse riding.

Crucial to the contrast is the comparison of their respective wilderness skills, a central criterion for the evaluation of a western hero.[31] For example, Sitting Bull laughs as he fires Buffalo Bill's pistol and discovers it is loaded with buckshot instead of bullets. (Halsey says, "Sitting Bull thinks you are a great marksman. He can see how you killed so many of his buffalo!") When Sitting Bull decides to establish his camp on the ridge across the river from the arena, a river that members of Bill's troop assure him is impassable ("We've already lost three horses, six Blackfeet Indians, and a barge load of show equipment valued at . . ."), the chief and his companions easily cross to the other side. And, most important, when Bill is called upon to perform the kind of action upon which his legend was built, gathering a posse of the best men in his company to go after Sitting Bull and his companions, who have taken off to the mountains, he goes out into the wilderness accompanied by a musical fanfare and, despite the fact that the Indians were in sight when they set out, returns empty-handed, his bedraggled posse betraying their inability to carry out the simple tracking task. Sitting Bull and Halsey return to the Wild West of their own volition, explaining that they had not tried to elude their perusers, but were simply visiting the sun in the mountains as they do each month during the day of the first moon.

Another significant area of comparison between Buffalo Bill and Sitting Bull is their respective use of language. Bill and the other members of the troop speak in inflated show-business language, which varies from producer Nate Salsbury's malapropisms ("We just signed the most futurable act in our history," and, "Gentlemen, I don't think that it's dispropriate to play a personal chord here.") to press agent Colonel John Burke's flamboyant alliteration ("Buffalo Bill, Monarch of the West, it delights me to present this compellingly cornucopious canary, this curvacious cadenza in the compendium of classical chanson . . ."). The Wild West's language is marked by its hyperbolic introductions, celebratory extravagance, and double dealing.

Sitting Bull, on the other hand, gains immeasurable dignity simply by not speaking. He is portrayed as moving, fragile, and poignant, a "mute victim condemned to the loss of pastoral innocence," which, as Stephen Greenblatt suggests, is one of the central prototypes of Native American representation.[32] William Halsey, identified in the opening credits as "The Interpreter," speaks for the chief. His language is measured, his words carefully chosen and absolutely to the point. While the film's representation of Native Americans is a variation of the Noble Savage, the argument between Buffalo Bill and Sitting Bull privileges the Native American perspective. The effect of the extended comparison is to critically parody Bill, to expose the gap between his image and his reality.

On the story level, their duel is best understood as Bill's attempt to colonize Sitting Bull. Buffalo Bill's possessive, like his portrait, is stamped on everything in the show (banners, drums, tents, props, pressbox, etc.). The first time we hear his voice, he is saying that "anything"—later corrected to "everything"—historical is his. Sitting Bull rejects having the possessive applied to him. Bill continually tries to conquer Bull by bending him to the Wild West's image, and Bull consistently refuses to be co-opted. During the dream sequence near the end of the film, Bill tries to convince Bull of the naïveté of his outlook with a logic that betrays his self-interest: "In one hundred years, I'm still gonna be Buffalo Bill, star! And you're gonna be the Indian." Buffalo Bill's legitimacy—and financial gain—are premised on the construction of natives as degraded and dangerous *others*. Sitting Bull's refusal to play that part—indeed, the metaphysical clarity of his existence—is a transgression against the image of Buffalo Bill and the frontier myth.

The duel is also an ironic reversal of the captivity myth, one of the primal narratives of white/Indian relations (and portrayed in the scene being rehearsed in the pretitle prologue), with Sitting Bull, rather than the helpless white woman, held captive.[33] Here Sitting Bull symbolizes the values imperiled by commercial mass culture and his captivity consists of the horrors suffered under capitalist enslavement, a descent into hell. In a nightmarish mirror inversion, the audience gets a hint of what it might be like if the captive were contaminated by his captors (or integrated into "civilization"): when Buffalo Bill objects to Sitting Bull and Halsey standing next to Annie Oakley in the company photo, Sitting Bull offers to move away "for twenty-five American dollars."

Sitting Bull refuses to allow himself to become entertainment, an object of false nostalgia. By resisting white "civilization" he vindicates "[his] own moral character and the power of the values [he] symbolizes."[34] The film undercuts the religious fervor of the early captivity narratives and blood-and-gore sensationalism of the latter commercially-inspired nineteenth-century captivity narratives by drawing out the essence of the myth: it is not so much a test of conscience as a text of conquest. Unregenerate, Sitting Bull gratefully returns home, only to fall victim to the federal government.[35]

Dreams and dreaming provide a central motif in the film, which is introduced through the figure of Sitting Bull. Halsey explains that Sitting Bull was not physically present at the Battle of Little Bighorn; he was "making medicine and dreaming." Halsey also explains that Sitting Bull has agreed to come to the Wild West because he has dreamt that there he would meet the "Great Father" (the president of the United States). Ned Buntline expresses respect for Sitting Bull's dreams, which he thinks are more sensible and "a hell of a lot cheaper" than the Wild West show, which is "just dreamin' out loud." Several of Buntline's saloon disquisitions sound the motif of dreaming so that the motif frames the matter and method of the film's last three major scenes.

Right after the news comes over the wire that President Grover Cleveland and his new bride are coming to a performance of the Wild West ("Uncle Will, it's just like in Sittin' Bull's dream!"), Buntline observes that "things are beginnin' to take on an unreal shape." "First you sit in your teepee and you dream. Then you go to wherever your dream might . . . come true, and wait for real life to catch up." This dialogue is heard as voice-over in relation to the first shot of the performance for the president, as if to confirm the performance as a realization of Sitting Bull's dream. As it turns out, Sitting Bull's dream is utterly rebuffed. When he shows up for the postperformance reception (to which he was not invited) to address the president, Cleveland uses political double-talk to deny him even the right to speak. Sitting Bull departs, defeated in his dream for his people's future.

On the other hand, the president's command performance plays as a bravura instantiation of the white man's dream. ("The only time [white men] dream [is] when things are going their way," Buntline had observed.) It spells out the Wild West's relation to the mythology of American nationhood. Cleveland is portrayed as an extension of Buffalo Bill: he is acknowledgd as a star, the biggest man the Wild West has ever seen ("He's bigger than Buck Taylor!"). His political pronouncements equal—perhaps exceed—Bill's in their hollow platitudes. He has a speech writer, as Bill has his legend makers. Bill, for his part, performs his act resplendent in a costume festooned with American flags.

The performance relates the Wild West to the imperatives of the nation. President Cleveland's presence and the pointed parallels with Buffalo Bill underline the degree to which the Wild West's mythology coincides with national ideology. The president's denial of Sitting Bull's dream demonstrates that the Wild West's racial politics are supported at the highest level of nationhood. The Wild West is the nation's collective fantasy, its "dreamin' out loud."

The dream motif is even more directly dramatized in the oneiric quality of Buffalo Bill's phantasmagoric soliloquy. Just before this sequence, the report of Sitting Bull's death circulates around the arena. Everyone is afraid to tell Bill. As if to verify the story, the camera leaves the Wild West for the first time for a long and eerie zoom in on a burnt-out campfire, with Sitting Bull's wooden cross and string of beads recognizable on the circle of stones (his remnants as relics, fit for a museum) and "naturalistic" bird (hawks, crows, ravens), animal (buffalo?), and wind sounds in the background. The sounds of nature merge with a creaking noise as the film cuts to Bill rising from his bed. Could it be a dream? Or is it an ongoing nightmare? In the eight-minute sequence, unmarked by any specific temporal cues, Bill wanders about the Mayflower, his headquarters and living space, drinking, rummaging through mementos, looking in the mirror, contemplating his life, speaking to the sometimes present and other times absent Sitting Bull, the phantom other. The indeterminacy of Sitting Bull's presence parallels Bill's own crisis of focalization.

The sequence itself is a tapestry of confusion in which Buffalo Bill questions betrayal and self-deception and the part they both have played in the creation of his legend and stardom. In trying to make sense of his life and history, his legend begins to unravel. Like Alice in Wonderland, Bill is in an unknown world of ominous confrontation, correspondences, and nostalgia and, like Alice, he struggles for an identity. Caught in a tangle of the heroic as an ideal and hero as "goodfellow" or "everyman," he is perplexed about his own image. He must be right, or why (he says, with an accusatory glance toward the camera) would people have taken him for a king? "God meant me to be white," his voice wanders off, "God meant me to be white and it ain't easy. I've got people with no lives living through me." He feels that he has to give his fans what they expect and he tells Sitting Bull, "You can't live up to what you expect and that makes you more make-believe than me because you don't even know if you're bluffing."

The sequence posits difference as a prior condition of identity, but at the same time challenges the assumed superiority of the white man's power and cultural dominance. Buffalo Bill explains to Sitting Bull, with a reasoning that reveals his insecurity, that "the difference between the white man and the Indian in all situations is that the Injun is red, and the Injun is red for a real good reason, so we can tell us apart!" The questions of illusion and reality that are raised by the way the story is told at the beginning of the film become part of Bill's own confusion at the end, the arena of bad dreams where the characters themselves can't distinguish between story and storytelling.

There is a preoccupation with what things mean, yet the speech and the editing often provoke us to question the security of meaning. That is, the relations between word and referent and in a larger sense between image and referent is often unclear. Different and dissonant logic systems play, diverge, and compete. Time and sequence are in abeyance. Did he kill that buffalo when he was nine, or when he was eleven? He tells Sitting Bull, "You want to stay the same; well that's going backwards." Recollection comes into conflict with and confuses narrative causality and continuity. In his dream, Custer did the Indians a favor by giving them a reason to be famous. Bill renegotiates his-story, disrupting sentiment and nostalgia; past events and past desires are recognized for their use value, their ability to be transferred into real rewards. Bill's virulent self-defense is both a questioning of and an attempt at protecting his fragile identity. He wonders whether his "self" can ever live up to his "performance." "My Daddy died without ever seeing me as a star: tall, profitable, good looking." Bill looks at his portrait, "My God, ain't he riding that horse right?" The switching between first person and third complicates any notion of unitary meaning or centered subjectivity. At the same time, it inscribes and destabilizes both the subject and the narrative.[36]

This confusion about history, spectacle, illusion, and real life inflects the story, the storytelling, and the spectatorial activity: it produces a superimposition of belief and disbelief. Bill's problem with his identity is associated with his estrangement from his image, a bit like Alice thinking of sending her feet a pair of boots for Christmas. In his muddle, Bill obsessively questions Sitting Bull's image: it's not right, so Bull can't be real. He declares that Halsey doesn't mean a word he says—"that's why he sounds so real." In Bill's enterprise, fiction engenders truth; as Nate had declared earlier, they are in the "authenticity business."

The reverie evaporates (or does it?) as the sound of the final scene of the film overlaps a tight frontal close-up of Sitting Bull, a shot so emphatic that it seems to be an authorial assertion of his posthumous power: "Ladies and Gentlemen . . ." Buffalo Bill is once again in performance, "The Challenge of the Future," fighting the great Chief

Sitting Bull (in lowered tones: "played by William Halsey") "... staged with spectacular realism." Out rides Halsey dressed in battle regalia (bare chested, in war bonnet and war paint); the curtain parts again and out rides Buffalo Bill with smiling bravado to the tune of his by-now-familiar Wild West theme song. As the curtain parts, we see the purple mountains in the distance juxtaposed against the anemic mountains crudely painted on the backdrop in the foreground. The two warriors face off to a dramatic drum roll; they dismount, then struggle briefly, Halsey wielding a knife, Bill bare-handed. Bill easily wrestles Halsey to the ground and, with the enthusiastic approval of the crowd, triumphantly brandishes the knife and "The Chief's" ornate headdress in the air. With Halsey's performance of the act, the honorable, wise, proud, noble, moral "savages" have irretrievably disappeared.

The camera's authorial zoom in for an extreme close-up of Bill in the penultimate shot of the film seems to reveal both joy and terror in his eyes; the emotions attached to triumph, already soured, are charged with both longing and melancholy. The last western hero and the first western star seems to understand his part in the construction of a genre, as he finally gets to "scalp" the ersatz Sitting Bull, once again enacting the idealized moral violence that had become so marketable.

A cut to a long shot of the Wild West from behind the arena breaks the spell of the star's magical sway and the end credits begin to roll as the camera pulls back until the arena and encampment are very small, a lone outpost in a wilderness, and we see the beautiful mountains once again in the background.

How are we to understand this scene? What is its narrative and representational status? Is it to be taken as a depiction of Buffalo Bill's subjectivity, his obsession with Sitting Bull, a continuation of the previous sequence? Or does it escape the character's perspective and function on a different level?

To a certain degree, the scene can be taken as a representation of Buffalo Bill's interests and desires: Custer's Last Stand is performed in the Wild West as he had wished, with Bill standing in for Custer and Halsey replacing Sitting Bull, and, very important, with the outcome of the battle remedied. Buffalo Bill's identity with Custer is suggested early in the film by his makeup, costume, beard, and long blond wig ("Someday it will be as long as Custer's"). He had tried before to convince Sitting Bull to perform "his Custer act," demonstrating the scenario in a mocking travesty of Little Bighorn with the smallest actor in the Wild West playing Custer, his too-large coat, vest, and hat, his obviously fake wig and beard mocking the hero's image[37] and an African American playing "the heroic villain" ("Oh Chief, we got a colored to stand in place for you 'cause he's the closest thing on our staff to a real Indian."). Sitting Bull refuses to perform the act; Halsey, speaking for him, notes simply, "Sitting Bull says the battle did not happen that way."

Understood in these terms, this scene could be seen as a representation of Buffalo Bill's fantasy, his desire to "possess" Sitting Bull. However, unlike the dream sequence, there are no visual or aural cues to mark it as a product of Buffalo Bill's consciousness. Understanding it as merely a projection of Bill's personal desires is a limited reading.

It might be more fruitful to think of the final scene in metaphoric symbolic terms, as representing a highly significant and ironic statement on the nature of historical and racial representation in western mythology. Don Russell claims that the Battle of the Little Bighorn is the most frequently depicted event in American history.[38] Richard Slotkin argues that Custer's Last Stand is one of the central metaphors of the Frontier myth.[39] Its importance lies in the ways the legend encapsulates a conception of American history as a heroic-scale Indian battle with "progress achieved through regenerative wars of extermination against a primitive racial enemy."[40] Because Custer was killed in the battle and his cavalry company wiped out by the Sioux, the Last Stand myth has attained a special status from the threat that, as Slotkin puts it, "the race war might really end up in victory for savage darkness."[41] As Richard White points out, Buffalo Bill's spectacles (drawing on iconography stretching back to the Puritans) showed Indian aggression and white victimization, an odd inversion to the modern historian.[42] The Battle of the Little Bighorn has been a great military icon for white America precisely because it confirms this inversion: the Indians are to be feared after all. The final scene of the film inverts this inversion. Buffalo Bill as Custer nullifies the threat of Sitting Bull.

In addition, the myth gains special resonance from its two principal protagonists. Custer is a contradictory figure, admired as a tragic hero in conservative interpretations and as a blatant villain in others. Sitting Bull has been traditionally portrayed as a potent example of the "great antagonist," the Indian who sees clearly that "the advance of the whites means doom for Indians' power and even their existence."[43] It is his bridging of the two cultures, especially his learning political conspiracy and corruption from whites, that makes the "great antagonist" a danger.

Buffalo Bill's battle with "Sitting Bull" in the final scene of *Buffalo Bill and the Indians, or Sitting Bull's History Lesson* could, then, be understood as one more version of an event that has played an extensive and highly significant role in western symbolic conceptualization. It is one more representation of the Last Stand myth. What can we say about this particular version? Most obviously, it is ironic; it rewrites history from the white man's perspective, reversing what we know to have been the outcome of the battle.[44] As an example of catachresis (literally, "misuse") which Hayden White describes as a "manifestly absurd Metaphor designed to inspire Ironic second thoughts about the nature of the thing characterized," it affirms tacitly "the negative of what is on the literal level affirmed positively."[45] Sitting Bull is easily and ignominiously defeated and Custer/Buffalo Bill is heroically triumphant. Whereas the film's first "Custer act" had been a comic travesty, this one is a serious postmodern parody, a "repetition with critical distance that allows ironic signalling of difference at the very heart of similarity."[46]

The sequence's status as the film's closure is highly ambivalent; it is even more temporally unstable than the previous sequence. With no clues to place it clearly as the representation of a unique or specific action within a causal chain of narrative events, it seems more iterative in nature. It may be helpful to think of the scene as representing not only Buffalo Bill's fantasy of the Custer act, but also the continuing way that the Last Stand myth, and, on a more metaphoric level, the relations of white man and Native American, have been represented in the western over the course of most of the twentieth century. The representation of a collective national fantasy, a "social imaginary," it triumphs despite the fact that everything we have seen in the film up to this point denies its validity. As a synecdoche for the western as national myth, this "closure" points to the future, the future of a particularly American mode of entertainment.[47]

The film interrogates the logical system of narrative causality that permeates most Hollywood film in which closure is usually attained through the actions and effectiveness of the movie's star, the western hero. If the classic Hollywood western builds a coherent and authentic narrative world, Altman's film deploys ambiguity, contradiction, and interference to destabilize these conventions. It employs irony as a self-critical discursive strategy to debunk and demystify the central motifs and icons of the genre. The film's narrative structure both problematizes and exploits the convention of conclusive closure.[48] And, if the classical Hollywood western emphasized story so it could entertain, the episodic structure of *Buffalo Bill and the Indians, or Sitting Bull's History Lesson* draws our attention away from story toward plotting, in particular, to how a nation and a hero have been built by their histories, endowed with illusory coherence by the way their stories have been told.[49] Self-consciously calling attention to its historicity as well as fictionality, it compromises the assumed correspondence of history to experience and narration to event. Disrespect for the dead, as Sitting Bull had called history, has been transformed into a spectacle for the future, making ambiguous whether the "lesson" of the film's second title was taught by Sitting Bull or learned by him.

notes

Parts of this essay were presented at Florida State University's Conference on Literature and Film, Tallahassee, January 1993. We are indebted to Christopher Sharrett's response at FSU, to Jim Diverio for identifying the bird calls, and to Elena Pinto Simon's comments on an earlier, shorter version of this essay. Originally published in the *Journal of Film and Video* 47, nos. 1–3 (1995), this essay is reprinted here in expanded form courtesy of the journal editor.

1. Benedict Anderson points out that "members of even the smallest nation will never know most of their fellow-members. . . ., yet in the midst of each lives the image of their communion." It is "the style in which they are imagined" that distinguishes communities. Anderson, *Imagined Communities: Reflections on*

the Origin and Spread of Nationalism (London: Verso, 1983), 6. As an exploration of the relations between the entertainment industries' heroes and the social construct "America," *Buffalo Bill and the Indians* might be seen as an extention of the ideological project of Altman's 1975 film *Nashville*.

2. Richard Slotkin, *The Fatal Environment: The Myth of the Frontier in the Age of Industrialization, 1800–1890* (Middletown, Conn.: Wesleyan University Press, 1985), 20.

3. See Patricia Nelson Limerick, *The Legacy of Conquest: The Unbroken Past of the American West* (New York: W. W. Norton, 1987), 21. Revisionist historians have problematized the criteria, cultural themes, and periodization that have been employed in describing "the West." Limerick, for example, sees the "quaintness of the folk" and "the popularization of tourism" as an important indication of the "closing of the frontier" (25). William Cronon, George Miles, and Jay Gitlin suggest that one telltale sign of the transition between "frontier" and "region" was a feeling among the inhabitants that they were "no longer inventing a world but inheriting one." Cronon, Miles, and Gitlin, eds., *Under an Open Sky: Rethinking America's Western Past* (New York: W. W. Norton, 1992), 23.

4. Frederick Jackson Turner's address to a gathering of the American Historical Association during the World's Columbian Exposition would become the dominant model of western historiography for generations. Turner's explanation of American history was based on the idea of "free land," ignoring the legitimacy of Native American claims to the continent. See Turner, "The Significance of the Frontier in American History," in *The Frontier in American History* (Tucson: The University of Arizona Press, 1986) and Cronon, Miles, and Gitlin, *Under an Open Sky*, 14. Interestingly, at the same time that Turner was giving his address to scholars at the American Historical Association meeting, just outside the Chicago fairgrounds Cody was performing his own interpretation in Buffalo Bill's Wild West. Both Richard Slotkin, in *Gunfighter Nation: The Myth of the Frontier in Twentieth Century America* (New York: Atheneum, 1992, 63–69), and Richard White, in "Frederick Jackson Turner and Buffallo Bill" (in James R. Grossman, ed. *The Frontier in American Culture* [Berkeley and Los Angeles: University of California Press, 1994]) elaborate the significance of this coincidence.

5. Alan Trachtenberg, *The Incorporation of American Culture and Society in the Gilded Age* (New York: Hill and Wang, 1982), 12.

6. Lonn Taylor and Ingrid Marr, *The American Cowboy* (Washington, D.C.: Library of Congress, 1983), 67. Rhodes was speaking to a group of filmmakers. The *BFI Companion to the Western*, ed. Edward Buscombe (London: British Film Institute, 1988), 91, states that William F. Cody's experiences as an army scout were no different from dozens of others. Richard Slotkin, in an extensive discussion of Buffalo Bill in *Gunfighter Nation*, identifies Cody as "a minor actor on the stage of Western history until 1869," when he was "discovered" by Ned Buntline (69).

7. Richard White, "Frederick Jackson Turner and Buffalo Bill," 9.

8. Cited in Sarah J. Blackstone, *Buckskins, Bullets, and Business: A History of Buffalo Bill's Wild West* (Westport, Conn.: Greenwood Press, 1986).

9. Cited in Richard White, "Frederick Jackson Turner and Buffalo Bill," 7.

10. Ibid., 35.

11. Linda Hutcheon, *Poetics of Postmodernism: History, Theory, Fiction* (New York: Routledge, 1988), ix–x, 5–6, 119.

12. Ibid., 110.

13. There is a slight variation: Altman declares his enterprise "Unique," whereas Cody claimed his was "Original."

14. These are the central themes that scholars of western legend have long identified as its core thematic material. See Turner and, more recently, Henry

Nash Smith, *Virgin Land: The American West as Symbol and Myth* (Cambridge, Mass.: Harvard University Press, 1978), John G. Cawelti, *The Six-Gun Mystique* (Bowling Green, Ohio: Bowling Green Popular Press, 1975), and Richard Slotkin, *The Fatal Environment*.

15. While we do not wish to suggest a monolithic response to the film, we will argue that a simultaneous engagement with and reflection on the spectacle is suggested by the film's narrative methods and its publicity and exhibition strategies—the film's text and intertexts.

16. As reported by Joanna Mermey, *Soho Weekly News,* May 6, 1976, 11.

17. Interview with Bruce Williamson, *Playboy,* August 1976, 55.

18. Mermey, *Soho Weekly News,* 11.

19. As reported by *The Christian Science Monitor,* June 17, 1976, files of the Billy Rose Collection, New York Public Library.

20. As reported by Dan Rottenberg, *Chicago Magazine,* July 1976, 84.

21. Jean-Louis Comolli, "Historical Fiction: A Body Too Much," *Screen* 19, no. 2 (1978): 44.

22. Ibid., 47–48.

23. Including Douglas Fairbanks, Roy Rogers, Charlton Heston, Joel McCrea, and Michel Piccoli (*Monthly Film Bulletin* 43, no. 512 [1976], back cover).

24. More recently, spectators would know him as the king of salad dressings, salsa, and marinara sauce.

25. See Michael Henry's interview with coscreenwriter Alan Rudolph, "Entretien avec Alan Rudolph," *Positif* 192 (1977): 47–48.

26. Authur Kopit, *Indians* (New York: Hill and Wang, 1969), scene 7, 40–42. The play was first performed by the Royal Shakespeare Company in London on July 4, 1968.

27. See Walter Benjamin's comments in "Theses on the Philosophy of History" that "[h]istory is the subject of a structure whose site is not homogeneous, empty time, but time filled by the presence of the now." In his *Illuminations* (New York: Schocken Books, 1976), 261.

28. The film's representation of Ned Buntline as voice of historical veracity is highly idealized. Two decades before "discovering" Buffalo Bill, Buntline, a popular author and journalist known for his urban tales, had a somewhat sullied notoriety when he was convicted of being a key perpetrator of the Astor Place Riot of May 1849. Historian Peter G. Buckley suggests that Buntline's biography itself demonstrates the confusion of "life" and "art" that his creation Buffalo Bill experiences in the movie. See "The Case Against Ned Buntline: The 'Words, Signs, and Gestures' of Popular Authorship," *Prospects* 13 (1988): 249–72. The film's authors have transformed him into an insightful and relatively unambiguous demystifyer.

29. The film's title valorizes Buffalo Bill in a way that Kopit's title *Indians* avoided.

30. As an example of the pervasiveness of this association of heroic stature with size, see Andrew Sarris's complaint that Paul Newman is too short for the role of Buffalo Bill in "Bottom Line Buffalos Altman," *Village Voice,* July 5, 1976, 108.

31. See, for example, Cawelti, *The Six-Gun Mystique,* 40; and Slotkin, *The Fatal Environment,* 374–75.

32. Stephen Greenblatt, "Columbus Runs Aground: Christmas Eve, 1492," public lecture, New York University, October 29, 1992.

33. See Richard Slotkin, *Regeneration through Violence: The Mythology of the American Frontier, 1600–1869* (Middletown, Conn.: Wesleyan University Press, 1973), 94–115.

34. Slotkin, *Gunfighter Nation,* 15.

35. Sitting Bull was killed by Sioux police operating under the command of the reservation federal agent. See Edward Lazarus, *Black Hills/White Justice: The*

Sioux Nation versus the United States, 1775 to the Present (New York: Harper Collins, 1991), 114–15.

36. Hutcheon describes this dynamic as one of the main projects of the poetics of postmodernism.

37. In the play, Bill is less ambiguous about Custer, calling him in the first scene, "one 'o the great dumbass men in history." Kopit, *Indians*, 4.

38. Don Russell, *Custer's Last, or the Battle of Little Big Horn* (Fort Worth, Tex.: Anon Carter Museum, 1968), 3.

39. Slotkin, *The Fatal Environment*, 32.

40. Ibid., 477.

41. Ibid.

42. White, "Frederick Jackson Turner and Buffalo Bill," 27–29.

43. Slotkin, *The Fatal Environment*, 101.

44. As defeat reinterpreted as victory, it is interesting to compare this with the myth of the Alamo, its historical glorifications and recent contestations.

45. Hayden White, *Metahistory: The Historical Imagination in Nineteenth-Century Europe* (Baltimore: Johns Hopkins University Press, 1973), 37.

46. Hutcheon, *Poetics*, 26.

47. In the cynical art-house culture of 1976, the irony and moral tone of the scene certainly suggested that the end of that tradition might be warranted.

48. Dialogue in the film discusses the narrative structure of a Wild West act: "What's the plot? String the pearls together and devise us a nice little Buffalo Bill fable, uniquely original." Cody once described one of his five-act frontier melodramas as "without head or tail," making it possible to start the performance with any act. Quoted in Don Russell, *The Lives and Legends of Buffalo Bill* (Norman: University of Oklahoma Press, 1960), 253.

49. Hayden White, *The Content of the Form: Narrative Discourse and Historical Imagination* (Baltimore: John Hopkins University Press, 1989), ix.

life-like, vivid,

and thrilling

pictures

buffalo bill's wild west

and early cinema

j o y   s .   k a s s o n

The stagecoach, pulled by six mules, travels through a Western landscape. Suddenly, a band of Indians appears from behind a rocky outcrop, whooping and shooting arrows. The stagecoach speeds up as passengers and drivers fire rifles and guns at the attacking band. Indians fall from their horses; defenders are wounded. Just when all hope seems to be lost, a band of soldiers rides to the rescue with blazing guns and the Indians disperse. Grateful passengers thank their rescuers, and the stagecoach continues on its way.

Scenes like this were staples of western filmmaking from early cinema through 1950s television and beyond. But before Tom Mix or John Wayne or Roy Rogers rode the silver screen, millions of people around the world had already seen the attack on the stagecoach with their own eyes as dust flew and shots rang in their ears. The film western sprang to life with uncanny vividness because its most memorable scenes and incidents had been part of the popular imagination for a quarter-century, made familiar throughout the United States, Canada, and Europe by the colorful

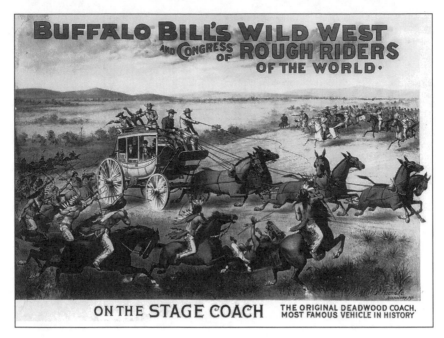

Fig. 5.1. On the Stage Coach, c. 1887, poster. Buffalo Bill Historical Center, Cody, Wyoming.

Fig. 5.2. *Stagecoach* (John Ford, 1939).

performance and vigorous ballyhoo of a show business sensation: Buffalo Bill's Wild West. From 1883 until its founder's death in 1917, Buffalo Bill's Wild West brought gripping enactments of western adventures to cheering audiences at thousands of performances. By transposing western melodrama from the already familiar venues of the dime novel and proscenium stage to an outdoor arena, and by bringing audiences face-to-face with real cowboys, Indians, horses, steer, buffalo, stagecoaches, and gunpowder, the Wild West blurred the lines between reality and entertainment, fact and fiction, history and invention. As enthusiastic viewers from Mark Twain to Susan B. Anthony attested, Buffalo Bill's Wild West persuaded viewers they had privileged access to a time and place both mythic and realistic. Its representation of American identity became a part of the national memory, creating a reservoir of images that filmmakers would tap from the flickering kinetoscope images through heroic mid-century westerns to the ironized anti-westerns of the late twentieth century.

How, exactly, did Buffalo Bill's Wild West assume this powerful position in American cultural memory? What legacy did it provide for the nascent film industry? How did it leave its stamp on everything from art to advertising to politics? The Marlboro Man rides in Buffalo Bill's shadow, and postmodern artist Richard Prince, who revisits commercial art in his own canvases, rides in the shadow of a shadow. Two presidents—Theodore Roosevelt and Ronald Reagan—have galloped to office in the guise of Buffalo Bill. Politics and advertising are useful points of reference, for Buffalo Bill's Wild West employed sophisticated selling techniques, clever promotional campaigns, as well as image creation, and product branding to make the show and its star instantly recognizable around the world.

This show-business spectacle drew its energy and credibility from the history and person of its star performer.[1] William F. Cody acquired the nickname "Buffalo Bill" when he worked as a hunter supplying meat for railroad crews on the Great Plains after the Civil War. He had grown up in Kansas and worked at a variety of transient occupations, including pony express rider, wagon train escort, Civil War soldier, and civilian scout for the U.S. Army during the Indian Wars. In 1869 he met dime novel writer Edward Zane Carroll Judson (Ned Buntline), who used him as a character in a story about another frontier hero, Wild Bill Hickok. When a stage play drawn from the novel made Buffalo Bill's name familiar, the scout moved from the world of plains showmanship (guide to wealthy tourists and participant in horse races and shooting contests) to that of the stage, starring from December 1872 onward in frontier melodramas based loosely on dime novels. In 1883 he organized an outdoor frontier exhibition that combined melodramatic narratives with demonstrations of shooting and riding skill, and featured a variety of cowboys and Plains Indian performers. The show floundered in its first season but became an international sensation when Cody joined forces

Fig. 5.3. Col. William F. Cody, c. 1887, cabinet photograph. Buffalo Bill Historical Center, Cody, Wyoming.

112

with Nate Salsbury, an experienced stage personality who supplied money and direction for the new entertainment.

Salsbury brought to the partnership imagination, energy, and considerable show-business savvy. As one admiring reporter described him, he was "a man who understands his business, attends to his business and minds his own business . . . shrewd, intelligent and practical off the stage as well as on it."[2] Salsbury had experience not only in theatrical performance but management as well, having toured his own company throughout the United States and abroad. His skills in planning and promotion complemented Cody's charming, but maddeningly improvident, affability. Early in their partnership, Salsbury addressed head-on the drinking problem that would hover on the edge of control throughout Cody's career. In response to an admonitory letter from Salsbury, berating him for a drinking binge, Cody responded with contrition and the hint of humor that must have made him a delightful companion and exasperating partner: "Your very sensable [*sic*] & truly rightful letter has just been read. And it has been the means of showing me just where I stand. And I solemnly promise you that after this you will never see me under the influence of liquor. I may have to take two or three drinks today to brace up on."[3] Although Cody continued to drink heavily (and sometimes baited Salsbury by promising to go on "a drunk that is a drunk. Just to change my luck,") his biographer claims that he never let his alcohol consumption interfere with his performances.[4]

Toward the end of his life, ill and feuding with Cody, Salsbury produced a bitter memoir he planned to entitle "Sixteen Years in Hell with Buffalo Bill," some of which was published in the 1950s. By no means should this angry reminiscence, which he never planned to make public, be taken as the only word on Salsbury's relationship with Cody. According to all accounts, including his own correspondence, the creative years were exciting, satisfying, and fun for Salsbury as well as Cody. But the very qualities that made Cody such an appealing performer could be hard to live with from day to day: he was openhanded and easily distracted, loved a good time, and could be self-indulgent. In his blackest mood, Salsbury put a harsh construction on his relationship with Cody, emphasizing his own role in shaping the frontiersman's worldwide celebrity:

> There were two of him to me. One the true Cody as he has always been from his birth, and the other was a commercial proposition that I discovered when I invented the Wild West, and picked him out for the Figure Head. Mind you, I am not trying to depreciate his physical courage at all. I have no doubt that he filled his position of Bull Whacker, and Express Rider, perfectly, and a man to do that must have physical hardihood, and courage of a certain kind. But there are others. And there were others, and there will be others, and if any of the three classes had had the good fortune to be good looking, tall, dashing, and the subject of romantic tale telling for a decade, there would have been some other commercial propositions that could have been developed.[5]

Filtering out the bitterness of an aging man who had been suffering from an injury received at the Wild West and who had recently beaten back Cody's effort to drop their partnership and wiggle out of paying his debts, we can still see the justice of Salsbury's claim. The celebrity Buffalo Bill was compounded of the natural man and the constructed hero. He was undoubtedly a "commercial proposition."

The Wild West became both popular and lucrative. With the aid of a brilliant publicity team of writers, advance men, and billposters, Cody and Salsbury made Buffalo Bill a familiar figure throughout the United States and Canada, then solidified this success with a series of European tours in the late 1880s and early 1890s. Photographs and drawings of Cody and his cast with Queen Victoria, Kaiser Wilhelm II, and Pope Leo XIII increased the hunger of audiences at home and abroad to see the show for themselves. Performing across the street from the World's Columbian Exposition in Chicago in 1893, the Wild West reportedly earned more than a million dollars and delighted several million spectators who had come to see the acclaimed World's Fair.

The Wild West mobilized all its resources of publicity and promotion to assure viewers that they were seeing both an entertaining performance

Fig. 5.4. Buffalo Bill's Wild West and Congress of Rough Riders of the World, 1893, program cover. Collection Joy and John Kasson.

and a truthful representation of western life. Advertisements never described Buffalo Bill's Wild West as a show but as an educational exhibition. The program booklet for the 1893 season, like those of seasons before and afterward, took pains to stress the Wild West's claims to authenticity. "The exhibitions given by 'Buffalo Bill's' Wild West have nothing in common with the usual professional exhibitions," wrote Salsbury. "Our aim is to make the public acquainted with the manners and customs of the daily life of the dwellers in the far West of the United States, through the means of actual and realistic scenes from life."[6]

Wild West performances, the publicity machine insisted, could be both pleasurable and accurate. A western writer whose glowing review was excerpted in the program booklet described the show as "a great living picture" of the frontier and recommended that it should be seen by "every person east of the Missouri River."[7] Furthermore, the program booklet reprinted a series of testimonials vouching for Buffalo Bill's status as an all-American hero. "His eyesight is better than a good field-glass," attested a former commander. "William F. Cody is one of the best scouts and guides that ever rode at the head of a column of cavalry on the prairies of the Far West," wrote a military historian. "Young, sturdy, a remarkable specimen of manly beauty, with the brain to conceive and the nerve to execute, Buffalo Bill *par excellence* is the exemplar of the strong and unique traits that characterize *a true American frontiersman*," gushed his publicist.[8]

Program notes also vouched for the authenticity of cast members, offering background information on cowboys, scouts, and Native American performers. Only three years after the Wounded Knee massacre, the Wild West's program included an article on Native American spirituality, providing an interpretation of the Ghost Dance as a religious expression and acknowledging the failure of the United States government to keep its promises in negotiations with the Sioux.[9] Yet at the same time that Cody and Salsbury insisted on the historical accuracy of their representations, they filled the show with melodramatic episodes drawn directly from the popular stage, including hand-to-hand combat and heroic rescue. The stagecoach raced away from its attackers in every show; Indians attacked a settler's cabin, only to be repelled by a band of soldiers led by Buffalo Bill. Famous incidents from the Indian Wars were reenacted, including Custer's Last Stand and Cody's subsequent battle with an Indian named Yellow Hand, whose death was celebrated as "the first scalp for Custer." Buffalo Bill's Wild West gloried in its ability to engage the viewer's emotions with vivid, dramatic vignettes and at the same time convince them that they were seeing a "realistic" representation.

The Wild West's producers bragged about the authenticity not only of the human performers but of the animals and props in the show as well. The program booklet contained pictures and articles designed to familiarize viewers with the bucking bronco and the bison, both guarantors of the show's "wildness." The special relationship between riders and their horses was also emphasized, both in what was sometimes called "The Race of Races," a horse race in which riders and mounts shared an exotic identity—an Arab on an Arabian horse, a Mexican on a Spanish-Mexican mount, an Indian on a western pony, for example—and in a reenactment of a Pony Express ride. Buffalo Bill's favorite horses were named and pictured, including "Old Charlie," who had died and was buried at sea, according to the caption on his portrait. A long essay in the program booklet attested to the authenticity of the stagecoach that appeared in the show. "A Historical Coach of the Deadwood Line," the vehicle was described as a "scarred and weather-beaten veteran of the original 'star route' line of stages, established at a time when it was worth a man's life to sit on its box and journey from one end of its destination to the other."[10] The program text heightened the sense of excitement that made the attack on the Deadwood Stage one of the showstopping acts that remained in the Wild West's repertory for more than three decades. (The Deadwood Stage is still a featured attraction at the Buffalo Bill Historical Center in Cody, Wyoming.)

As symbol, star, and impresario of the Wild West, Cody introduced and ended the show. Each performance began with the "Grand Review" of performers, the thundering horseback entrance of cowboys, Indians, Mexican vaqueros, Russian Cossacks, Arabian horsemen, and whatever other colorful participants Salsbury had recruited for that particular season. When all had circled the ring and lined up in formation, Buffalo Bill rode up on his big gray horse, swept off his famous Stetson hat, and addressed the crowd: "Ladies and Gentlemen, Allow Me to Present the Congress of Rough Riders of the World!" Cody's presentation of his cast was both an endorsement of their authenticity and a consummate act of showmanship. After a varied menu of acts, including races, roping contests, sharpshooting exhibitions, and dramatic vignettes, the show ended with a "salute," reassembling the cast under Buffalo Bill's leadership, dissolving the fictive premises of acts like "Attack on a Settler's Cabin" and presenting the show's performers once more to the public.

By the last decade of the nineteenth century, as the Indian Wars faded into the past and the Great Plains began to open for settlement and tourism, the Wild West represented by Cody's show came to be understood by its audience as a nostalgic re-creation rather than a representation of the world of the present. The scholars who heard Frederick Jackson Turner proclaim the closure of the American frontier in his famous address of July, 1893, may have arrived with shouts and gunfire ringing in their ears after visiting Buffalo Bill's Wild West earlier in the afternoon. Performing just outside the gates of the World's Columbian Exposition, Cody had extended a special invitation that very day to participants in the American Historical Association conference. Yet the Wild West created a special kind of memory landscape. It had the ability to persuade its viewers that the past it depicted was *their* past, something they had viewed with their own eyes. According to French historian Pierre Nora, memory has taken on a new significance in the modern era, with its alienation from traditional sources of communal identity. What Nora calls *lieux de mémoire*—sites of memory or memory places—are repositories for shared meaning in a modern world. "*Lieux de mémoire*," writes Nora, "are fundamentally vestiges, the ultimate embodiments of a commemorative consciousness that survives in a history which, having renounced memory, cries out for it." Buffalo Bill's Wild West appeared in just such a cultural moment, in a society emerging into modernism, urbanization, and participation in world politics and military operations, in the midst of a culture, as Nora described the modern world, "fundamentally absorbed by its own transformation and renewal."[11] The Wild West's legacy to the western film would include this remarkable ability to embody a shared memory.

In the 1890s, then, at the very moment that film technology was just beginning to open the possibility of a different form of mass entertainment, the Wild West had already created a popular spectacle that combined the excitement of stage melodrama and dime novel with an illusion of authenticity, infusing the show with a hyperreality that stemmed from the spectators' sense that they had actually witnessed the events represented before them. Salsbury and his team promoted the Wild West in language that eerily anticipated motion picture rhetoric, inviting spectators to imagine they were seeing pictures miraculously springing to life. The 1884 program for the Wild West had announced that it offered "life-like, vivid, and thrilling pictures of western life."[12] In a torrent of inspired rhetoric, Salsbury's advertisement for the 1893 engagement in Chicago promised "life, action, skill, daring, danger defied; one thousand animated pictures in two hours given by flesh and blood; . . . an affair of magnitude second to none in novel enjoyment, instruction, interest and educative merit."[13] No wonder the creators and distributors of early motion pictures turned in overwhelming numbers to western subjects. Buffalo Bill's Wild West had already assembled the tropes and images of the American West into a convincing and popular entertainment form. Cody and Salsbury created the template early filmmakers could adapt and embellish.

In 1894, Cody and Salsbury reached out directly to the emerging world of film entertainment. They had met Thomas Alva Edison in Paris in 1889, when the Wild West was performing at the Exposition Universelle. According to press accounts, the Wizard of Menlo Park had encountered a group of the Wild West's Indian performers on the summit of the Eiffel Tower, and Cody entertained the inventor and his wife at an elegant luncheon that ended with shouts of "Vive Edison."[14] For their 1894 season in Brooklyn, Cody and Salsbury had contracted with the Edison Illuminating Company to install a powerhouse for the showgrounds.[15] Perhaps on the strength of these connections, groups of performers from the Wild West visited Edison's laboratory that summer and fall to be filmed in his new kinetoscope technology. Edison's Wild West films featured individual performers, such as Buffalo Bill firing a rifle, Mexicans throwing a lasso or fighting with knives, horsemen on bucking broncos, and Annie Oakley shooting at targets; but they also included several short pieces focusing on the Indian war narratives that were so important to the Wild West. *Buffalo Bill, Sioux Ghost Dance, Buffalo Dance*, and *Indian War Council* were among the kinetoscope productions Edison advertised.[16]

During the next few years, the Wild West's show-business spectacle was recorded on film several times. Edison's cameramen photographed the Wild West's parade through the streets of New York and in a smaller city, and the American Mutascope and Biograph Company shot footage of the Wild West's arena performance, including Buffalo Bill's trademark sweep of his hat and announcement of the Rough Riders of the World. Biograph filmed one of the Wild West's signature vignettes, *Attack on an Emigrant Train*, in 1907. In 1910, the Buffalo Bill and Pawnee Bill Film Company produced three reels of film showing acts from the Wild West.[17]

Although these early filmmaking efforts focused on documenting the show itself, recording with the camera's eye what a spectator might see in the Wild West arena, it was soon apparent to Cody and others that cinema could also attempt to tell the story of the Wild West directly, replicating in a new medium the powerful blend of documentation and fictionality the arena show deployed so successfully. In 1912, the Buffalo Bill and Pawnee Bill Film Company produced a three-reel film, *The Life of Buffalo Bill*, that juxtaposed an appearance by Cody with an actor's representation of adventures from his earlier career. The film begins as the "real" Buffalo Bill, Cody himself, rides along a trail. He demonstrates his tracking skills, dismounts, unsaddles his horse, and lies down to sleep. Intertitles announce "A dream of the days of his youth," and an actor playing his younger self stars in a series of vignettes drawn directly from the arena show. Indians attack a wagon train, Buffalo Bill saves a stagecoach and captures a notorious gang of bandits, and the "Famous Duel Between Chief Yellow Hand and Buffalo Bill" produces "The First Scalp for Custer." As in the Wild West show, other scenes demonstrate the everyday life of the Indian camp and the wagon train, and soldiers and Indians ride furiously across the landscape. The film ends when the present-day Buffalo Bill awakes from his dream, saddles his horse, and rides off.[18]

The Life of Buffalo Bill was Cody's first attempt to transfer the Wild West's themes and images to the medium of film, and it drew on the two most powerful techniques he had developed as a showman: the evocation of western events and landscapes as memory and the claim to authenticity derived from the participation of "actual" western figures, in this case himself and the Indians from his company. As in the Wild West performances, the "historic" Buffalo Bill opened and closed the show, giving a stamp of historicity to the fictional scenes. The new medium of film gave the impression of "real life" to scenes that were also highly dramatic; in holding these claims in balance and creating a convincing impression of shared memory, this early film sketched the contours that would define the film western for a half-century.

By the time Cody appeared in *The Life of Buffalo Bill*, western themes had already become a staple of early cinema. Edwin S. Porter's landmark 1903 film *The Great Train Robbery* could be seen as a variant on the stagecoach drama Buffalo Bill had made so famous. Porter's most startling image, that of a gunman firing point-blank at the audience, used the resources of the cinematic close-up to mimic and intensify the face-to-face encounter with performers that had always thrilled Wild West audiences. The year after the American Mutascope and Biograph Company filmed Buffalo Bill's Wild West parade, cameramen for that company began to shoot a film released in 1904 as *The Pioneers*, which contained a series of episodes closely related to the Wild West's famous "Attack on a Settler's Cabin." Although archivists are not entirely sure how the film was assembled when it was distributed, the individual parts seem clearly to reflect the melodramatic structure of one of the Wild West's featured episodes: its reels are entitled "Settler's Home Life," "Firing the Cabin," "Discovery of Bodies," and "Rescue of Child from Indians."[19] In 1910, more than twenty percent of the films made in America were westerns.[20] By 1912, Biograph had already produced more than seventy film westerns,

Fig. 5.5. *The Great Train Robbery* (Edwin S. Porter, 1903).

119

and D. W. Griffith had directed at least fifteen of them, including a version of Helen Hunt Jackson's *Ramona* starring Mary Pickford in 1910.[21] From its very birth, the film western drew on a set of audience expectations formed partly by the popular dime novels and story magazines, but especially, these examples make clear, the Wild West performances so many millions had seen and were still seeing.

In 1913, Cody tried another approach to translating the Wild West to the new medium of film: he diminished the element of fictionality and heightened the claims to authenticity in an ambitious film, *Indian War Pictures*, that reenacted battles from three campaigns of the Indian Wars on the original sites and with the participation of many of the survivors.[22] Eliciting the cooperation of several of his old army friends, including Lieutenant General Nelson Miles, Major General Jesse M. Lee, Major General Charles King, Brigadier General Marion Maus, and Brigadier General Frank Baldwin, Cody attempted to create a "historically correct" motion picture. Unlike *The Life of Buffalo Bill*, the film would feature no performances by actors, but all scenes would involve actual participants.

The task of recreating the Indian Wars for film was daunting, but its components were very similar to the problems Cody had handled for years in arranging for his traveling companies. He had to seek permission from the Secretary of the Interior, the Commissioner of Indian Affairs, the secretaries of the War Department and the Army Board; he had to arrange for horses, equipment, and support staff, enlist participants, and publicize his operations. He also had to find the money to fund his operations, and it is important to realize that the film project came into being at a time when his own financial situation was distressingly precarious. Despite the enormous success of Buffalo Bill's Wild West for three decades, Cody had never managed to save his money, and had sunk ruinous amounts into a failed mining scheme. After the death of Nate Salsbury in 1902, Cody had allied himself with partners who did little to arrest his financial slide, and by 1913 his show had been forced into bankruptcy, his property was mortgaged, and he was about to begin touring with a three-ring circus. Cody was desperate for a plan to recoup his finances as well as his self-respect. The film project incorporated all the aspects of the Wild West he would have to leave behind when he performed in the circus ring: the enactment of battle scenes, the claim to authenticity, the association with army generals and Indian chiefs. It would also allow him to provide salaries to American Indian performers who had been dismissed without pay when his show was closed down. Cody turned for financial support to Denver publisher Harry Tammen, although the latter had been responsible for forcing him into bankruptcy. Tammen, eager for more profit, helped to underwrite the production, sent a reporter from the *Denver Post* to cover the filming, and secured the filmmaking expertise of the Essanay Film Company of Chicago, in which he had an interest.

Fig. 5.6. Filming *Indian War Pictures*. Buffalo Bill Museum and Grave, Lookout Mountain, Golden, Colorado.

Essanay was a partnership between two movie producers, with *S* (ess) standing for George K. Spoor, a long-time associate of Tammen's, and *A* (ay) for Gilbert M. Anderson, who had played the role of a passenger in *The Great Train Robbery* in 1903, and had already starred in more than 150 films as the movie cowboy Bronco Billy. Of course, the Wild West had helped to create and popularize the cowboy mystique so effectively evoked in these early films, and even Anderson's assumed name suggested the bronco-busting displays of Buffalo Bill's show. Essanay's participation in the Indian War film completed a circle: the Wild West established a popular understanding of and hunger for dramatic representations of the frontier, which the emerging film industry could tap; now a film company gave a new look to the putatively historical features of the Wild West.

Indian War Pictures was a breathtaking enterprise. Enactments of the battles of Summit Springs (1869) and War Bonnet Creek (1876) had been staples of the Wild West program for years, so the contours of their presentation were already familiar to Cody and his audiences. Transferring them to the film medium added little thematically, bringing mainly technical challenges, choreographing movements through the landscape and adding scenes to take advantage of the outdoor location. But the Battle of Wounded Knee (1890) was a different matter. Although the printed program had referred to this event for years, Cody had never staged it in the arena.[23] And because the episode was far more recent and involved not merely a battlefield encounter between warriors but religious ceremonies and the slaughter of Sioux women and children by the United

121

States army, memories of the event were still poignant and contested for many participants, and would prove to be disturbing to audiences as well. Bringing Indian survivors to the scene of the massacre, representing Ghost Dance ceremonies, reenacting their terror-stricken flight into a ravine, simulating the firing of the deadly Hotchkiss gun that killed so many— Cody found all this unleashed more passion than he had anticipated. According to one account, Indian women chanted death songs and wept when they returned to the scene of the slaughter, and it was reported that some of the young men vowed to use live ammunition in the battle scene to avenge their fathers.[24] Opting for the greater realism made possible by the film medium, Cody had disrupted the delicate balance between role-playing and memory that his show had managed to maintain for thirty years. Although he avoided a disaster at the time of the filming, the powerful emotions these scenes engendered would come back to haunt him at the box office.

Oddly enough, this confrontation with the past also produced a schism between Cody and his old military friends. General Miles insisted that the film should show all eleven thousand troops that had come to Pine Ridge for the surrender of the Sioux, and spent several hours marching his much smaller contingent of troops in circles around the camera so there would appear to be more of them. He quarreled with Cody over his insistence that the company had to be transported to the Badlands for authenticity in shooting the scenes that occurred there. Although this was finally done, the friendship between the two men suffered.[25]

Finally, *Indian War Pictures* enacted what must have been one of the most painful episodes in Cody's own career, his inability to prevent the murder of Sitting Bull, the Sioux chief who had toured with the Wild West in 1885, and whose goodwill Cody retained when they parted. As the Ghost Dance religion gained strength among the Sioux in 1890, Indian agents had grown increasingly nervous about Sitting Bull's interest in the movement. Two weeks before the massacre at Wounded Knee, Cody had persuaded General Miles to let him act as an emissary to negotiate with Sitting Bull; but his orders were rescinded and he was prevented from reaching Standing Rock Reservation. Meanwhile, trigger-happy Indian police rushed to arrest the Sioux chief. Pushing and shoving led to gunfire, and Sitting Bull was killed together with his son and five of his followers as well as six Indian policemen. The printed program for *Indian War Pictures* places this event in the first reel of the second section of the film; it appears to be Cody's only appearance in this section.[26] Playwright Arthur Kopit imagined that Cody was haunted by remorse over his inability to save Sitting Bull, making their relationship the crux of his play *Indians* (1969), and of the script for Robert Altman's *Buffalo Bill and the Indians, or Sitting Bull's History Lesson* (1976). Unlike the killing of Yellow Hand, which the Wild West had always presented as heroic, and the death of Custer, which it portrayed as tragic, the murder of Sitting Bull and the slaughter of the Ghost Dance adherents were difficult to depict with the note of triumph that marked both Wild West performances and early film westerns.

The filming of *Indian War Pictures*—between September 26 and November 1, 1913, under the direction of Theodore Wharton—produced over thirty thousand feet of negatives. After a screening for the Secretary of the Interior and other government officials, an edited version of the film was released to the public. Judging from surviving advertisements and promotional materials, there were at least three versions, one of eight reels, one of six, and another of five. The eight-reel version, like a Wild West performance, started and ended with references to present time: introductory glimpses of Buffalo Bill and his advisors, and concluding vignettes of contemporary reservation life including a ceremony of reconciliation that featured a tree planting by Buffalo Bill. This framing structure was like the opening and closing processionals of the Wild West performance, and also recalled the visit to the Indian encampment on the showgrounds that was always part of the audience experience of the Wild West. The film then devoted one reel each to the battles of Summit Springs and War Bonnet Creek, but Wounded Knee (described as the Rebellion of 1890–91) was treated in much more detail, spanning five reels. As if to acknowledge the complexity of this event, the film proceeded from one vignette to another, including the rise of the Ghost Dance religion, the escalation of tensions, Buffalo Bill's failed mission to Sitting Bull, the death of Sitting Bull, the flight and capture of Big Foot's band, the outbreak of violence at Wounded Knee Creek, and the surrender at Pine Ridge. The final reel depicted life at Pine Ridge, scenes from an Indian school, and "the TRANSITION OF THE RED MAN, from the WARPATH TO PEACE PURSUITS, under the American Flag—'The Star Spangled Banner.'"[27]

Many indications suggest that, unlike Buffalo Bill's Wild West, *Indian War Pictures* never found its ruling principles of coherence. It was apparently edited and reedited, released in different versions at different lengths. It never seemed to acquire a single, defining title. Announcements of screenings called it, variously, *Last Indian Battles*, *Indian Wars*, *Buffalo Bill's War Pictures*, *Indian War Pictures*, and *Indian Wars Refought by United States Army*. It was shown under varying conditions, from theaters to clubs, in Washington, New York, and Denver.[28] By November 1914 advertisements in *The Moving Picture World* were cajoling exhibitors to show it, promising "Fifteen Different Styles of Posters, Heralds, Slides, and Lobby Displays," praising its "beautiful Photography and Realistic Scenes," and asserting that "Nothing more picturesque, more thrillingly entertaining was ever staged. Nothing to equal it will, perhaps, ever be done again. No boy, girl or grown-up should be allowed to miss this picture."[29] Perhaps the promoters' overeager rhetoric tips their hand: although the film was widely publicized, few theaters were booking it for exhibition.

Fig. 5.7. Scene from *Indian War Pictures*, "First Scalp for Custer." Buffalo Bill Museum and Grave, Lookout Mountain, Golden, Colorado.

Even more completely than *The Life of Buffalo Bill*, *Indian War Pictures* tried to embody the essence of Buffalo Bill's Wild West in the medium of cinema. But the format that Cody chose for his film failed to produce that magical blend of authenticity and melodrama that his show so vividly delivered. When audiences watched a sixty-seven-year-old Cody reenacting deeds he had done at the age of thirty, they would always be aware that they were bearing witness after the fact, substituting the pleasure of thinking "that is the real man" for the satisfaction of imagining "that is what it must have looked like." The film emphasized the passage of time rather than its erasure, and so crossed a crucial line, choosing the claims of historical accuracy over dramatic believability. While the makers of western fiction films were reaping box office success by expanding the Wild West's aura of glamour and melodrama, *Indian War Pictures* insisted on its stature as documentary, and so fizzled with audiences.

Cody's supporters did their best to promote the film. Tammen's *Denver Post* ran special reports from the filming site in 1913, and anticipated the Denver screenings by publishing an article "from the facile and brilliant pen of Lieutentant General Nelson A. Miles" in March,

1914. Reviews stressed the film's "terrible realism," and reported that viewers were "spell-bound." "Bill, I didn't think it could be done," a veteran of the Custer campaign was said to have remarked after the Washington performance. "I didn't think until I saw these pictures that it would be possible to reproduce what we went through out there." "Nothing like this has ever been done before," a Denver review read. "Nothing to equal it will perhaps ever be done again. It is not a 'photo play.' It is not a series of 'staged spectacles.' It is War itself; grim, unpitying and terrible." In Denver, a surprise appearance at the movie theater by Cody himself enhanced the film's claims to realism. After the segments that featured his exploits, Buffalo Bill appeared live on stage, riding his horse Isham. Sweeping off his hat as if he were introducing the Wild West, he patted his horse and delivered his lines: "Gee, old pard, that was a hot one; we are going swift; two victories of forty-five and thirty-eight years ago in forty minutes, and another campaign to move on for." Cody's publicist gave press interviews touting "the sudden rise in [Cody's] fortune by the Historic Picture company's sensation in the moving film world."[30] But despite the ballyhoo, the film failed. Tammen tried to revive it in the surge of nostalgia after Buffalo Bill's death in 1917, and Essanay reedited some of the scenes for a film released that same year, *The Adventures of Buffalo Bill.* Neither effort gained national attention. Although Cody had announced that he was depositing the original footage with the United States government, it is now lost.[31] A copy of *Indian War Pictures* owned by the Buffalo Bill Museum in Cody, Wyoming, deteriorated long ago due to exposure to heat and cold. [32] Some fragments have been found, and the film is also known from a remarkable series of stills, but there is little left of the enterprise on which Cody staked the recovery of his fortunes and the translation of his historical claims into the new medium of film.

Nonetheless, Buffalo Bill's Wild West left an indelible mark on the history of cinema. Although this live outdoor entertainment was not the only source for the western theme that so dominated film and later television programming, it established a vocabulary of incident and image that would become standard—even clichéd—to filmgoers around the world. Like Buffalo Bill, cowboy heroes were devoted to their horses, from William S. Hart and Tom Mix to Roy Rogers and Gene Autry. The cavalry rode in, bugles blaring, to save settlers threatened by Indians in countless western movies, and the suspenseful chase and desperate gunfight are recognizable as western motifs whether they occur in *The Birth of a Nation* or *Star Wars.* Similarly, old-fashioned stagecoaches raced away from pursuing desperados, whether Indians or bandits, in film after film. It is not too much of a stretch to see John Ford's 1939 classic *Stagecoach* as another in the long line of film tributes to the Wild West's frantic Deadwood Stage chases.

And the look of the film western was familiar to a generation schooled by Buffalo Bill. The generalized "Indian" dressed in feather headdress, war paint, and mounted on a racing pony moved directly into film from the Wild West, where differences between tribes were minimized and all Indians took on a generalized Plains Indian identity. The Stetson hat, which Buffalo Bill popularized (and advertised), became the standard costume for the western film star. As western films took on a life of their own in the 1920s, '30s, and into the middle of the century, they did begin to depart from the Wild West's cast of characters. The figure of the cowboy, the focus for western films and novels, had occupied a relatively small place in Buffalo Bill's Wild West, and the gunfighter, a western film and television staple, never appeared. But to the extent that he was heroic, the western film protagonist drew on the vocabulary of frontier virtues so successfully embodied by Buffalo Bill's performances: masculinity, courage, self-possession. As critic Lee Clark Mitchell has written, the western film is defined by "a set of problems recurring in endless combination: the problem of progress, . . . the problem of honor, . . . the problem of law or justice, . . . the problem of violence, . . . and subsuming all, the problem of what it means to be a man."[33] Thematically, Buffalo Bill's Wild West had set the stage for all of these preoccupations.

The Wild West anticipated the film western's extraordinary emphasis on the male body. Cody's celebrity was always based on the palpable fact of his own dynamic presence, a living individual in whom all the western virtues appeared to be collected. The crowds flocked to see "Buffalo Bill Himself," the actual man. As Cody's partners from Salsbury to Tammen had always understood, the Wild West's most valuable asset was the person of its star. This was true even in death: Tammen convinced Cody's widow to bury the Wild West star in Denver instead of in the town he had founded in Wyoming, so that even his mortal remains would continue to be a profitable tourist attraction. The adulation of Cody's fans prompted them to overlook troubling indications of personal excess and weakness during his lifetime, from the scandal of his 1905 divorce trial to the evidence of intemperance and infirmity. When an aging Buffalo Bill took to wearing a wig to maintain his famous long hair, fans and the press pretended not to notice, even when a sweep of the famous Stetson dislodged the hairpiece during a performance.[34] The body of the performer, complete with costume and props, attracted a sort of reverence and gave audiences a feeling of familiarity that was an essential part of their hero worship.

In the age of cinema, the body of the western hero became even more intimately available for the audience's gaze. Lee Clark Mitchell points out the importance of the western hero's physicality: "Not only is the Western a genre that allows us to gaze at men, this gaze forms such an essential aspect of the genre that it seems covertly about just that: looking at men."[35] Whether the intense engagement of the camera with its subject evokes erotic responses to the male hero, or asserts his power and charisma, many critics agree that the western film constitutes an important arena for the contemplation of the male body. The twentieth-century western actor whose personal appeal most nearly approached that of Buffalo Bill, John Wayne, has attracted critical attention for his powerful physicality. Critic Garry Wills has analyzed Wayne's importance as a physical embodiment of cultural values, giving him an authority that transcends the particular roles he plays: "Wayne is among the most expressive of those who move about in the moving pictures. . . . His body spoke a highly specific language of 'manliness,' of self-reliant authority. It was a body impervious to outside force, expressing a mind narrow but focused, fixed on the task, impatient with complexity."[36] Like Buffalo Bill, John Wayne convinced audiences that, whatever narrative he engaged in, he himself was the spectacle they had come to see. And like Buffalo Bill, Wayne represented himself as the embodiment of a set of values that spoke to issues of national importance: patriotism, toughness, masculinity.

Fig. 5.8. Production still of John Wayne in *The Big Trail* (Raoul Walsh, 1930). Bettmann Archive.

The substance of Buffalo Bill's legacy, then, lies in the dramatization of cultural issues that are basic to American national identity: the use of violence and conquest in the formation of the American nation, Americans' love-hate relationship with unspoiled nature and native peoples, gender and the meaning of heroism, and the role of the individual in an increasingly urban, industrial, and corporate society. But the Wild West's importance also lies in its very form: a mass medium that blurs the lines between fact and fiction, history and melodrama, truth and entertainment. And this form provided the framework on which the film western could build.

Buffalo Bill died in 1917, although his show had lost its independence four years earlier. Wild West shows continued for decades to come, but the film industry inherited its cultural legacy after the smash of Cody's fortunes. Filmmakers assumed Cody's practical legacy as well. At his bankruptcy sale in 1913, livestock, wagons, saddles, and bridles from Buffalo Bill's Wild West were bought by purchasers including the Bison Motion Picture Company (whose very name allied them with Cody) and the Miller Brothers 101 Ranch, a rival Wild West show that furnished personnel and equipment to the burgeoning film industry. The Sioux who worked for Thomas Ince and 101 Bison Films were recruited from the same group of show Indians who had traveled with Buffalo Bill and other Wild West entrepreneurs.[37]

The Wild West show declined, not only because Cody himself lost control of his medium, but also because film replaced it. By the 1910s it was the western film that carried out the mission the Wild West had set for itself: to provide living pictures of a time and place increasingly remote and romantic, increasingly imagined as the crucible of American virtues. Cinema drew upon the plots, characters, and settings of the West to create an entertainment that was, like the Wild West, both realistic and fictional, historic and heroic. But, unlike the Wild West, cinema was infinitely repeatable, and could play to audiences in Chicago, Brooklyn, and Omaha simultaneously. Cody's instinct had been correct: film was the inevitable successor to the Wild West and the medium that transmitted its message to succeeding generations.

notes

Material in this chapter is drawn from my book, *Buffalo Bill's Wild West: Celebrity, Memory, and Popular History* (New York: Hill and Wang, 2000), and is reprinted courtesy of the publisher. This essay expands and focuses the discussion of the western film and its relationship to the historical claims of Buffalo Bill's Wild West. Thanks to the University Research Council, University of North Carolina at Chapel Hill, for support for the purchase of photographs and permissions.

1. A solid starting point for Cody research is Don Russell, *The Lives and Legends of Buffalo Bill* (Norman: University of Oklahoma Press, 1960). Nuanced and revealing discussions of Cody's significance can be found in Richard Slotkin, *Gunfighter Nation: The Myth of the Frontier in Twentieth-Century America* (New York: Atheneum, 1992); Richard White, "Frederick Jackson Turner and

Buffalo Bill," in *The Frontier in American Culture, An Exhibition at the Newberry Library, August 26, 1994–January 7, 1995*, ed. James R. Grossman (Berkeley and Los Angeles: University of California Press, 1994), 7–66, and all of the essays in the Brooklyn Museum catalog *Buffalo Bill and the Wild West* (Brooklyn, N.Y.: Brooklyn Museum, 1981).

2. Unidentified clipping, Nathan Salsbury Papers, Yale Collection of American Literature, Beinecke Rare Book Library, YCAL MSS 17, Box 1, Folder 26.

3. William F. Cody to Nate Salsbury, 1884. Nathan Salsbury Papers, Yale Collection of American Literature, Beinecke Rare Book Library, YCAL MSS 17, Box 1, Folder 4.

4. William F. Cody to Nate Salsbury, March 9, 1885. Nathan Salsbury Papers, Yale Collection of American Literature, Beinecke Rare Book Library, YCAL MSS 17, Box 1, Folder 4. See Russell, *Lives and Legends*, 303.

5. Nate Salsbury, "Cody's Personal Representatives," Typescript of Reminiscences, c. 1901, Nathan Salsbury Papers, Yale Collection of American Literature, Beinecke Rare Book Library, YCAL MSS 17, Box 2, Folder 63.

6. *Buffalo Bill's Wild West and Congress of Rough Riders of the World, Historical Sketches and Programme* (Chicago: Blakely Printing Company, 1893), 4.

7. Brick Pomeroy, quoted in *Buffalo Bill's Wild West*, 10.

8. Ibid., 6, 8, 7.

9. "Ghost-Dances in the West," *Buffalo Bill's Wild West*, 38–45.

10. Ibid., 23.

11. Pierre Nora, ed. *Realms of Memory: Rethinking the French Past.* Vol. 1, *Conflicts and Divisions*, trans. Arthur Goldhammer (New York: Columbia University Press, 1996), 6. Originally published as *Les Lieux de Mémoire*, 1992.

12. *Buffalo Bill's Wild West, America's National Entertainment*, 1884 program, Harvard Theatre Collection.

13. Advertisement, n.d., n.p. Harold McCracken Research Library, Buffalo Bill Historical Center, Cody, Wyoming. MS 6—William F. Cody Collection, Series IX: Scrapbooks, etc. Box 8, Scrapbook 1893, Chicago Season.

14. *The Illustrated London News*, Sept. 1, 1889, and *New-York Herald*, Aug. 28, 1889. Wm. Cody France 1889, Red Book, Microfilm Roll #2, Harold McCracken Research Library, Buffalo Bill Historical Center, Cody, Wyoming.

15. "Electricity at the Wild West Show," *The Electrical World*, September 15, 1894. Col. Cody Brooklyn Season 1894, Tan Book, Microfilm Roll #2, Harold McCracken Research Library, Buffalo Bill Historical Center, Cody, Wyoming.

16. Charles Musser, *Edison Motion Pictures, 1890–1900* (Washington, D.C.: Smithsonian Institution Press, 1997), 125–45.

17. Karen C. Lund, "American Indians in Silent Film, Motion Pictures in the Library of Congress," pamphlet for Motion Picture, Broadcasting and Recorded Sound Division, Library of Congress, April 1995. Also John L. Fell, "Motive, Mischief, and Melodrama: The State of Film Narrative in 1907," in John L. Fell, ed., *Film Before Griffith* (Berkeley and Los Angeles: University of California Press, 1983), 274.

18. "The Life of Buffalo Bill," Ernst Collection, Motion Picture, Broadcasting and Recorded Sound Division, Library of Congress, FLA 1982. Corey Creekmur's discussion of this film, "Buffalo Bill (Himself): History and Memory in the Western Biopic" (in this volume), emphasizes the device of the dream and its significance for the claims of memory; in a complementary reading, I point out that the film recapitulates the structure of the Wild West performance: introduction and conclusion presented by Buffalo Bill, then well-established vignettes that blur the lines between documentary and fiction.

19. "Settler's Home Life," FLA 5202; "Firing the Cabin," FLA 4624; "Discovery of Bodies," FLA 4580; "Rescue of Child From Indians," FLA 5185. Paper

Print Collection, Motion Picture, Broadcasting and Recorded Sound Division, Library of Congress.

20. Edward Buscombe, ed., *The BFI Companion to the Western* (London: British Film Institute/ New York: Da Capo Paperback edition, 1988), 24.

21. See Lund, "American Indians," and Buscombe, *BFI Companion*, 28.

22. See the pathbreaking discussion of this film in Kevin Brownlow, *The War the West and the Wilderness* (New York: Alfred A. Knopf, 1979), 224–35.

23. My review of the extensive collections of printed programs in libraries including the Harold McCracken Research Library; the Buffalo Bill Historical Center, Cody, Wyoming; and the Western History Collection of the Denver Public Library, has yielded no examples of the enactment of the Battle of Wounded Knee.

24. Brownlow, *The War*, 230–32.

25. Ibid., 323–33.

26. "Indian War Pictures," program for the Tabor Grand Opera House, Denver, Harold McCracken Research Library, Buffalo Bill Historical Center, Cody, Wyoming, MS 6, Series ID, Box 3, Folder 1.

27. Ibid.

28. "First Public Presentation at the Columbia Theatre, Washington, D.C.," MS 6, Series ID, Box 3, Folder 1.

29. *The Moving Picture World*, November 21, 1914, 615; files of Motion Picture, Broadcasting and Recorded Sound Division, Library of Congress.

30. *Washington Herald*, February 28, 1914; two unidentified clippings from Denver, *Albuquerque Morning Journal*, March 19, 1914; Col. Cody Motion Picture Venture, Historic films, 1914, Black Scrap Book, Microfilm Reel no. 1, Harold McCracken Research Library, Buffalo Bill Historical Center, Cody, Wyoming.

31. Kevin Brownlow suggests that the U.S. government may have tried to suppress the film because of its stark content. Brownlow, *The War*, 233.

32. Don Russell, "Buffalo Bill—In Action," *Westerners Brand Book* 19 (1962), 33–35, 40.

33. Lee Clark Mitchell, *Westerns: Making the Man in Fiction and Film* (Chicago: University of Chicago Press, 1996), 3.

34. Dexter W. Fellows and Andrew A. Freeman, *This Way to the Big Show: The Life of Dexter Fellows* (New York: The Viking Press, 1936), 84–85.

35. Mitchell, *Westerns*, 159. Jane Tompkins also suggested that violence in western films and novels constituted a way to affirm masculinity. Jane Tompkins, *West of Everything: The Inner Life of Westerns* (New York: Oxford University Press, 1992).

36. Garry Wills, "John Wayne's Body," *New Yorker*, August 19, 1996, 45. See also Garry Wills, *John Wayne's America: The Politics of Celebrity* (New York: Simon and Schuster, 1997), 22.

37. See L. C. Moses, *Wild West Shows and the Images of American Indians 1883–1933* (Albuquerque: University of New Mexico Press, 1996), especially chapter 11.

buffalo

bill

(himself)

history and memory

in the

western biopic

corey k. creekmur

Of this past epoch of our national life there remains but one well-
known representative. That one is my brother. He occupies a unique
place in the portrait gallery of famous Americans to-day. It is not alone
his commanding personality, nor the success he has achieved along
various lines, which gives him the strong hold he has on the hearts of
the American people, or the absorbing interest he possesses in the eyes
of foreigners. The fact that in his own person he condenses a period of
national history is a large factor in the fascination he exercises over
others. . . . He is the vanishing-point between the rugged wilderness of
the past in Western life and the vast achievement of the present.

— Helen Cody Wetmore, *Last of the Great Scouts*
(Buffalo Bill) (1899)

He said the Messiah might not come for many years. He would ride a
white horse and put to shame every enemy of the Jews.

Would he look like Buffalo Bill? I asked.

No. He would be pale, young and peaceful. He would not shoot people down, but would conquer them with love.

I was disappointed. I needed a Messiah who would look like Buffalo Bill, and who could annihilate our enemies.

— Michael Gold, *Jews without Money* (1930)

Early in *My Darling Clementine* (1946), John Ford's classic and of course historically inaccurate retelling of the story of the gunfight at the O.K. Corral, the hero played by Henry Fonda introduces himself as Wyatt Earp, and in speaking his name aloud momentarily silences the film's snickering villain and his neanderthal sons. Newly arrived in Tombstone, Earp has a reputation that clearly precedes him, and his self-identification suddenly transforms the anonymous rube whose cattle have just been rustled and whose brother has just been murdered into a figure to be reckoned with: Earp is now a man with a past, a man with a history. The guilty Clantons have obviously heard this name before, but, more importantly, so have we, the film's audience: the name resonates within the re-created world of the film, across the genre of the western that contains it, and further outward, into the pages of American history. Earp's name circulates through both the fictional western and the history of the American frontier the genre evokes because "Wyatt Earp" is not only a recurrent character in the canon of fictional westerns, but Wyatt Earp (1848–1929) was a historical subject whose name and biography have been frequently appropriated to tell many of the genre's most memorable stories.[1] Of course, the dramatic pause for the announcement of a resonant name is in itself a common trope in popular narratives, but when, for example, a legendary British secret agent ritually identifies himself as "Bond . . . James Bond," this declaration also trades upon instant recognition but does *not* extend beyond textual borders to recall a historical referent. In the western, on the other hand, the identification of characters by name often serves as an implicit announcement, however legitimate or tenuous, of that work's persistent attachment to the facts and characters of American history.

The history of the American West and its ongoing re-presentation through the popular western maintain a lengthy roll call of individuals whose names simultaneously evoke a genuine and a mythic time and place, but perhaps no single figure summarizes the transformation of the reality of the American frontier into commercial entertainment—of the West into the western—as fully as William F. "Buffalo Bill" Cody (1846–1917). Though contemporaneous names (or nicknames) like Billy the Kid, Jesse James, Doc Holliday, Wild Bill Hickok, Judge Roy Bean, Calamity Jane, or Belle Starr also retain rich narrative connotations—and perhaps some historical significance—for many audiences, Buffalo Bill remains unique insofar as his life story was regularly represented by himself, playing himself in a range of media. Of all the figures commonly included in the pantheon of Wild West legends, Buffalo Bill is the only one to have frequently appeared on stage and in early documentary as well as narrative films. (Cody's frequent employee and costar Annie Oakley was also documented by early motion pictures but she did not appear in fictional films.) Cody first played himself in western stage melodramas beginning in 1872, and, after 1869, was the subject of hundreds of dime novels published when he was a living celebrity, unlike Deadwood Dick, his fictional rival for the hearts and dimes of young readers. But Cody's enduring fame rests upon his self-presentation as the central figure in the Wild West, the live exhibition—Cody disdained the tag "show," which implied artifice—that recreated the fading frontier for audiences in the United States and Europe between 1883 and 1910.

Despite his keen recognition of the power of various new reproductive technologies, Cody was a performer who understood the pleasures and aura of the live, personal appearance, the uniquely autographed souvenir, and of the direct, unmediated address to his fans. However, Cody was also aware that the rapid development of mass media like the photograph, cinema, and phonograph, all of which he eventually employed for publicity purposes, could establish extensive links (as well as alienating gaps) between the individual star and his many admirers. While Cody apparently enjoyed his international fame, like most celebrities he frequently found himself negotiating the awkward division between his private life and public persona: in later and financially desperate years, Cody's appearances with the Sells-Floto circus were advertised as exhibitions of "Buffalo Bill (Himself)," a promotional construction that seems to anticipate the postmodernist fascination with the contradictory ways in which "authentic identity" might always be understood as constructed and performed. "(Himself)" functions as both a promise of authenticity and perhaps as a veiled threat, a bracketed qualification allowing at least the hint that "Buffalo Bill" could increasingly designate a sign free of any living referent, like "Deadwood Dick" or "The Lone Ranger," or a representation, such as a motion picture, that did not require the star's live appearance. "Buffalo Bill (Himself)" of course must also refer to William Frederick Cody, the individual whose proper name often became obscured behind his more colorful and widely circulated nickname and commercialized image. However, even when Cody's physical presence was not guaranteed by the price of a ticket, all of Buffalo Bill's multimedia appearances were fundamentally biographical in their advertisement and appeal. As the figurehead of the Wild West, Cody consistently insisted upon the event's realism, demonstrated in part by the regular import of western animals and Native Americans to the urban east and beyond; but the Wild West's authenticity was most emphatically secured by Cody's own documented and elaborated biography, his own demonstrable participation in the expansion of the western frontier that the historian Frederick Jackson Turner famously declared complete at the 1893 meeting of the American Historical Association held in downtown

Chicago while, on the city's south side, Buffalo Bill's Wild West was appearing daily under a massive tent pitched alongside the World's Columbian Exposition. Like the world's fair itself, which combined the genteel and informative White City with the rowdy and disorienting midway, Cody's Wild West announced itself as both educational and entertaining, a collection of genuine artifacts displayed with showmanship and all the trappings of arranged spectacle.

While most film genres, including the most fantastic, often make some claims upon prior historical reality, the western appears unique in its regular, perhaps even inherent, reference to a geographically and historically delimited space and time. (In other words, while most individual genre *films* locate themselves within an identifiable historical setting, genres *themselves* are clearly free to range across historical periods: even war films, while almost always specifically grounded, are not limited *as a genre* to the depiction of a single historical conflict.) Although recognized and increasingly criticized for its distortion of historical facts, the western's embedding in actual locations, events, and a rather narrowly circumscribed time frame—roughly 1865 to 1900—provides a consistent historical specificity that remains central to the meaning and popularity of the genre. This delimitation has also led to a persistent and often pedantic strain of criticism that seeks to "correct" the genre's frequent historical errors, noting for instance the inaccurate use of particular firearms or costumes, or criticizing the genuinely troubling misrepresentations of the languages, customs, and behavior of Native Americans. Indeed, one might argue that the decline in the western's popularity is directly related to the increased recognition that the genre, though ostensibly embedded in American history, has distorted more of that history than it has accurately chronicled.[2] Just a little less often, the western has also been questioned for its common rewriting of actual biographies, especially when it elevates common criminals to the status of romantically rebellious heroes, or, more recently, when it demotes once heroic figures (such as Wyatt Earp, General Custer, or Buffalo Bill) into the deeply flawed and neurotic characters that must be, we simply assume, more realistic than earlier hagiographic portrayals.

In a recent essay updating his groundbreaking study of the Hollywood biography film, or biopic, George F. Custen notes, "Unlike the fictive discourse out of which the rest of Hollywood's canon is acknowledged to be fabricated, biopics' putative connection to accuracy and truth makes them unique. At the outset, each member of the category is defined as being a true story."[3] Certainly this broad claim cannot be applied to all westerns, which often appear just as fabricated or stylized as musicals or horror films: the real West's imprecise firearms alone, we are often told, would have made the regular and deadly accuracy of gunfighters in most fictional westerns impossible. But I believe that the considerable extent to which the western frequently, perhaps implicitly, asserts its basis in history hasn't been adequately considered. (Like Custen discussing the biopic, I am allowing for a significant gap between the regular assertion and the rare achievement of historical accuracy.) Moreover, the fact that the western often claims this historical grounding through biographical references suggests a consistent blurring between the western and the biopic that also hasn't been fully investigated. Custen, for instance, does not always clarify—perhaps following Hollywood's own practice of seeking the broadest possible audience for its products—the precise generic distinction that might isolate biopics and westerns. For instance, he includes Alan Dwan's 1939 film *Frontier Marshall*, based upon Stuart N. Lake's (notoriously novelistic) 1931 biography *Wyatt Earp: Frontier Marshall*, among his listing of Hollywood biopics, but does not include the "original" 1934 *Frontier Marshall* directed by Lew Seiler, the earlier film *Law and Order* (1932) directed by Edward Cahn and clearly based upon Earp's life but employing pseudonyms (itself remade in 1940 and 1953), nor Ford's classic *My Darling Clementine*, which is in large part a consciously artistic remake of the earlier films, and which again explicitly credits Lake's biography—a 20th Century-Fox property—as its source. Later films featuring the character of Wyatt Earp and the most famous incident in his life, like *Gunfight at the O.K. Corral* (1957), also do not appear in Custen's ostensibly complete overview of Hollywood biopics. If 1939's *Frontier Marshall* is a biopic, why aren't the original 1934 version or Ford's famous remake biopics as well? Why aren't all westerns featuring the character of Wyatt Earp also identified as biopics?

Custen's straightforward definition of a biographical film is "one that depicts the life of a historical person, past or present." Narrowing his definition somewhat, Custen specifies that a biopic "is minimally composed of the life, or the portion of a life, of a real person whose real name is used."[4] Except for *Law and Order*, which obscures Earp's name, all of the films I've just mentioned seem to qualify as biopics under this minimal definition: the same is true for hundreds of other films conventionally categorized as westerns. In Custen's table of "Biopics by Profession," we find films that might otherwise be identified as westerns under the subcategories of Entertainer (*Annie Oakley* [1935] and *Buffalo Bill* [1944]), Outlaw (*Billy the Kid* [1930 and 1941], and *Jesse James* [1939]), Military Figure (*Geronimo* [1939, 1962, and 1993], *Chief Crazy Horse* [1955], and *Sitting Bull* [1954]), and Law Enforcement (*Frontier Marshall*). At some level this grouping simply reflects the western's common tendency to construct stories around the names of actual westerners whose biographies might otherwise play little or no part in those narratives: though it employs a nickname associated with a historical figure (the outlaw William Bonney), the horror-western hybrid *Billy the Kid vs. Dracula* (1966), for instance, appears to make no biographical claims at all regarding either of its title subjects, unlike the ostensibly more straightforward "biographical" westerns *Billy the Kid* (1930 and 1941), *Pat Garrett and Billy the Kid* (1973), or *The Left-Handed Gun* (1958), which all base some of their plots and audience

135

interest on "authentic" historical referents. As with the many musicals that also narrate the life story of a famous composer or performer, the western seems to allow and even encourage generic blending, though the musical does *not* share the western's tendency to invoke historically resonant names in works that are not also conventional "life stories": a range of actors playing significantly different characters in westerns have all been called Wild Bill Hickok, whereas Cole Porter and Fanny Brice (the subjects of *Night and Day* [1946] and *Funny Girl* [1968]) are not names shared by distinct characters in a variety of Hollywood musicals. In short, while some films commonly identified as musicals, war films, romances, or comedies may also function as biopics, a much larger number of films typically categorized as westerns suggest a biographical core even if they do not choose to follow a historically "responsible" plot line. Since westerns are almost always "historical" recreations of an earlier era and often feature heroes taken from the historical record (perhaps in name only), the western may in fact be the most consistently "biographical" of all Hollywood genres.

The cinematic representation of Buffalo Bill Cody usefully demonstrates some of the common interplay between the western and the biopic as Custen defines it, though again, Cody's example retains distinct features because he—unlike, say, Judge Roy Bean or Sitting Bull—played himself in films. As a public figure, Cody was often filmed by early cameramen (and of course was photographed much more often)[5]: his first film appearance was, appropriately, for fellow mythmaker Thomas Edison, at the Wizard of Menlo Park's New Jersey laboratory shortly after Cody's successful appearance at the Chicago Columbian Exposition, along with members of Buffalo Bill's Wild West, including Native Americans and Annie Oakley.[6] Cody eventually appeared in approximately eleven films between 1894 and 1917, some the products of his own production companies.[7] Between 1923's serial *In the Days of Buffalo Bill* and Robert Altman's 1976 *Buffalo Bill and the Indians, or Sitting Bull's History Lesson*, Cody has also been a character embodied by actors in some thirty-five films. (Altman's film, which clearly seeks to debunk the mythology of Buffalo Bill, is finally no more historically accurate than most Cody films, and frequently relies upon cheap shots to imply its revisionist view: for instance, the film suggests that Cody's celebrated long hair was really a wig, and that Annie Oakley's marriage to Frank Butler was unhappy, whereas the actual "scandal" of that partnership seems to have been in Butler's complete willingness to accept a subservient role to his celebrity wife.[8])

Among the many self-representations and dramatic recreations of Cody's career, at least two examples directly motivate a discussion of the biographical impulse that I believe frequently underlies the narrative surface of the western. Before proceeding to discuss these, however, I should briefly emphasize that Cody's representation through written biographies is at least as complex as his representation through cinema—

which is to say that he both participated in and played no direct part in the production of available biographical materials. In addition to the plays, dime novels, and especially the Wild West, an autobiography entitled *The Life of Hon. William F. Cody, Known as Buffalo Bill, The Famous Hunter, Scout, and Guide* was published in 1879 by Frank E. Bliss in Hartford, Connecticut. Against the now commonly expected view that any star autobiography must have been ghostwritten, Cody biographer Don Russell has convincingly argued that most of the work must have indeed been written by Cody.[9] A later volume, *Buffalo Bill's Life Story: An Autobiography* (identified otherwise on its own title page as *An Autobiography of Buffalo Bill (Colonel W. F. Cody)* appeared in 1920, three years after Cody's death, though it too may include earlier material written by Cody. An early biography, *Last of the Great Scouts, The Life Story of Colonel William F. Cody* appeared in 1899, "as told by his sister" Helen Cody Wetmore (with later editions, following Cody's death, emphasizing a short preface and epilogue by the famous western novelist Zane Gray). A later biographical manuscript by one of Cody's other sisters, Julia Cody Goodman, aimed to counter some of Helen's claims. Other biographical works, including publicist Frank Winch's 1911 intertwined biography of Cody and his later business partner, *Thrilling Lives of Buffalo Bill and Pawnee Bill,* relied upon then-familiar stories until Don Russell's 1960 *The Lives and Legends of Buffalo Bill* approached the standards for modern biographical research. (These texts are by no means irrelevant to film representations, since thirty-three years later Winch was credited with the original story for the biopic I will discuss shortly.) Russell's careful work did not prevent the ongoing appearance of curious works like Nellie Snyder Yost's *Buffalo Bill: His Family, Friends, Fame, Failures, and Fortunes,* a lengthy catalog of fairly innocent local gossip. Biographies of Cody written for children also contribute to the body of work seeking to narrate this singular life, and reinterpretations of Buffalo Bill have been central to a number of novels, including Loren D. Estleman's *This Old Bill* (1984) and Thomas Berger's *The Return of Little Big Man* (1999).

Competing for the public's attention with many of these written artifacts, *The Life of Buffalo Bill (Col. Cody)* was, on the evidence of an apparently original title card, produced and copyrighted in 1912 by the Buffalo Bill and Pawnee Bill Film Company, 145 E. 45th Street, in New York City. (The only print I have been able to examine was apparently shortened by about a third to appease later tastes when it was copied in 1959: long, static shots seem to have been trimmed, but so far as I can determine no shots have been completely removed, nor was the sequence of the film altered.) Some sources list the film as a 1910 production, while a film commonly identified as *The Adventures of Buffalo Bill,* released in 1917 following Cody's death, is likely a retitled, possibly reedited version of the now lost film generally known as *Indian War Pictures,* though some sources conflate these first and last works (suggesting perhaps that "life" and "adventures" were synonyms for

Cody). As one of dozens of films representing Cody, *The Life of Buffalo Bill* is unremarkable and even rather disappointing. The film's consistent reliance on static long shots is numbing, and its dramatization of three discrete events does not cohere as a narrative: intertitles rather than progressive plot construction carry the film from one unrelated incident to the next. While the action of the entire film takes place in exterior locations, none provide the dramatic visual backdrop that Cecil B. DeMille's first westerns, produced a few years later in southern California, would successfully exploit.

Nevertheless, the film is exceptionally interesting insofar as its truncated, episodic "biography" features the notable spectacle of its actual subject. The short film opens with three shots and closes with one more of a sixty-six year old William F. Cody (himself), alone with his white horse in a wilderness setting, falling asleep and waking: an intertitle isolates the longer middle of the film as "A Dream of the Days of His Youth" consisting of "Memories of the Old Santa Fe Trail [,] The Way to the West Before the Railroad Came." All that follows is explicitly presented as a dream until a final intertitle unnecessarily clarifies that "Buffalo Bill Awakens from His Dream." The film therefore relies upon a structure common to Hollywood cinema (from *Sherlock Jr.* [1924] and *The Wizard of Oz* [1939] to *The Matrix* [1999] and *The Sixth Sense* [1999]) that encloses most of the events depicted on screen within borders that demarcate the majority of the film as subjective fantasy, though unlike most Hollywood examples, *The Life of Buffalo Bill* doesn't recognize even the basic effects of displacement performed by the dreamwork and summarized by Sigmund Freud a decade before the film was made. (By representing Cody's rich life in only three reels, the film is also certainly condensed, but not in Freud's sense.) An intertitle that shifts the film from its first section, in which Cody defends a group of pioneers against an Indian attack, to a dramatization of Cody's foiling a stagecoach robbery clarifies the film's understanding of what it means to dream: "Another Memory of His Past." While two intertitles identify the body of the film as a dream, an equal pair compete for the designation of the film as more properly the narrativization of "memories." Since the film doesn't recognize the distorting quality of dreams, it seems more rewarding to think of this dream as indistinguishable from memory, which might also be personal and subjective but not altogether a fantasy: the film implies that the content of these dreams *happened*. But given the national status of this particular dreamer, these memories might also be described as history. If Cody, a notable historical figure, recalls an American past rather than just his own wishes, the subjective taint of dreams and memories might be overcome by the objectivity ideally promised by the claim of historical fact.

Given its clearly marked borders, *The Life of Buffalo Bill* thus divides itself into two realms, which might be summarized through interlocking terms: present and past, retrospection and action, memory and event, and

138

(a tension I will return to) old age and youth. But the explicit isolation of the shots of the *actual* older Cody from the remainder of the film, featuring an *actor* recreating Cody's youthful exploits, suggests that the film's principal structural distinction is between reality and artifice, or what we have come to call documentary and fiction.[10] All of the film's operative tensions rely upon the audience's critical awareness that the obvious representation before us is nevertheless contained by the mechanically recorded images of the genuine living legend at the film's borders. Even though we might describe Cody's actions at the margins of the film as acting, the fascination generated by these shots, then and now, derives from the recognition that we are viewing Cody himself.[11] Indeed, the quality of Cody's acting is simply irrelevant, since the fact that he has been recorded or documented overwhelms the halfhearted attempt to dramatize his limited actions. (Curiously, in a brief summary of the film in R. L. Wilson and Greg Martin's *Buffalo Bill's Wild West: An American Legend*, an invaluable resource for gauging the vast material production of Buffalo Bill souvenirs and memorabilia, the fact that Cody is played by a younger actor for most of the film remains unacknowledged, though this finally seems appropriate for a work devoted to Cody's mass media image rather than his life.[12]) To use the appropriate term from the period (before *documentary* secured its place), but also to draw upon the term's ontological claims, we see Buffalo Bill in an "actuality"—and in actuality—before and after we witness his more active but ultimately less compelling impersonator. Although the dramatic middle of the film would seem to provide more obvious action and spectacle than the framing shots, the aura of fame, celebrity, and legend circulates around the attraction of Cody: the overwhelming appeal of the images of the old man on the edges of this otherwise undistinguished cowboy movie carries the considerable fascination of the real thing, and the aged scout's white hair and slowed movements function as the powerful physical register of history—or at least the sweep of passing time—that the film otherwise ineptly recounts.

Of course, Cody's own career as the figurehead of the Wild West was premised on the fascination of the live appearance and of the physical body on display, and the rising popularity of the early western film should be recalled in light of the increasing historical distance between mass audiences and the color, sounds, and smells of the early frontier. By 1944, however, the Hollywood western could provide at least the colors and sounds of the Old West for viewers less and less likely as time went on to have also seen Cody and the Wild West in the flesh. Though cited in Custen's study, *Buffalo Bill* (1944), starring Joel McCrea and Maureen O'Hara and directed in Technicolor by William A. Wellman for 20th Century-Fox, does not receive extended attention but is employed to reinforce general characteristics common to the biopic as a Hollywood genre.[13] But this example, like many others in Custen's book, troubles his exclusive focus upon it as a biopic when its trappings as a western are simultaneously evident. For instance, the film's relatively brief running time of ninety minutes is padded with action-packed shots of Indian battles and cavalry charges that do not always directly involve the main character. But for the most part, *Buffalo Bill* certainly adheres to well-established biopic conventions, especially in its central tension between the celebrated public life and semitragic private life of a famous and eventually triumphant individual. Like other biopics set in the past but released during World War II, *Buffalo Bill* also finds ways to comment upon the social and political context of its immediate audience; for example, at a key moment Cody chooses to serve his country in battle rather than retreat to a quiet civilian life with his wife and infant: Cody's morally correct, selfless decision is clearly set against his wife's misguided, selfish desire.

As Custen and other writers on biopics have recognized, detailed correction of a film biography's distortions and omissions seems to miss the cultural and aesthetic point of biopics as mass entertainment, even if the genre implicitly and "irresponsibly" presents itself as historically accurate. I won't, therefore, bother to trace the many errors in *Buffalo Bill*, or, to be fair, cite the many details in the film that seem historically justified. Overall, *Buffalo Bill* seems typical in its balance of such elements; again, it's at least as fair as Altman's *Buffalo Bill and the Indians*, though the latter's cynicism might more easily be mistaken for accuracy by contemporary audiences. Instead, I would like to focus upon *Buffalo Bill*'s self-aware treatment of historical and textual distortion, and of the possible effects of mediation and dramatization on historical events and figures. This self-reflexivity is hardly unique to *Buffalo Bill*, and in fact often marks the biopic as a Hollywood genre, though it's perhaps most common in musical biopics: the dizzying moment in *Jolson Sings Again* (1949), the sequel to 1946's blockbuster *The Jolson Story*, when the actor Larry Parks, playing Al Jolson, meets the character Larry Parks in 1945, played by actor Larry Parks, who will go on to star in *The Jolson Story*, is only a slightly excessive example.[14] Most conventionally, *Buffalo Bill* relies upon a stentorian voice-over narrator to signal historical status, employing an anonymous male voice who serves in effect as the voice of authoritative, retrospective history: this story is known and can be told. Apparently slipping in from the newsreel that would have typically preceded a 1944 feature, and after announcing that the film "is the story of [Cody's] life," the narrator intrudes five more times to summarize not only the events of Cody's life but to clarify the film's and the broader western genre's central themes. The significance of Cody's marriage to the senator's daughter Louisa Frederici is thus identified as a moment when "the lady from the East became the bride of the man from the West. . . ." To the extent that control is possible, *Buffalo Bill* does not risk misinterpretation: its narrator functions as the work's storyteller, critic, and historian.

Early in the film, after rescuing a cavalry stage containing Louisa and her father, an extreme close-up of a letter from Louisa inviting Cody to dinner begins a visual motif of on-screen letters and documents that continues the voice-over narration's function of providing objective evidence for what has been dramatized in film. In a comic bit, Cody copies a reply to Louisa from the blackboard of the school room run by an Indian maiden (Linda Darnell) who will explicitly function as Louisa's dark, western "other" throughout the film, until she is finally sacrificed in a battle. Eventually, additional documents and signatures will appear in printed, handwritten, and hieroglyphic form, and montages of newspaper headlines will rhyme with sequences of Indian communication via smoke signals. But when Louisa's father visits the married Codys later in the film, his arrival is a surprise because the letter he sent announcing his trip has only arrived with him on the same coach; the comic driver and mailman, Chips McGraw (Edgar Buchanan) notes that a previous letter, containing a reprieve, only arrived for a soldier ten days after he was hanged. In a film so explicitly based upon historical and biographical events, the frequent recourse to documentary evidence is suddenly put into question. The film thus shifts toward a recognition that mediation might defer or deflect meaning as often as it effectively delivers messages: this historically based film, in short, begins to admit the disturbing possibility of miscommunication.

This theme also intersects with the film's barely sublimated fear of aging: just before Louisa gives birth to a son, she and Cody encounter an elderly Indian woman who begs them for tobacco. Cody informs Louisa that the old woman has been left alone, with a few provisions, to eventually die, according to the "ways of her people." Cody explains, "That's nature's way, Louisa. When anything becomes too old to be useful, it's just pushed aside." Louisa then reestablishes the meaning of her symbolic position within the film, a position more common to the genre of the western than the biopic: "But it shouldn't be. That's why we have civilization." Soon thereafter, Louisa, fully representing eastern femininity as a cultured realm, will propose taking her son east to expose him to the "advantages of civilization," and when she and Cody separate a few days later, his clear moral choice is between the "civilization" and "safety" she represents and the dangerous adventure inevitable in the patriotic mission requiring Cody to remain in the West to participate in the Indian wars. Manly duty becomes additionally opposed to effeminate civilization when the Codys' son, Kit Carson Cody, dies in the East of dyptheria, which is, as an attending doctor tells Cody, who has never heard of the disease, "a crowd disease . . . a disease of civilization." Buffalo Bill then mutters the word *civilization* as if it were an obscenity, now associated as much with the deadly eastern city as with as the weakly feminine perspective of Louisa.

But the weakness and uselessness of civilization also become directly associated with age: Cody only comes east because a letter from the president of the United States has informed him that he is to receive a

141

Congressional Medal for his role in the battle of War Bonnet Gorge, where he killed his childhood friend Yellow Hand. At the same time, the old cavalryman Chips, who has delivered mail throughout the film, receives an official letter, misdirected for thirty years, announcing his retirement and demanding his trip to the Old Soldier's Home in New York. (This important plot point does not bear careful calculation.) Bitter that the first letter he has ever received puts him out to pasture, Chips tears an array of medals off the wall and begins to rip down a tattered American flag before Cody stops him with a shout. With his national duty restored by the younger man, Chips provides a final salute as another flag outside is raised with a bugle call. But because the film will end with Buffalo Bill's (notoriously oft-repeated) farewell speech before a Wild West audience, the fear of aging and enforced retirement—and of course death in forgotten anonymity rather than through the glory of adventurous violence—continues to haunt the film. Chips is indeed removed from view when he is removed from his profession. Eventually, in a rapid summary, the movie ages Buffalo Bill through the transformation of Joel McCrea's hair and beard from ginger to snow white, but the majority of the film avoids the older image of Cody: the fascination with the actual aged body of Cody that marks the earlier *Life of Buffalo Bill* is in this case withheld as long as possible. No one, the film suggests, wants to see the handsome movie star Joel McCrea play an old man, though of course McCrea's own role in Sam Peckinpah's elegiac *Ride the High Country* (1962) would eventually provide exactly that spectacle. Although Cody maintained his international celebrity into relatively old age, the biopic decides that the period just before his widespread fame, when his accomplishments cannot be so easily interrogated, matters most. Relying upon the simple understanding of history as passing time, most obviously marked in human terms by the signs of physical aging, *Buffalo Bill*, one might say, both dramatizes and fears history itself: Cody's passage toward immortality is only achieved through the rapid visualization of his physical mortality. The final scene of *Buffalo Bill* depicts Cody's decision to retire from the public arena, on his own terms and in his own time, unlike Chips, whose enforced retirement literally banishes him from the film. Retirement is what occurs after time passes, when one's own history is running out. Although *Buffalo Bill* finally stages Cody's farewell as a triumph, it does not let us easily forget the possibility of quiet and forgotten disappearance into the Old Soldier's Home.

142

First, however—and again building upon the misdirected communications produced by earlier delayed letters—the film works toward the tarnishing of Cody's name and reputation. If the battles in which Cody participates as a young man serve the nation, the battles in the latter half of the film revolve around the accurate writing of Cody into history. When Cody first heads East with Chips, he comments that he may be lonely in Washington since "Nobody in the East ever heard my name."

When their train stops at a depot in Council Bluffs, Chips finds a newsstand full of illustrated Buffalo Bill dime novels written by Ned Buntline, and when a clerk spies the actual Cody looking through the stories, fans chase the startled cowboy back to his train. This begins another montage sequence—like the voice-over narration, evocative of the contemporary newsreel—summarizing Cody's growing fame, with larger advertisements and crowds marking his progress toward the United States capitol. This sequence does not emphasize, as other westerns from *Annie Oakley* (1935) to *Unforgiven* (1992) do, the gap between fact and fabrication summarized by the precinematic western dime novel. Although we know that the verbose and heavy-drinking Buntline (here played by Thomas Mitchell, the drunken doctor of John Ford's earlier *Stagecoach* [1939]) is likely to exaggerate, *Buffalo Bill* does not emphasize the distortion of reality into myth that most entertainment forms may have practiced. Indeed, the tacit suggestion of accuracy in Buntline's dime novels is demanded by the film's association of deliberate historical distortion with influential newspapers rather than boys' adventure stories. After Cody, at a banquet at the Astor Hotel (announced by yet another inserted text), defies the greedy locomotive magnate Schyler Vandervere by identifying Indians as "free-born Americans" and insulting monied interests by declaring the Indian-head penny the only Indian white men really care about, Vandervere begins a smear campaign against Cody through the newspapers. Another montage sequence features headlines that question Cody's character by undermining his history: "Who Killed Yellow Hand?" is followed by "Buffalo Bill's Story of Battle with Indian Warrior Doubted" and "Buffalo Bill Deemed as Fraud: Facts Fail to Prove Cody Really Killed Cheyenne Warrior." Like the contradictory newspaper headlines in Fritz Lang's *You Only Live Once* (1937) or Orson Welles's *Citizen Kane* (1941), these headlines—which the audience of the film can only see as lies since we have witnessed the events they describe being rewritten—clearly warn us of the possible manipulation of truth when money, power, and the media are allowed to intertwine. The personal attack on Cody is reprehensible but the willful distortion of the truth, or history, appears to be even more odious, since Cody can only fight back to defend his name but not the doubts now inserted into the recorded pages of history. Buntline's hyperbolic narratives, like the "white lies" common to Hollywood biopics and westerns, only distort the truth in order to entertain more effectively: these forms of communication should not be held, the film insists, up to the standards we demand from the press, whose lies are scurrilous insofar as they insult not only great men but historical truth itself.

Curiously, the doubt raised for the public about Cody's reputation will never really be vanquished in the film, despite the eventual resurrection of our hero. Down and out after his reputation has been soiled, Cody wanders into the Wonderland Museum and tries to trade his Congressional Medal for the dollar prize at a shooting gallery. When the

143

barker running the shop calls over an Irish cop, Cody declares his identity: "I'm Buffalo Bill Cody." The incredulous cop retorts, "And I'm Jenny Lind," and then presses his point: "You know, if I was pretending to be someone I wouldn't be that faker." When Cody demonstrates his remarkable marksmanship—in the manner of his future employee Annie Oakley—the cop relents, though with a comic equivocation: "Pleased to meet you Mr. Cody. 'Tis the King of Siam you are if you're sayin' so." Although presented in both heroic and comic terms, this scene quietly troubles the film's otherwise secure restoration of Cody's identity and pride. The cop suggests that Cody's possible fraud is absurdly doubled: why would anyone pretend to be someone known to pretend? And when the policeman acknowledges Cody to have proven his identity through his actions, he nevertheless allows that such impressive actions should allow even more outrageous impersonations: undeniable proof offers credit to even the most outrageously false claims. The doubt encouraged by this scene is reinforced shortly thereafter, when Cody has been hired to exhibit himself at the shooting gallery. Louisa, informed by her father (who now admits his friend Vandervere's deception) that her estranged husband is "posing at the Wonderland Museum in New York—on a wooden horse," flies in horror to the spectacle of Cody's public humiliation. After we see Cody emerge on his fake horse, with a shot treating the film audience as "insiders" via a glimpse of the mechanism behind this illusion (which of course obscures the actual mechanism—the camera—recording this illusion), the barker announces that Cody will shoot a dollar out of the hand of any man, woman, or child up to the challenge. When a skeptical patron asks the barker why he doesn't hold the coin, the showman replies that "it is an unfortunate weakness of human nature not to trust a man of my profession. . . ." Louisa will then step forward and hold not a dollar but a penny—the Indian-head penny that summarized Cody's disgust with white materialism—in her delicate hand.

In the film's final minutes, Buffalo Bill responds to boys who want to know what Indians are like, including a small black boy who declares "I sure wish I was an Indian!" leaving us to ponder which history of oppression would in fact serve him better. Cody and Buntline then come up with the idea for the Wild West, which Buntline declares "will bring the West to the East" if "the East won't go to the West." In true biopic fashion, this declaration efficiently synthesizes American history, show-business success (with the popular film western riding the coattails of the Wild West show), and Cody's restored marriage. The film thus prepares us, even while it deflects our attention through the markers of success, to recognize that Cody, having cleared his name of its association with fraud, has now entered into the questionable profession that the barker admitted generated mistrust from the public. As the voice-over narrator emphasizes while we watch Cody rapidly age in front of audiences including Queen Victoria and Teddy Roosevelt (surely the stand-in for the other Roosevelt in the White House when the film was first released), "because the most lasting of all is the fame which passes from one generation to another, his name came to typify performance, frontier and freedom, adventure and fair play, the spirit of the West." The final balancing act of the film is to suggest that performance and fair play go hand in hand. While a performance may be feigned, it must not seek to deceive. In a sense, this was also the moral code of Cody's Wild West, the Hollywood biopic, and frequently of the film western, three entertainment forms invested in historical claims as well as the distortions of dramatization. In spite of Cody's rejection of the appellation *show* to describe his Wild West, the exhibition was clearly understood to be a representation rather than original reality, but its higher purpose apparently checked any nagging doubts regarding complete accuracy. Cody's sister, in her biography of her brother, summarized the Wild West in similar terms:

> An exhibition which embodied so much of the historic and picturesque, which resurrected a whole half-century of dead and dying events, events the most thrilling and dramatic in American history, naturally stirred up the interest of the entire country. The actors, too, were historic characters—no weakling imitators, but men of sand and grit, who had lived every inch of the life they pictured. The first presentation was given in May, 1883, at Omaha, Nebraska, the state Will had chosen for his home. Since then it has visited nearly every large city on the civilized globe, and has been viewed by countless thousands—men, women, and children of every nationality. It will long hold a place in history.[15]

Like the child in Michael Gold's radical novel *Jews without Money*, who fantastically blends Buffalo Bill and the promised, avenging Messiah, Helen Cody Wetmore suggests that Buffalo Bill's task as a public figure involved resurrection—the restoring of current life to the dead past—rather than mere recreation. The Wild West "will long hold a place in history" because it was constructed out of "historic characters." Like the Hollywood biopic and the westerns that draw upon biographical figures for their grain of historical truth, the Wild West, in this account, also accepts and even demands historical revision, at least as long as the show remains entertaining.

notes

I would like to thank Janet Walker for her encouragement and patience, and Teresa Mangum for inspiring me to think about the spectacle of aging cowboys.

1. For discussions of various film versions of Earp's life, see Edward Gallafent, "Four Tombstones 1946–1994," in *The Book of Westerns*, ed. Ian Cameron and Douglas Pye (New York: Continuum, 1996), 302–11; and John Mack Faragher, "The Tale of Wyatt Earp: Seven Films," in *Past Imperfect: History According to the Movies*, ed. Mark C. Carnes, Ted Mico, John Miller-Monzon, and David Rubel (New York: Henry Holt, 1995), 154–61. I have also discussed Ford's film in "Acting Like a Man: Masculine Performance in *My*

Darling Clementine," in *Out in Culture: Gay, Lesbian and Queer Essays on Popular Culture*, ed. Corey K. Creekmur and Alexander Doty (Durham, N.C.: Duke University Press, 1995), 167–82.

2. This is one of David Thompson's claims in a recent article on the television remake of *High Noon*. According to Thompson, "the Western died (slowly) because of our rising discontents over its accuracy." See David Thompson, "The Winding Road of the Western Hero," *New York Times*, August 20, 2000, 29–30.

3. George F. Custen, "The Mechanical Life in the Age of Human Reproduction: American Biopics, 1961–1980," *Biography* 23, no. 1 (2000): 139. This essay is Custen's contribution to an excellent special issue on biopics edited by Glenn Mann.

4. George F. Custen, *Bio/Pics: How Hollywood Constructed Public History* (New Brunswick, N.J.: Rutgers University Press, 1992), 5–6. On the underanalyzed biopic, one should also cite Carolyn Anderson's bibliographical essay "Biographical Film," in *A Handbook of American Film Genres*, ed. Wes D. Gehring (Westport, Conn.: Greenwood, 1988), 331–51, and Ronald Bergan, "Whatever Happened to the Biopic?" *Films and Filming* 346 (1983): 21–22. A very illuminating analysis of the "musical biopic" can also be found in Bruce Babington and Peter William Evans, *Blue Skies and Silver Linings: Aspects of the Hollywood Musical* (Manchester: Manchester University Press, 1985), 114–40.

5. I discuss photographs of Cody (and his contemporary Oscar Wilde) in relation to Victorian codes of masculinity in the first chapter of my book *Cattle Queens and Lonesome Cowboys: Gender and Sexuality in the Western* (Durham, N.C.: Duke University Press, 2001).

6. Information on Cody's film appearances is sparse, and where available, often contradictory. For information on his film appearances, and on later cinematic representations of his character, see William Judson, "The Movies," in *Buffalo Bill and the Wild West* (Brooklyn, N.Y.: The Brooklyn Museum, 1981), 68–83. Judson's "Chronology of Buffalo Bill on Film" builds upon a list first published in *Monthly Film Bulletin* 43, no. 512 (1976), back page. Both contain titles that do not in fact appear to feature Cody. Charles Musser's recent, magisterial filmography of Edison productions clarifies the extent to which Cody and members of the Wild West appeared on film between 1894 and 1900 and reprints a number of interesting newspaper accounts of Cody being filmed. See Charles Musser, *Edison Motion Pictures, 1890–1900: An Annotated Filmography* (Washington: Smithsonian Institution Press and Le Giornate del Cinema Muto, 1997), 125–29, 296–97, 442. The American Film Institute catalogs identify (discounting repeated titles and films with alternate titles) approximately fourteen additional (non-Edison) films featuring Buffalo Bill. See *The American Film Institute Catalog of Motion Pictures Produced in the United States: Film Beginnings, 1893–1910*, compiled by Elias Savada (Metuchen, N.J.: Scarecrow Press, 1995), 128–29 (*Buffalo Bill Fight*, unknown director, 1905; *Buffalo Bill's Parade*, Selig Polyscope, 1903; *Buffalo Bill's Street Parade*, Lubin, 1903; *Buffalo Bill's Wild West and Pawnee Bill's Far East*, Buffalo Bill and Pawnee Bill Film Co., 1910; *Buffalo Bill's Wild West Parade*, American Mutoscope and Biograph Co., 1900 and 1901; *Buffalo Bill's Wild West Show*, American Mutoscope and Biograph Co., 1900; and *Buffalo Bill's Wild West Show*, Lubin?, 1902); and *The American Film Institute Catalog of Motion Pictures Produced in the United States: Feature Films, 1911–1920*, executive editor Patricia King Hanson, (Berkeley and Los Angeles: University of California Press, 1988), 5–6 (*The Adventures of Buffalo Bill*, 1917), 108 (*The Buffalo Bill Show*, 1917), 452 (*The Indian Wars*, 1914), and 666 (*Official Motion Pictures of the Panama Pacific Exposition Held at San Francisco, Calif.*, 1917).

7. Though many of the numerous studies of Cody briefly mention his filmmaking activities, the only extended discussions of one of Cody's film productions appear in Kevin Brownlow, *The War the West and the Wilderness* (New York:

Alfred A. Knopf, 1979), 224–35, and Joy S. Kasson, *Buffalo Bill's Wild West: Celebrity, Memory, and Popular Culture* (New York: Hill and Wang, 2000), 255–63. Kasson's work appeared as this essay was in press, and her focus on the balance of authenticity and fiction throughout Buffalo Bill's career obviously resonates with my discussion. For sparser accounts of Cody's filmmaking activities, see Richard J. Walsh (in collaboration with Milton S. Salsbury), *The Making of Buffalo Bill: A Study in Heroics* (Indianapolis: Bobbs-Merrill, 1928), 344–47; Henry Blackman Sell and Victor Weybright, *Buffalo Bill and the Wild West* (New York: Oxford University Press, 1955), 249–51, which wrongly suggests the unnamed *The Indian Wars* was "the only movie [Cody] ever made"; and Joseph G. Rosa and Robin May, *Buffalo Bill and His Wild West: A Pictorial Biography* (Lawrence: University Press of Kansas, 1989), 203–9.

8. While Joy S. Kasson is generally wary of the many spurious "facts" cited in the earlier literature on Cody, she seems to accept a single report from the 1930s claiming that Cody wore a wig, and notes that in Altman's film "the secret of Buffalo Bill's wig is at last exposed to the public." See Kasson's *Buffalo Bill's Wild West: Celebrity, Memory, and Popular Culture*, and Kasson's chapter in this volume. If Cody indeed wore a wig, one might at least wonder why he did not dye his increasingly white hair, which clearly demonstrated his aging, if not actual baldness. I discuss contemporary comparisons between Cody's and Oscar Wilde's hair in *Cattle Queens and Lonesome Cowboys*. On Annie Oakley's marriage, see Tracy C. Davis, "Annie Oakley and Her Ideal Husband of No Importance," in *Critical Theory and Performance*, ed. Janelle G. Reinelt and Joseph R. Roach (Ann Arbor: University of Michigan Press, 1992), 299–312.

9. See Russell's extremely helpful foreword to *The Life of Hon. William F. Cody, Known as Buffalo Bill: The Famous Hunter, Scout, and Guide, An Autobiography* (Lincoln: University of Nebraska Press, 1978). Joy S. Kasson has carefully addressed and clarified many of the questions surrounding Cody's autobiography in *Buffalo Bill's Wild West, Celebrity, Memory, and Popular Culture*, 27–41.

10. This curious little film might thus anticipate the "placing in abeyance of the distinction between the real and the imaginary," which Hayden White associates with the postmodernist docudrama or historical metafiction. See White, "The Modernist Event," in *The Persistence of History: Cinema, Television, and the Modern Event*, ed. Vivian Sobchack (New York: Routledge, 1996), 19.

11. Joy S. Kasson describes and analyzes the film in similar terms; see her chapter in this volume and *Buffalo Bill's Wild West: Celebrity, Memory, and Popular Culture*, 256–57.

12. R. L. Wilson with Greg Martin, *Buffalo Bill's Wild West: An American Legend* (New York: Random House, 1998), 227–28.

13. See, however, Custen's interesting note on producer Darryl F. Zanuck's alteration of the film's original dedication to Native American soliders in *Bio/Pics*, 265–66. Ronald Bergan cites *Buffalo Bill* as his sole example of a "Western biopic" when making the point that "[t]he biographical picture, affectionately known as the biopic, is as much part of cinema history as the Western, the Musical and the Gangster movie and, although a genre in itself, it encompasses all other genres." See Bergan, "Whatever Happened to the Biopic?," 21.

14. Babington and Evans treat the Jolson films as paradigmatic examples of the musical biopic in their *Blue Skies and Silver Linings*.

15. Helen Cody Wetmore, *Last of the Great Scouts (Buffalo Bill)* (New York: Grosset and Dunlap, 1918), 261, originally published in 1899.

film

history:

widening

horizons

how

the west

was sung

k a t h r y n   k a l i n a k

In James Cruz's 1923 silent western *The Covered Wagon,* a young boy strums a banjo as the lyrics of the Stephen Foster tune "Oh! Susanna" appear in the intertitles. The diegetic representation of song is not unique to *The Covered Wagon,* nor is the film's use of period music. In fact, the use of period music, both diegetic and nondiegetic, has provided something of a touchstone for the genre of the western. The prototypical dime novel *Deadwood Dick, The Prince of the Road,* for instance, includes a scene in which a miner picks up a banjo and sings "Gwine to Get a Home, Bymeby." Owen Wister's tonier opus *The Virginian* has the eponymous cowboy protagonist singing "Jim Crow."[1] It is this tradition that *The Covered Wagon* extended into film when it used "Oh! Susanna," paving the way for sound westerns to exploit music in the same way. To cite but a few examples: "Kingdom Comin'" (aka "Year of the Jubilo" or "Jubilo") in *The Telegraph Trail* (1933) and *Virginia City* (1940); "Dixie's Land" (aka "Dixie") in *Royal Rodeo* (1939); "Camptown Races" and "Ring, Ring de Banjo" in *Virginia City;* and "Oh! Susanna" in *Virginia City, The Telegraph Trail, Royal Rodeo, Gunsmoke Ranch* (1937), and *Oh,*

Susanna, starring Gene Autry (1936). What all these examples (and more) have in common is the use of a specific kind of period song to signal authenticity to their audiences.

In their reach toward authenticity, filmic westerns adopted a number of codes—among them costume, setting, props, and historical reference—to signify the real. Music, and especially diegetic song, become one of those markers, functioning as shorthand to the spectator that the representations on the screen were historically accurate. Thus, when audiences recognized a song as western (or thought they did), the film seemed more genuine. But the use of period song in the western is anything but simple and straightforward, and many frontier songs are not western in the way that we have assumed them to be. In fact, when westerns tapped into period song, they often accessed something else: minstrelsy. What we thought were folk tunes generated on the frontier often turn out to have been written expressly for and performed on the minstrel stage. *The Royal Rodeo*, a 1939 Vitaphone short, encapsulates this slippage between folk tune and minstrelsy in its very plot: a young European monarch invites a traveling rodeo to perform for him. The cowboys sing, among other things, the minstrel songs "Oh! Susanna" and "Dixie."

My purpose here is to begin an archeology of American popular song in an attempt to understand its resonance in the western. What I am prepared to argue is that much of the music that we have come to associate with the frontier is authentic only in a deeply complex way. While it is true that many songs reproduced in westerns were actually sung on the frontier, it is equally true that many of those same songs trail in their wake a complicated, overdetermined, and multifaceted discourse of blackface minstrelsy that has been all but elided for contemporary audiences. Unpacking the meaning in minstrelsy itself and examining its use in westerns has much to tell us about the ways we access the historical West, and especially about the centrality of race and ethnicity to the formation of American national identity.

Song, historically, played an important role in the West: as a form of diversion to those making their way and living in places where professional entertainment was not readily available; and as a form of cultural transmission, reinforcing key terms in America's cultural lexicon. When these two functions of song overlap, as they often did in the West, they produced and sustained a powerful cultural fiction about American national identity and destiny, reinforcing a particular definition of "Americanness" during a historical period when that definition was called into question.

Some of the earliest Anglo writings about the West included descriptions of music. At least two of the men on Lewis and Clark's expedition played the violin; square dances among the men in the expedition were not uncommon. In fact, violins were widely available across the frontier in the second half of the nineteenth century, costing about ten dollars apiece.[2] Naturalist John Bradbury reported hearing singing among

fur traders at work for John Jacob Astor's Pacific Fur Company, and cal-
liopes, brass bands, cabin orchestras, and singers were a staple of riverboat
travel up and down the Mississippi River.[3] Songs sung on the Oregon
Trail included "Oh! Susanna" and "Old Folks at Home" (aka "Swanee
River") by Stephen Foster; "Old Dan Tucker" by Daniel Decautur
Emmett; "The Girl I Left Behind Me," and "Seeing the Elephant" by
David G. Robinson (to the tune of "De Boatman Dance" by Emmett).
Homesteaders sang "Old Joe Clark" and "Skip to My Lou." Popular
among miners were "Carry Me Back to Old Virginny" by James K. Bland
and, again, "Oh! Susanna." Soldiers sang "The Girl I Left Behind Me," as
did cowboys, later.

Music about the West, however, was a function of the East, of ways of
thinking about the frontier constructed by those who did not live there.
James K. Bland, who wrote "Carry Me Back to Old Virginny," lived on
Long Island. Daniel Decautur Emmett, who wrote "Old Dan Tucker,"
and "Dixie," hailed from Mount Vernon, Ohio. "Seeing the Elephant," a
mining song, was actually written by New Englander David G. Robinson
for his stage play of the same name. "Oh! Susanna," and "Swanee River"
were penned by Stephen Foster, a native of Pittsburgh, Pennsylvania, and
later resident of Hoboken, New Jersey and New York City who never got
any farther west than Kentucky.

George and Ira Gershwin wrote "The Real American Folk Song is a
Rag." I would like to argue something different. The real American folk
song is a minstrel song, the first type of music in this country to be
considered uniquely and natively American. If the other in America's
story about the West is the Indian, the other in American popular song is
the African American. How minstrel songs came to be defined as
American and functioned in the popular imagination of the nineteenth
century has much to tell us about the construction of American identity.

Minstrel song debuted in the same year as "The Star Spangled Banner,"
but it was minstrel song, not patriotic music, that came to be explicitly
defined as American.[4] Music of nineteenth century America was highly
derivative of Anglo models; in fact, many of the patriotic songs that we
consider so central to our identity, "The Star Spangled Banner," "My
Country 'Tis of Thee," and "Yankee Doodle Dandy," among them, were
adaptations of well-known English melodies.[5] Thus, while these songs
may have been a source of national pride, they did not signal Americanness to their listeners. Nor did the sentimental ballads that were so popular
throughout the nineteenth century. Largely replicating English and Irish
models, songs such as the wildly popular "Woodman! Spare That Tree" by
Henry Russell were often indistinguishable from their Anglo prototypes.
With the War of 1812 not quite a distant memory, songs associated with
Britain (Russell, for instance, was an English transplant), were not likely to
be embraced as a native form and a borrowed musical genre, such as the
sentimental ballad, did not trigger a public discourse about American
music. Minstrel song did.

Foreign writers were among to first to comment on the Americanness of minstrel songs, describing them as "*volkslied,*"[6] and "the only original people's songs which the New World possesses."[7] American journalists were quick to join the bandwagon. Bayard Taylor, in the *New York Tribune*, described minstrel songs as "the national airs of America"[8]; J. Kennard, in *Knickerbocker*, deemed minstrels "our ONLY TRUE NATIONAL POETS" and their music as "the quintessentially American song."[9] Henry Franklin Belknap Gilbert composed his orchestral suite, "Americanesque," from minstrel songs. No less than the venerable Walt Whitman praised the performances of minstrel troupes.[10] This discourse about the Americanness of minstrel song not only helped to establish minstrelsy as an archetypally American form, it also created a climate in which it was possible for minstrel songs to become redefined as folk music. (More on this later.)

Certainly minstrel song had its critics, and some writers, initially enamored of "Ethiopian melodies," changed their opinion in the tumultuous years preceding the Civil War: James Russell Lowell, for one, and Whitman for another. Interestingly, those critics who chose to assail minstrelsy did so by attacking the connection between minstrelsy and the American character.[11] Some African-American writers, such as Frederick Douglass, penned venomous attacks;[12] others wrote new lyrics for minstrel melodies, adapting them for abolitionist purposes.[13] Minstrel song, however, proved critic-proof. It was the most popular type of music in America from the 1840s through the two decades following the Civil War.

No other composer left as indelible a stamp on minstrelsy as Stephen Foster, the first composer in America to actually make a living from his craft. Foster hit upon a nerve in American consciousness: anxiety about what it meant to be an American. When the wrenching divisions first of slavery and then of the Civil War divided the young country, Foster's songs offered a vision of a unified America. At a time of massive immigration (America's population doubled in the two decades preceding the Civil War) and large-scale population shifts from rural to urban areas, his work offered a stable American identity. When the boundaries of America, geographic and otherwise, were expanding, Foster provided national coherence. During the 1850s and especially in the years following the Civil War, his songs, and those of other minstrel composers, were carried west, bringing with them a nexus of ideas about Americans, their identity, and their destiny, which resonated in that new landscape.

Foster published nearly two hundred songs in his lifetime,[14] about 90 percent of which are sentimental ballads, or parlor songs, of one kind or another (such as "Jeanie with the Light Brown Hair").[15] But Foster made his living from the income generated by the twenty "others": blackface minstrel songs. Foster struck a resonant chord. None of his sentimental ballads equaled the success of the blackface ouevre.[16] Despite what appears to have been a growing discomfort with the minstrel songs and an effort to establish a reputation as an art composer through sentimental ballads and parlor songs, Foster knew where his bread was buttered, so to speak, and cranked out a blackface tune when his precarious finances necessitated it.[17]

The function of blackface was to reinforce white superiority, but its condensed representation of race did not function in a totalizing manner. Minstrelsy is a multifaceted cultural practice embracing ambivalence and contradiction. I agree here with Eric Lott, whose revisionist work on minstrelsy, *Love and Theft: Blackface Minstrelsy and the American Working Class*, posits the phenomenon as a "mixed erotic economy of celebration and exploitation."[18] Although I might choose to reverse those terms and prioritize the exploitive dimension of minstrelsy, I am in essential agreement with Lott's argument that minstrelsy is an "unsettled phenomenon."[19]

The stage impersonation of blacks by whites did not begin with the minstrel show. Stage performances by white actors in blackface existed well before the American Revolution, a carryover from English practices of the period. By the middle of the nineteenth century, the minstrel show, absorbing blackface performance, was the most popular form of stage entertainment in America. Even the tony John Hill Hewitt, composer of "Wilt Thou Think of Me" and "Mary, Now the Seas Divide Us" wrote minstrel songs.[20] Most histories of the period cite the centrality of George Washington Dixon's blackface performances of his own songs "Coal Black Rose," "Long Tail Blue," and "Zip Coon" and the Jim Crow impersonations of Thomas "Daddy" Rice to rise of blackface. Initially, whites performing in blackface, called "Ethiopian delineators," helped to round out the variety format of a typical evening's entertainment. But Daniel Decautur Emmett hit upon its most popular form: the minstrel show, an entertainment built around blackface performances of song and dance as well as comic routines. Emmett's troupe, the Virginia Minstrels, landed in New York in 1843, soon to be imitated and superceded by others. The height of the minstrel show's popularity occurred in the decades following the Civil War. Waning popularity eventually spelled the demise of the minstrel show, but blackface continued well into the twentieth century. (Witness Al Jolson immortalized in *The Jazz Singer*, or more recently Ted Danson at Whoopi Goldberg's roast at the Friar's Club in New York.)

The blackface song reinforced white superiority; its weapon was ridicule—of African Americans, or anyone else, who thought that blacks were the equal of whites—and its function distinctly nationalistic: to provide a definition of Americanness at a historical moment when the country was searching for that definition. Blackface song was a social construction, defining what it meant to be an American by default, constructing an image of the other against which white Americans, many newly arrived from foreign shores and hailing from a variety of national backgrounds, could measure themselves and feel superior. Eric Lott describes whiteness in the nineteenth century as precarious;[21] minstrelsy helped to establish in the definition of Americanness a connection between whiteness and the

155

American nation and to allow the release of tension required in sustaining that definition amidst mounting evidence to the contrary. It is not surprising that the minstrel song became connected to the settling of the frontier and found its way into any number of texts that were concerned with defining the frontier experience. The frontier was the place where American character was supposedly forged and minstrel song was the first American music to be perceived of as embodying the American character.

America was in the process of constructing that other in the nineteenth century, and blackface entered into a psychic discourse that helped to circumscribe the boundaries of American identity. This is one of the most compelling reasons for the explosion of blackface song in the 1830s, an era when Andrew Jackson was president, and nationalism, in a number of guises, comprised his political agenda. Minstrel song tapped into and reinforced the fragile American identity by providing an other against which that self can be imagined.

Annette Hamilton has developed the concept of "the national imaginary" to refer to "the means by which contemporary social orders are able to produce not merely images of themselves but images of themselves against others."[22] Since the advent of nations in the eighteenth and nineteenth centuries, national identity has hinged on the function of difference; a nation self is not sustainable without "an image of another, against which it can be distinguished."[23] In America, the other is nonwhite and constructed through racial difference from that perceived norm. Thus, Native Americans, African Americans, Latinos, and Asian Americans have functioned as points of difference against which American culture defines its essential self. Each of these others has had a specific function in the development of American identity across a variety of contexts defined by historical era, geographic region, and various social and political tensions. America's master narrative of national origin revolves around the Indian. In American song, it is the African American—amoral, avaricious, lazy, sexually profligate, and mentally inferior—who functions as the other against which white America defines itself.[24] The filmic western unites the two.

Stephen Foster's first success, "Oh! Susanna," provides a fascinating and disturbing case in point. Reprinted in countless songbooks for schoolchildren, the song is almost never reprinted in its original version, complete with blackface dialect and all four verses. It will shortly be apparent why. Although dismissed by critics (the venerable music historian Charles Hamm describes it as "nonsensical"[25]), the song has much to tell us about the extent to which Americanness depends upon constructions of the other. The song's humor derives from its representation of the African-American male as innately illogical, mentally dull, shiftless, superstitious, and, interestingly, innately musical. The power of minstrel song derives from its ability to ridicule this other while insistently reinforcing values of the dominant white culture.

The song opens with a set of contradictions known to schoolchildren everywhere: "It rained all night" but "the wedder it was dry"; "The sun so hot" while "I froze to def."[26] Later, "I shut my eyes to hold my breath." This irrationality, which when divorced from its historical context may appear quaint or folksy, wouldn't have surprised nineteenth-century listeners, who would have recognized the stereotype, a staple of minstrel song: the illogical African American, incapable of higher thinking, more suited to the emotional language of musical expression than to rational thought. "Oh! Susanna" is quite deliberate in setting up this stereotype. The song is aided by the use of blackface dialect, one of the most pernicious aspects of minstrel song. Although nominally an approximation of a deep Southern accent, blackface dialect actually functioned by creating deliberate mispronunciations and ungrammatical constructions ("I'se gwine to Lou'siana / My true lub for to see"). These linguistic deficiencies were attributed to the weak-mindedness and mental impairment of African Americans. Thus, every minstrel song that uses dialect (and almost all of them do) carries with it a socially constructed connection between African Americans and lessened mental powers. I would like to believe that a growing awareness of the racism inherent in blackface dialect is the reason why contemporary editions of "Oh! Susanna"(and other minstrel songs) fail to reproduce it, often substituting a more genteel Southern accent in its place.

Mental confusion is at the heart of the second verse of "Oh! Susanna," as well. A seldom reprinted or quoted verse, these lines embody an overt racism, difficult, if not impossible, to explain away as quaint, nonsensical, or even as "irresponsible fun"[27]:

> I jump'd aboard the telegraph
> And trabbled down de ribber
> De lectrick fluid magnified,
> And kill'd five hundred Nigga.
> De bulgine bust and de hoss ran off,
> I really thought I'd die;
> I shut my eyes to hold my bref
> Susanna don't you cry.

Here the complications of technology are far beyond the mental abilities of the speaker. The humor, if you will, of the verse depends upon the comedy generated by the speaker's complete and utter confusion about recent innovations such as the steamboat, the telegraph, and the locomotive. It is a steamboat, of course, that the speaker travels down the river upon, not a telegraph. The name of one of the most famous of the era's steamboats—one, in fact that plied the Ohio River between Louisville and Pittsburgh, Foster's hometown—was the *Telegraph*. The simple use of capitalization here would have changed the meaning of this line entirely. It is interesting how deliberately Foster created the image of the African American incapable of higher understanding. A bulgine is a locomotive engine, not the boiler of a steamboat. Electricity does not create steam, what the speaker calls "lectrick fluid," or cause a boiler explosion, what the speaker calls "lectrick fluid magnified." The insidious racism of this verse, of an African American who cannot possibly understand the frightening complexities of technology, is accompanied by the overt racism of the death of "five hundred Nigga." What Ken Emerson calls the "casual slaughter,"[28] as well as the magnification of numbers (one of the most famous and horrendous steamboat accidents in America claimed the lives of 150 people—500 killed at once is a telling exaggeration), speaks for itself.

Superstition figures prominently in the third verse, a dream scenario in which the speaker imagines a reunion with Susanna:

> I had a dream the udder night,
> When ebry ting was still;
> I thought I saw Susanna dear,
> A coming down de hill,
> De buckwheat cake was in her mouf,
> De tear was in her eye,
> I says I'se coming from de souf,
> Susanna don't you cry.

One of the things that makes Foster's minstrel songs so fascinating (and is it one of the things that made them so popular in his lifetime?) is their complexity, a level of psychological depth that brings with it complication, ambiguity, and ambivalence about the very subject they are, supposedly, simply and straightforwardly addressing. "Ring, Ring De Banjo" is a famous example that begins by invoking the plantation myth, the supposedly idyllic relationship of slave to master, but ends with the possibility that the slave has killed his master. In the third verse of "Oh! Susanna" something interesting along these lines happens. In a song clearly adopting minstrelsy's pejorative stereotypes of African Americans, there is a suggestion of something else, too. Is the speaker imagining his own freedom in the North, or in the West? There are some tantalizing clues: the bounty attendant upon Susanna (she's eating cake), her freedom of movement and even nonchalance ("A coming down the hill"), the reference to the speaker's arrival *from* the South (to the North?), the "tear" that "was in her eye" (is she waiting for him there?). A verse that begins by marking African Americans as highly superstitious ends, as I read it, with an acknowledgment of the emotional toll of slavery. If I may be a bit psychoanalytic for a moment, I'd like to suggest that it is the collective unconscious of white Northerners (who created minstrelsy, after all) rising to the surface of the text. White Northerners needed to represent enslaved African Americans as inferior and minstrelsy proved the perfect vehicle for this agenda. Blackface minstrelsy was clearly a racist response to challenges to American identity in the nineteenth century. Yet the guilt that lurks beneath minstrelsy, that its "comedy" cannot completely cover over, can be glimpsed in "Oh! Susanna."

In fact, a standard song type within minstrelsy was devoted to the horrors of slavery, often focusing on the destruction of the family or the blighted love between a young couple. Ambivalence about slavery, however fleeting, surfaces in any number of these songs. "Lucy Neal," "Dinah Clare," "Mary Blane," and "Rosa Moon," for instance, all chronicle the demise of female slaves attendant upon the loss of their family or husband/lover at the hands of a white master.

Not surprisingly, this ambivalence is more pronounced in early minstrelsy. As the Civil War loomed and there was more at stake in voicing abolitionist sentiments, references to the horrors of slavery in minstrelsy become far less common. I hasten to point out, however, that one of the most important of the abolitionist Civil War songs, "Jubilo," composed in 1862 by Henry Clay Work, was a smash hit for the Christy Minstrels. (More on "Jubilo" later.) After the Civil War, the antebellum plantation myth of happy slaves, or its inverse, the Reconstruction myth of dandified, irresponsible, shiftless, freed blacks took center stage. Sam Dennison, in his important study of African-American imagery in American popular song, points out that minstrel songs that overtly strayed from stereotypical formulas paid the price—failing, for the most part, to achieve widespread popularity.[29] And one might rightly question the extent to which such songs stirred anything other than mawkish sentiment. White America did not want to confront the horrors of an institution it condoned. Yet as I read minstrelsy, even some of the most popular and mainstream of its successes (such as "Oh! Susanna" and "Jubilo") present a complicated and even contradictory response to dominant representations of race. Eric Lott draws parallels between the legislative compromises of the pre–Civil War America and minstrelsy, both of which "incorporated certain antislavery images and arguments into their generally complacent acts."[30]

Consider the publication history of "Oh! Susanna." The original published version ends with the third verse and its tantalizingly ambivalent references to slavery. The fourth verse, which retreats from these implications, was added to subsequent editions, almost as if Foster (or his publisher) recognized a subtext that came too close to the surface. In this new verse the speaker's direction is identified as western: he is heading to New Orleans. He is not finding his way to freedom, but to Susanna. Yet, I hear resonance from the previous verse in the insistence of the speaker's quest for Susanna and in his emotional tie to her: "But if I do no find her / Dis darkie'll surely die." Were the speaker and Susanna separated by slavery? Is he now free to find her? "Oh! Susanna" ultimately leaves us with questions and ends on a deep sense of longing: for Susanna; for freedom; for a past in which the speaker and Susanna were together.

There is an emotional resonance to this song that catches up in its representation (and ridicule) of the other certain characteristics that white America saw *itself* as embodying: a kind of wanderlust that takes the form of westward expansion (remember that the speaker begins in Alabama and ends in New Orleans); anxiety about the Industrial Revolution and its

159

attendant technological change; and a nostalgia for what progress was leaving behind: the agrarian and rural American past, a past that it was imagined could be re-created on the frontier. Like the sentimental ballad, America's other popular genre during the nineteenth century, "Oh! Susanna" traded on nostalgia, specifically a nostalgia for an idyllic agrarian way of life, close to the land and the virtues it imparts. This ideal was envisioned to exist in the South by Northerners, many of whom had never been there. (Stephen Foster appears to have traveled south only once in his lifetime, on a riverboat trip to New Orleans that he took *after* he wrote the majority of his minstrel songs.) In fact, blackface enjoyed its largest audiences in the cities of the Northeast, where urban decay and the Industrial Revolution rendered its vision obsolete, or at least very difficult to obtain for the vast majority of the working classes. Little wonder, then, that "Oh! Susanna" became a national anthem for white America. It created both an other against which white America could measure itself and find itself superior, as well as an idealized, pastoral America that could be carried to the only place where it seemed possible to reproduce it: the West.

Psychoanalytic arguments about the function of blackface for white America offer another vantage point. Ken Emerson argues that blackface afforded white America psychic release from decorum and respectability, noting that "more than simply a revolt against decorum, blackface was also a veil and a vehicle for discussion of sex and violence, money and class—all the dirty stuff of life that white Americans preferred to sweep under the parlor rug."[31] Foster's "Lou'siana Belle" tells just such a story, one of illicit and even dangerous sexuality. The nature of the relationship between the African-American speaker and his lover is unmistakable: "Oh! Belle don't you tell, / Don't tell Massa, Don't you Belle, / Oh! Belle, de Lou'siana Belle, / I's gwine to marry you / Lou'siana Belle." The stereotype of the sexually promiscuous African American, a staple of the minstrel repertoire, is complicated, as things often are in Foster, by the fact that the Lou'siana Belle is also the mistress of her white master: Is this why the speaker must implore her, "don't you tell"? Would their lives be in danger if "Massa" found out? In a draft version of the song, "Massa" does find out and sells Lou'siana Belle, a powerful reminder of the horrors of slavery that obviously gave Foster pause. It was not included in the final published version.[32]

The psychic resonance of pretending, however momentarily, that one is something other than what one is has been more thoroughly explored by Michael Rogin in *Blackface, White Noise: Jewish Immigrants in the Hollywood Melting Pot*. Arguing along lines similar to those of Emerson, Rogin contends that "minstrelsy enacted the urban white desire to acquire African-American expressive power and supposed emotional freedom without actually freeing the slaves."[33] However, when Rogin explores blackface as a potentially subversive act through theories of masquerade, he reaches a somewhat unsatisfying conclusion: "Cross-racial identification may or may not have had its transgressive moments. . . ."[34]

Certainly, on the whole, racial masquerade reinforced racial inequalities. I think a much more productive avenue to explore in terms of understanding the subversive potential of blackface is its relationship to African-American culture and to African-American performers.

One of the factors complicating an attempt to understand the relationship between minstrelsy and African-American culture is the fact that minstrelsy is a construction, and not a direct appropriation, of that culture. This fact has tended to obscure the actual contribution of African-American culture to minstrelsy, and even to erase it. Although most of the celebrated "Ethiopian impersonators" claimed to have learned their craft directly from actual African Americans, evidence suggests that it was a bit more complicated. If Foster was in any direct contact with African Americans on any kind of regular basis, none of his biographers note it. Stories of direct appropriation from African Americans may have added authenticity to early performances, and white performers were understandably eager to create an audience, but serious studies of minstrelsy dismiss such anecdotal evidence as "absurd," "rarely confirmable," and dependent upon an "astonishing lack of solid fact."[35] Minstrelsy itself is not an authentic African-American form.

The musical construction of most minstrel songs would seem to belie much African-American influence as well. What we do know about the music that the earliest slaves brought over with them from Africa is that it was constructed along the lines of a unison call-and-response without the conventions of Western harmony. Minstrel song is characterized by a verse and chorus structure that relies heavily on four-part harmony. It is an exceptional minstrel song that departs from the verse and chorus format.[36] The melodies for minstrel songs were, instead, characterized by the influence of Irish and Scottish melodies popular at the time. "Zip Coon," known to most contemporary listeners as the sanitized "Turkey in the Straw," is based on Irish dance music. "Backside Albany" borrows from Irish balladry.[37] These circumstances have led many critics to claim, as Ken Emerson does, that "[t]he blackest thing about blackface singing may have been the burnt cork."[38]

Yet the dominant white culture has never been entirely separate from or uninfluenced by African-American culture, and I am prepared to argue that minstrelsy is no exception. In fact, minstrelsy borrowed heavily from African-American culture, but that borrowing was not direct and thus not readily apparent. The influence of African-American culture on minstrelsy was so mediated that it was possible for white performers and/or their audiences to fail to recognize it.

Nineteenth-century popular culture is a distinctly different phenomenon from that of the twentieth century, especially in terms of exhibition and circulation. Popular entertainment was a much more fluid entity for much of the nineteenth century, more likely to be a shared experience crossing ethnic, racial, and class lines. The concept of distinct entertainment forms, practices, and vocabularies aimed at different audiences did

161

not characterize the life of the nineteenth century to the extent that it does today. African Americans in the North, for instance, even before the Civil War, were entertaining themselves in much the same way that white folks did. In New York, the African Grove, an outdoor theater for African Americans, offered a program of excerpts from Shakespeare (*Richard III*), "fashionable songs," including "Eveleen's Bower" from Thomas Moore's *Irish Melodies*, a prototypical minstrel song, "Opossum Up a Gum-Tree," and pantomines.[39] In Philadelphia, the African-American conductor Frank Johnson, performed Strauss waltzes, English sentimental ballads, and American patriotic tunes. The African Theater Company in New York City presented *Hamlet*.

Minstrelsy, which developed as a distinct form in the 1830s and '40s, evolved in this shared culture. Minstrel songs were sung by both white and black performers and circulated through nineteenth-century America across a wide range of subcultures, including immigrants in urban areas such as New York City, farmers throughout the Midwest, slaves in the South, socialites in eastern cities, pioneers on the Oregon Trail, and miners in the California Gold Rush. Minstrel songs were even performed for Queen Victoria. The shared nature of entertainment in the nineteenth century as well as the fluidity of its transmission more freely allowed for the absorption of material generated from the margins. Thus, circulating through the mainstream were contributions from individual subcultures, often masked, but discernible nonetheless. One of the cultures that found a place in nineteenth-century entertainment through this process was African-American culture, which would have met serious roadblocks in its free absorption into the mainstream had it been recognized as such.

Cultural interaction between different ethnicities and even races would have been a part of that entertainment landscape in the nineteenth century. Davy Crockett described the music he heard at a tavern in New York as: "[b]lack and white, white and black, all hug-em-snug together."[40] It was not the South that provided source material for minstrelsy, but places where such cultural exchanges occurred. One point of such exchange was the urban setting. It is interesting to me that none of the biographers point out Foster's access to this kind of cultural exchange;[41] he spent a significant portion of his young adult life working for his brother's shipping company on the docks of Cincinnati.

Another point of cultural exchange was the frontier. Within a decade of the Virginia Minstrels' debut in New York City, minstrel troupes were traveling and performing on the frontier. Elements of African-American culture, white folk culture, and European traditions found an especially conducive place to coalesce out west. Like the city, the frontier provided a melting pot of cultural practices. As one miner described his experience of California, "Yankees watch and listen to Southerners, or as both of these watch and listen to Missourians and the hill folks of Arkansas. Strange worlds—customs, dress, dialects and manners—here meet together."[42]

One aspect of frontier culture that found its way into minstrelsy was white folk culture and its legendary frontiersmen, such as Mike Fink and Davy Crockett. Another was African-American culture in its many forms, including dance (an argument could be made that African-American dance largely defined minstrel performance);[43] polyrhythms, particularly in banjo accompaniment and instrumental pieces; the banjo itself, an instrument with an African heritage; syncopation (the collision of African rhythms and European song); and elements from African-American folklore. (The contradictory verse structure of "Oh! Susanna" comes into sharper focus as the nonsense humor of African-American culture seeping through.) Here, as I see it, is the most subversive aspect of minstrelsy: in its absorption of certain aspects of African-American culture, minstrelsy made that culture a part of the mainstream. In fact, much of what we consider uniquely American in terms of entertainment is highly influenced by and derivative of African-American culture.[44]

It is no coincidence that those decades in the nineteenth century that saw the most disturbance in America's national identity formed the height of minstrelsy's popularity, a popularity that coincided with massive immigration westward. On one level, minstrelsy's popularity in the West is quite easy to explain. When settlers came to the frontier from the South, from the Northeast, and from the Midwest, they sang the music that everyone in America was singing: minstrel song. As William Swain, one of the thousands of hopeful miners who found their way to California after 1849, described the gambling halls he frequented, "Some of the establishments have small companies of Ethiopian melodists, who nightly call upon "Susanna" and entreat to be carried back to Old Virginny. These songs are universally popular, and the crowd of listeners is often so great as to embarrass the player at the monte table and injure the business of the gamblers."[45] An anonymous miner put the matter even more precisely, saying, "I wonder if I am putting it too strongly to say that we American people never really got together until now? ... While travelers from both North and South have visited beyond the Mason and Dixon line, and while minstrel troupes have carried darkey songs far and wide, I think negro melodies never acquired the popularity which is accorded to them here and now."[46] Minstrel song provided a kind of common cultural currency that held a disparate population together on the frontier.

There is an aspect of the connection between minstrelsy and the West, however, that exceeds such pragmatic explanations. It is important to remember that it was homesteading, the western migration of white settlers to the newly opened frontier, that catapulted slavery into the center of public debate in the 1840s and '50s. In fact, it was the West that provided one of the most volatile flashpoints in pre–Civil War race relations, combusting slavery with working-class demands for a free labor force, class tensions and prejudices, abolitionist sympathies, and the growing popularity of Manifest Destiny. Eric Lott describes blackface as "the political unconscious of Manifest Destiny," and certainly minstrelsy gave expression to the unspoken racism behind a doctrine which envisioned settlement of the frontier as white settlement only. It is interesting to consider the inverse—what part Manifest Destiny might play in the unconscious of minstrelsy. Indeed, submerged in minstrelsy's conflicted subtext is western migration, glimpsed in the recurrence of one of minstrelsy's prototypical narrative tropes: the westward journey. This catching up of the West with unsettled and unsettling questions of race is a buried subtext of minstrelsy. If a cultural form can have an unconscious, then this is part of minstrelsy's unconscious.

Minstrel song must have seemed ideally suited to a western landscape that was envisioned as empty space, there for the taking. What better way to fill it with than with America itself, or, to be more precise, with a lost America, with an idealized, agrarian, pastoral existence that had become largely obsolete. This is what settlers brought with them to the frontier when they brought minstrel song: a dream of something that was already lost, an imagined definition of America. By the close of the Civil War, the frontier was vanishing, too, but the minstrel song helped to keep it alive.

Gradually, subtly, but unmistakably, minstrel song became detached from its roots, becoming redefined as folk music. Much of minstrelsy became attached to the South in this way ("Dixie," "Old Folks at Home"), but frontier culture absorbed its fair share, too, where it became transformed into cowboy songs, dance-hall tunes, and pioneer melodies. "Oh! Susanna," minstrelsy's best-seller, came to be regarded as authentic western folk material in this way, and "Jubilo" became the prototypical dance-hall tune. By the early twentieth century, scholarly works on music history were mistakenly describing "Oh! Susanna," for instance, as indigenous folk song. (Listen to recent recordings of Civil War songs to hear the slippage between Confederate music and minstrel song.) Minstrelsy's connection to the settling of the West has been elided and frontier song deracinated in the process. Although the legacy of minstrelsy has largely been lost to today's audiences, that legacy was not as thoroughly elided even a generation ago, and filmmakers and viewers in the past were more able to access issues of race through minstrel song. Even today there are viewers and filmmakers who recognize minstrelsy and through it the racial undercurrents swirling deeply within the genre of the western become available. (I'm thinking of Mel Brooks's *Blazing Saddles* [1983], with its opening rendition of "Camptown Races," a humorous but hardly unconscious acknowledgment of race on the frontier.[47])

The genre of the western established itself early in the history of moving images as a successful formula. Cinema's first blockbuster was a western: *The Great Train Robbery* of 1903. (And it wouldn't surprise me a bit if minstrel song was used as live accompaniment in the dancehall sequence.) As the genre began to develop and authenticity became a defining criterion, its makers sought historical connections to the West and turned to minstrelsy. In doing so, filmmakers of the western entered into a discourse that might be defined as "complexly authentic." The use of "Oh! Susanna" clearly reflects aspects of historical reality: it was widely sung by settlers on the Oregon Trail, by miners in California, and throughout the frontier. But "Oh! Susanna" carries with it another historical reality that is not acknowledged and that in fact has been repressed: minstrelsy, and the racism of the nineteenth century on which the frontier was constructed. To understand something of the history of "Oh! Susanna" is to glimpse that other historical reality packed into the "westernness" surrounding the song. It is through minstrelsy that the specter of the other haunts the western, repressed on the level of the text, but returning in a variety of ways, not the least of which is through the score.

I would like to turn now to several films that use "Oh! Susanna" and other minstrel songs so that I may argue that the textual complications of minstrelsy can find their way into the western and become especially potent when they collide with the textual complexities of the genre itself. Minstrel songs in westerns function most conventionally by covering over the presence of African Americans and the problems of racism, affirming the films' construction of Americanness as white. In these cases, minstrel song becomes doubly deracinated: minstrelsy itself is prone to denying its African-American influences, and this denial is doubled when the minstrel origins of frontier song are unacknowledged. Here minstrelsy mirrors the film's politics of white superiority and the exclusion of racial others. Yet, in other films, minstrel songs express covertly what is elided by the dominant machinations of the text: the function of race on the frontier. Here minstrelsy's own contradictions bring to the surface the textual contradictions that such filmic repressions of race engender. In some cases, minstrelsy can even open up an antiracist perspective.

A film such as James Cruz's silent opus, *The Covered Wagon*, provides an archetypal case in point of how the use of minstrel song catches up, in its quest for authenticity, the very other that the film is trying to erase. The film's subject is, quite literally, the settling of the frontier; its narrative follows the fortunes of a wagon train of white settlers on the Oregon Trail. Like so many other westerns, this one tells the story of the coming of white civilization to the wilderness. It is about, among other things, the power of community and the enfranchising of that white community as the natural inheritors of the frontier. "Oh! Susanna" is part of this enterprise.

One of the ways in which the community coalesces in the western is through rituals, ceremonies that bind together the people who enact them. Often in the western, these rituals revolve around music: weddings, funerals, sing-alongs, and dances of all sorts. In *The Covered Wagon*, the fragile community of settlers, awaiting the start of the wagon train's westward journey, amuses itself with music. As the film opens, young Johnny Wingate, the son of the wagon master, strums a banjo, singing "Oh! Susanna" as the actual sheet music for Foster's tune appears in superimposition over the boy's performance. There is to be no mistake as to what the boy is singing: an "authentic" frontier song sung to the accompaniment of an "authentic" western instrument, the banjo. The

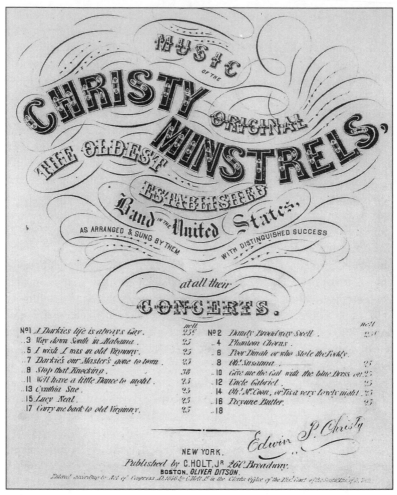

Fig. 7.1. In its original 1848 printing, "Oh! Susanna" is defined by its minstrel origins. Stephen Foster, whose name does not appear on the cover, was an unknown composer at the time and the Christy Minstrels America's most successful minstrel troupe. University of California, Los Angeles, Music Library special edition.

lyrics of the song itself, with its narrative construction around a journey west and its emphasis on restless wandering, optimism, and determination evokes the myth of white America's unproblematic and preordained mission to settle the frontier. Of course, settling the frontier meant taking it away from the Native Americans, whose land it was, and disenfranchising the Mexican Americans, who got there first. But the use of "Oh! Susanna" with its resonance of authenticity and western folk attachments helped to cover over just these troublesome aspects of America's national venture.

But "Oh! Susanna" has more to tell us here, or more to reveal about the complex and convoluted history of the frontier and its representation

Fig. 7.2. By 1935, the minstrel origins of "Oh! Susanna" had been elided. In this edition, the covered wagon displaces Christy's Minstrels. University of California, Los Angeles, Music Library Special Collections.

in the filmic western. A community, of course, exists in relation to what it is not, to what it has come together to protect itself against or to eliminate. The community in *The Covered Wagon* is established in a way characteristic of the genre as a whole: through exclusion of the other, who is defined as racially and/or ethnically different. The western is always, on some level, about American identity, about who is American and who is not. And in *The Covered Wagon* it is clear who is who. The film's opening intertitle reads, "The blood of America is the blood of pioneers—the blood of lion-hearted men and women who carved a splendid civilization out of an uncharted wilderness." Here is white America's entitlement to the wilderness.

167

That the white settlers who move across the frontier from Kansas to Oregon are uniquely American is established by default: absent from the assembled group of pioneers are any African Americans, Mexicans, or Native Americans. In fact, the film goes to some lengths to rationalize the exclusion of these groups, constructing the Native Americans who appear in the film as wild Indians, murderously possessive of land they do not know how to utilize, and defining Mexicans and Mexican-Americans as the mortal enemy in a recent war (the Mexican American War of 1848).

One of the most resonant occurrences of "Oh! Susanna" is the one that ends the film. Will Banion, the protagonist, has been an outcast for most of the film because he has been labeled, unfairly, a cattle rustler. Upon his arrival in Oregon, he seeks out his true love, Molly Wingate. It is only after Molly learns that Will, as an officer in the Mexican American War, commandeered (not rustled) cattle to feed his hungry men, that she forgives him. As they reconcile at her family's farm, they are serenaded by young Johnny Wingate to the strains of none other than "Oh! Susanna." The film ends as it began, with reference to one of the western's most potent markers of authenticity: a minstrel song by Stephen Foster. Its effect is to ratify the union of the white heterosexual couple as the archetypal American family unit and the true inheritors of the West.

The presence of African Americans, at least on the narrative level, is more invisible. There are no African Americans in the film, nor references to slavery or the impending Civil War. African Americans haunt the film in a different way. In its appropriation of minstrelsy, the film activates their presence. It seems to me that the banjo is an especially telling connection here. Thus trailing in the wake of "Oh! Susanna" comes exactly what the film has worked to exclude: the African-American other, a presence the film cannot entirely repress.

The Covered Wagon is not the only film explicitly about the settling of the frontier to use minstrel song. There are scores of other films that do so. Westerns often use minstrel song to harness historical "authenticity" to ideology. For instance, in Republic Picture's *Gunsmoke Ranch*, a contemporary western about settlers in Arizona, "Oh! Susanna" is used not only to reconstitute the historical West but to enfranchise controversial Depression-era homesteading in the Arizona desert. The Gene Autry vehicle *Oh, Susanna* exploits its title song in a similar fashion. "Oh! Susanna" connects the contemporary West of the thirties in which the film is set to the nineteenth century frontier and its values. This connection between the Old West and the New West renders less problematic the appearance of outdated notions of frontier justice that appear in the film (a public execution, by hanging, for instance, or the protagonist being "forced" to take the law into his own hands). *The Telegraph Trail*, a Warner Brothers western, similarly uses minstrelsy to authorize its ideological project, Manifest Destiny. *The Telegraph Trail* tells the story of the transcontinental telegraph and its transformation of the wilderness into civilization. What the telegraph protects white settlers from is, of course, "infernal redskins," and the film's dramatic conclusion, an Indian attack on a wagon train, demonstrates the power of the "singing wires." Settlements not yet connected to the telegraph are vulnerable: the frontier is constructed as threatening and potentially terrifying, subject to both lawlessness and the ever-present threat of Indian attack. What the telegraph brings is the power of white authority to control these elements by expelling them and that is just what happens in the film's dramatic conclusion: in the midst of an Indian attack on a wagon train, Army scout John Trent (John Wayne) rides to a telegraph pole to tap out the urgent cry for rescue. The cavalry soon appears and the Indians are sent back into the wilderness from whence they came (minus their chief and their white instigator). There is a real sense in this film that whites are under threat: the town cannot control the lawless elements within it and the army troops sent to erect the telegraph are prey to the Indians who pick them off as they climb the poles. The cavalry in this film is on the vanguard of white settlement, carving out a safe space in the wilderness through the technology of the telegraph. But until the final link is connected, danger lurks everywhere. As in *The Covered Wagon*, in *The Telegraph Trail* civilization is defined as white, the wilderness is there for the taking, and Indians are bloodthirsty savages with no claim to the land they inhabit.

But race turns out to be a slippery business in *The Telegraph Trail*. The most reprehensible "Indian" in the film is Gus Lynch, a white man who instigates insurrection among the Indians for his own profit. And during the climactic Indian siege at the end of the film, John Trent exchanges clothing and weaponry with a dead Indian in order to reach the wagon train safely. These moments of confusion and exchange between whites and Indians bring the submerged politics of race to the surface of the film to confound its narrative trajectory. If the Indians are not murderous savages hell-bent on exterminating white settlers (but only whipped up by irresponsible whites), why is it of the utmost importance to protect oneself from them? Who is the real enemy? What is it that the telegraph is protecting settlers from, exactly? For these reasons, the film's narrative conclusion lacks conviction.

Trent's masquerade as an Indian troubles the film even more. After telegraphing the fort for rescue, Trent must sneak back to the wagon train, now surrounded by Indians. He removes his shirt, dons the headdress of a dead Indian, and exchanges his gun for a tomahawk. His masquerade is so successful that he is almost shot by his friend, Jonesy (Frank McHugh), who, luckily for Trent, is a poor shot. Again, race cracks open the narrative. If Indians are so completely other, how is it that a white man can so easily masquerade as one? Here *The Telegraph Trail* taps into the unconscious of the western through one of its most persistent undercurrents: the collapse of difference between the white man and the Indian and the consequence of the identification between them. In its more sinister version, the exchange of identity between whites and Indians results in violence

(John Ford's *The Iron Horse*, for example, or even *The Searchers*). In its more benign form, whites embrace Indian culture, willingly taking on the other's identity often, but not always, with tragic results (*Broken Arrow*, Kevin Costner's *Dances with Wolves*, Cecil B. DeMille's *The Squaw Man*, John Ford's *The Searchers*). In either version of this scenario, social constructions of race and racial difference begin to collapse and the endings of these films bear the burden of containment, often unsuccessfully. In *The Telegraph Trail*, the telegraph link is completed and, as if in direct consequence, the defeated Indians ride back into the wilderness. Yet one can't help but think how precarious the telegraph is: one snip of the wire at any point on its journey and it is useless.

There are no African Americans in *The Telegraph Trail*, but the racial turmoil stirred up by the conflation of white men and Indians bubbles up on the soundtrack in another form. In one sequence, the cavalry camps for the night and the men gather around the fire to entertain themselves. With a banjo, guitar, and harmonica, they perform three "western" songs: "Jubilo," "Oh! Susanna," and "Mandy Lee," two of which are minstrel songs. Through "Oh! Susanna" and "Jubilo," what the film represses—the presence of African Americans on the frontier—returns. "Oh! Susanna," as I have already argued, functions as a marker of and replacement for African Americans. "Jubilo" provides an even stronger marker.

"Jubilo" is an abolitionist song, published in 1862 and sung on the minstrel stage that same year. With its exaggerated blackface dialect and its abolitionist message, the song is one of the best examples of the contradictions contained (or more precisely, not contained) in minstrelsy. Written by Henry Clay Work, who grew up in a noted abolitionist family (his childhood home was a part of the underground railroad), "Jubilo" tells the story of a plantation awaiting the arrival of Abraham Lincoln's soldiers. The master, described as "six foot one way, two foot tudder" and weighing "tree hundred pound," has departed in advance of the Union Army and the slaves have tied up the overseer and taken over the plantation. This was not a sentimental ballad filled with helpless African-American women and children. Here were powerful African-American men who had seized control of the master's property. This was pretty heady stuff for 1862, a year ahead of the Emancipation Proclamation and three years from the end of the war. Yet within a week of the song's publication, the Christy Minstrels successfully included "Jubilo" in their act. The exploitation of minstrel conventions to tap into the public's consciousness was a commonplace strategy for abolitionists and this wasn't the first song that Work had written for the Christys. "Jubilo" was popular throughout the North and especially among African Americans. Reportedly, African-American troops liberating Richmond, Virginia, sang the song as they marched into town. It was even popular in the South, where it passed into folklore. In the 1930s, "Jubilo" was published as an Ozark folk song; by the fifties it became a North Carolina folk song and finally an Alabama folk song.[48]

Of all the minstrel songs that voiced antislavery sentiments, "Jubilo" seems to have retained the most of its abolitionist past. Like "Oh! Susanna," it has had a remarkably long shelf life: it was a part of the popular repertoire in this country for at least fifty years after its publication and is regularly anthologized in American songbooks. (A colleague of mine showed me a piano book she had studied as a child with "Jubilo" arranged for young players by the eminent piano pedagogue John Schaum.) Two John Ford Civil War films use the song and connect it to African Americans: in *The Horse Soldiers* (1959) it can be heard on the soundtrack during an African-American church service, and in *Sergeant Rutledge* (1960) it is connected to Rutledge, an African-American soldier. Abolition, slavery, and race are close to the surface of "Jubilo," creating resonances from which the song has not entirely shaken free. Thus, when a film such as *The Telegraph Trail* uses "Jubilo" in the guise of cowboy entertainment, it is not without some friction. Narrative conventions of the western can well absorb a sequence of cowboys unpacking guitars and harmonicas around the campfire. But when a banjo appears on the open range and the trio of musicians play a minstrel song with abolitionist sympathies, race, the absent but organizing principle of the film, surfaces. Films about the settling of the West, such as *The Telegraph Trail,* are at some pains to establish what the settlers stand in opposition to: the Indians, the visible menace, and African Americans (and others), the invisible one. "Jubilo" and "Oh! Susanna" trouble that invisibility, bringing into focus, if only momentarily, what the film has worked to repress.

Minstrel song entered popular culture as "American," defined in public debate as a singular expression of American values and character. It is interesting how many western film scores depend upon minstrelsy's associations with Americanness to cover over problematic gaps or contradictions in their narratives. A film such as *The Royal Rodeo*, distills in its soundtrack an association that many westerns would use: the convergence of minstrel song and American patriotic tunes. Thus minstrel song becomes encoded with patriotism, its sound a rallying point for American values. *The Royal Rodeo* begins with the introduction of mythical Avania's adolescent monarch, seated on his throne and reading pulp fiction, *Bill Stevens and the Indians.* Much to the bored youngster's delight, the actual Bill Stevens (John Payne) and his Wild West Rodeo soon arrive in Avania with cowboys on horseback and Indians in tow. The king convinces Bill to perform in the palace itself, where a full-blown rodeo materializes. After some palace intrigue and a failed coup d'état, Bill and the Wild West Rodeo celebrate the monarch's restoration with a songfest and square dance to the accompaniment of the cowboy performers singing "In the Good Old American Way," an arrangement of original material, patriotic tunes, and minstrel songs. That this climactic celebration is harnessed to the restoration of a European monarchy creates a slightly edgy moment.

Music, and specifically minstrel song, is a part of the process by which such ideological contradictions (cowboys celebrating the return of the monarchy) are covered over. When "Oh! Susanna" and "Dixie" find themselves in the company of "Yankee Doodle Dandy," "Columbia, the Gem of the Ocean," and the refrain "In the good, old American way," questions about the nature of democracy and the relationship between America and European monarchies (a question not without contemporary import in 1939) recede into the film's subtextual background. When the young king reveals that underneath his princely garb he is wearing a cowboy outfit and packing two pistols, the triumph of American values is complete, and Manifest Destiny has changed directions and found its way to Europe.

Virginia City plays out the connections among minstrelsy, patriotism, and Americanness more fully, and not as successfully. Mapping the Civil War onto the western landscape, the film chronicles the story of two men, one fighting for the North and one fighting for the South, as they make their way west and meet in Virginia City, Nevada, at the close of the war. Supposedly based on a true story, as the film's titles triumphantly announce, the film posits Virginia City as a Union stronghold filled with Confederate sympathizers launching a desperate scheme to transport five million dollars in gold to Jefferson Davis. Many of the conventions of Civil War dramas are grafted onto the western: two men of like minds separated by war and positioned as mortal enemies; a woman shared between them; and a reconciliation scene as one of them dies. Minstrel songs appear, along with patriotic songs, in the saloon sequences, where they help to establish historical authenticity. The conjunction of minstrel song and patriotic song in *Virginia City*, however, is not entirely successful in covering over the potentially threatening presence of race embodied in the historical context of the film. Here the contradictions regarding race contained in minstrelsy collide with contradictions occasioned by the historical context of the film, resulting in narrative moments in which race bubbles to the surface.

It's interesting to note the relative absence of African Americans in this Civil War saga. The initial scenes of the film transpire in the besieged South. The film works hard to activate the plantation myth: male slaves jovially converse with retreating Confederate soldiers (one slave complains about his wife), a plantation is used as the headquarters for Confederate President Jefferson Davis, and a southern belle and gentlemenly Southerners fill the scenes. This is the only place in the film where African Americans literally appear. But the other, generally, and the issue of slavery, particularly, return in the frontier portion of the film.

Even before the protagonists reach Virginia City by stage, they meet and must confront a Mexican bandit (played by Humphrey Bogart!). With his dark makeup and thick accent, Bogart's character Murrell provides the western's ever-ready stand-in for African Americans: the Mexican outlaw. The arrival of the protagonists into Virginia City occasions a different type of substitution. A rally celebrating the Union victory at Vicksburg precedes the arrival of the stage. Union supporters sing "The Battle Hymn of the Republic" and carry placards bearing messages such as

"Death to the Rebels." One of those placards is privileged with a close-up: on it a stick figure is being lynched. It is a powerfully disturbing image that contains a potent (and presumably unconscious) reminder of the historical reality of lynching as a tool for the repression of African Americans. A few scenes later, we see an actual mock lynching of a sawdust figure of Jefferson Davis, as the assembled crowd sings a version of "John Brown's Body": "We'll hang Jeff Davis from a sour apple tree." The reference to the abolitionist song "John Brown's Body," itself the precursor to "The Battle Hymn of the Republic," helps to anchor the images of lynching to the historical context of slavery and abolition. In these moments the subtext of race that the film has worked both to redefine and repress, surfaces. It is immediately after this sequence that minstrel song appears.

Minstrel songs in *Virginia City* become part of the dance-hall tunes in the diegetic background of the Sazarac saloon sequence.[49] Here minstrel songs alternate with one of the most popular Union songs of the Civil War, "The Battle Cry of Freedom" (aka "Rally Round the Flag, Boys") by George Frederick Root. In fact, "The Battle Cry of Freedom," (outsold in the north only by "The Battle Hymn of the Republic"), with its lyrics highlighting the Union's cause, is diegetically performed at the saloon. The patina of patriotism attached to this song rubs off on the minstrel tunes that bracket its performance, and the minstrel heritage of "Camptown Races," "Oh! Susanna," "Jubilo," and "Ring, Ring de Banjo" is subsumed into some larger sense of Americana. Minstrelsy's historical legacy as blackface performance is elided and minstrelsy itself redefined as patriotic music.

"Jubilo" troubles this textual operation, however, as does "Ring, Ring de Banjo"; these songs are two of minstrelsy's most explicit evocations of the potentially violent relationship in slavery between master and slave. Additionally, the title and chorus of "Ring, Ring de Banjo," with their direct references to the banjo, are a reminder of the song's minstrel heritage. And "Jubilo" in the forties retained at least some of its abolitionist attachments. Because of the explicit subject matter of the film (the Civil War), the inability of the image track to completely control the subtext of race, and the inclusion of "Jubilo" and "Ring, Ring, de Banjo" on the soundtrack (minstrel songs that are not as fully detached from their nineteenth-century roots and whose contradictory position on race is not fully controlled by the film's discourse), *Virginia City* offers an opportunity for the subject of race to emerge. I would argue that, on one level at least, an antiracist subtext emerges, a subtext that the film cannot entirely repress or control.

Minstrel song was an intricate part of America's frontier experience in the nineteenth century. But in the twentieth century, we have experienced what might be termed a cultural blindspot when it comes to minstrelsy, obscuring the fact that many frontier songs are minstrel songs of one sort or another. The diversity of the American frontier has been elided in

America's cultural memory, covered over by a powerful frontier mythology that constructs American identity in terms of whiteness. What I have tried to do here is recover that connection between frontier song and minstrelsy, both historically and in its filmic traces. In dime novels, popular literature, the melodramatic stage, and, of course, in motion pictures, the minstrel legacy of many frontier songs brings with it more than a reminder of the diverse experience the frontier presented. Minstrelsy brings with it the other, and the complicated discourse on race that has always been at the center of American identity.

notes

I would like to extend my thanks here to Janet Walker, whose intelligence, insight, and patience helped shape this article.

1. Edward J. Wheeler, *Deadwood Dick, The Prince of the Road: Or, The Black Rider of the Black Hills*, repr. in *Reading the West: An Anthology of Dime Novels*, ed. Bill Brown (Boston: Bedford, 1997), 339; Owen Wister, *The Virginian* (New York: Signet, 1979), 134.
2. For an illuminating history of song on the frontier, see David Dary, *Seeking Pleasure in the Old West* (New York: Knopf, 1995). Dary quotes the price of violins on page 28.
3. Bradbury's journals are summarized in Dary, *Seeking Pleasure*, 9–10.
4. The first successful minstrel song is generally credited to Micah Hawkins, whose "Backside Albany," written in 1814, was the first American song in blackface dialect to enjoy widespread popularity.
5. Margaret Fuller, for instance, writes deprecatingly of "Yankee Doodle" in 1842: "Our only national melody, *Yankee Doodle*, is . . . a scion from British art." *Dial* 3, no. 1 (1842), quoted in William W. Austin, *"Susanna," "Jeanie," and "The Old Folks at Home": The Songs of Stephen C. Foster from His Time to Ours* (New York: Macmillan, 1975), 59.
6. Moritz Busch, *Travels on the Hudson and the Mississippi* (Lexington: University of Kentucky Press, 1971), quoted in Austin, *"Susanna,"* 42.
7. Frederika Bremer, *The Homes of the New World* (London: A. Hall, 1853), 369 ff., quoted in Austin, *"Susanna,"* 45.
8. Bayard Taylor, *Eldorado (or Adventures in the Path of Empire, Mexico, and California* (New York: Putnam, 1882–83), 314, quoted in Austin, *"Susanna,"* 29–30.
9. J. Kennard, "Who Are Our National Poets?" *Knickerbocker* 26 (1845): 331, quoted in Austin, *"Susanna,"* 54; emphasis in the original.
10. Walt Whitman, *Walt Whitman Looks at the Schools*, ed. Florence Bernstein Freedman (New York: Kings Crown Press, 1950), 216, quoted in Austin, *"Susanna,"* 61.
11. Thus the English writer Charles Mackay, who published his reminiscences as *Life and Liberty in America*, writes that "the United States have done nothing in music. . . . The airs called "negro melodies," concocted for the most part in New York, . . . [are] old English, Scotch, and Irish melodies altered in time and character." The poet James Russell Lowell similarly assails the connection between minstrelsy and Americanness. In "The Power of Sound," Lowell writes, "But have we nothing that is wholly ours? / No songs commensurate with our growing powers?/Answer, whose ears have felt the torturing blows / Of lays like "Jump Jim Crow" and "Coal-black Rose." See Charles Mackay, *Life and Liberty* (New York: Harper, 1859), 299, quoted in Austin, *"Susanna,"* 48; and James Russell Lowell, "Fable," *Oxford Book of American Verse*, ed. F. O. Matthiesson (New York: Oxford University Press, 1950), 261, quoted in Austin, *"Susanna,"* 51.
12. Frederick Douglass wrote about minstrelsy in no uncertain terms. In 1848 he

attacked "the 'Virginia Minstrels,' 'Christy's Minstrels,' the 'Ethiopian Sere-
naders,' or any of the filthy scum of white society who have stolen from us a
complexion denied to them by nature, in which to make money ... [with]
'Old Zip Coon,' 'Jim Crow,' 'Ole Dan Tucker,' ... and a few other specimens
of *American* musical genius" (emphasis in the original). Quoted in Austin,
"Susanna," 66.

13. The most important of these is "I'm on My Way to Canada," sung to the tune
of "Oh! Susanna."

14. Only one, "Beautiful Dreamer," was published posthumously.

15. Some of Foster's sentimental ballads have also found their way into the mythology of the West. Ford's *Stagecoach* uses two: "Jeanie" and "Gentle Annie."

16. The possible exception is "Old Dog Tray," which although published as a minstrel song contains none of its characteristics, including the defining one: blackface dialect. For this reason, some music historians have chosen to classify "Old
Dog Tray" as a sentimental ballad, in which case it would be the one exception
to the claim that Foster's success came exclusively from minstrel songs.

17. As Ken Emerson puts it, "There was one problem with Foster's attempt to
branch out beyond blackface: He was going broke." The average return for a
blackface song was ten times that of a parlor song. See Ken Emerson, *Doo-Dah!
Stephen Foster and the Rise of American Popular Culture* (New York: Da Capo,
1998), 174.

18. Eric Lott, *Love and Theft: Blackface Minstrelsy and the American Working Class*
(New York: Oxford University Press, 1993), 6.

19. Ibid.

20. So did the eminent composer George Root, who studied composition in Paris
and wrote the popular Civil War song "Battle Cry of Freedom." Influenced by
Stephen Foster's success with the Christy Minstrels, Root wrote minstrel songs,
being careful to publish under the name F. Friederich Wurzel (*Wurzel* is "root"
in German).

21. Lott, *Love and Theft*, 4.

22. Annette Hamilton, "Fear and Desire: Aborigines, Asians and the National
Imaginary," *Australian Cultural History* 9 (1990): 16.

23. Ibid.

24. While minstrel song was primarily concerned with the African-American male,
it did occasionally represent the African-American female. She appears fraught
with contradiction: emasculating and/yet sexually alluring; domineering
and/yet sexually promiscuous. The representation of women in minstrelsy
would be a fascinating study in itself.

25. Charles Hamm, *Yesterdays: Popular Song in America* (New York and London:
Norton, 1979), 210.

26. Stephen C. Foster, "Oh! Susanna," in *The Music of Stephen C. Foster: A Critical
Edition*, vol. 1, ed. Steven Saunders and Deane L. Root (Washington, D.C.:
Smithsonian Institution Press, 1990), 41–43. (The fourth verse is also cited in
a number of sources, including Emerson, *Doo-Dah!* and Austin, *"Susanna."*)
All subsequent references to Foster's work are taken from this source.

27. Austin, *"Susanna,"* 7.

28. Emerson, *Doo-Dah!* 133.

29. Sam Dennison, *Scandalize My Name: Black Imagery in American Popular Music*
(New York: Garland, 1982), 78.

30. Lott, *Love and Theft*, 202.

31. Emerson, *Doo-Dah!* 66.

32. For a publication history of "Lou'siana Belle," see Emerson, *Doo-Dah!* 105–6.

33. Michael Rogin, *Blackface, White Noise: Jewish Immigrants in the Hollywood
Melting Pot* (Berkeley and Los Angeles: University of California Press, 1995),
22.

34. Ibid., 39.

35. For work that disputes this position, see Howard L. Sacks and Judith Rose
Sacks, *Way Up North in Dixie: A Black Family's Claim to the Confederate Anthem*
(Washington, D.C.: Smithsonian Institution Press, 1993). The Sackses make

an intriguing but not entirely convincing case for their position that "Dixie" was not written by its credited composer, Daniel Decautur Emmett, but plagiarized by him from a family of black performers, the Snowdens. The practice of blacks and whites sharing music and performance techniques in the nineteenth century has been well documented, but the Sackses case depends upon a sparse historical record and scant personal testimony. For Dan Emmett's dubious version of the circumstances surrounding the composition of "Dixie," see Hans Nathan, *Dan Emmett and the Rise of Early Negro Minstrelsy* (Norman: University of Oklahoma Press, 1962), 243–75.

36. In Foster's ouevre, there is one song that deviates from standard practice and approximates call-and-response structure: "Camptown Races," with its "Doo-Dah" refrain.

37. See Hamm, *Yesterdays*, 125.

38. Emerson, *Doo-Dah!* 70–71.

39. See Hamm, *Yesterdays*, 114.

40. Davy Crockett [pseud.], *An Account of Col. Crockett's Tour to the North and Down East,* 10th ed. (Philadelphia: E. L. Carey and A. Hart, 1837), 48, quoted in Emerson, *Doo-Dah!* 69. I would hasten to add here that this multiracial mix did not erase the pernicious effects of discrimination for African Americans.

41. This possibility is not lost on Eric Lott, however. See Lott, *Love and Theft*, 52.

42. Emerson, *Doo-Dah!* 10.

43. There are numerous sources documenting the influence of African-American culture on minstrel dance. Two particularly influential texts are Marshall Stearns and Jean Stearns, *Jazz Dance: The Story of American Vernacular Dance* (New York: Schirmer, 1968), esp. 35–60; and Marian Hannah Winter, "Juba and American Minstrelsy," *Dance Index*, ed. Lincoln Kirstein, Paul Magriel, and Donald Windham (New York: Arno, 1970), 28–47.

44. African-American minstrelsy, which began before the Civil War and blossomed after it, is a bit more of a mixed bag. While the form allowed African Americans performance opportunities and access to large, mainstream audiences, it also severely restricted the ways in which they could perform. (How African Americans performed in front of black audiences would be an important historical question to pursue.) Minstrelsy opened up careers for African Americans, but it determined the shape and direction of those careers. James K. Bland, the composer of "Carry Me Back to Old Virginny," was African American. During his lifetime, Bland published several hundred songs, many of which were wildly popular and some of which are still sung today. But all of them were written for the minstrel stage (and are largely indistinguishable from those written by whites). While African-American minstrelsy provided the forum for many entertainers to perfect their craft and move beyond its confines (W. C. Handy, Ma Rainey, Bessie Smith, to name a few), it also reinforced white stereotypes by having actual African Americans performing the parts constructed for them by whites. I agree with Michael Rogin's estimation of African-American minstrelsy: "Certainly . . . [it] pushed the form as far in the direction of Afro-American self-expression as it could go, though the spread of burnt cork to cover those it supposedly represented is hardly evidence of progress toward racial equality." See Rogin, *Blackface*, 44.

45. William Swain, quoted in J. S. Halliday, *The World Rushed In: The California Gold Rush Experience* (New York: Simon and Schuster, 1981), 322.

46. Anonymous miner, quoted in Emerson, *Doo-Dah!* 10.

47. Thanks to Nathaniel Shrout for bringing this example to my attention.

48. See Vance Randolph, *Ozark Folksongs*, vol. 2 (Columbia: State Historical Society of Missouri, 1948); Frank C. Brown, *The Frank C. Brown Collection of North Carolina Folklore*, vol. 2 (Durham, N.C.: Duke University Press, 1952); and Byron Arnold, *Folksongs of Alabama* (Birmingham: University of Alabama Press, 1950).

49. "Dixie" appears nondiegetically in this Max Steiner score in both major and minor modes as a marker of the Confederacy.

drums

along the

l.a. river

scoring

the indian

c l a u d i a   g o r b m a n

Film music is like the medium of a dream: it's largely forgotten in the
waking state, but this medium is itself not neutral. It conveys meanings
that are all the more powerful in not actively being noticed. How does
music represent the cultural or ethnic other in movies, and what might
be the implications of such musical encoding on moviegoing? This essay
examines the American western's music for Indians onscreen, and
explores the kinds of cultural and political meanings constructed through
these musical representations. Can we trace a history of the musical
coding of Indians, and what has been its heritage in the poststudio era
since the 1960s?

The western's pervasiveness in literature, drama, painting, film, and
television testifies to its significance as a rich reservoir of material about
what it means to be American. Its setting in a particular historical period,
roughly 1865 to 1900, embodies a defining moment in the nation's
psychosocial evolution. These years embrace the aftermath of the Civil
War, the American Industrial Revolution and the building of the
railroads, the ongoing establishment of markets and routes for westward

expansion, the apogee of the Indian Wars, and the reservation movement. The movie western centers on the white male hero in some aspect of the process of pushing ever westward the borderline between "civilization" and "wilderness."

Among the hero's adversaries are nature, outlaws, and Indians. It is well understood that the Indian plays a key role as the cultural other. The nature of this otherness has changed in tune with social and political history through the twentieth century. Using a very broad brush, one might say that the Indian served in films of the 1930s and 1940s as an obstacle to the fulfillment of Manifest Destiny. In the 1950s and beyond, the Indian continued to be a symbolic repository of various American fears and preoccupations, such as black-white relations and the "Red (read Communist) scare." Precious few of these social preoccupations pertained to actual Native American people's history or politics, especially before the American Indian Movement of the early 1970s.

What role does *music* have in determining the spectator's reception of the other—or better yet, how does music inflect the nature and degree of the Indian's otherness?

Let us begin with the familiar musical clichés. In the classical, pre–World War II western, the film score represented Indians through a small inventory of stable and unambiguous musical conventions. Often accompanying the onscreen Indian savage is the "tom-tom" rhythmic drumming figure of equal beats, the first of every four beats accented (DUM-dum-dum-dum). This percussive figure is typically heard either played by actual drums or as a repeated bass note or pair of notes in perfect fifths, played in the low strings.

Additionally, a modal melody might be heard above the tom-tom rhythm, sometimes monophonically, sometimes in parallel fourths, often with a falling third (e.g., F–D) concluding a melodic phrase. A more "threatening" variant of the melody line consists of a two-note motif, the initial note being brief and strongly accented, followed by a longer note a second or third lower. Examples of these patterns abound in popular culture, from movies to recorded song to television commercials.[1]

The Indian-on-the-warpath cliché accounts for most Indian music before 1950, but not all. Just as the feminine other in Hollywood cinema appears as a binary set—as either the madonna/wife accompanied by violins, or the vamp/whore introduced by a sultry jazz saxophone or clarinet, movie Indians are manifested either as bloodthirsty marauders or romanticized noble savages. The noble savage trope comes from the literary tradition of Henry Wadsworth Longfellow and James Fenimore Cooper,[2] depicting the Indian as the natural man, the emblem of the lost Eden. Movies musically stereotype the romantic Indian by deleting the tom-tom rhythm and featuring a legato, rather than staccato and angular, modal melody played by flute or strings, accompanied by sweet, pastoral harmonies.[3]

antecedents: musical stereotypes and the "indianists"

Where did these musical stereotypes come from? Part of the answer is that they descend from a Euro-American all-purpose shorthand for representing primitive or exotic peoples. By the nineteenth century, musical representation of Turks, the Chinese, Scots, and generic peasants tend toward pentatonicism, rhythmic repetitiveness, and intervals of fourths or fifths.[4] Reviewing these devices in concert music of the nineteenth century, musicologist Michael Pisani pinpoints what he calls a "ready-made toolbox of exotica whenever nineteenth-century European or Europe-trained American composers undertook Indian topics for the stage."[5] Pisani finds an example of the stereotypical features as early as 1859 in Robert Stoepel's symphony *Hiawatha*. His hypothesis is that the clichés emerge mostly on the popular stage throughout the century. This development was most probably inflected later in the century by actual exposure to Indian song through the new availability of ethnographic recordings, and through Wild West shows, to sound a bit more Indian and a bit less all-purpose exotic. Virtually all the ephemeral music for popular stage entertainments is lost. But by the 1910s, it is the clichés developed for these entertainments that make their way into silent movie music collections for movie-house accompanists, such as those of Erno Rapée (1924) and the Sam Fox volumes of the 1910s (composed by J. S. Zamecnik).

Whatever factors determined the development of the musical clichés for Indians, let it be clear that the resultant conventions bear little relation to authentic Indian music, which is entirely different in instrumentation (no violins!) and most often consists of sung monodic melodies or chants, in any of a number of scales, accompanied by a regular drumbeat without that Hollywood downbeat. Furthermore, there is great variety in the musics of the great variety of nations or tribes, yet the stage, and then Hollywood, assigned the same formulas to all.

I have noted that ethnographers' transcriptions (and later, field recordings) of actual songs of American Indian tribes beginning in the 1880s seem to have had less direct bearing on the evolution of the popular stereotypes. Authentic tribal music was, however, appropriated by certain art composers in the period 1890–1920.[6] A digression into these art-song adapations by the so-called Indianist composers will prove illuminating. In the context of romantic composers' fascination with the exotic, the music of the Negro and American Indian offered a new source of inspiration as these composers consciously strove to develop an American school of composition. This movement was inspired by Antonin Dvořák, who, during his stay in the United States from 1892 to 1895 famously declared that such indigenous music could provide "all that is needed for a great and noble school of music."[7]

The Indianist impulse caught on and saw a vogue. At the popular end of the spectrum was the composer Charles Wakefield Cadman, who had

179

a gift for facile expression. His song "At Dawning" was taken up by the celebrated tenor John McCormack and enjoyed phenomenal success, eventually selling over a million copies. Cadman's song "In the Land of the Sky-Blue Water" did comparably well.

The more accomplished composer Arthur Farwell (1872–1951) stood at the vanguard of the movement. His 1901 collection of pieces for piano, *American Indian Melodies*, adapted ten tribal songs from transcriptions by Harvard University ethnologist Alice C. Fletcher.[8] Farwell set these melodies in a nineteenth-century harmonic idiom, thus fashioning what sounds to the modern-day ear like conventional salon pieces out of vocal monody from an entirely alien culture.[9]

In the introduction to this collection, Farwell stated that his piano adaptations were engendered by the spirit of the occasion on which the songs would be sung in their native cultural context, thus gaining a new cachet of the exotic. As he explained, "I realized that if the musical imagination could be fired by a consideration of the particular legend pertaining to a song, it will give rise to a combination of harmonies . . . vitally connected with the song's essence, its spiritual significance. . . . The final result is the consequence of a trained intellect seizing upon, and expressing in a mode comprehensible to its kind, a feeling already developed in a race whose mode of expression is more primitive, or perhaps merely different."[10]

A century later, the reader of Farwell's comments may find the musical appropriation and remarks by a "trained intellect" to be a rather bald example of imperialism. As progressive an impulse as this was at the time, does it not have as its end result the self-consciously liberal, high-art equivalent of the tom-tom stereotype that prevailed in popular culture of the period? Farwell's early songs, as well as those of other Indianists, are sentimental arrangements. Their faithfulness to the Indian melody in the top voice produces little variation from turn-of-the-century convention, aside from shifts in time signature and an often repetitious upper melody. "The song's essence, its spiritual significance," leading to its "more complete expression," is determined through Farwell's Euro-American sensibility.

But looking beyond the inadvertent cultural imperialism, we recognize here an issue central to any cross-cultural understanding, which we might call the issue of translation or mediation. In what respects can a listener "understand" the musical language of an alien culture without some form of mediation, whether this be the listener's education, a mixing of idioms, or a translation in some other sense? This issue is, of course, more pressing now than ever before, as commercial interests pick and choose among the world's musicians and musical traditions in the insatiable search for new sounds to add to the global pop mix. Musicologist Richard Crawford has discussed the dialectical tension between *authenticity* and *accessibility*: something is always lost in even the most faithful transporting of music from one culture into another, in each stage of presenting original music to a mass audience.[11] What can an Osage chant "mean" to a Euro-American listener in 1890? To what degree can we consider the transcriptions of the Plains songs, then their harmonizations, faithful? Farwell's final sentence above clearly if self-servingly indicates the problem of bringing such alien music to white America "in a mode comprehensible to its kind." I shall return to this question of mediation further on, especially in discussing the score of *A Man Called Horse.*

Temporarily leaving the art song aside and returning to the cinema's tom-tom and modal stereotypes, we can summarize that the formulas we now know so well arose in tandem with the Indian conflicts of the nineteenth century and entered popular culture primarily through melodrama, fairs and Wild West shows, and other forms of popular theater. Presumably when the Indian became a stock character on the stage, stock Indian music developed accordingly. Certainly stock Indian music for the cinema had come into full bloom by the second decade of the 1900s.[12] Hugo Riesenfeld's incidental music for *The Covered Wagon* (1923) borrowed liberally from clichés circulating in his day, and was widely imitated in subsequent silent westerns.

the classical western

The coming of sound to the cinema may actually have pared down and consolidated the already limited range of representations of Indians. For the most part, the Indian in 1930s westerns was a threat to the white hero, and the music playing behind him was de rigueur stereotypical. The score of John Ford's *Stagecoach* (1939, by the team of Richard Hageman, John Liepold, W. Franke Harling and Leo Shuken) is a locus classicus of Indian music in the pre–World War II sound western, and demonstrates how such music functioned as an efficient narrative cue.

The main titles include a few bars of Indian music. Over shots of silhouetted Indians, the tom-tom motif enters in the form of fifths in the low strings; then one hears the two-note motif in French horns, joined by trumpets, with a brief section of the treble voices moving in parallel fourths (see figure 8.1, section A). Barely two minutes into the story, soldiers at a cavalry post learn that the telegraph line to Lordsburg has been cut. The villain responsible, and the last word that got through before the line went dead? Geronimo! and the Indian theme plays behind the uttering of his name.

Much later, during a rest stop on the stagecoach's odyssey from Tonto to Lordsburg, the Ringo Kid (John Wayne) looks off toward the hills. The camera has no need to pan to the smoke he sees on the horizon: we hear a modal melody in parallel fourths (see figure 8.1, section B). And so it goes with each reference to the Indians. What may well be the quintessential moment of this encoding for Hollywood westerns arrives in the scene showing the stagecoach from a high angle, wending its way through Monument Valley. The familiar main title theme (an orchestral version of "O Bury Me Not On the Lone Prairie") plays—until the camera flash-pans over to the ridge to reveal a group of Apaches on horseback, spying on the stagecoach from above—accompanied by a fortissimo line of trumpets in parallel fourths, a drum thundering the requisite tom-tom beat, and trombones (playing the two-note motif) in dialogue with the trumpets (see figure 8.1, section C). Cut back to the stagecoach, the western music for a few seconds—and a second flash-pan to the warriors, again with the Indian-on-the-warpath music.

Fig. 8.1. "Indian Music" from the score of *Stagecoach* (1939).

What to say about the insistence, and automatism, of this welding of stereotypic music and image? Wordless throughout the film, and virtually invisible until this scene and the climactic chase sequence on the plain, the Indians serve as the faceless antagonist, often signaled by music alone. One must bear in mind that the Indian musical clichés are sonic signs, useful bearers of meaning in the system of classical Hollywood film music, whose overriding drive is to convey narrative and emotive meanings with hyperexplicit clarity. Were the Indian music to stray from the well-established conventions, it would not be doing its job. Both visually and musically, the Indians are reduced to bits of local color, narrative functions. The paucity of musical language for designating them of course stands in direct contrast to the variety of musical expression for the hero and other individualized white characters as they move through their narrative trajectory.

postwar westerns

After the war, the western hero became a man of reflection as well as action. Older, more battered and worn, he was not so certain of "civilized" America's moral superiority and divine right. The hero's faltering machismo becomes identified with a political uncertainty, with the increasingly questionable prerogative of Manifest Destiny. As part and parcel of the new psychological and politically relativist tendencies of the period, some postwar westerns took on the project of humanizing the Indian. *Devil's Doorway* (Anthony Mann, 1950), *Broken Arrow* (Delmer Daves, 1950), and others would serve as catharses for national guilt, portraying the Indians as proud, intelligent, misunderstood and oppressed. The Indians' aggression is revealed as a defense against encroachment on their lands, and against the cruelty and ignorance of white settlers and soldiers. What prompted one French critic to call 1950 "the 1789 of the western" is the sheer number of films whose project was to rehabilitate the Indian.[13] Of course, many movies after 1950 continued to portray Indians with the traditional faceless-savage stereotypes, but here we are interested in the liberal or revisionist western and its musical portrayals. It should be clarified that the true subject of the liberal western is rarely the Indian, but the white hero as reflected in the Indian's otherness. The Indian remains a foil for the hero's negotiation of his identity. Indian characters with speaking parts are portrayed by white actors, and there are rarely any efforts made to portray them authentically, or to distinguish among tribes.

Let us now focus on three representative liberal westerns, from 1950, 1970, and 1990. All three—*Broken Arrow*, *A Man Called Horse* (Eliot Silverstein), and *Dances with Wolves* (Kevin Costner)—have similar plots. A hero slowly befriends a tribe considered by the whites to be hostile and dangerous. Each hero learns the ways of the tribe; each falls in love with an Indian woman and marries her. The Indians emerge as people of honor, and white society is revealed in its boorish, destructive ignorance; the hero finds himself in a tragic position between the two cultures. *Broken Arrow* is a manifestation of postwar antiracism and anti-anticommunism. It is also a product of its time in its optimism; its revisionist history making depicts fair treaties being drawn up between the U.S. government and the Native Americans as equals.[14] *A Man Called Horse* was released at the height of U.S. military involvement in Vietnam and Cambodia; the Indian community it depicts stands metaphorically for both Southeast Asia and a hippie fantasy counterculture—organic, natural, spiritual, psychedelic, and free of the constraints of conventional society.[15] *Dances with Wolves*, for its part, responds to 1980s cultural debates on postfeminism, multiculturalism, and environmentalism. The truly civilized society here belongs to the Sioux; white society is shown to be decadent, mad, and brutal.

Indians in 1950s westerns variously represent actual Indians (in a new spirit of historical revisionism), communists (in the context of the McCarthy era), and African Americans.[16] On this latter point, Thomas Cripps traces the depiction of blacks in postwar American film, and shows that the touchy subject of race emerged in disguised form. Since so many African Americans had fought in the armed forces overseas, political pressure came to bear on the studios to move beyond the degrading stereotypes for black characters. A number of postwar films began to portray black characters and racial problems with new depth, in a cycle of message movies that included *Pinky* (1949), *Intruder in the Dust* (1949), and *No Way Out* (1950). But race relations could be treated with even more frankness once safely couched in the guise of a western. So movies from *Broken Arrow* and *Devil's Doorway* to *Flaming Star* (1960) explored in a remarkably candid way the virulent hatreds of white society.[17]

Delmer Daves's *Broken Arrow* is emblematic of the new meanings overdetermining the Indian. Tom Jeffords (James Stewart) comes upon an injured young Apache in the wilds. Instead of shooting him, he realizes that "an Apache woman would cry over her son like any other woman," and nurses him to health. "Tired of all the killing," Jeffords learns Chiricahua Apache ways and succeeds in befriending the Apache chief Cochise (Jeff Chandler), as well as marrying an Apache girl, Sunseeahray (Debra Paget). He serves as an intermediary between Cochise and General Howard, whose mandate is to establish peace in Arizona. Racist whites raid the Apaches, killing Jeffords's wife in the process and threatening the fragile truce. But Cochise exercises even greater conciliatory restraint than the sacrificial liberal Jeffords, and resolves to keep the peace: "As I bear the murder of my people, so you will bear the murder of your wife."

The success of *Broken Arrow* spawned many socially conscious westerns in the 1950s that rewrote history in terms of peaceful coexistence and reconciliation, and which seriously probed racism in dominant white society.[18]

postwar western music: the 1950s and 1960s

Once the western began to diversify in its depiction of Indians, what happened to the musical score? Logically we might expect that the simple labeling via the classical "Indian motifs" would no longer suffice. But even in the 1950s liberal western, musical representations evolved slowly at best.

Hugo Friedhofer's score for *Broken Arrow* is typical in remaining well within the established conventions. The principal Apache motif for Cochise and his tribe draws on the hoary clichés, and the music for Jeffords's romance with his Indian beloved, in its flute-and-strings modal sweetness, is also in keeping with the pastoral side of the Hollywood Indian. The greatest difference from prewar western scores arises from the story's very emphasis on the Indian. Since the movie dwells at some length on events in the Apache village, the score is called on to elaborate on characters, moods, and action in a more varied and sustained way than the classical western demands. This does not mean that the score is much more nuanced, however: the Apaches are still treated musically as either savage or noble.

The main title theme, associated with the Apaches, is predictably modal. As the film opens, the Apache theme plays as soon as Jeffords (James Stewart) comes upon an injured brave (see figure 8.2). Later, Jeffords travels to Cochise's stronghold deep in Indian territory, and the theme is announced in full force by brass instruments, accompanied by the tom-tom figure on the tympani. At the climactic peace conference bringing Cochise and the other Apache leaders together with Jeffords and General Howard, we hear the Apache theme: fifths in the bass, the melody played by the brasses in fourths, and more dissonances than usual in a particularly serious and grave arrangement.

Figure 8.2. Apache theme from *Broken Arrow* (1950).

The treatment of diegetic Indian music is also significant. On his first visit to the village, Jeffords makes his pitch to Cochise about allowing the U.S. mail riders to travel undisturbed through Apache territory. When they have finished talking business, Cochise invites Jeffords to stay overnight in the village, where a ceremony happens to be in progress. This scene has been described by Anne Dhu McLucas as the film's "big musical surprise," for what we see and hear are the actual music and dance of the Mountain Spirit from the girls' puberty ceremony of the White Mountain Apache. It is a surprise, because Hollywood cinema as a rule does not worry about authenticity—one chanting voice with drums is just as good as another.

In truth, seeing Indians singing and dancing in a western has the same effect as seeing Indians speaking their language. Such sights show the Indians as the impenetrable other. Their language and music bestow their aura, give them the stamp of authenticity. Sometimes a character—a white old-timer, a half-breed, or an Indian leader—will explain what is said or sung. *Broken Arrow* adopts the conceit that when we hear the Indians speak English, we are to understand that they are speaking Chiricahua. Some movies after the 1960s provide subtitles as Indians speak. But singing—whether really that of the tribe depicted or not—is most often unmediated for the white listener.

Recall that the Indianist composers' idealizing harmonizations of Indian tribal songs are in part an attempt to make the songs intelligible to Euro-American listeners. It is curious that such a strategy of musical mediation did not occur to Friedhofer or indeed any Hollywood composers at the time. There must have existed a desire to preserve the diegetic music as *sound effects*, rather than a language to be understood, and simultaneously to retain the clichés of orchestral "Indian music" on the other hand: both strategies *keep the Indians alien.*

In *Broken Arrow*, then, the system of authentic diegetic tribal songs and orchestral modal-and-tom-tom music preserves the basic self/ other dichotomy. Someone made a considerable effort to represent Apache culture with a modicum of fidelity. All the same, when it comes to clueing the filmgoer in on an important dramatic development such as the surge of feeling between Jeffords and Sunseeahray when they embrace after the colorful ceremony scene, romantic orchestral background music quickly takes over, featuring a celeste as well as the requisite strings, as if to ensure complete readability.

A musical theme is assigned to the romance between Jeffords and Sunseeahray. This features a modal flute melody accompanied by simple harmonies in the strings; in later iterations, flute, oboe, or violins carry the melody (see figure 8.3, section A). Curiously, after their nuptial night, a viola dripping with sentiment plays a different, nonmodal (and non-"Indian") melody as Jeffords promises he'll never leave her for his own people (see figure 8.3, section B).

claudia gorbman

Fig. 8.3. Romance themes from *Broken Arrow* (1950).

Has their marriage canceled out Sunseeahray's otherness? Although the film shows Jeffords now living among the Apache, the music suggests that ethnically the union of white man and Indian woman is white. The music, verbal language, and use of Caucasian actors encodes the hybrid sexual union as assimilated not to Indian but white culture—signifying encompassment of the other by the (white) self.

The second romantic melody is the theme upon which the film ends. Sunseeahray has been killed in the white men's ambush, and as Jeffords rides off into the future, his heart full, violins play their nonmodal romantic theme. When push comes to shove, Friedhofer seems to suggest, local color must cede to "real" musical language. Music in the film belies the film's ostensible cross-racialism.

Despite its beauty and variety of expression, Friedhofer's soundtrack for *Broken Arrow* is well ensconced in the late-Romantic tradition of the classical film score. Other liberal westerns, with rare exceptions such as David Raksin's modernist sound for *Apache* (1954), treat Indians in much the same way, with only slight variations on the musical stereotypes described.[19]

The basic set of conventions continues to characterize "Indian music" of the 1950s and '60s. Toward the end of a thousand-mile trek upriver in *The Big Sky* (Howard Hawks, 1952), the frontiersmen's boat becomes entangled in brush and trees. Hope wanes; and as if this misfortune did not already spell doom, Indians appear on shore. Low bass notes and a drumming in fours supply the menace music. The Indians do not attack immediately; over the tom-tom rhythm we hear a minor-modal melody. Then the moment of recognition occurs: the Indians are friendly Blackfeet, coming to aid the travelers and trade with them. Triumphantly the melody switches into major, then segues into happy western frontier music. The same melodic motif thus works for both moods; instrumentation, mode, and presence or absence of the tom-tom musically define the difference between friend and foe.

the 1970s

I have noted that the humanizing of the Indian occurred more slowly in musical scoring than in onscreen characterization, and it is intriguing to speculate on reasons for Hollywood music's conservatism. Composer Dimitri Tiomkin (responsible for scoring some of the most famous westerns of the 1940s to 1960s), when asked in the 1950s why less stereotypical music should not be used to represent Indians, responded that audiences simply wouldn't understand who was who on the screen. Indeed, one constantly has to wonder why the neo-Romantic style persisted as long as it did in Hollywood's musical language—as well as the stereotypes for actions, ethnic groups, gender, geography, and social class that evolved within it. The classical model was driven by the desire to "cement" musically the meanings onscreen, and thus became highly codified, calling on a style of music that antedated the musical modes of the day. Not until a series of structural shifts—the Paramount decision (when the major movie studios were ordered to divest themselves of their theaters) and the subsequent reallocation of capital in the film industry; the gradual transition to younger generations of composers influenced by television, jazz, and rock and roll; and the entry of film studios into the recording industry and their consequent strategy of marketing sound-tracks as commodities in themselves—did the unity, redundancy, and stylistic conservatism of the traditional western score begin to loosen its grip. Beyond 1960 it is difficult to make generalizations about the musical coding of Indians in westerns. To be sure, Indian stereotypes continued to prevail in all audiovisual media, but new scoring solutions arose as well—especially in the liberal westerns where the Indian was no longer the faceless enemy.

In the early 1970s western, the Indians' floating symbolic significance moored itself onto both Vietnam and the hippie generation, notably in the cluster of films including *A Man Called Horse* (Elliot Silverstein, 1970), *Little Big Man* (Arthur Penn, 1970), and *Soldier Blue* (Ralph Nelson, 1970).

In *A Man Called Horse*, Richard Harris plays a bored English nobleman on a hunting trip in the American frontier in the 1820s. A party of Sioux capture him with a lasso, and thus name him Horse as they bring him to their encampment. He is awarded as a slave to old Buffalo Crow, chief Yellow Hand's mother. Little by little, Horse gains respect in the village, and also wins the love of Running Deer, the chief's sister. He marries Running Deer after his initiation and purification by the excruciating Sun Vow ritual. A devastating Shoshone attack kills many in the village, including Yellow Hand and Running Deer, and only through the British military strategy and prowess of Horse do the Sioux remain unconquered. His wife dead, he is resigned to return to the world of white society.

A Man Called Horse has a unique tone among the liberal westerns, a

187

tone one might call *faux* ethnographic. The Sioux are depicted as primitively violent, and they appear to define family and community in a decidedly foreign way. The film strains to give us the feeling of shocking immersion in an alien culture. Sioux language is not translated by the use of English-speaking actors (as in *Broken Arrow*), nor by subtitles (as in *Dances with Wolves*); occasionally Horse's fellow slave and sidekick, the Frenchman Baptiste, will translate into broken English.

But the viewer does understand everything that needs to be understood, through a combination of mediating forces: Baptiste's occasional oral translations, the meanings embedded in the mise-en-scène and editing, the Indians' frequent expressive use of hand signals instead of speech, and their body language. The film is predicated, it seems, on the notion that body language is universal. The best "speakers" of this body language in the Sioux village are Buffalo Crow—played not by a Sioux but by a famous British actress, Dame Judith Anderson—and Horse's Indian bride—played by Corinna Tsopei, a Greek heiress and Miss Universe for 1964.

But beyond the undeniable fact that the film is a white self-idealizing fantasy—after all, it has a white protagonist, who rises to greater success as a warrior than any Sioux in the story[20]—there's still the distinction of its effort to preserve the Indians' otherness by means of the hero's trajectory through it. These Indians are "uncouth" and "impolite": Jeff Chandler would have no role here as the eloquent and earnest statesman-chief he plays in *Broken Arrow*. The acceptance James Stewart acquires through politeness in *Broken Arrow* Richard Harris acquires only through the passage of time, tests of courage, and great physical pain in *Horse*.

Leonard Rosenman's music matches this pseudo-anthropological project. For the first time, a musical score draws a relationship between onscreen chanting/drumming and the composer's background score. Rosenman cast his score in a distinctly twentieth-century idiom, well beyond Romantic tonalities (with the exception of a major-key choral theme). For the most part, the filmgoer has no easy tonal language to fall back on; the score alternates between Indian chanting and modernist choral/orchestral music. Furthermore, key sounds from the Indian chanting carry over into the background score: singing voices, the Indian flute, rattle, drum, and high-pitched whistle.

In short, Rosenman's score *translates* the Indian music. Take, for example, a scene early in Horse's life among the Sioux. The hobbled slave Baptiste has agreed to teach Sioux ways to Horse in hopes that the two might eventually escape together. A montage shows the passage of summer to winter, during which we see villagers drumming, singing, and dancing, animals in nature, Horse at work, and Baptiste teaching warrior skills to Horse. The authentic diegetic chant heard at the beginning of this montage, over the images of chanting tribesmen and women, segues into Rosenman's background score, here featuring the orchestra with a male chorus singing a modal melody in unison. Rosenman's instrumentation includes the Indian drum, rattle, and flute heard previously in crowd scenes of Sioux music making. The strings play a chord using the first, second, and fifth tones of the scale in an interesting, repeated rhythm. A women's chorus joins the men's, singing a modal melody in counterpoint. They sing in "ha-ya" syllables, and the men's line imitates the Sioux tradition of vocal pulsation on the longer notes. The sequence is therefore predicated on an audition of the actual chant, then segues into a westernized "version" that retains some original features. It de-alienates the Indians (on white terms).[21]

Rosenman's score does not follow the same strategy the Indianists followed at the turn of the century, for unlike Farwell, for example, he invents his own melodic lines and harmonies. But his incorporation of certain aspects of authentic vocal style and instrumentation certainly reflects the intention to write not Hollywood clichés but a white composer's eye view of Sioux music (he spent a month on a Sioux reservation in preparation for composing the score).

What is lost in this musical translation, and what is gained? Rosenman falsifies the original, but not as flagrantly as the tom-tom formulas that held sway in film music from the 1920s to 1960s. His music represents the Sioux chants through a western filter, making it "readable" for viewers. Reading a translation is, of course, a far cry from learning the original language itself, and the cultural translation necessary to make a linguistic translation readable is always political. But given that a translation is always itself a reading, Rosenman's score is new in being a reading at all, rather than a series of clichés. Perhaps this is the farthest a Hollywood score of the era can go without becoming incoherent and unreadable.

Once the film has identified with the Sioux via Horse's relationship with them, the Shoshone come to fill in as the racial other. Rosenman's musical treatment of the Shoshone raids is interesting in this regard. In the first raid, just outside the village, Horse jumps from a rock and surprises an attacker. An Indian whistle trills, and stridently dissonant sounds from the orchestra are heard. The high point has yet to come: once he has killed the second marauder, a number of Sioux spectators have arrived from the village, and Horse knows he must scalp the victim to show his membership in the tribe. As he does so in emotional agony, we hear a climactic blare of trumpets in parallel fourths sound a descending motif.

Thus, in representing the other, Rosenman reverts to two tried-and-true kinds of musical language: the parallel-fourths technique from the classical western, and also strident atonality (the Shoshone-as-other are represented by clichéd modernist tropes). This strategy of locating a new racial scapegoat occurs in many liberal westerns, as we will see shortly in *Dances with Wolves*.

The scene just described signals another musical turning point as well. When Horse, having killed and scalped his Shoshone, triumphantly reenters the village to general acclaim, we hear not the usual orchestral pomp befitting the conquering hero, à la Erich Korngold, but Indian whistles and drumming, and above all the shouting and chanting of the villagers. Similarly, near the end of the film, the tribe mourns their dead after the climactic battle. No war requiem plays, no 120-piece orchestra in a minor key externalizing the grief of a people, but a Sioux elder intones a mourning song, wandering among the dead and wounded, accompanied solely by an Indian rattle. In both these scenes, the real Indian music has been allowed to carry the emotion, and does so effectively since the score has accustomed us to that music and its performers. We have learned to read a bit in a foreign language that has become ours. It no longer acts as sound effects but as music.

the 1980s to the present

Following a period of hibernation, a spate of westerns on film and television in the mid- to late 1980s revived the genre. *Lonesome Dove, Dances with Wolves, Tombstone, Unforgiven, Wyatt Earp, Posse, The Ballad of Little Jo*, and others continued to examine and revise the myths through the lenses of contemporary concerns. *Dances with Wolves* (Kevin Costner, 1990) owed its box-office success to its combination of "political correctness," compelling story, stunning cinematography, star actor-director, and lavish score by John Barry that became a best-selling soundtrack CD. The film draws on precisely the same strategies as any liberal western since *Broken Arrow*. The white protagonist Dunbar—the film's liberal—comes to know the nobility and wisdom of the Indians, mourning their vulnerability in the face of advancing white civilization. As in *Broken Arrow* and *A Man Called Horse*, the hero in *Dances with Wolves* virtually becomes an Indian but in the end leaves the doomed tribe to wander the white world.

Dances with Wolves offers itself to a variety of different readings, ranging from current American preoccupations with gender roles and masculinity to concerns over dwindling natural resources and, environmental quality, multiculturalism, the encroachment of big business and government on daily life, the loss of community, and, not least this time, Native American rights. In an ironic reversal of their position in classical westerns, the Indians here represent traditional American community and values. They discuss important matters in town meetings; the chief listens to their reasoned arguments and makes decisions that reflect a consensus. Unlike the Sioux in *A Man Called Horse*, these Indians are reasonable and well groomed—the original smalltown conservatives.

John Barry's score hails from the grand, lush, neo-Romantic 1930s tradition of Erich Korngold and Max Steiner, which continues into contemporary movies with John Williams, some work of Thomas Newman, and others. It is replete with beautiful themes that give narrative clarity and emotional force to the story. The numerous themes in *Dances with Wolves* include the main title, a beautiful motif for Dunbar's travel through the west, a 3/4 melody for the wolf Two-Socks, a lush "vista" theme (heard when Dunbar first beholds the Sioux village, and also on first sight of the huge buffalo herd), a theme for the buffalo, a love theme, and a theme for the Pawnee. But there is a most striking difference between Barry's score and the music for liberal westerns of the 1950s. The compulsive depiction of Indians as other through the standard background "Indian music" techniques seemingly disappears. The Sioux receive a musical treatment free of tom-tom and modal-melody clichés. Dunbar's new allies are graced with occasional real Lakota chants on one hand (to establish their authenticity on the musical level) and a set of lovely western-sounding themes on the other. In contrast to the stern Indian music that plays when Jeffords, in *Broken Arrow*, first rides over the pass and sees the Apache village, an exquisitely expansive orchestral theme is heard as Dunbar arrives with the wounded squaw and first casts eyes on the Sioux village (see figure 8.4, section A).

The Sioux may be assigned Euro-American music, but—as in *A Man Called Horse*—there is another racial other here: the Pawnee tribe, whose visual representation (negroid features, mohawk and other fanciful hairdos) strongly evokes both blacks and skinheads of 1990. In contrast to the romanticism of the rest of the score, the Pawnee's theme is angular and nonmelodic, and though it is based on the tonal center of E, it is clearly more harmonically indeterminate than the rest of the score (see figure 8.4, section B).

Fig. 8.4. Contrasting treatments of Sioux and Pawnee in *Dances with Wolves* (1990).

As I've already noted, this isolated use of musical modernism is itself a Hollywood cliché, connoting danger and otherness in contrast to the standard tonal conventions of the rest of the score.[22] Thus, Barry has found a less hackneyed means to replicate Indian otherness in the context of an otherwise traditional musical language, achieving a newly displaced racism.

So the Sioux are treated to the same musical language as Dunbar. The accessibility of this musical language is a key to understanding that the Sioux are "us." In fact, late in the film, when the hero is captured by the newly arrived white soldiers, they ask him his name. He answers in Lakota, "I am Dances-with-Wolves"— and the Sioux theme plays![23] The film has completed the protagonist's metamorphosis, and the musical score has completed the shift in spectator identification by identifying Costner's character with the Indians.

Once "we" perceive the army as the second enemy, the music announcing them conveys a number of associations above and beyond their threat. Trombones play a sustained minor triad while a snare drum beats out a simple 4/4 rhythm—not the DUM-dum-dum-dum denoting the tom-tom, but a regular pulsation nevertheless. Is it a coincidence that the score's depiction of the ugly Americans combines conventions of military music with those of savage Indians?

Barry's decision to depict the Sioux in *Dances with Wolves* in the same lush musical language as the good white protagonist is a political one. It turns the tables on the traditional distinctions between self and other—although not completely, as we have seen in noting that the Pawnee are musically scapegoated as the new focus of racism, and also in the sense that the diegetic Sioux singing and drumming remain distinctly alien, "untranslated," more irreducibly exotic than in *Horse*, which effectively trains us to understand it. But in general, the depiction of the Sioux as subjects rather than objects reinforces a reading of *Dances with Wolves* that sees the Indians as the traditional Americans. They stand in nostalgically for the American values that prevailed before meaningful physical communities were replaced by the ersatz community of tele-communications and by intrusive big government. From this perspective, the film expresses dark pessimism about Americans' ability to retain a sense of self-determination at the end of the twentieth century, just as the film's fiction recounts the end of the Sioux as a self-determining nation at the end of the nineteenth.

conclusions

The political rehabilitation of the Indians in many westerns since 1950 by no means shifts the central focus on American masculine identity worked out against a mythologized landscape. But the Indians' position changes in this landscape in relation to the hero, and film music's status in the background of consciousness inflects this relation in subtle and forceful ways.

Walter Hill's *Geronimo: An American Legend* (1993) illustrates the suggestive power of music. This film takes up roughly where Jeffords and Cochise had left off in *Broken Arrow*. Its white liberal is Lieutenant Gatewood (Jason Patric), saddled with the task of negotiating with the legendary Apache leader Geronimo (Wes Studi) for his surrender. The villainous force is the army, this time in the person of the machiavellian General Miles. Gatewood carries out his duty with distaste, aware that Miles is deceiving Geronimo. An Indian hunter (Robert Duvall) sums up Gatewood's predicament: "You don't love who you're fighting for, and you don't hate who you're fighting against."

Ry Cooder's score creates a global dimension to this chapter in American history by means of an eclectic selection of folk and "world" musics. In the context of world music, diegetic Apache chanting takes on an avant-garde mystique; it sounds *interesting*. Cooder's score, punctuated with reverb and other electronic effects, includes zither, Indian flutes and/or recorders, the high-pitched Indian whistle, a plucked stringed instrument like the Chinese lute, the very low vocal productions of Tuvan throat-singing, period brass-band music, snare drums, Scottish bagpipes, a solo cello playing "Wayfaring Stranger," traditional American shape-note singing, and the Boston Camerata intoning a hymn.

How can we make sense of such music in such a setting? First, independent of narrative meaning, this movie was calculated to sell CDs, as commercial films are these days. In the 1980s, as exotic ethnic musics became raw materials to pass through the mills of global media commodification and consumption by western markets, a world music soundtrack began to stand for a "style" in itself, defining the film audience as much as the film. Whereas by the 1930s neo-Romantic orchestral underscoring took hold as a "universal" language whose effects depended in large part on not being attended to, the song score since the 1980s enables a more immediate social identification. Hence the success of such movie soundtracks in the 1990s as *Dead Man Walking* (1995, a drama with music by Nusrat Fateh Ali Khan and Tom Waits, among others) and *Addicted to Love* (1997; a comedy that includes a song by Malian star Ali Farka Touré in collaboration with Ry Cooder).

Second, *Geronimo* becomes a meditation on the nineteenth-century nationalistic way of conceiving identity (the Apaches) in conflict with the twentieth-century dissolution of nations through U.S. imperialistic assimilation and domination (the army). Like the Indian in liberal westerns of the last fifty years, Geronimo stands for what America has lost: virility, purity of spirit, community, commitment.

The liberal western seems to be more and more elegiacal with respect to this perceived loss. The classical western's Heroic West has ceded to images of an Aging America, increasingly limited by technological progress, corporate capitalist interests at the expense of people, and ethical relativism. Whereas the prewar Indian was an obstacle to overcome, the postwar Indian has emerged as the ideal American. As we have seen, film music has responded to this changing repository of cultural meanings in a number of ways. For the moment, it seems, the prettiest music belongs to the Indian.

193

notes

This chapter was originally published, in slightly different form, in Georgina Born and David Hesmondhalgh, eds., *Western Music and Its Others: Difference, Representation, and Appropriation in Music* (Berkeley and Los Angeles: University of California Press, 2000), 234–53.

1. A few examples among many are the American pop song "Running Bear" (1960), the 1960s TV cartoon song "Powwow, the Indian Boy" (see figure 8.5 below), the Hamm's Beer publicity campaign of the 1980s, the motif for the Apaches in *Stagecoach* (1939), or Max Steiner's motifs for the Sioux in *They Died with Their Boots On* (1942) and for the Seminoles in *Key Largo* (1949).

Pow -wow, the In-di - an boy   Loved all the a-ni- mals in the woods

Fig. 8.5. "Powwow, the Indian Boy."

2. Cooper's Leatherstocking Tales, novels written between the 1820s and 1841 (including *The Last of the Mohicans* and *The Deerslayer*), and Longfellow's epic poem *The Song of Hiawatha* (1855) are perhaps the best-known embodiments of this image.

3. Surely the movies contain other Indian types, but these are individual characters: the town drunk, the comical Indian (e.g., the squaw in *The Searchers*), the old sage, the sidekick (e.g., the Lone Ranger's Tonto).

4. Pentatonicism: a pentatonic scale contains five notes from "do" to the octave above, as opposed to, say, the familiar major scale, which has seven. Use of pentatonic scales in Euro-American music connotes the exotic and/or primitive. A perfect fourth refers to the interval of four steps between two notes, e.g., C–F. Perfect fifths are pairs of notes five steps apart, e.g., C–G. Often, Euro-American music will accompany a "pastoral" or "exotic" melody with repeated perfect fifths in the bass.

5. Michael V. Pisani, "'I'm an Indian Too: Creating Native American Identities in Nineteenth- and Early Twentieth-Century Music," in *The Exotic in Western Music*, ed. Jonathan Bellman (Boston: Northeastern University Press, 1998), 218–57.

6. Among these composers are Charles Wakefield Cadman, Arthur Farwell, Charles Sanford Skilton, Henry Gilbert, and Amy Beach.

7. See his article "Music in America," *Harper's*, February 1895, 428–34, repr. in *Dvořák in America, 1892–1895*, ed. John C. Tibbetts (Portland, Ore.: Amadeus Press, 1993), 370–80.

8. Fletcher, an active voice for Indian culture in the late nineteenth century, collaborated with an Omaha Indian, Francis La Flesche, in collecting songs among Plains Indian tribes. Her published collections and studies of 1893 and 1900 (in addition to transcriptions by others such as the musicologist Theodore Baker) were invaluable resources for Indianist composers. Fletcher's songs were transcribed and harmonized with hymnlike piano accompaniments by music historian and theorist John C. Fillmore, who elsewhere wrote "how monophonic Indian music could be harmonized and made palatable to cultured tastes" (Pisani, "I'm an Indian Too," 242).

9. Farwell's passion for Indian tribal music continued all his life. Some of his later compositions are remarkably daring in their departure from Euro-American convention and their exploration of tribal song patterns. The most "authentic" of his works is a "Navajo War Dance" (Op. 102, no. 1, 1937) for unaccompanied chorus. A recording exists on *Farwell, Orem, and Cadman, Recorded Anthology of American Music* (New World Records NW 213, 1977).

10. Arthur Farwell, *American Indian Melodies* (Wa-Wan Press, 1901); repr., ed. Maurice Hinson, Chapel Hill, N.C.: Hinshaw Music, 1977.

11. Richard Crawford, *The American Musical Landscape* (Berkeley and Los Angeles: University of California Press, 1993), 86.

12. Anthologies of selections for silent-film musical accompaniment provide evidence. *Sam Fox Moving Picture Volumes* of 1913, 1914, and 1923, composed by J. S. Zamecnik, include selections on American Indian music.

Some of this material is difficult to distinguish from the Chinese and Arabic entries. All include pentatonic composition, and some open fifths; moreover, some of the "Indian" cues do not use the stereotypes outlined here. (The cue "Indian Attack" cited by Pisani does, however, have the standard devices.) The selections under "Indian: West" in Erno Rapée's piano scores late in the first decade of the twentieth century are musically more sophisticated and complex, and also include but are not limited to the stereotypes described. Rapée's selections from various composers include dances, war songs, and scenics.

13. Yves Kovacs, *Le Western* (1963); repr., Paris: Gallimard, 1993, 167.

14. Blacklisted screenwriter Albert Maltz wrote the film using a front. For an interesting account of the film's problematic relation to the historical events to which it refers, see Frank Manchel, "Cultural Confusion: *Broken Arrow*," in *Hollywood's Indian: The Portrayal of the Native American in Film*, ed. Peter C. Rollins and John E. O'Connor (Lexington: University Press of Kentucky, 1998), 91–106.

15. Georges-Henri Morin, *Le Cercle brisé, L'Image de l'indien dans le western* (Paris: Payot, 1977), 254. See also Philip French's essay "The Indian in the Western Movie," on the changing cultural meanings of Indians in westerns from 1950 to 1970; originally published in *Art in America* (July–August 1972), reprinted in *The Pretend Indian: Images of Native Americans in the Movies*, ed. Gretchen Bataille and Charles Silet (Ames, Iowa: Iowa State University, 1980).

16. "Directors, fearful of censorship if they denounced contemporary injustices (social, economic, or resulting from the United States's imperialist policies in Korea, then Cuba, Santo Domingo, and Vietnam), found in their depiction of outlaws and redskins new ways to construct a satisfactory means of criticism." Ralph E. Friar and Natasha A. Friar, *The Only Good Indian ... : The Hollywood Gospel* (New York: Drama Book Specialists, 1972), 162.

17. Thomas Cripps, *Making Movies Black: The Hollywood Message Movie from World War II to the Civil Rights Era* (New York: Oxford University Press, 1993).

18. Some films in this cycle include *Devil's Doorway* (Mann, 1950), *The Big Sky* (Howard Hawks, 1952), *Apache* (Robert Aldrich, 1954), *The Last Hunt* (Richard Brooks, 1956), *Run of the Arrow* (Samuel Fuller, 1957), *The Unforgiven* (John Huston, 1960), *Flaming Star* (Don Siegel, 1960), and even some of John Ford in the 1960s—*Two Rode Together* (1961) and *Cheyenne Autumn* (1965).

19. Even Raksin's score ultimately invokes the stereotypes. His main theme can sound warlike when accompanied by rhythmically repeated fifths in the bass, and romantic when the strings bring out its lyricism.

20. Native American singer Buffy Sainte-Marie said in 1970, "It's the writers' fault. That's what I object to. Hollywood keeps using the same old white writers over and over again. They don't say anything important and they don't know what they're writing about. There's no empathy. Even the so-called authentic movies like *A Man Called Horse*—that's the whitest of movies I've ever seen. Everything they do, everything they write has to go through layers and layers of white cheesecloth and it's all bound up in rolls and rolls of white tape. And it's the audience that ends up getting gypped. . . ." Friar and Friar, *The Only Good Indian*, 124.

21. Rosenman's music here bears comparison to Arthur Farwell's 1937 piece, the "Navajo War Dance," for unaccompanied chorus (Op. 102, no. 1, 1937). A recording of the latter exists on *Farwell, Orem, and Cadman, Recorded Anthology of American Music* (New World Records, NW 213, 1977).

22. The exception is where a composer has written an entire score in this idiom, in which case the music can become perfectly expressive of moods, emotions, and actions within its own language.

23. In *Dances with Wolves*, dialogue in Lakota is subtitled.

beyond

the western

frontier

reappropriations of the

"good badman" in france,

the french colonies, and

contemporary algeria

peter j. bloom

American western films were an international sensation during the interwar period. They were among the most coveted American cultural imports, featuring action-packed visual landscapes of settlement and "civilization" on the frontier. The polysemic nature of the western, which has contributed narrative elements to so many international genres, still remains a vital point of reference for cinema and serves as a compelling metaphor for political and social conflict.

This essay addresses an evolving process of reception and reappropriation of the western film genre in France and the French colonies. Focus will be on the "good badman," a well-known stock western character, to establish conflicting perceptions of French colonial authorities and spectators. In France, colonial Algeria and Morocco were represented as the French frontier most frequently compared to the climate, opportunities, and moral dilemmas of the American West. As a case study, I will examine the accumulated historical legacy of the western in France and Algeria by addressing a recent Algerian adaptation of an early French "spaghetti" (or "Camembert") western. Without changing the visual montage, two French-based Franco-Algerian comedians created a new post-synchronous Franco-Algerian Arabic voice track. Initially entitled *Dynamite Jack* (1961, directed by Jean Bastia), Fellag and Allalou bought the rights to this obscure film and transformed it into a satire on contemporary Algerian politics, renaming it *Dynamite "Moh"* (1996)— where the familiar "Moh," as in Mohammed, refers to the name of the prophet in the Koran and, by association, the holy war on secular institutions declared by the GIA (Groupe Islamique Armée [Armed Islamic Group]), an armed separatist faction of the Islamic Salvation Front (FIS).[1]

Jean Bastia's *Dynamite Jack* (1961) was itself a spoof of the American western. The immensely popular French Marseillaise comedian Fernandel stars in the two title roles of the film, Dynamite Jack, the fastest (and badest) gunslinger in the West, and Antoine Esperandieu, a naive French fortune hunter invited by a friend to share in the gold rush of Arizona (which he has confused with the California Gold Rush). But as soon as Antoine arrives, he finds his friend, Jules Lavisse, being buried after a shoot-out with Dynamite Jack. Though primarily a vehicle for Fernandel, who had starred in more than one hundred films by 1961, this film was part of a cycle of French-styled Camembert Westerns, most often produced near Paris, in Fountainbleu. *Dynamite Jack*, however, was filmed near Aix-en-Provence,[2] in the southwestern Camargue region, French cowboy territory.

Joë Hamman, the best-known French cowboy film star of the silent era, a native-born Camargue cowboy himself, was made famous in a series of twenty Gaumont films, in which he starred as Arizona Bill, from 1907–1913, in films such as *Les diables rouges* (Red Devils; 1911) and *Aux mains des brigands* (In the Hands of Crooks; 1912). In the French public sphere at the turn of the century, "Arizona" referred to the primitive settler state of American social organization on the western frontier and "Bill" registered as a passing reference to William Frederick "Buffalo Bill" Cody and his world-renowned Wild West shows.

A longstanding tradition of the American West in the French imagination is bound up in depictions of the American Indian as the purest example of "natural man," superior to civilized man, pace Jean-Jacques Rousseau,[3] especially superior to the American pioneers. The settlement of the American West, geographically and culturally removed from the realities of French colonial settlements, was depicted as a new frontier of the imagination in the popular nineteenth-century children's fiction of Gustave Aimard, which featured French heroes and their Indian companions.[4] French translations and adaptations of James Fenimore Cooper's dime novels and the presentation of Buffalo Bill's live Wild West shows to the general public were featured at the Parisian ethnographic exhibitions,[5] which continually featured quasi-theatrical ethnographic troupes. These small-scale live exhibitions were held in urban park settings, such as the Jardin d'Acclimatation, located in the

Fig. 9.1. Video jacket sleeve for *Dynamite "Moh,"* the Algerian version of *Dynamite Jack: The Terror of Laghouat*, a film originally made by Jean Bastia in 1961 and subsequently given a completely new Franco-Algerian voice track by the comedian Fellag, with Allalou, Samia, and Zaoui.

Bois du Boulogne. The popularity of Buffalo Bill's live Wild West shows demonstrated the appeal of the social and physical geography of the American West in France.

The popularity of silent American western films in France served as a subsequent model for fast-paced French adventure films. It was not until after the First World War that American westerns, melodramas, and Charlie Chaplin comedies dominated French movie screens. After all, French film production maintained a dominant share in international film markets prior to the war. The shifting fortunes of the French film industry are well-illustrated in statistics on American film exports. Clarence J. North, chief of the Motion Picture Section of the U.S. Department of Commerce, reported in 1926, that "France is our second market in Europe and our fifth for the whole world. Starting with about 275,000 feet [of film] in 1913, France took from us over 4,000,000 feet ten years later, doubled it in 1924 and for 1925 reached a total of over 14,000,000 feet."[6] This increase in American film imports marks a shift from 15 percent of all commercially released films shown in France in 1913 to 70 percent in 1926.

The international reach of American cinema and its domination of world markets in the aftermath of the First World War has been well-documented in a number of important books and articles. Kristin Thompson convincingly argues that the subsequent international domination of the American film industry was founded upon pre-1918 film exports to Latin America and Australasia.[7] Victoria de Grazia, among others, points to the massive scale of the American domestic market and the Hollywood majors (Paramount, Loew's [MGM], and Warner Bros.), which operated as industrial cartels controlling an international network of distribution and exhibition venues.[8] Beyond the control of foreign markets, the American film industry also developed an industrial "mode of production" that drew on the scientific industrial management principles of Frederick W. Taylor and the assembly-line organization of Henry Ford.[9]

Thomas H. Ince's western films were most often associated with the development of Fordist assembly-line techniques for film production. Although Ince produced other film genres, his westerns represent the application of Taylorist management principles and a Fordist logic of standardization and interchangeability. The Bison Film Company (later renamed 101 Bison), where Ince was hired to make his first westerns, put the Oklahoma-based 101 Ranch Wild West show on the payroll. By contracting the entire company, 101 Bison obtained the services of trained horses and buffalos, authentic cowboys and Indians, stagecoaches, teepees, and other props essential to the setting of an authentic western film.[10] The authentic mise-en-scène associated with 101 Bison contributed a documentary-style dimension to narratives of capture, gunfights, and honor on the frontier. Ince, as a director and producer for Bison 101, was best known for his managerial acumen associated with the detailed shooting script, which specified props, costumes, and camera set-ups.

Ince is the figure most associated with the organization of the expansive facilities of the Santa Ynez ranch, known as Inceville. While other studios developed a managerial-based industrial mode of production concurrently, Inceville set a standard for a steady flow of films with relatively high production values. Ince's westerns, starring William S. Hart, were among his best-known productions. The melodramatic expressionism of Hart's characters became an international trademark of the morally conflicted western protagonist, contributing to the expansion of American film exports.

Hart's morally ambiguous characters gave depth to the "good badman" theme, pioneered in the one-reel westerns starring G. M. "Bronco Billy" Anderson (a.k.a. Max Aronson). Unlike "Bronco Billy" however, Hart was a trained Shakespearean actor with some historical interest in depicting the moral dilemmas of the western frontier. Close-ups revealing Hart's moral ambivalence were used to great advantage in so many of the films produced by Ince. As Kalton C. Lahue describes, "Hart appeared on the screen many times larger than life—hat brim pulled down over his slowly narrowing eyes, nostrils flaring slightly with a deep rhythmic breathing—while [Hart] considered his opponent. Kids shook in their seats as the stern visage of Bill Hart glared down at them."[11] The concentrated figure of Hart, able to stand down any challenge, was rendered believable through his magisterial posture.

Hart's characteristic determination was tempered by the theme of the outsider in search of redemption. In *Blue Blazes Rawden* (W. S. Hart, 1918), Hart plays Blue Blazes Rawden, a fledgling strongman in a logging town, who kills the dishonest, bullying owner of the tavern, Ladyfingers Hilgard (Robert McKim). Rawden initiates a duel with Ladyfingers in a play for his half-Indian, half-French girlfriend, Babette du Fresne (Mande George), while also seeking to protect Babette from Ladyfingers' abusive behavior. In spite of the fact that Ladyfingers loaded blanks in Rawden's gun, Rawden still prevails, demonstrating his superior moral and physical bearing.

Nonetheless, Rawden is bound to honor Ladyfingers' dying wish, to host his visiting mother and brother. Ladyfingers' mother (Gertrude Claire) takes an immediate liking to Rawden and even treats him like her own son. Blazes forbids anybody in the logging town from telling the mother that he killed Ladyfingers. Once Babette spitefully defies Blazes's ultimatum, who has since lost interest in her, and reveals his secret, Rawden leaves in disgrace and embarks on a search for his own redemption. Hart's depiction is of a physically powerful and morally ambivalent outsider on the western frontier who exists beyond the reach of the law. But the vulnerability of Hart's characters also softened the depiction of the nomadic western outsider.

Westerns such as these starring William S. Hart, "Bronco Billy" Anderson, J. Warren Kerrigan, and Tom Mix, among others, were part of an early wave of westerns that were shown in North Africa as well as France following the First World War. According to American consul reports from Algiers in 1924, "Moving pictures have spread throughout Algeria and have become very popular among all classes . . . , Arabs as well as Europeans. Cinematograph houses have been established in all the towns and some exhibitors travel about the country with an automobile equipped with [a] projection apparatus. A screen is placed in the open field or in an old barn to which a small admission fee is charged."[12]

Most of the American films that were shown in Algeria in these traveling caravans had been previously circulated in France. After export duties were paid on these films in Paris, these "junk prints," as they were known, were sent on to Algeria, Morocco, and French Indochina for presentation in film caravans, among other theatrical venues. (Traveling film caravans were part of an early fairground history of film attractions in France, prior to the First World War,[13] and they were tied to military recruitment campaigns and American-supported film hygiene campaigns.) In addition to circulating "junk prints," new prints of American films were provided by American film representatives based in Algiers and Casablanca. In Algeria, several first- and second-run movie theaters were established in Algiers, Oran, and Constantine by the mid-1920s. The theaters drew a mixed audience of Spanish, Italian, Maltese, French, and Arab filmgoers, seduced by fast action adventures and melodramas on the American frontier.

Algeria was colonized under a policy of French assimilation, such that most of the country was considered an administrative unit of France, with a firmly established secular French education system and a history of cinema that began at the turn of the century with the early Lumière cinematograph. The Lumière-trained film operator Félix Mesguich, who previously served under French command in Algeria as a *spahi*,[14] later returned to Algiers where he filmed daytime crowd scenes and projected them in a theater to willing customers in the evening.[15] The flexibility of the Lumière cinematograph, which recorded and projected films, established the cinema as a transportable spectacle of moving images. With successive normalizations of film projection equipment, the moving image was projected in a vast array of settings and established the vitality of motion pictures as an international form of visual communication.

Penetrating seemingly inviolable temporal, geographic, and psychological boundaries, narrative cinema represented a new way of seeing the world. The international domination of American cinema after the First World War meant that themes in American cinema were locally adapted and interpreted. The local interpretation of American films was reinforced by additional inserts and alternate endings that were not available in the United States. Somewhat cryptically, the American consul based in Algiers wrote that "the ending of American films do not agree with French ideas and for that reason it is suggested that films be given alternate endings—to let Algerian leasees pick the one most likely to appeal to audiences."[16] This assertion suggests that the local adaptation of American films was not about adapting American films to Algerian audiences per se, but it does suggest an uninhibited notion of what it might mean to entertain "French ideas."

Hollywood was accused of double-shooting films during the 1920s—presenting a relatively tame version for American audiences, under the industry self-censorship regulations of the Hays Office, and a livelier, more provocative version for foreign audiences.[17] Creating a more risqué version for foreign audiences might have contributed, as Kerry Seagrave suggests,[18] to the international appeal of American films, when so many American films were not translated into local languages. The practice of adding "ginger scenes" was reported in the trade press and was even subject to investigation by the Federal Bureau of Commercial Economics (FBCE). The FBCE acknowledged the existence of "ginger scenes," but claimed that smaller production companies unaffiliated with the Hollywood majors added them.[19] Adding "ginger scenes" and a practice known as "quota quickies," which were American-financed European films designed to meet quota restrictions on American film imports, suggests an increasingly aggressive American trading posture for American film exports.

Beyond the excesses of American film export practice, American films were popular as spectacles, appropriated by various audiences in Algeria during the interwar period. American films were so popular, in fact, that the very same American consul in Algeria, writing in 1924, reported that "acrobatic pictures, wild west episodes, comic and sentimental films appeal to the local public, which likes quick action. American films have enabled theatre owners to double and triple charges without cutting down attendance."[20] In 1928, Hollywood films commanded 85 percent of the screens in French North Africa.[21] Fox Film, Metro-Goldwyn-Mayer, and Paramount-Famous-Lasky maintained representatives in Algiers and Casablanca. The appeal of American modernity, representing an alternative to a totalizing French-styled modernist hierarchy of "civilization," cut across national, racial, class-based, and spatial boundaries in French colonial North Africa.

Paul Saffar, a French journalist based in Casablanca who wrote regularly about film production and exhibition in French North Africa during the interwar period, explains that American Westerns starring Art Acord, "Bronco Billy" Anderson, Buck Jones, William S. Hart, Tom Mix, Eddy Polo, and Richard Talmadge were among the most popular films in Algeria, Morocco, and Tunisia in 1931.[22] Saffar also reported that there were 210 movie theaters throughout North Africa at the time. He distinguishes among three types of film theaters in North Africa: the thirty or so large first-run picture palaces with higher ticket prices, grandiose architecture, and newer "talkie" film prints primarily drawing a clientele of European expatriates; the smaller, less technologically sophisticated, second-run theaters, located on the outskirts of the major cities which drew working-class Arab and foreign laborers from the factories, ateliers, and manufacturing plants in the nearby area;[23] and the third-run theaters, or all of the rest, which were smaller theaters located in more strictly Arab and Berber neighborhoods.

Saffar describes the ambiance in a second-run Arab cinema hall in Casablanca with a mix of condescension and wonder with this telling anecdote:

> The audience loves watching actors on screen gesticulate in spite of the fact that most of the films are incomprehensible. This is partially due to the numerous missing scenes and the uselessness of the intertitles, as most of the audience cannot read [English or French]. When the film becomes too difficult to follow, spectators loudly proclaim what they see on screen to the person sitting next to them, as if they were blind. Being that so many people are talking, you can easily imagine this kind of "talkie" ambiance. The Arab spectator participates in the action and drama of the film, encouraging the actors on screen with taunts and cheers while drowning out the pathetic live piano accompaniment or sound pick-up. They throw their fez [hats] in the air to show their satisfaction, once the hero successfully accomplishes a dangerous deed. During the course of these enthusiastic shows, red hats are scattered throughout the theater and they must wait to reclaim them. In most cases, spectators don't find their hats and a series of altercations might ensue.[24]

Saffar's description was supposed to reflect Arab reactions to American films and was part of his larger argument for introducing French sound films that would educate Arab audiences about European morality ethics, while entertaining them with American-inspired acrobatic scenes. By 1931, there were calls for stricter film censorship regulations on all films shown in the French colonies. French film censorship committees were already established by 1928 in French Indochina as a form of market protectionism against American- and British-produced Chinese films.

Saffar's description of the Arab movie-theater experience evokes some of the same themes evident in the enormously influential crowd psychology of the day. Gabriel Tarde's work on crowd psychology, *L'opinion et la foule* (Public Opinion and the Crowd; 1901),[25] ties the question of social knowledge to a series of imitative acts that follows a geometric pattern of extension through a chain of intermediaries. Tarde's theory of imitation is tied to the universalizing acts of repetition, opposition, and adaptation, in accordance with an evolutionary model in natural history.

Saffar claims that if films demonstrate proper moral standards, Arab filmgoers would be be educated through a process of "imitative reform."

Saffar's description of throwing red fez hats in the air during the course of a film exemplifies a form of unthinking imitative behavior—an important term in crowd psychology that is still used as part of contemporary marketing lexicon. The negative critique of imitative behavior was associated with Tarde's description of *imitative contagion,* which is grounded in the same principle as that of an army of ants at work, where individual initiative is followed by imitation.[26] For Tarde, imitation was a theory of repetition, education, and the somnambulistic state of social organization. Tarde's discussion of imitation is based on the notion that flows or waves of imitation are powerful unconscious cues.

For Tarde, the crowd is an undifferentiated mass existing at the intersection of rhythms, undulations, and vibrations of an abundant flow. It is in this sense that Tarde writes, "The state of the social, like a hypnotic state, is only that of a dream, a dream of ultimatums, a dream of action. Hypnotic suggestion encouraging spontaneous belief—that is the illusion of the sleep-walker as well as socialized man."[27] Perhaps this is one of the clearest statements from the fin-de-siècle period that describe how public spaces under French civil authority were constituted and sustained through a series of hypnotic, imitative flows.

While Tarde himself was not writing about the effect of cinema on audiences, his notion that social organization, like a hypnotic state, takes the form of commands and actions in a dream state may be likened to Metzian ideas of the film spectator's dream state in the darkened cinema hall.[28] We are then led to ask how does the dream state of film spectators influence their perceptions of an immediate political and social reality? This very question has been a source of ongoing scholarship in film studies and has given rise to an important psychoanalytic literature on theories of identification, gender difference, and spectatorship.

Tarde's theory of imitative contagion and the discourse of crowd psychology elucidates a more historically nuanced understanding of Saffar's discussion of the cinema hall experience in Casablanca and the generalized fear of the cinema hall as a site for political and social unrest in the colonies. Furthermore, crowd psychology emphasized public assembly as a negatively charged undifferentiated mass rather than a form of enlightened democratic assembly. This facile dichotomization of "the popular" in crowd psychology has been an influential source for political and social commentary since the mid-nineteenth century. More crucially however, crowd psychology historically locates the cinema hall as a scene of potential insurrection, or, rather, of political and social resistance both in the gathering of communities at the theater and, as I will further argue, through the interpretation of the narrative film experience. The popularity of American westerns among Arab spectators suggests a textual referent for such resistance.

Returning to the popularity of American westerns in North Africa, I suggest that the "good badman" theme was interpreted against the grain of civil authority by audiences in French North Africa, as it was in the

United States at the time. Let us look at a more detailed example of this theme in *The White Outlaw* (Robert J. Horner, 1929) starring Art Acord, who Saffar mentions as one of the popular American western matinee idols in North Africa.

In *The White Outlaw*, Johnny Douglas (Acord) is a well-known "good" outlaw who is accused of a federal holdup that he did not commit. Jed Isbell, Johnny's former associate, committed the crime while wearing Johnny's distinctive white scarf and costume in order to make it seem to be the work of the mysterious White Outlaw. Though an adept outlaw who would always avoid hurting anyone, Johnny gives up the art of the holdup after being called to the bedside of his dying mother. Soon thereafter, Johnny is framed by Jed Isbell. On the run several months later, Johnny finds work on the cattle ranch of Colonel Holbrook in Wagnerville, Texas. Johnny befriends a fellow cattle rancher, who is in love with Holbrook's daughter, Janice. Colonel Holbrook cannot pay off his debts to the biggest creditor in town, Chet Wagner, and Janice agrees to marry Wagner if he agrees to cancel all of her father's debts. Ted, who also wants to marry Janice, holds up a stagecoach in order to pay off Colonel Holbrook's debts but is quickly arrested on suspicion of having committed the crime.

While Ted is in jail, Johnny confides in Ted. He explains that he is the true White Outlaw; in turn, Ted tells Johnny where he hid the cash box so Johnny can return it and shift the blame for the hold-up from Ted to the mythic White Outlaw. After all, the White Outlaw is an empty category with an indeterminate identity. In the meantime, a $5,000 federal bounty is put out for the capture of the White Outlaw. Jed Isbell, in need of money, leads a posse to hunt down and arrest Johnny as the "real" White Outlaw. Instead, Johnny hunts down Jed, punches him out, and dresses him in the White Outlaw's signature white scarf and costume. When the sheriff and his posse arrive, they are led to believe that Jed is the real White Outlaw. Once Jed is arrested, Ted is released and the sheriff gives Johnny the $5,000 reward. Johnny then gives the money to Colonel Holbrook such that he can pay off his debts to Wagner. In turn, Ted is now free to marry his true love, Janice. And finally, true to the "good badman" formula, Johnny moves on to his next destination alone, like a religious figure in search of spiritual and moral redemption.

The changing perceptions of the White Outlaw's true identity are the centerpiece of the film. The various interpretations of the White Outlaw's role in the film serves as an illustration of how breaking the law is a matter of interpretation. The shifting identity of the White Outlaw demonstrates the possibility for redemption but also points to an operative interpretative framework. That is, Johnny acted in the interests of Colonel Holbrook, Janice, and Ted, and opposed to the manipulative behavior of the wealthy Chet Wagner and the villainous Jed Isbell. The sheriff, as the representative of civil authority, stands outside of the moral universe of the film's characters.

During the interwar period there were a number of criticisms leveled at the morally questionable themes in American films and their impact on colonial audiences. The well-known English journalist and novelist Aldous Huxley (1894–1963) criticized American films for depicting the white race as capable of criminal behavior. Following Huxley's travels around the world, recounted in his novel *Along the Road: Notes and Essay of a Tourist* (1925), he wrote an influential article about the ill effects of American cinema abroad. Huxley wrote, "Over the entire globe the producers of Hollywood are the missionaries and propagandists of white civilization. [. . .] But the share of Hollywood in lowering the white man's prestige is by no means inconsiderable. A people whose own propagandists proclaim it to be mentally and morally deficient, can not expect to be looked up to."[29]

Huxley was pointing to the fact that so many of the themes in American cinema did not reflect well on American morals and, by association, European moral and civil authority in the colonies. Huxley's criticisms were echoed and expanded by the British colonial expert, Sir Hesketh Bell, who claimed that American cinema was "caricature-like" and its portrayal of the intimate side of Euro-American life was the perpetrator of political instability. Bell's expanded critique of American cinema, later translated into French,[30] became part of a French critique of the ill-effects of American films in the colonies. And more significant than simply branding American films a form of cheap sensationalism, critical commentary about American films also revealed French insecurities with native populations in the colonies.

Themes such as that of the "good badman" indirectly challenged the legitimacy of French colonial authority and revealed its fear of local assembly. Second- and third-run theaters presenting American films were considered sites for potentially dangerous local agitation. Aimé-François Legendre, a French sinologist charged with conducting numerous geological surveys throughout Asia, described popular American cinema as a potentially powerful instigator of civil unrest. He wrote, "The cinema has become the master of the masses through [. . .] the power of its images, its realism, its appeal to the emotions, to all internal vibrations. Its control over the indigenous masses, dominating their child-like spirit, has been accomplished with great immediacy and totality. The cinema is all-pervasive, and its reach extends from the largest to the smallest village, even drawing the peasant from the distant rice paddy fields."[31]

In Legendre's extended discussion of cinema in French Indochina, he associates cinema with a great humanizing potential and yet decries unscrupulous work of businessmen, especially the Americans who have infiltrated it with values that undermine the civilizing forces of empire. The so-called pernicious influence of this predominantly American cinema is tied to the redeeming qualities of vagabonds, bandits, and prostitutes, appearing in melodramas and westerns—the very same social actors that were associated with criminality in crowd psychology.

Legendre did not consider these films indecent, but rather inappropriate for indigenous spectators, who he claimed were incapable of seeing beyond the veracity of the photographic reproduction into the narrative at hand. He wrote, "They understand the brutal realism of the images that pass before them due to their well-developed visual memory, but usually miss the moral lesson. A theatrical piece treating the same narrative does not produce the same consequences but the image creates a permanent impression in their mind forever."[32] Legendre imagined a cinema of the instincts that indelibly marks the memory of the colonized subject, the way a child's mind is marked at a formative stage of maturity.

In spite of Legendre's ill-informed and racially hierarchized vision of how natives think, he nevertheless saw foreign audiences as capable of reappropriating themes from the American cinema. The continued penetration of American westerns created a stable stock of characters and situations that created yet another resource for political allegory and political parody. It is possible that the figure of Johnny Douglas in the *White Outlaw*, which appeared in the second- and third-run theaters of Casablanca in 1931, might have rekindled recent memories of Abd el-Krim, the Moroccan resistance fighter. Abd el-Krim successfully drove the Spanish out of the Rif mountain region of Morocco, and threatened French imperial interests in Morocco and neighboring Algeria,[33] culminating in the 1925–1926 Rif War with France. As a world-class rodeo rider from Stillwater, Oklahoma, Acord could conceivably thrill North African audiences with his clearly evident skill as a rider professional stuntman. Paul Saffar's description of the Casablanca movie theater in which Arab spectators are narrating the film's action to the person sitting next to them suggests such a scenario.

Just as American western heroes might have been associated with local North African independence leaders during the interwar period, Italian spaghetti westerns reappropriated the western hero as a figure of kitsch and violent excess. Moreover, I contend that this redeployment of long-standing western characters, symbols, and situations in *Dynamite Jack* and *Dynamite "Moh"* is both dependent upon and points to the fact that a critical mass of early American westerns were already popularly reappropriated in the French, Algerian, and Moroccan *café-concerts* acts and streetside humor during the 1930s and 1940s. In other words, the intertextual relationship between *Dynamite Jack* and *Dynamite "Moh"* suggests the heritage of resistant readings and readers.

The search for the identity of the western bandit and hero is the centerpiece of *Dynamite Jack*. It begins with the unsuspecting Antoine Esperandieu in search of gold in Arizona. His name, Esperandieu [as in *espère en dieu*], literally means that he hopes for god's intervention, which would be the only way to find gold, when there is none to be found. Through Antoine's journey as a failed gold prospector and subsequent tax collector, he is comically transformed into a mirror image of Dynamite Jack, serving as his cowardly comic double.

The theme of the gold rush was one of the best-known themes in early American westerns, and Bastia's parody of this story recalls one of the most widely circulated American westerns, *In the Days of the Thundering Herd* (1914). Starring Tom Mix, and later released during the 1920s and 1930s as *The Wagon Train*, it featured familiar elements of the Pony Express and the 1849 gold rush to California. The gold rush serves as a backdrop for a burgeoning love affair between Tom Mix, who plays a rider for the Pony Express, and Sally Madison (Bessie Eyton). As the intertitles suggest, "Sally was more interested in the arrival of the *male* than the *mail*." Tom and Sally embark on their journey with a group of villagers only to be ambushed and taken hostage by an Indian tribe. Through a series of near escapes, assisted by the Indian chief's sister Starlight, they finally prevail, forging a new couple and family on the frontier.

The numerous battle and chase scenes easily could have been appropriated beyond the film's moral and narrative boundaries—Tom and Sally's abduction by Chief Swift Wind could have been interpreted within the context of resistance movements in Algeria, Morocco, and Indochina during the interwar period. The reinterpretation of western morality tales, which were presented in questionable condition with largely incomprehensible English intertitles, is an argument for the possibilities of the early American western as a polysemous narrative resource—a form that was continuously appropriated beyond the film's narrative intention.

The parody of the search for gold on the western frontier is made explicit in *Dynamite Jack*. In fact, before Esperandieu arrives in Arizona, he was attacked by various groups of Indians and dodged numerous brush fires on the prairie. Esperandieu's search for gold is thwarted by the fact that none remains and instead of creating the paterfamilias on the frontier, he is subject to a form of feminine coercion. In the final scene of the film, Esperandieu is taken at gunpoint to the altar, to abide by his promise to marry the character Dolorès.

In *Dynamite "Moh,"* Antoine Esperandieu is recast as Atamane Lamane (Fernandel/Fellag),[34] an extremely gullible city slicker from Algiers in search of oil in the Algerian provinces. Atamane believes the tales of the town pharmacist who tells him that if you scratch the surface, oil spurts out. Just as there was no gold to be found in Arizona, the hardheaded Atamane Lamane does not believe the sheriff (Lucien Raimbourg/Allalou), who wryly contributes that all of the oil wells have dried up or are in the hands of British Petroleum and Elf Aquatine. The sheriff's suggestion that these companies have since robbed the area of its oil reserves is made all the more comical because it is at once a preposterous proposition, again at Atamane's expense, and yet accurate if this western frontier-like desert setting were to be contemporary Algeria. In this scene, the gap between the visual track, which remains unchanged from Bastia's 1961 *Dynamite Jack*, and the contemporary Franco-Algerian audio remake contributes to an uncanny verisimilitude of the western film genre as French parody in present-day Algeria.

The name *Atamane* draws on the significance of the Ottomans in Algeria, formerly serving as French-backed mercenaries, and his last name, *Lamane,* is a play on the first name of the previous president of Algeria, Liamine Zéroual, who was put into office by the Algerian Army in 1995, three years after the election of the Islamic Salvation Front candidates was revoked by the army. Atamane goes to the Algerian frontier in search of his friend Djelloul Elvisse, based in Laghouat. This name is yet another play on words: following the Parisian North African back-slang for Lavisse in the original *Dynamite Jack*, we get Elvisse, as in Elvis Presley. In the opening scene of the film, there is the implication that Atamane is one of the visiting pilgrims to Elvis's tombstone in Graceland, making the journey because he believes that Elvis is still alive. *Dynamite "Moh"* begins to graft itself onto the visual content of *Dynamite Jack* upon renaming Jules Lavisse, whose name is clearly engraved on a tombstone, as Djelloul Elvisse, setting the stage for the back-slang linguistic, historical, and social universe of the film.

Atamane arrives to find that his friend Elvis, or Elvisse, was killed by Dynamite Moh, known as the fastest gunslinger in Algeria. While *Dynamite Jack* is a parody of the western genre, *Dynamite "Moh"* takes the Camembert western one step further into the realm of Algerian political allegory. The character of Dynamite Moh (also played by Fernandel/Fellag) is most likely a reference to a former leader of the GIA (Armed Islamic Group), Mohammed Allel, a.k.a. Moh Léveilley. Allel was one of the founding members of the GIA in the early 1990s. A native of Algiers, he was the leader of the GIA for a short time after its previous leader, Mansouri Miliani, was himself killed in December 1992.[35] Allel was himself killed shortly after becoming the leader of the GIA. His nom de guerre, Moh Léveilley, suggests the continued readiness of Mohammed as part of a holy jihad. In English, the name Léveilley, as in *l'éveillé,* means "on the alert."

The terror tactics associated with the GIA, such as the murder of entire villages near Algerian military garrisons, have led human rights advocates and journalists to claim that the GIA was infiltrated by Algerian security forces with specialized French counterterrorist tactics to discredit the Islamic Salvation Front (FIS). The FIS won the majority of parliamentary seats in the freely held elections in 1992, but the results were subsequently annulled by the Algerian military. Apart from the brutality of the massacres and their proximity to Algerian military installations, Algerian soldiers would rarely appear to protect village populations against "Islamic terrorists"; furthermore, none of the perpetrators of the massacres were identified or brought to justice. The mark of French counterterrorism, with the brutal throat-cutting of entire families and reports of torture, harkens back to terror tactics used by the French during the Algerian War of Independence.

Dynamite "Moh" parodies the Algerian military, Islamic terrorists, and the attitudes of the Algerian people. Allalou and Fellag explain that their interest in creating the audio remake was to "dynamite" political and social taboos of political and social life in contemporary Algeria. This redubbed film was first shown surreptitiously on video in cafés in Algeria as early as 1996 and was recently subtitled in French (March 1999) with the support of the director of the Guides du Routard travel books, Philippe Gloaguen. According to a recent article in the French television weekly *Télérama*, the proceeds of the video sale will be donated to Algerian refugees and to an orphanage for abandoned children.[36]

Atamane Lamane's transformation into the mirror image of Dynamite Moh begins with the arrival of a military sergeant who was called in by the villagers to protect them from Dynamite Moh. The arrival of a lone sergeant is a caricature of the army's claim that they are protecting the common people against Islamic terrorists. The sergeant proves his muster as a capable fighter to the doubting villagers by shooting a bullet through a coin that he tosses in the air. When he shoots at the coin, the same bullet enters Atmane Lamane's hotel room, shattering the bathroom mirror, which Atamane is using to shave off his mustache. To this Atamane replies, "Is there something wrong with you? Stop playing with guns! I might have slipped and cut my own throat!" Finally the sheriff, who had been urging on the sergeant, throws Atamane a gun belt with two pistols and says, "Listen, good looking, take this. It is more useful than your brylcream."

Atamane is shaving and changing his hairstyle in order to present a new, more intimidating appearance as tax collector. His earlier excursion in search of oil ended in return to the village on a stretcher in a state of delirium, subsequently recounting a traumatic encounter with fifty armed terrorists. Upon hearing Atmane's convoluted ramblings, the sheriff has realized that Atmane may serve as the perfect replacement for the tax collector, who recently quit.

Returning from his first day on the new job, Atamane unknowingly befriends Dynamite Moh at the saloon and they begin playing poker. Atamane cheats Dynamite Moh at poker, winning every hand until he recognizes him. From this point on, Atamane desperately tries to lose, but he cannot because Moh is such a bad poker player. Atamane finally tries to walk away from the game, rhetorically offering him his ATM card. To this Dynamite Moh quips, "Where is the secret code?" The offer of the ATM card does not match the visual cues in this scene. It registers as a joke precisely because it interrupts the strangely appropriate parallel between the "good badman" in *Dynamite Jack* and *Dynamite "Moh"*.

Following this scene a shoot-out ensues, led by Lady Han'fa (Adrienne Corri/Samia), the widow of Dynamite Moh's last victim. The next day, the sergeant rides into town. Upon his arrival, he proclaims that the state never abandons the people. The sergeant explains that he was the only person sent because all the other soldiers are busy guarding the voting booths. This is a passing reference to the 1994 rigged elections, in which Liamine Zéroual of the National Liberation Front, or FLN,[37] reportedly won 60 percent of the vote after being put in office ten months earlier by the Algerian military junta, officially known as the High Security Council.[38] When Atamane finally emerges after his shave, with two pistols and an all-around more dapper outlaw look, he self-mockingly asserts that he has now become a patriot, or a secular *moujahadid* activist for the FLN, which now serves as the progovernment establishment. Ironically, Atamane has been transformed into a mirror image of the Islamic terrorist, Dynamite Moh.

The first test of his new appearance is when the Indian maidservant enters his room. She passes out upon seeing him. Attributing her reaction to his striking good looks, Atamane peeks under her dress before proceeding down the staircase, where the bartender sees him in the mirror behind the bar, and begins to lower the mirror as he also ducks down. The mirror plays a vital role throughout the film as the site of misrecognition. The role of the mirror and the fact that Fernandel plays both Dynamite Moh and Atamane Lamane transforms the western theme of the "good badman" into a schizophrenic political identity crisis in Algeria. The "good" though traitorous and self-serving Atamane is transformed into an image of the "bad" Dynamite Moh without knowing it. A series of comic scenes reinforce Atamane's complete misunderstanding of the situation.

Atamane, now appearing as Dynamite Moh, continues his work as the tax collector with much greater success. The townspeople are so frightened of him that one man with a loaded rifle cannot even muster the courage to shoot at him. When Atamane arrives at a funeral for Dynamite Moh's last victim, Ahmed, all of the mourners leave in fear of him. Highly susceptible to other people's reactions, Atamane also becomes afraid and tries to escape with them. Instead, they think that he is chasing after them, while he begs them to wait for him. As the sun begins to set, Atamane arrives in town and begins to realize that some kind of transformation has occurred. He looks at himself in a mirrored window and then notices a $10,000 "wanted" poster with a drawing that looks remarkably similar to his reflection. The pathos of his discovery is revealed when he turns and sees another wanted poster, a third, and then he sees the real Dynamite Moh, accompanied by his three associates on their way to rob the baker's safe.

Zoubida (Eleanor Vargas/Samia), Dynamite Moh's lover who also happens to be the proprietor of the saloon and innkeeper, mistakes Atamane for Moh and tells him to be careful of the newly arrived sergeant. She sends him away on her white horse in search of a safe haven for the evening. The inseparability of Atamane and Moh continue as they choose the same empty house in the mountains as a hideout. Atamane hides under the bed when he sees Moh and his accomplices enter the house. At an opportune moment, Atamane knocks Moh over the head and pushes him under the bed while he lays on top of the bed. One of

Moh's accomplices becomes confused when he sees both of them on and under the bed. It is only when Moh recovers from being knocked out that Moh's remaining accomplice, the one-eyed man, who is convinced that he has double vision, understands the situation. The tongue-in-cheek humor of the film is based on the blurring of Dynamite Moh and Atamane Lamane's identities.

The indeterminacy of the warring factions in Algeria, with various relationships to the army and the French government, has led to a full blown civil war in which 100,000 people have died since 1992. The circumstances that led to the civil war might also be interpreted as yet another, more deadly, variation on the western film genre. In 1988, 7.5 million acres of public land were to be sold to foreign-based companies for oil and natural gas excavation as part of the Algerian government's general privatization of the economy. Of this land, 250,000 acres are part of a collectively organized farming delta known as the Mitidja, which was transformed into a collective farm when Algeria declared independence from France. The Mitidja Plain, which stretches from the capital Algiers to the garrison town of Blida, thirty miles to the south, is one of the main arenas of conflict between the FIS and government forces. Some journalists speculate that it has been the site of a deliberate terror campaign by factions within the government to clear the land for further privatization to increase government revenues.[39] With each successive massacre, farmers abandon their farms in search of work in the cities.

When Atamane is mistakenly captured by the villagers, it is Zoubida, a crack shot, who saves him from the hangman's noose. With her shotgun she pierces the hangman's rope and escapes with him to the safety of a granary. Zoubida takes off her clothes and they are suddenly in bed together. After making love, Zoubida professes her love to him and spins out her fantasy of a married life with him. Throughout this sequence, the masculinity of the western gunfighter is upended by an all-powerful woman, infinitely brave, powerful, and desirous. Once Zoubida and Atamane are discovered in the granary, the sergeant holds up a white flag, the sign of surrender in the western, and tells them that he knows that he is not the real Dynamite Moh and asks them to come out. When Atamane hesitates, the sergeant mockingly quips, "Do you want a U.N. peacekeeping force with Boutrous-Boutrous Ghali?" This serves as yet another humorous reminder of the how the audio track grafts the gravity of the Algerian conflict onto this comic western situation. Zoubida is angry for having been duped and turns the rifle on Atamane, who, professing his love for her and promising marriage, makes a swift exit.

The saga of mistaken identity continues. Dynamite Moh returns to town and is heralded as Atamane, the hero. He is made sheriff of the town and offered hard currency from the villagers. Moh becomes so profoundly disgusted as the double of the inept Atamane that he escapes from the village, never to return again. As the anti–"good badman" Moh must leave the village in order to maintain his profile as a self-respecting

213

terrorist. He is not in search of redemption, but a new identity as a true terrorist when nobody believes in him any longer.

Successive reappropriations of the "good badman" character, and its recent culmination as a farce of Algerian politics in *Dynamite "Moh"*, points to a Baudrillardian simulacrum. That is, politics follow cinema— western-style stock characters and events are replayed as political forces. The relationship of political farce to the actual tragedy of the Algerian situation not only places humor as the final defense against political power but is a testament to the underlying forces of narrative to make sense of conflict and scenarios that promise a form of psychic relief. I have cast *Dynamite "Moh"* as a variation on the western "good badman" in order to underscore a symbolic American logic of standardization, the western film genre, and its effects on globalization in postcolonial Algeria.

Dynamite "Moh" demonstrates an ongoing historical process in which the subversion of dominant meanings is a dynamic system of meaning production nearly simultaneous with the reception of the speech act itself. The ease of ignoring, misunderstanding, or willfully subverting the English or French intertitles in some of the earliest westerns makes it clear that the international circulation of the American western served as an infinitely adaptable cinematic form—serving as a malleable parable for contemporary political realities.

notes

A version of this paper was presented at the Symposium on the Black West, organized by Bennetta Jules-Rosette, under the auspices of the African and African-American Studies Research Project at the University of California, San Diego, April 22–23, 1999. Thanks to Janet Walker, the editor of the present volume, for her excellent suggestions for revision. Note: All translations are mine unless otherwise noted.

1. The Islamic Salvation Front (FIS) was founded in 1989 as a grassroots political and religious movement that initially attracted the dispossessed. In 1992, the FIS was banned as a political party after winning a majority in the elections.
2. Jacques Lorcey, *Fernandel* (Paris: PAC Editions, 1981), 270. Alain Petit, a French film commentator for the French television station Canal+, claims that this film was shot in Spain and the backdrop in *Dynamite Jack* was later used by Sergio Leone. Petit, however, does not cite any sources to substantiate his assertion. For further information see [http://www.cplus.fr/html/magazine/mai98/quartier.htm].
3. Jean-Jacques Rousseau, *Discourse on the Origin of Inequality*, trans. Donald A. Cress (Indianapolis: Hackett Publishing House, 1992).
4. Popular mid-nineteenth century French novels about the American West were written by Gustave Aimard, such as his thirty-volume "His Indian Tales" series which included titles such as: *The Gold-Seekers, The Indian Chief, The Last of the Incas, The Missouri Outlaws, The Prairie Flower,* and *The Trappers of Arkansas,* among other titles.
5. William B. Cohen, *The French Encounter with Africans: White Response to Blacks, 1530–1880* (Bloomington: Indiana University Press, 1980).
6. C. J. North, "Our Foreign Trade in Motion Pictures," in *The Annals: The American Academy of Political and Social Sciences,* special issue, "The Motion

Picture in Its Economic and Social Aspects," ed. Clyde L. King and Frank A. Tichenor, vol. 78, (1926), 102.

7. Kristin Thompson, *Exporting Entertainment: America in the World Film Market, 1907–1934* (London: British Film Institute Publishing, 1985).

8. Victoria de Grazia, "Mass Culture and Sovereignty: The American Challenge to European Cinemas, 1920–1960," *Journal of Modern History* 61 (1989): 58.

9. David Bordwell, Janet Staiger, and Kristin Thompson, *The Classical Hollywood Cinema: Film Style and Mode of Production to 1960* (New York: Columbia University Press, 1985), 87–95.

10. Edward Buscombe, ed., *The BFI Companion to the Western* (London: BFI Publishing, 1988), 26–28.

11. Kalton C. Lahue, *Winners of the West: The Sagebrush Heroes of the Silent Screen* (New York: A. S. Barnes, 1970), 154.

12. "American Films Lead World; Algeria Sees Them on Fly," *Variety* 75, no. 2 (1924): 1, 43.

13. Guy Olivo, "Aux origines du spectacle cinématographique en France. Le cinéma forain: l'exemple des villes du Midi méditerranéen," *Revue d'histoire moderne et contemporaine* 33 (1986): 210–28.

14. *Spahis* were a North African Cavalry contingent organized in 1834 on the model of Ottoman cavalry units and dissolved in 1962 at the end of the Algerian War. Those who joined were obliged to remain for three years. Half of the officer positions were reserved for North Africans. There were *spahis* in Algeria, Senegal, Tunisia, and Morocco.

15. Félix Mesguich, *Tours de manivelle, souvenirs d'un Chasseur d'images* (Paris: B. Grasset, 1933).

16. "American Films Lead World," 43.

17. Charles Merz, "When the Movies Go Abroad," *Harper's Monthly Magazine* 152 (1926): 163.

18. Kerry Segrave, *American Films Abroad: Hollywood's Domination of the World's Movie Screens from the 1890s to the Present* (Jefferson, N.C.: McFarland, 1997), 62.

19. Ibid., 32.

20. "American Films Lead World," 43.

21. "North Africa: Morocco," Algeria, Tunisia, French Colonies," in *The Film Daily Year Book [of Motion Pictures]*, ed. K. D. Mann (New York: J. W. Alicoate, 1928), 1010.

22. Paul Saffar, "Comment les Arabes aiment le cinéma," *Pour vous* 143 (1931): 4.

23. In this article, Saffar assumes that all Moroccans and North Africans are Arabs, which is not strictly accurate, especially in Algeria and Morocco. Many of the ethnic tribes are polytheistic and several groups, such as the Berbers were converted to Christianity.

24. Saffar, "Comment les Arabes," 4.

25. Gabriel Tarde, *L'opinion et la foule* (Paris: Félix Alcan, 1901).

26. Gabriel Tarde, *Les lois de l'imitation* (Paris: Editions Kimé, 1993 [1890]), 4.

27. Ibid., 84.

28. Christian Metz, *The Imaginary Signifier: Psychoanalysis and the Cinema*, trans. Celia Britton (Bloomington: Indiana University Press, 1982 [1977]).

29. "Our Films Disillusioning the East," *Literary Digest* 90 (1926): 26–27.

30. Sir Hesketh Bell, *Foreign Colonial Administration in the Far East* (London: E. Arnold, 1928), 121–23. As cited by A. J. W. Harloff, "L'influence pernicieuse du cinéma sur les peuples de l'Orient" (1934), 1–2. (Centre des Archives d'outre-mer, Aix-en-Provence, Dossier 64384, Fonds du Gouvernement général de l'Indochine.

31. Aimé-François Legendre, *La crise mondiale: L'Asie contre l'Europe* (Paris: Librairie Plon, 1932), 287.

32. Ibid., 289.

33. David Slavin, "The French Left and the Rif War, 1924–25: Racism and the Limits of Internationalism," in *Journal of Contemporary History* 26 (1991), 5.

34. When possible, I list the French actor who plays the role on-screen and the name of the person who performs the new Arabic voice-over.

35. "Brothers and Enemies: A War for Leadership, A Profile of Two Top Terrorist Leaders in Algeria," in *The North Africa Journal,* January 1999 [http://north-africa.com].

36. Marie Cailletet, "Eclats; Algérie: Fellag, Fernandel, même combat," *Télérama* 2567, (1999): 20.

37. The National Liberation Front (FLN) was founded in 1954 by the nine historic leaders of the Algerian revolution and has served as the unique ruling party of Algeria since 1962, when Algeria was declared an independent republic. The goal of the FLN was the restoration of Algeria as a democratic and sovereign state in accordance with Islamic principles and with respect for all fundamental human liberties, without regard for race or religion. Jean Martin, *Lexique de la colonisation française* (Paris: Dalloz, 1988), 176.

38. Akram Ellyas and Hatem Jamani, "Civil War to Reconciliation? Algeria Hopes and Prays," trans. Derry Cook-Radmore, *Le Monde Diplomatique*, September 1999, 5.

39. Patrick Forestier, "Algérie: Derrière les tueries, de sordides intérêts immobiliers et financiers?" *Paris Match*, October 9, 1997, 93.

216

part four

history

through

narrative

captive images

in the

traumatic

western

the searchers, pursued,

once upon a time in the

west, and *lone star*

j a n e t   w a l k e r

Included on the laser disc and DVD editions of *The Searchers* are some striking images from the making of the film. Apparently linked together in the 1950s for a Warner Brothers promotional program hosted by Gig Young, these images, and the accompanying narration, echo the film's historiographic agenda. Where *The Searchers* tells the story of two pioneer families, the Edwardses and Jorgensens, carving out a living in Indian territory, this early "making of" document tells a parallel story of occupation. Images of tractors gouging roads "into a wilderness where roads had never existed" are followed by images of buses and trucks bringing "pioneers from Hollywood" (John Ford and company) into a formerly "trackless Navajo country . . . a thousand square mile domain of the yucca, the cactus, and the bones of earlier pioneers who had died." A sequence of shots of the Jorgensen home under construction is followed by shots of the Edwards homestead, which the narrator promises will be "entirely destroyed by fire in an Indian raid." As Natalie Wood recites after obvious coaching, "the raids of the renegade tribes were the greatest dangers that faced the frontier people." The set-building sequence culminates in a high-angle shot from atop a ridge picturing *The Searchers'* company town "set down in the middle of a brooding wilderness."

One story of spirited physical conquest (that of the daring cast, crew, and stuntmen) echoes another (that of two unstoppable men who ride for five years to rescue a girl taken captive by the Comanche). And in both cases the landscape is crisscrossed and furrowed—scarred, if you will—by the territorial markings of the Euro-American arrivistes. Furthermore, both stories conform to the pattern of thousands of other westerns, planned and shown as fictional renditions of what Richard Slotkin, Richard White, and Ward Churchill among others have so eloquently exposed as America's own creation myth: the conquest of "the Indians" as a by-product of necessary and defensive westward expansion.

We know that the western is a historical genre, and that the history it presents is conventionalist. What I want to examine here is a particular formal feature of western film conventionalism: the catastrophic past event. I have come to the realization that westerns are not only grandly historical (peopled by historical personages and referencing actual occurences), but that very many of them are *internally* historical as well. In countless westerns, events of disturbing proportions, events that are markedly anterior to the fictive present, propel the actions and the retaliatory violence of the narrative: the Ringo Kid must kill the Plummer brothers because they victimized his family and murdered his brother (*Stagecoach*); Lin McAdam spends years tracking the man who killed his father—we find out later that that man is his very own brother (*Winchester '73*); Union soldiers kill a man's wife and burn his house down, so he goes out for revenge (*The Outlaw Josey Wales*); a bad man stuffs a harmonica into a boy's mouth and leaves that boy supporting his elder brother hanging from a gibbet (the brother meets his inevitable end); the boy grows up with a mission, hunts down the evildoer, confronts him, and relates the haunting memory in the context of a fatal duel (*Once Upon a Time in the West*); Will Munny killed women and children (*Unforgiven*). And so they go.

The commonality of these narratives is striking, as is the way the past is handled, traumatically, as I will contend, in a series of quick flashes—rapid cuts, odd angles, lots of movement; or perhaps as a fully formed flashback, sometimes of uncertain origin (in *Once Upon a Time in the West* the two men "share" the memory[1]); or as a trail of signifiers strewn across the landscape (a bloody guidon, a burning wagon, a shred of gingham); or, finally, as a structuring absence—the unseen past that animates present action and gives it its charged violence, or, at the other extreme, its extraordinary but characteristic *lack* of affect (Martin in *The Searchers*: "I hope you die!"; Ethan, laconically: "That'll be the day."). In retrospective westerns such as these, past events elude the realist register to suggest another way of knowing, one marked by ellipsis, uncertainty, and repetition.

The aim of this essay, then, is to identify a prominent subgroup of westerns, made up of what I'll call "traumatic westerns," in which past events of a catastrophic nature are represented so as to challenge both the realist representational strategies of a genre that often trades on historical authenticity and the ideological precepts of the myth of Manifest Destiny. Traumatic westerns, it might be said, are counterrealistic and counterhistorical. They are those films in which the contradictions of American conquest—a kind of generalized trauma—become invested in particular narrative scenarios.

There are two preeminent abodes where trauma lodges, whether found separately or together in one film: the western captivity narrative and the narrative of familial succession. Both rely more than most other western narratives on the sequela of events, capture and rescue in the former case and generational accession in the second, and both are represented very often through ellipses and marked temporal warping.[2]

Consider *Blazing the Trail* (Thomas Ince, 1912), *The Searchers* (John Ford, 1956), and *Dances with Wolves* (Kevin Costner, 1990) as examples of the captivity narrative in action. In *Blazing the Trail* Indians stand on a bluff overlooking a pioneer encampment. Their strategy planned, they approach a family of settlers who greet them, offer food, and proffer guns to "curious Indians." But the Indians have other ideas: grabbing the guns, they shoot the father and mother of the family, wound the adult son Jack, carry off the unmarried daughter, and leave the wagon burning.

Maureen Turim, in *Flashbacks in Film*, is right to emphasize the "disruption and postponement" that characterize *Blazing the Trail*'s particular rendition of the flashback.[3] In a twelve minute film, delay has got to be hard won and deliberate. And here the capture is bracketed by both delay and distance: our hero, the daughter's sweetheart, sees the telltale smoke but just . . . can't . . . get . . . there in time to stop what he "should" have been on hand to prevent. All he can do is kneel beside the dead father at the smoking campsight and then take off after the daughter. What adds interest to the sequence is the fact that we, too, are given to be late arrivals at the scene. As spectators, we arrive before the hero, but only after the parents have been shot—we don't actually see the shooting at that point. All we see is the struggling daughter disappearing around the back of the wagon in the arms of Indian braves. But here the mind's eye is enabled by filmic representation. Jack has stumbled to his feet and staggered off in search of help. Although he collapses, he revives sufficiently to tell the wagon train of settlers what has happened. This we see in a flashback that fills in the events of the massacre itself from the time we left the family making welcoming gestures to the Indians to the moment of the daughter's abduction. Thus is capture in *Blazing the Trail* marked as a trauma, one that seems to haunt the young men of the narrative, and one whose "pastness" is marked by delay and the flashback device.

Though perhaps difficult to recall in the context of an ostensibly pro–Native American film, there is also an Indian attack scene in *Dances with Wolves*. The sequence is presented as the childhood memory of the film's heroine, Christine or Stands With A Fist, a woman who has been raised by a Lakota family after her own family was massacred by Pawnee. Indians approach a pioneer settlement. The men of the settlement, fathers of two children looking on from afar, walk out to meet them. In an instant, the Indians attack. As the pioneers turn to flee, they are mortally wounded with flung tomahawks that lodge in their backs. A young Christine, one of the children looking on, runs off across a field.

This is, in my view, the most frightening of all such massacres and the most reprehensible in its portrayal of Indian savagery: the children watching helplessly—little captive witnesses—as the tomahawks fly in slow motion, but inexorably, toward the turned backs of their unsuspecting victims; the disembodied voice of the mother calling for her daughter ... "Christiiine" ... the sound waves floating out across the sudden vastness of the homestead we know to be already as good as reclaimed by the wilderness from which it had been so tenuously carved; the mother as good as scalped.

The scenario abides here as an example of what Mikhail Bakhtin calls "genre memory": the continuing existence of an earlier generic paradigm in the narrative sediment of a later one.[4] The pointed pastness of this flashback differentiates Pawnee savagery from the noble Lakota of the film's present, and old filmic conventions from supposedly enlightened new ones. And Christine is not actually taken captive. She escapes across the plains to find safety with the Lakota. But, in *Dances with Wolves* on this occasion of Stands With A Fist's traumatic memory, long-held stereotypes erupt through the thin crust of liberal sediment, belying the film's pretense to present an enlightened picture of Native Americans.

Moreover, this seemingly exceptional moment actually does penetrate the larger meaning of the film. As Ward Churchill has observed in passing (but monumentally), the whole film may be construed as a captivity narrative that ends as "Lt. Dunbar and the female 'captive' he has 'recovered' ride off into the proverbial sunset, leaving their Lakota friends to be slaughtered by and subordinated to the United States."[5]

In *The Searchers,* the massacre of Aaron, Martha, and Ben Edwards, and the abduction of the two girls, Lucy and Debbie, is not, technically, an event of the past. It occurs in its proper chronological place in the narrative, offscreen, yes, but still simultaneous with events in the present mode. The men ride out after what they think are Kiowa cattle rustlers, while back home the Comanche stage a murder raid on the largely unprotected homestead.

Yet, technicalities apart, the massacre belongs securely to the traumatic past. Steven Spielberg has said that the film "contains the single most harrowing moment in any film I've ever seen,"[6] and one possible supposition would be that he's referring to what Janey Place has called "the astounding close-up of [John Wayne's] face" taken over the back of his horse, as he realizes his brother's family is lost.[7] So many things are indeed astounding about this moment.[8] For one thing, it is the mature expression by director John Ford of a previously existing cinematic trope. In *Blazing the Trail* the hero senses the worst when he sees from afar the line of smoke wafting over the bluff from the direction of the campsite. But we see only the back of his head, and, of course, this silent short in no way offers the character identification of a feature narrative. Perhaps it is *Red River* that inspired Ford,[9] for it contains a shot of Wayne's face at the moment he realizes that the smoke visible over the rise comes from the burning wagon train and signals the death of Fen, the woman he loves . . . and that there's nothing he can do about it. In *Red River* Tom Dunson (Wayne) doesn't bother to investigate, as far as we know. All he can do is hunker down for a fight with the Indians who come after him, and cherish the bracelet he had given Fen once he recovers it from the wrist of an Indian brave.

What I find most compelling about this trope, and in particular Ford's rendition of it in *The Searchers*, is what I'll call the "prospective pastness" of this sequence in future preterite. At the moment of the character Ethan's (Wayne's) close-up, the family may still be alive, but by the time he gets there, the family will have been killed (or abducted). It's already too late, even though it hasn't happened yet. Another paradox is that slowness now equals quickness. Ethan stops to feed and rest his horse, and by so doing bypasses the other men and arrives home first. But then there's nothing to be done upon arrival except to read the signs of what has already transpired: the smoking buildings, the ravaged bodies, the abandoned rag doll (and in the novel, a bit of buffalo robe where Debbie had gone to hide, and Martha's severed hand, a toy the Comanche "tossed . . . from one to another, capering and whooping, until they lost it in the dark").[10]

Ethan's "look back"—a last look, in a way—is one of premature grieving (since they are not yet dead). The present of the look back (when they are still alive) is already being made past from the standpoint of an imagined future (when they are dead). And all of this is mixed instantly with Ethan's guilt over his inability to help them and his failure to properly protect them. It is the "future past" now "present" in his look back that becomes the trauma that will haunt him . . . is already haunting him . . . in advance of their deaths. Of course he will never really see what happened at the massacre, but can only imagine. And he will continue to look for that scene/seen, to search for whatever can be recovered (like Fen's bracelet in *Red River*)—be they scraps and artifacts or a girl captive. Thus, it is Ethan's instant recognition as expressed by his look and not the massacre per se that is the traumatic event for him because his imagination summons the horrible images of what has not yet occurred. And his subsequent search for the captive girl will be his attempt to "recover" his (normal, pretraumatic) memory. Thus, the western landscape becomes a mental landscape. This thought is also suggested by the poster for *The Searchers*: two mounted men, tiny in the distance of a desertscape over which they ride, and the words "He had to find her. . . ."

in wavy script as if to evoke an echoing call or thought,[11] the graphic merging of landscape and mindscape.

The massacre scene is doubly elusive for the spectator. Not only do we not see the massacre itself (parallel editing has placed us with Ethan, the properties of cinema spectating have made us helpless to act, and no flashback will be provided), but also we are not given (thankfully) the sight of Martha's corpse.[12] This is what Ethan sees, presumably, when he ducks into the burned cabin (the camera is in there too, but angled toward Ethan and not toward what he sees), emerges reeling, and bars Martin from entering. And the smoking ruins that further veil the scene help induct the spectator into Ethan's (and Martin's) realm of horrifying imagination and loss. Now we, too, have a stake in the "ruins of memory."[13]

The ability to discern the meaning of prior events by the traces they leave is highly valued. Martin Pauley notices "something mighty fishy" about the trail the Comanche left to lure the men. But his interpretive insight comes too late anyway, even if Ethan had paid him any mind. In the novel, the men initially debate the significance of subtle signs they spot along the trail until their meaning becomes obvious to all: "This here's a murder raid. . . . They drove your cattle to pull us out."[14]

And, again, in the novel, the futility of hindsight, of missed signs and tardy interpretations is underlined by a joint reflection that the narrator has the characters engage in as they follow the trail of dead cattle: a reflection that contrasts impending catastrophe with the sharper vigilance of prior years. In it we read, "The last five minutes had taken them ten years back into the past, when every night of the world was an uncertain thing. The years of watchfulness and struggle had brought them some sense of confidence and security toward the last; but now all that was struck away as if they had their whole lives to do over again."[15] This passage echoes, in turn, the fatalistic reverie of Aaron Edwards ("Henry" in the novel) with which the book begins. As he scouts his property at sundown, knowing something's wrong and pretty sure he knows just what, he reflects on "eighteen years of hanging on" in the face of danger ever more apparent. Yes, there had been signs: "Sometimes a man's senses picked up dim warnings he didn't even recognize."[16] But he had not realized their meaning, nor had he acted . . . in time: "If he could have seen, in any moment of the years they had lived here, the endless hazards that lay ahead, he would have quit that same minute and got Martha out of there if he had had to tie her."[17] Again, we have a realization that comes too late: a powerless vision of impending events; and an equally powerless vision of present events from the perspective of an imagined, inevitable, lethal future. He already didn't get Martha out in time. His novelistic reverie matches Ethan's filmic gaze: the future passes before their eyes and renders the present past. Temporal elasticity is there in film and novel both, as is the work of imagination. Reading *The Searchers* as novel we must imagine what people and things look like (as we would reading other novels), but we are given Aaron's thoughts. Watching *The Searchers* in film we are given an open landscape—a certain amplitude of space—in which to conjure Ethan's thoughts. The look and the land: this film exemplifies the power of the trauma western to transform physical landscape into a mental traumascape for character and spectators alike.[18]

As the narrative unrolls its five years of searching, the massacre's pastness will be cinched. But the reminders of its torments will resurface in the form of objects scavenged from the landscape: Lucy's dress, the shred of Debbie's apron, the Civil War medallion.

Cathy Caruth writes that "to be traumatized is precisely to be possessed by an image or event."[19] In this sense *The Searchers*, and other westerns in which the catastrophic past event is a prominent feature of the narrative, are *traumatized*—and now I use the term technically. They are "possessed by" certain events and images (those swatches of gingham) that keep turning up both in single films and in multiple westerns of the traumatic cycle as a whole.

Specifically, traumatic westerns share the formal features of traumatic memory as associated with and described by the literature of post-traumatic stress disorder (PTSD). The American Psychiatric Association defines PTSD as a response to an event or events that takes the form of "distressing recollections," "recurrent distressing dreams," "illusions, hallucinations, and dissociative flashback episodes."[20] This, to my mind, describes very well how certain ostensibly classical westerns depart from strictly realistic conventions to depict catastrophic events in a subjective style marked by nonlinearity, repetition, emotional affect, metonymic symbolism, and flashbacks. I'm not saying that the characters suffer from PTSD (though if one were to psychologize a fictional character, that diagnosis would be as good as any). What I do want to say is that the films themselves display the formal and stylistic characteristics of the traumatic mindscape in which disturbances of memory are prominent.

As Judith Herman expresses it, "trauma simultaneously enhances and impairs memory.... On the one hand, traumatized people remember too much; on the other hand, they remember too little."[21] Writing about the mental changes found in "casualties of war and political oppression—combat veterans, political prisoners, and concentration camp survivors; and in the casualties of sexual and domestic oppression—rape victims, battered women, and abused children,"[22] Herman reports that such individuals may relate stories about their experiences in which large parts of the story are missing or misplaced. Or, the survivors of such experiences may not have ready access to the memory of the things that befell them. Specifically, whereas people relating terrifying experiences tend to be unusually accurate in describing their "gist" and "central detail," they tend to be inaccurate in the "peripheral detail, contextual information, [and] time sequencing."[23] From a broader perspective, Herman delineates what I have called, elsewhere, the "traumatic paradox."[24] That is, the very fact that an event of horrifying proportions really did occur interferes with the ability of a witness, survivor, or participant to remember and report accurately the actual details of that event. The catastrophic event is, literally, mind-boggling.

Herman and others, including Lenore Terr and Elizabeth Waites, have done pathbreaking work in the area of PTSD,[25] and theirs is a convincing argument that traumatic experiences change peoples' ability to remember what they went through.[26] Yet there remains a dearth of literature documenting the specific nature of the alterations people make and/or the embellishments they add to their stories. What these clinicians and authors *have* established is that such material must come either from the realm of the rememberer's own experiences, including her experience of interactions with others and with media texts, and/or from her fantasy life. Traumatic memory, these researchers show, mingles the realms of fantasy and reality.

If all this is so, then what is the nature of the underlying traumas with which audiences are presented in traumatic westerns? How can we account for the perseveration that produces and reproduces these particular stories? What is achieved in the recourse to the nonrealist register? What insights can be gained from sorting out the realms of fantasy and reality in the traumatic western? My answer is historiographic in nature, and also psychological. Traumatic westerns feature the American mind and bodyscape in history; their internal pastness doubles the western's historical setting, interpolating the spectator into the terrain of history and memory.

As PTSD literature teaches us, traumatic memories, due to the incomprehensible nature of the events that produced them, tend not to resolve themselves into clearly demarcated facts and falsehoods. Instead, traumatic memories are made up of veridical *and* revised elements; that is, of elements that refer directly to determinate past happenings, and elements that have been mentally "shade[ed] and patch[ed] ... combine[ed] and delete[d]" according to the exigencies of the current world of the rememberer.[27]

And, when the rememberer is a perpetrator of violent crimes, denial and prevarication along with the unconscious vicissitudes of memory are all the more common. Although relatively little is known about the mental life of people who perpetrate violent crimes, Herman suggests that one common line of defense used by perpetrators is to "attack the credibility of the victim and anyone who supports the victim.... The victim is deluded; the victim lies; the victim fantasizes; the victim is manipulative; the victim is manipulated." Herman stresses the eagerness of the perpetrator to put his own "spin" on reality and explores the relative power of perpetrators to do so: "The more powerful the perpetrator, the greater will be his prerogative to name and define reality, and the more completely his arguments will prevail."[28]

This is the sort of "shading" and the sort of relationship to history that obtains in captivity westerns. It must be partially true that people have long enjoyed scenes of Indians massacring settlers and taking captives because these scenes represent both the enormity of conquest's obstacles ("the greatest dangers that faced the frontier people" à la *The Searchers* promo) and because they seem to justify retribution, leading to the gratifying search and rescue portions of the captivity narrative in which the Indians wind up dead. But might this not be a perpetrator's view of traumatic events? It is true in reality, as seen in conventional fictionalizations, that some Native Americans killed or abducted European settlers. But it is also true that the vast majority of the victims of these encounters were Native Americans. Thus I contend that while captivity sequences do recall and "justify" the settlers's perspective, because they are traumatic texts they also do more than that. Repeated in multiple films, characterized by fragmentary imaging and stereotypical portrayals, these texts represent the "gist" and "central details" of Indian/settler confrontation—the conquest of American Indians—in a form in which "contextual information, [and] time sequencing" are altered (see Herman). In other words, at the same time that captivity sequences ascribe an insistent false consecutiveness ("they started it—we were only fighting back") to rewrite conquest as defense, they also delete, dissociate, and reverse the genocidal onus. In short, these texts represent the massacre of American Indians *as* the massacre of settlers.[29] Indian savagery redux shadows white vengeance as the misbegotten marker of Native American dispossession and death, and the subjugation of Indians by whites is referenced only obliquely through the shifting roles of fantasy structures in traumatic texts. Traumatic captivity sequences represent indirectly a historical reality they cannot really justify: the conquest of Native Americans and the appropriation of their land.

Memory work sees through such deceptive textual operations. The ellipses, symbols, and smoke that characterize captivity sequences: also signal their status as traumatic texts and the concomitant need to approach them through what Ian Hacking calls a "memoro-politics" of reading.[30] As Robert Burgoyne has argued in relation to the more recent film *Thunderheart*, so too in captivity sequences: attacking Indians function as projections of Euro-American selves.[31] This is facilitated by the commonplace doubling of Hero and Savage (as with Ethan and Scar), and (at another level) by the commonplace casting of caucasian actors in the roles of Indians ("racial drag" signaling reversal). Moreover, the fictional westerner's consistent failure to act in time to prevent what he knows is coming—experience in future preterite—is a better description of what must have been the Native Americans' and not the conquerors' experience of conquest. American Indian history in traumatic westerns is not unrepresented. It is there. But it is there in another guise, legible through the reading practices appropriate to the traumatic text.

As suggested at the outset, the captivity theme is not the only one through which the western's engagement with the traumatic past is realized. Perhaps more narratively diffuse but of equal significance is the theme of fathers, sons, and familial succession. Here, too, the past abides as an unrecoverable time of wrenching trauma. *Pursued, Once Upon a Time in the West,* and *Lone Star* are all films in which grown men are driven to action by traumatic boyhood events. More specifically, in these films and others like them, the death of a father, or a father figure, looms large. In *Little Big Man* a boy bursts into a bar and fatally shoots Wild Bill Hickok, all the while shouting, "I've been looking for you all my life—you killed my father." The joke—that a mere boy could lay claim to a protracted past, and that he could successfully ambush the gunfighter Hickok—wouldn't work if dead fathers (mentors, or brothers) and lives exhausted by family loyalty were not common in western films. These themes are indeed central to a significant number of westerns, especially those, including *Stagecoach, Winchester '73, The Man From Laramie,* and *Nevada Smith,* that define what Will Wright has called the "vengeance variation" of the genre.[32]

Of particular interest here, for course, are films in which past events pertaining to familial succession now are visually and/or aurally evoked as the memories, dreams, and/or hallucinations of central characters. Represented, once again, through nonrealist devices including the deliberate blurring of past and present time frames, uncertain narration, and nonsynched sound, these hazy evocations of times past suggest a traumatic logic at work here as in the captivity sequences.

Virginia Wright Wexman has provided what I take to be the most extended and insightful exposition of dynastic progression in the western, "the family on the land."[33] Westerns about familial succession represent, she argues, a regulated system of property inheritance ensuing from father to son, threatened by exterior agencies, but sufficiently entrenched to counter even the "genre's pervasive emphasis on violence and killing."[34] And, by attending to the role of the family in this subgroup of westerns, Wexman is able to bring gender issues to the fore, showing the centrality of gender to a genre so often regarded as one that leaves women out. She reveals, in short, the inseparability in the western of formations of gender and the frontier.[35]

Wexman begins her section "The Land as Property and the Ideal of Dynastic Marriage" by stating, succinctly, "What is most conspicuously at issue in westerns is not the right to possess women but the right to possess land."[36] But as we see, tracing Wexman's developing argument, the right to possess land is after all based on an "ideal of dynastic marriage," returning ultimately to gender relations, specifically "the right to possess women." Bringing contemporary cultural studies literature on the west together with Friedrich Engels's ideas about and Edward Shorter's history of gender and property, Wexman shows that the couple in the western is not the romantic essense that nostalgic memory conjures up, but rather a supremely economic unit, a "created" couple. For example, in *Arizona*, Wexman recounts, "William Holden decides to marry Jean Arthur on first seeing her, and Arthur, who needs someone to help run her ranch, makes up her mind about Holden almost as quickly."[37] Not only do westerns abound with such "affectionless" marriages "held together by considerations of property and lineage,"[38] but the "economic struggles involved in establishing the presence of the family on the land" and "issues of inheritance" very often outweigh depictions of any kind of courtship at all in western narratives.[39]

Then what's the problem (apart from the all too historical conception of women as property)? If familial succession westerns are to be seen as traumatic, wherein lies the catastrophe? What is the motive force of traumatic representation in this subgroup of westerns? Although Wexman seems to regard dynastic progression as a largely positive force that "counters" or perhaps compensates for the violence of the western, she does mention the frequent theme of rivalry between brothers and the "odd aura of incest prohibition,"[40] usually of the mother-son variety, that pervades these films. To my thinking these insights could be extended. Familial succession films harbor a landscape that is every bit as traumatized as that of the captivity western, and traumatized precisely at the point where property informs intergenerational conflict.

In *Pursued*, Jeb Rand (Robert Mitchum) is in a position to inherit precisely because his father has been killed. In a distinct echo of Sigmund Freud's family romance, Jeb finds himself adopted into a wealthier family, one that is, conveniently for the boy's prospects, already missing its patriarch. The events he struggles to remember against defensive forgetting have already accrued to his economic benefit. And in *Once Upon a Time in the West*, the sadistic act that the boy sets out to avenge (the hanging noted at the beginning of this chapter) is perpetrated by a land-hungry bad man whose representation locates him simultaneously outside of and inside the film's core family unit. As with captivity narratives where the external threat posed by Indians veils the homicidal impulse of settlers, so with westerns of familial succession the family itself harbors a murderous rivalry, veiled but not obviated by the demonization of the evil antagonist.

These are Oedipal issues and Wexman is right to bemoan the dearth of psychoanalytic analyses of the western. The westerns she discusses are unmistakeably "anchored by issues of a compelling psychological nature,"[41] as are traumatic westerns by definition. In view of this lack, two lengthy articles on *Pursued,* one by Paul Willemen (1974) and one by Andrew Britton (1976), are still unsurpassed early contributions to the psychoanalytic study of the western.[42]

Both authors attribute to the film an ambivalence about the family, and specifically about the father: "It is one of the film's main strategies to imply that, whether protective or aggressive, the parent generates anxiety in the children," writes Britton.[43] Willemen argues that the traumatic sequence presented multiple times in flashback is in fact a "primal fantasy" expressing the child's wish to eliminate the father. It's particularly interesting, given this consistency of thought, that the Britton article is a refutation of Willemen's, with the main point of attack being precisely Willemen's identification of primal scene imagery and "incestuous overtones" in *Pursued*.

I agree with Willemen on both points. The film is frankly Oedipal and the rivalry is not just between the boy Jeb and the bad man Grant Callum who is after him, but also between the boy Jeb and his own father. It comes as something of a surprise, then, to note that in the same article that Willemen identifies father-son rivalry he also denies it, saying that virtually all of the men *except* Grant (who is bad) stand in for the father. In other words, both critics acknowledge *and also disavow* that the film couches a mutual murderousness between father and son.

If anything, Willemen could have been more, and not less, adamant about the Oedipal impulses that inform the film. But the blind spots of his otherwise brilliant and pioneering article are likely those of its time: his attributions of Oedipality wither because they are not grounded in historical exposition of the centrality of land ownership in the West/ western (Wexman's "*family* on the *land*"), and because the contemporary literature on posttraumatic stress disorder had not yet been written at the time.

I return to *Pursued*, therefore, to locate as traumatic representation some of Willemen's insights about the function of memory and imagination in the film, to add to some of his findings, and to suggest the film's intimations of Oedipality provide a counterreading of the inheritance structures that undergird American settlement.

In *Pursued*, the Robert Mitchum character, Jeb Rand, experiences recurring flashbacks to a scene he witnessed as a boy of about three or four years old. But he can't mentally pin down the details of what took place— nor will his adoptive mother, who was also present at the scene, tell him. Finally, in desperation to remember, Jeb returns to the place where the events occurred, the little house at Bear Paw Butte, and waits for the return of memory and for events to come to a head. This return is particularly prominant plotwise, for it forms the start of the film, the body of which is told in flashback from that beginning point as Jeb relates his life story to Thorley (Teresa Wright), his adoptive sister who became his wife. At the film's climax, Jeb "recovers" the memory of what he had witnessed from his childhood hiding place below a trap door: the death of his father, sister, and two brothers in a gun battle with the Callum brothers, one of whom is also killed. With the memory recovered, the film proceeds toward resolution.

What Jeb learns is that the basis of the feud was an extramarital affair between Jeb's father and "Ma" Callum, the woman who would carry young Jeb away when the shooting died out and become his adoptive mother. Her husband (the Callum who died in battle) and his brother, Grant Callum, killed Jeb's father because he provoked adultery in the Callum clan. And Grant left the battle with every intention of finishing the job by hunting Jeb down and killing him, too.

Because Jeb knew nothing of this before his final return to Bear Paw Butte, the autobiographical incidents he recounts to Thorley are introduced as a series of lucky escapes, near misses Jeb avoided through dumb luck alone. Audiences, however, are able to appreciate the depth of Jeb's predicament because we know more than he could have, either at the time events were occurring, or even later, when he relates them to Thorley.[44] For example, as a ten- or eleven-year-old, Jeb didn't know that it was Grant Callum who shot the colt out from under him, nor did he know that the intended target wasn't the colt at all but rather Jeb himself. Therefore, *we* know that Jeb's *not* knowing makes him a sitting duck for Grant Callum. Moreover, Jeb's not knowing keeps he and Thorley apart. He needs to know about his past in order to secure his future and to preserve his marriage to Thorley. Thus, as in *The Searchers*, the mood of the film is retrospective immediacy. Jeb must learn what he already did not know before it's too late. But this time, unlike in *The Searchers*, it's not too late.

The key to safety is memory, but memory is presented as a dicey proposition. As Paul Willemen points out, the most remarkable element of the flashback sequences in *Pursued* is the "doubt, or rather . . . ambivalence" that "is created regarding Jeb's memories: the distinction between memories and imagination has been blurred" and "the reality status of that memory is thereby evacuated."[45] The initial image whose reality status is in doubt is that of a man who "come[s] killing." This latter image is the inaugural memory of the film. "I don't know all of it, but I know some," says Jeb to Thorley. "I've been thinking and figuring," he continues. "This is where it started, this is where it's gonna end. See that rise? They'll be coming over that. They'll come killing." Jeb looks screen left and his words are supported by the blurred image of a single man superimposed on the desert landscape. The specter's threatening words (presented in voice-over) echo over the image: "Come out or we'll come in after you." A close-up of Thorley follows; she looks in the direction Jeb indicates. But the eyeline match yields only an empty landscape: "Jeb honey, there's no one out there. You're imagining." "I'm not imagining, I'm remembering," Jeb counters, and, at that point in the film, we can't tell for sure which it is.

Near the end of the film events occur that take up the action where it was interrupted by the extended flashback and they seem to bear out the validity of Jeb's memories. Grant Callum appears over the rise, this time with the intent to kill the grown-up Jeb. However, it is never completely certain whether Jeb was, as he claimed, "remembering," and not imagining or, as Andrew Britton suggests, "predicting." And, as Willemen further contends, this "distinction between phantasy and the real operates

Figs. 10.1 and 10.2. Jeb (Robert Mitchum) remembers or predicts what happened or is yet to happen in *Pursued* (Raoul Walsh, 1947).

only within the film [the diegesis]."[46] Objectively speaking, the formal operations of the film support no such distinction between fantasy and reality.

Willemen's other strand of argument is that the film functions according to a logic of Oedipal desire. What Jeb witnessed, a father shooting and a mother "lying down," constitutes a Freudian "primal scene" ("a scene of parental coitus, observed by the child or inferred and phantasized on the basis of a re-activation of unconscious memory-traces"[47]). And it is a scene that ends well for the boy. Willemen describes the events as follows: "After they have gazed into each other's eyes, she takes him into her arms. No wonder the child is not anxious to leave and grabs hold of the doorposts in an effort to remain at the scene of his triumph."

Moreover, the film's character roles are overdetermined and shifting: Thorley is not only Jeb's stepsister and then wife, but also a "(narcissistic) love object/mirror image to Jeb" and "stand-in for mother."[48] Adam, Thorley's brother, and Jeb's too after the latter's adoption into the family, is rightful heir to the Callum ranch and thus another occupant of the father role.

This is where Willemen could go further, both with the Oedipal issues he distinguishes and with the supporting stylistic analysis. Jeb's memory/hallucination is actually made up of two conjoined portions, and this doubleness is key to the film's central concern: the threat that adult men/fathers pose toward boys/sons. In the main, what Jeb struggles to recall is the gun battle that results in the death of his father and siblings. And we are given four more-or-less complete renditions of this emergent memory. But the other portion of the memory is its sort of prologue: the hallucination/memory of the man who "comes killing." And he *keeps on* coming. When he ambushes Jeb, killing the colt, he starts a train of actions that triggers one of Jeb's flashbacks. Next, he manipulates events so that Jeb has to go off to fight in the Spanish-American War, where Jeb is wounded and suffers another flashback. Finally, as the film's own flashback structure comes full circle, Grant Callum arrives at Bear Paw Butte to kill Jeb Rand, who is now a grown man.

But Grant Callum isn't "the father"—or is he? Willemen, before me, has discussed how the gun-battle-as-primal-scene couches disavowal and Oedipal fantasy. Jeb disavows the presence of his father in the first extended telling of the memory ("Daddy, Daddy," the boy Jeb cries. "He wasn't there," the adult Jeb narrates). And in the final telling Jeb recounts his father's death and his own flight from the scene in the arms of his new mother. But Willemen hesitates over the role of Grant Callum. He does perceive that "[a]ny representative of this scene," including Callum, "must bear the marks of both the father's castration threat, ie. the name of the Father, the Law, and of Jeb's blocking out of castration."[49] And Willemen acknowledges that "Grant Callum therefore functions as an incarnation of the conflicting elements at play in the phantasy."[50] But Willemen refuses what his own argument suggests: that Callum might occupy the father role. There is no shortage of other minor characters to whom Willemen *is* willing to grant the father role, including Thorley's beau Prentice and Jeb's mentor, Dingle; only Callum is left out. Callum, writes Willemen, is "not a representative of the father, but of the elements represented in the scene, he is a representative of the representation." And

Willemen concludes his study as a whole by arguing that the "center of interest of the phantasy" in *Pursued* is not, after all, the spectacle of Jeb's nightmare/memory, but rather the look itself. Thus, Willemen's title, "The Fugitive Subject," indicates that it is the condition of split subjectivity that is central to the film and not the threat posed by the father, denied or otherwise.

I beg to differ. Willemen's claim that Callum is a "representation of a representation" seems suspiciously like a disavowal of the elements he himself has identified, which elements include, of course, the mechanism of disavowal itself. Willmen stops short of arguing—he seems to deny—that a murderous character could occupy the father role. I believe a murderous father can and does. The Callum character functions precisely to embody the most potent of threats posed by fathers against sons: to come killing (sexual pun intended).

It is the conjoined nature of Jeb's memories that ensures that Grant Callum does indeed occupy the role of a murderous father in the film's fantasy logic. The image of the man who "come[s] killing" is not repeated in conjunction with the recovered memory of the gun battle, but *replaced* by it. The killer's image is followed by the first rendition of the gun battle scene in which Jeb's actual father is absent, never to be seen. Jeb usurps the place of his real/dead father with Ma, which makes him vulnerable to the father's wrath, here embodied by Grant, the man who "keeps coming." In this way a substitution is made: bad man for good; effectual man for ineffectual; killer for father.

Another aspect of the film that links Callum to the violent father is the fact that, while "they'll come killing" refers to a group of men, it is only Callum that we see in the flashback.[51] There's no sign of the others, including Callum's brother, who must have participated in the battle. Thus, the lone man in the image is *the* prominent male figure in Jeb's life and psychosexual makeup. And his intent is murderous. None of this is at all surprising in Freudian terms, where a boy may very well perceive his own beloved father as being eminently capable of violence against the mother and against the boy himself.

True, the film represents said threat only in fantasy form, "distorted to a greater or lesser extent by defensive processes:"[52] Callum is not *actually* Jeb's father, nor has *this* Callum known Jeb's mother. However, the appearance of the Callum mirage adjacent to a scene that depicts and erases a father's violence does indeed suggest that Callum incarnates a role that can't be represented more directly nor talked about critically without the urge to deny: the role of the violent father.

The father's threat has the further distinction of being at the crux of the film's productive "ambivalence" over memory, imagination, and, prediction. Not only do the conjoined memories substitute Callum for the absent father, but they clinch the substitution's violent import: what we see when we see Jeb mentally conjuring his father is the image (achieved through the technique of superimposition) of his father's spurred boots stomping on his face. Moreover, the dialogue given to the character Jeb when he finally (supposedly) remembers the traumatic scene downsizes a two-family feud into a one-family affair involving his own nuclear family. Two shooting men collapse into one: "The man shooting was my father. My sister lay on the floor dead. And my brothers were prone, too."

The plot justifies the son's desire to have the father eliminated by weaving a story of self-defense against an evil outside agent. In this film Grant is killed by Ma so that Jeb can go off (in possession of the Callum ranch?) with Thorley. But on the level accessed through trauma literacy, it is the father's death that reads as a necessary and desirable preamble to "dynastic marriage."

In a limited Freudian psychoanalytic reading, one could say that *Pursued* figures rivalry and castration as the "imaginings" (read: fantasies tout court) of the boy child—a fictional character.[53] But I think the film does more. What it also provides, and what psychological theories of trauma allow us to discern in it, is a meditation on the unpalatable nature of memory.

As Cathy Caruth explains, "[T]he impact of the traumatic event lies precisely in its belatedness, in its refusal to be simply located, in its insistent appearance outside the boundaries of any single place or time.... [Traumatic events] assume their force precisely in their temporal delay."[54] Jeb claims he is remembering and not imagining, but his purchase on the events that occurred is imperfect. For one thing, he has forgotten them until the rush of memory at Bear Paw Butte. But what is more significant is the fact that, even when he has supposedly remembered what transpired, gaps and inconsistencies remain. Why has he remembered only a solitary opponent? And shouldn't he have remembered his father's dead body rather than no father at all? What he claims to remember, then, is never borne out fully by the events of the film.

Trauma-generated delayed memory is applicable not only to character memory but to the viewer's experience as well. Trauma westerns invite a way of apprehending the world that is disorienting. When we take in Callum and characters like him in trauma westerns, we read realist representation pragmatically (all is what it seems) *and* we read traumatic representation fantastically (meaning and identity are shifting propositions): Callum is and isn't the father; Callum as father/not father is/isn't violent; fathers are/are not capable of violence toward sons.

That the theme of father-son rivalry and the rhetoric of ambivalent memory resonate for audiences is suggested by their presence in other films. *Once Upon a Time in the West* and *Lone Star* also pay sustained attention to the son's trauma and its ongoing effects and they, like many other westerns, deepen and complicate the "good but dead father" plot, or, as I see it, partial pretext.

Christopher Frayling writes that *Once Upon a Time in the West* is full of references to Hollywood westerns, and that this use of quotations as

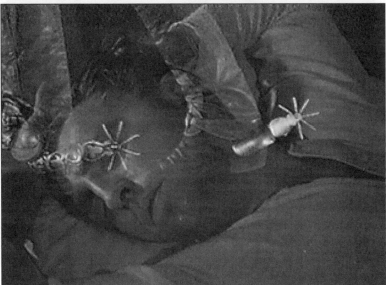

Figs. 10.3 and 10.4. A conjured image of paternal violence in *Pursued*. What the boy experienced. What the man remembers/dreams.

236

well as his "professional expertise in Hollywood film technique" are what allowed Sergio Leone, in his spaghetti westerns, to overturn the myths of Hollywood fare. *The Iron Horse, Johnny Guitar, High Noon, Shane,* and *Dodge City,* not to mention the themes and settings of any number of John Ford films, are all cited by Frayling as films "quoted" in Bernardo Bertolucci's three-hundred-page treatment for *Once Upon a Time* and/or in the finished film. That Frayling doesn't mention *Pursued* is surprising, for *Once Upon a Time* seems to draw from that psychological western not only its central character motivation (a man driven by a traumatic boyhood experience), but also its central memory fragment: the initially blurred image of a single man approaching, step by step, superimposed on the desertscape, his left arm (the same arm Callum lost to the gun battle in *Pursued*) raised to grasp a coat slung over his shoulder. This image, accompanied each time on the soundtrack by the nondiegetic wail of a harmonica, appears twice to the character Harmonica (Charles Bronson), and then once more, this time in focus, as a preface to the revelation of the traumatic past event.

Here, as in *Pursued*, a recurrent but unfocused and incomplete image and musical theme haunt a character's memory and also the film's mise-en-scène. The association with *Pursued* is even stronger for the fact that, while we assume Harmonica knows why he's hunting Frank (that is, we assume he recalls the incident he's avenging), the initial blurring and increasing clarity of Frank's (Henry Fonda's) image—for it is he who comes—evoke a process of memory retrieval that is unmotivated by the narrative alone but very suggestive of what Jeb undergoes in *Pursued*. Of course, the use of soft focus is a practical solution to the need to withhold Frank's identity from viewers. Whatever its intent, the device itself constructs the traumatic past as a quantity that may only be purchased on the installment plan. *Knowing* is represented identically to *remembering*, as a progressive transaction entered into jointly by viewers and characters.

Frayling may have neglected the association of *Once Upon a Time* with *Pursued* because he takes "the impact of technological developments on the Western frontier" to be the main theme of the film.[55] What I want to show is that such issues of frontier history *are* quite central but that, far from overwhelming the aspects of the film concerned with the man who came killing, they are inextricably bound to this image of adult male violence.

Frank is not only a killer, but a child killer and sadist to boot. Near the start of the film, and in the narrative present, he and his men sneak up on the McBain homestead where the (iconically European) wedding feast is being prepared. There they slaughter the entire family, minus the bride—McBain's second wife, who has not yet arrived. This is the "ballet de mort" that Frayling sees as the "'pessimistic' version of the family dance" in *Shane*, "enjoyed by the rugged homesteaders on Independence Day."[56]

The McBain massacre sequence is also a very appropriate precursor for the climactic flashback that recalls what Frank did to a young Harmonica and his brother years before.[57] Indeed, Frayling indicates several links between the two sequences: the chiming of a bell heard on the soundtrack as the youngest McBain son is shot reverberates with the ringing of the bell from which Harmonica's brother hangs; the subjective point-of-view shots seen as each McBain child meets his or her death are reflected in the ultimate subjective close-ups through which Harmonica and Frank share the final flashback.

237

Figs. 10.5 and 10.6. Harmonica's memory in *Once Upon a Time in the West* (Sergio Leone, 1968). Frank (Henry Fonda) approaches.

Frayling could go further. The "balletic" qualities, the "'fantasy' violence," the "flamboyance," and the intense stylization that Frayling locates in the film are, for me, telling indicators that the film's traumatic plot conveys a meaningful fantasy logic in which things are what they seem . . . and more. First of all, matching up the two sequences eyeball to eyeball editorially speaking, puts Timmy McBain (the youngest child) in the position of the boy Harmonica. The earlier sequence is constructed of alternating close-ups of the boy and his adult male killer, interrupted only by close-ups of Frank's gun barrel. A similar exchange of close-ups between Harmonica and Frank marks the climactic sequence, although this time the close-ups are periodically interrupted by shots of Harmonica's brother (the literal victim) and by Frank's men looking on (in both sequences Frank's actions are performed for an audience).

The first sequence ends focused not on Timmy but on a close-up of the gun that kills him. We never see him fall. Instead, the image that follows the gunshot is an out-of-focus shot of a steaming locomotive accompanied by the startling sound of the train's whistle. We have been transported into the adjacent scene, one that takes place elsewhere, geographically and narratively. However, the image of the boy's fall is provided after all—with a difference—in the climactic scene: here we see a boy fall, and that boy is Harmonica, falling to the ground as his brother hangs. Moreover, the climactic flashback sequence not only shows but *dwells on* the formerly elided fall by depicting it in slow motion and by repeating it a second time: we see it first as Harmonica's memory (we assume) and then as Frank's (we assume). Harmonica is Timmy.

Harmonica would then have to rise from the dead to take revenge on Frank. And, in fact, although Frayling does not discuss the fantasy logic in which Timmy and Harmonica are linked, he does see Harmonica as a revenant.[58] "The massacre at Cattle Corner station, which opens the film, ends with four bodies lying near the railroad line," writes Frayling. "[B]ut, some hours later, one of them rises from the dead, with work still to be done. Harmonica . . . exists in a different dimension to the rest of the characters. . . ."[59] His "extradimensionality" and his connection to Timmy are also expressed by his possession of Frank's name. Timmy is killed for knowing Frank's name. His death is preceded by the following exchange between Frank and one of his men:

> Man: "What are you gonna do with this one, Frank?"
> Frank: "Now that you've called me by name . . . "

Frank's sentence ends with a bang. But the knowledge of Frank's identity that died with Timmy lives on in Harmonica, whose first words in the film are "Where's Frank?" One could say that Harmonica rises from the dead three times: first, as the boy he once was, rising from the ground beside his brother's suspended body in the wake of Frank's cruelty; second, as a kind of reincarnated Timmy, in possession of the knowledge that killed him; and third, from the shoot-out at Cattle Corner. This is the triply overdetermined premature death and resurrection of the child/man Timmy/Harmonica that is avenged by Frank's fall. For fall he does when he loses the final duel, and from right to left into close-up as did the boy Timmy/Harmonica.

Frank, like Callum, is a bad and violent man. And, also like Callum, he is ultimately dispatched by a grown-up boy. The reader may not be surprised, therefore, when I argue further that Frank, again like Callum, occupies the role of the violent outsider *and* that of the (violent) father in the fantasy structure of the film. Three main scenes solidify this association: the McBain massacre, the final memory/duel, and an additional sequence that bears the marks of another primal scene analogous to the one in *Pursued.*

First of all, Frank is closely linked to the only father of the film, Brett McBain, and linked, furthermore, through images and acts of violence. If the last shot of the McBain massacre sequence is up the barrel of Frank's gun, the first shot of that same sequence is of the double barrel of McBain's shotgun (being employed on a partridge hunt with Timmy). And if Brett McBain isn't the child murderer Frank is, he is retrospectively linked to Frank by a violent act that turns out to be one of his last: he slaps his eldest son hard. Through a metonymic process, McBain's gun

239

Figs. 10.7, 10.8, and 10.9. A succession of shots in which Harmonica (Charles Bronson) appears at first to be watching Frank and Jill (Claudia Cardinale).

240

finds its substitute in Frank's hand and a shot takes the place of a slap. Director Sergio Leone is here modifying the Hollywood tradition. The good father whose death Timmy would have avenged had he survived is associated from the start with his own son's killer. Frank is McBain.

This substitution is furthered when Frank sleeps with (rapes) McBain's wife Jill in a delayed and distorted consummation of what would have taken place had McBain survived his marriage banquet. Frank rapes Jill, all the while threatening either to marry her or kill her, while Harmonica peers through the lace-curtained window. Or so we believe at first. In the subsequent shot we realize, retrospectively, that Harmonica's gaze through the window belongs not to the original scene but to the next one: the window Harmonica is looking through is not that of Jill's room but rather that of the hotel bar where her property is being auctioned off. Frayling provides this ambiguous transition as evidence of how Harmonica "is always there" even if it means being in two places at once.[60] I think the transition also simultaneously suggests and denies the familial relations and replacements that obtain in the film. Timmy as witness to paternal violence is hereby replaced by Harmonica as (non)witness to (extra)familial violence in this extended primal scene.

In light of these earlier scenes, the climactic duel is clearly Oedipal. In dispatching Frank, Harmonica not only achieves his long-sought revenge but gains free access to Jill as well. Where Ma Callum's desire for Jeb (apart from her desire for him as a son and later son-in-law) may be discerned only through an interpretive substitution of Thorley for Ma,[61] Jill's desire for Harmonica is referred to overtly by Cheyenne (Jason Robards), a character who loiters on the premises of the film. Thus, as was the case for the character Jeb Rand, Harmonica's manhood is secured in and through remembering and acting against a violent father figure, gaining the right to take his place.

Furthermore, Harmonica's authority over Frank is contingent on getting Frank to remember the assault he perpetrated years ago on Harmonica's brother, and on Harmonica himself, for it is Harmonica who is traumatized—the brother is merely dead. Harmonica bides his time throughout the film, waiting for just the right moment to shoot Frank. He waits for an unhurried interlude where time may be allotted not only to kill Frank but to remind him "at the point of death," of the incident that made this confrontation inevitable.

Thus the face-off, when it occurs, is handled as a mix of remembered and lived actions, past and present comingled. In the past, Frank approaches (his younger look achieved in part by the beard Fonda sports). Then we see Frank in the present, beardless, taking up his position for the duel. Harmonica's fall (a past event, twice represented) is echoed by Frank's fall to the ground as he is vanquished (in the present) by the grown-up Harmonica. And then we have Harmonica's memories of the hanging itself, represented here with a distinct antirealist bent featuring extreme angles (the high angle shot of the gibbet that would correspond to nobody's actual perspective) and asynchronous sound (as when we see the brother mouth a speech that isn't heard as dialogue).

Thus is emphasized the psychic dimension of trauma, and, significantly, the representation of memory as a receding vision. Traumatic westerns figure memory as compensatory, as a phenomenon that stands in for what can never be perfectly known. Frank's memory is a recovered one—he had forgotten the events that he is now being reminded of. Harmonica's memory is continuous, supposedly. And yet

241

these representational extremes, like the blurring of Frank's image in its initial appearances, suggest an incomplete purchase on the very memory that motivates the entire narrative. True, we are provided with a scene that fills in the motivation for Harmonica's otherwise enigmatic actions, and we're given no reason to doubt the veracity of the memory when it is finally provided—the "gist" of the traumatic events is intact. However, the formal qualities of this climatic sequence along with the earlier memory images suggest that there is something more at stake than the question of what, exactly, happened. Why, for example, is Harmonica not "cured" of his need to move on once the joint goals of killing Frank and making him remember are achieved? Why is his last line to Jill "Gotta go" instead of "Gotta come"? Why does Harmonica's "extradimensional" mood overspill the revenge framework?

I contend that all of these strategies, the mixing of past and present, the intercutting of a continuous memory (Harmonica's) with a recovered one (Frank's), the marked absence of synched sound in certain places, and the twisted violence of the traumatic scene, combine to achieve the film's symbolic annihilation of realist strategies as a means of knowing. But if it does annihilate realist strategies as a means of knowing, if this film is traumatic, then what is it that cannot be known, realistically? The murderousness of the son, I would argue, and the relationship of this to land possession.

In *Once Upon a Time in the West* the "primal scene" in which Harmonica seems to be peering in Jill's window is also securely tied to inheritance—in this case the inheritance of land worth "thousands of thousands" as the character Cheyenne puts it ("Millions," Harmonica corrects). As I have indicated, it isn't really Jill's window that Harmonica is looking through, but that of the auction house. We are fooled initially not only because of the editorial sequence (the shot of Harmonica looking follows a shot of Frank raping Jill but precedes a shot of Jill auctioning off her property), but because the lace at the window is more suggestive of a brothel or of Jill, a former prostitute who wears lace, than of a setting where business is transacted. In fact, this confusion between the two locales and between business and sexual conduct exemplifies Wexman's perception about the inextricable connection that obtains in westerns between "the right to possess women" and "the right to possess land." I would go even further to argue that, as with *Pursued*, the connection made in the interstices of these two scenes is one of generational conflict.

Structurally, Harmonica and Frank are constituted as rivals around the rape of Jill and the possession of property. Harmonica defends Jill from Frank's men, and yet he also stands in for Frank, with the dangling train station sign as a signifier of what's at stake. Harmonica haunts Jill's environs. Three visits prior to the shoot-out (which "happens" to take place outside Jill's window) seem particularly significant: first, we sense Harmonica's presence outside the window; we hear the strains of his instrument as Jill discovers the miniature train, train station, and town buildings that Brett McBain had stored in a trunk; second, Jill discovers Harmonica staring down at her from a jagged hole at the top of the barn as she prepares to abandon the farmhouse property; third is the visit that includes Harmonica's glance through the auction house window.

On the first occasion, Jill barricades the door and readies a rifle to defend herself against the unseen figure lurking outside in the dark. But the menace she senses is elided by the coming of morning, handled across a single, sudden cut from the dark of night framed by the window to the light of day. Any questions the viewers may have about what Harmonica would do to Jill were he to enter (or did do for all we know) are left unanswered.

Thus, the scene in which Harmonica appears, rather magically, atop the barn functions as a kind of delayed response. After a dolly in to his silhouetted figure against the sky, Harmonica comes forward toward Jill. He rips the lace from her bosom and states, "Once you've killed four, it's easy to make it five." He then pushes her down on a haystack, his palm pressed across her heaving breast. This is the cinematic language of rape.

We come to realize, retrospectively, that Harmonica acts to protect Jill from Frank's men who have "come killing" ("He not only plays, he can shoot too," observes Cheyenne), and that his dialogue about having killed four refers to Frank's actions and not to Harmonica's own. And yet the delay, along with the mise-en-scène and dialogue of the moment, combine to open a duration over which there abides the suggestion of an assault, sexual and otherwise. Thus the rivalry between Harmonica and Frank is figured not only as that of a good man against a bad one but also as that of an interchangeable pair. Harmonica is Frank.

And both are further linked to McBain. When Jill sees the piles of lumber her husband has ordered, she is mystified. Mystified, that is, until she sees the unpainted sign. Then she finally realizes the nature and extent of her late husband's plans: to build a town called Sweetwater around the water from his well, water that the future westward moving trains will require. A quick zoom into a close-up of Jill communicates the moment of her realization, and this is further supported by a cut to the toy station sign that she had previously held in puzzlement. Three shots later Jill is back at the house searching frantically for the miniature, which slowly comes into frame, suspended from Frank's extended hand. There follows Frank's rape of Jill. This sequence is interrupted, though, by a cut back to the piled lumber, which is now being surveyed by Harmonica and Cheyenne. In this way, parallel editing allows a close-up of Harmonica at the building site immediately to precede a close-up of Frank and Jill as his assault on her proceeds. In that shot the camera rotates ninety degrees in a counterclockwise direction and quickly pulls back out the window revealing, from that distance, the bars of the headboard that now frame Frank and Jill. At the end of the sequence comes the close-up of Harmonica referred to earlier, the one that precedes the auction scene.

243

Thus, not only is Frank's sexual assault on Jill fitted in between two close-ups of Harmonica looking, but the sequencing also forges a link between Harmonica's gaze at the lumber yard and his subsequent gaze through the window. Plotwise, Harmonica has no thought of marrying Jill to take possession of Sweetwater station. Editorially, though, the film's sequencing raises the stakes of sexual possession by anteing up economic issues. Harmonica is McBain.

Recall, though, that Harmonica is also Timmy. And these two premises lead to the crux of the matter. *Once Upon a Time in the West* pivots on two intergenerational pairs: (1) the good father and son, McBain and Timmy, and (2) the bad man and the good boy, Frank and Harmonica. The almost perfect interchangeability of these characters enables the violence of the Harmonica-Frank pair to bleed over onto the Timmy-McBain pair. Harmonica has his own reasons for wanting Frank dead. But if Frank takes McBain's place with Jill and the land, and Harmonica stands in for Timmy in the film's fantasy structure, then the violence of the primal scene in which the boy fears the father and wants him out of the way may be enacted covertly.

The supreme irony broached by the characteristic overtones of paternal violence in the familial succession western is that whereas the father's life can secure the son's dominion, it simultaneously blocks his succession. In other words, inheritance necessarily involves the death of the father. The option of mother-son incest may also be present (Ma Callum and Jeb, per Willemen; Timmy and Jill per yours truly if *Once Upon a Time*'s relations of looking were to be carried further), for that, too, allows intergenerational succession while keeping the estate in the family. Thus, for reasons of property as well as for reasons Freud described through the concepts of Oedipality and castration anxiety, the death of the good father is at the same time a fear and a wish. What we find here, then, are both Wexman's "odd incestuous aura" *and* an oddly patricidal impulse that these films are at pains to justify.

The larger argument that follows from the patterns I've set out is that violent conquest is as central to the paternal succession western as it is to the captivity narrative, and that the murderous father is as overdetermined a filmic creature as is the savage Indian. Both attract the brunt of the son's/settler's fears and both must be vanquished in the struggle for possession of the land. There are certain differences between the pattern of the captivity narrative and that of the familial succession narrative. In the captivity narrative the savage Indians serve as the projections of settler violence, whereas in the narrative of familial succession the bad man's badness (his infanticidal tendency) justifies the patricidal impulses of the son. There are also certain important differences in the historical bases for these respective narrative patterns and their function in the filmic imagination. Fathers are perennial in the sense that they return renewed, and in greater numbers even, with each successive generation. Indians, on the other hand, while demonstating a powerful centuries-long tenacity, have seen their various tribal ranks greatly diminished. Sons are always young. But America, for better and worse, has grown up. Nevertheless, the two groups of films evince a telling similarity in representing violent fathers and savage Indians, respectively, as the objects of the ambivalent memory of their heirs, and, specifically, as projections that serve to disavow but not to nullify the violence of the pioneer sons of America.

Virginia Wright Wexman draws on Patricia Limerick's paradigm-shifting conception of the frontier not as an "outpost of civilization" but as a "line of demarcation between different cultures" to argue that the western genre's emphasis on land goes hand in hand with issues of "cultural dominance" defined in terms of "racial privilege."[62] Limerick notes that "Western history has been an ongoing competition for legitimacy—for the right to claim for oneself and sometimes for one's group the status of legitimate beneficiary of Western resources. This intersection of ethnic diversity with property allocation unified Western history."[63] A scene in *Red River* provides Wexman with a particularly good filmic application of this principle when John Wayne as Tom Dunson shoots the representatives of Hispanic landowner Don Diego and appropriates his land, saying, "That's too much land for one man to own."[64] And the sequence is even more racially charged, I would add, since, historically speaking, one assumes that the acreage a real counterpart of Tom Dunson would have wrested from a real counterpart of Don Diego would have been land previously occupied by Native Americans.

It seems to me that the formal elements of paternal succession and of captivity westerns exemplify in filmic terms this revised notion of the frontier in western history in no small part because their point of contact is the intersection of "ethnic diversity" and "property allocation." The two groups are part of the same historiographic project within the western imagination.

John Sayles's 1996 film *Lone Star* interweaves the trauma of paternal succession with that of the trauma of race in a way that makes the film an apt one with which to conclude this chapter. Like *Pursued, Lone Star* revolves around a son who seeks knowledge of his dead father as a means of gaining insight into his own life. In both films there are adults of the father's generation who refuse to divulge the knowledge the son desires. In particular, both films contain a female character who harbors a secret: her adulterous relationship with the son's father, which relationship affords our respective protagonists with sisters of sorts and the films with an aura of incest. In *Lone Star*, even more so than in *Pursued*, all of this is placed in the context of disputed individual, national, and racialized land rights.

All these similarities notwithstanding, the most important one of all for this discussion is the two films' comparable emphasis on memory as an avenue to past knowledge. Where Jeb Rand wracks his own brain for the broken shards of memory, Sam Deeds (Chris Cooper) in *Lone Star* looks both within and to others, those who *will* speak, to piece together a record of his father's "deeds" and those of the father's contemporaries. As in *Pursued,* past events in *Lone Star* are rendered as subjective flashbacks.

These flashbacks are motivated by sheriff Sam Deeds's efforts to discover what role, if any, his father, the late sheriff Buddy Deeds played in the death of Charlie Wade, the corrupt sheriff of Frontera, Texas, whose job Buddy took over after Charlie's death. For reasons that are never fully explained, Sam's disrespect for his father is so great that he believes his father to have been capable of the murder of Charlie Wade, and the traumatic past events of the film mainly concern who killed Charlie Wade and why he deserved his fate.

But actually, of the seven flashback sequences in the film, three do not revolve around Wade and Deeds. Instead, they revolve around Sam's relationship with Pilar, a Mexican-American history teacher with whom he had a relationship when both were teenagers that is being reconsummated in the present. As it turns out, in seeking to know Buddy's past, Sam reveals an earth-shattering fact with major implications for his own life: Buddy had a long-term extramarital affair with Pilar's mother, Mercedes, a successful Latina restaurant owner; Buddy and Pilar are half brother and sister (as readers of this volume may well know from the film itself or from Tomás Sandoval's insightful chapter).

The revelation is handled, in a manner characteristic of the traumatic western, through the blurring of the boundary between past and present. Director Sayles's deliberate aesthetic choice, noticed by reviewers of the film, was to dispense with the convention of the editorial dissolve between past and present in this and other flashbacks in the film. In *Pursued,* for example, the pan right from the interior of the cabin at Bear Paw Butte to the boy Jeb hiding below the trap door is accompanied by a dissolve used to connote the spectator's backward time travel. In *Lone Star* the traditional dissolve has been replaced by a continuous pan that links two *contiguous* spaces but two *disparate* time frames. The result is a hybrid zone of memory.

In keeping with the film's revisionist impulse, the truth about the past is represented as being multifaceted, subject to competing interests, and contingent upon the memory and will of the teller—in this case the various narrators of flashbacks who include two African Americans, a Mexican man, and a Mexican American. Sam himself was not an actual witness to the events he seeks to retrieve. They happened during his childhood and are part of his father's life and identity. They are part of what Sam needs to know to mature. But these catastrophic events were lost to him even at the time of their occurrence.

In the end Sam finds out that it was not Buddy Deeds who killed Wade, but rather Deeds's deputy, Hollis, who pulled the trigger on Wade before Wade could slaughter an African-American barkeeper as he previously had a Mexican workingman. And yet a certain ambivalence about the father abides thoughout the body of the film, covertly, as in *Pursued*. Buddy Deeds the good (?) sheriff/father is linked to his predecessor in various ways. For one thing, the Rio County sheriff's badge identifies Wade (both when it is unearthed at the start of the film and when we see it on the door of his sheriff's car), but it also identifies Buddy Deeds. It is prominent on his chest on many occasions in the flashbacks, and also when Sam uses a magnifying glass to examine old photos of Buddy (in one of the film's several photo memoir sequences that are accompanied only by the nondiegetic sound of a wailing guitar). In fact, it is only when Buddy is shirtless in a photo, posed waist deep in water on a pleasure outing with his mistress Mercedes, that he is without his badge. Ironically, it is this image of Buddy, and not the incarnation of Buddy-as-sheriff, that does Sam the most damage, for this is the image Sam shows Pilar as evidence that they are half brother and sister. It is this photo that will force Sam to break off the romance with Pilar or to sleep with her ever after with the knowledge that theirs is an incestuous coupling. Thoughts of the past will not be banished from their union.

Sam's patrilineal researches in *Lone Star* backfire all around. That Buddy is not after all Wade's killer renders Sam's longtime animosity misguided. That the townspeople admire Buddy all the more because of their mistaken belief that he *is* Wade's killer is simply more of the same old elitist disregard for truth that has galled Sam all along.[65] That Buddy had to have Mercedes before Sam could have Pilar must be the last straw. The trauma of succession in *Lone Star* lies in its impossibility. Sam can't have Pilar because Buddy had her mother. Or can he? As with *Pursued* and *Once Upon a Time in the West*, here too in *Lone Star* a series of substitutions simultaneously mask and reveal the violence of the father-son relationship and the salience of generational conflict. Fathers: can't live with 'em, can't live without 'em.

Poised on the border between the fictional narratives they inhabit and the real history of American settlement, traumatic representations such as those discussed here are best read through a vernier attuned to memory and history both—*they cannot be taken at face value*. Sometimes the best evidence that a traumatic event really did occur is the impossibility of its overt expression. This is true for the pioneer sons in westerns where succession and/or land acquisition form the wrenching problem of the narrative. Past events are intransigent and ungraspable. They cannot be worked through, but only reexperienced as "distressing recollections," "recurrent dreams," "hallucinations, and dissociative episodes." This is also true for spectators for whom "distressing recollections" and the lot become a traumatic mise en scène. Thematized catastrophic past events are only partially perceptible—they happened before the plot got underway, they are revealed only later, in flashback, their particulars are obscured by the rising smoke of half-burned homesteads. And for the spectators, all of this is magnified both by the shifting character

247

identifications that typify the traumatic westerns—the spectator's trauma is pervasive and inchoate—and by the actual relationships that inhere among what was, what is, and what is being shown. The trauma these fictions embody is also profoundly historical.

Here I want to affirm that even where they are fictional or inauthentic, westerns still elicit a reading practice based on historical and generic understanding. Captivity narratives are compelling because the fantasy structures they entail veil at the same time that they express another, even grislier, trauma—that of Native-American genocide. The same goes for familial succession westerns. The Oedipal conflicts that mark these narratives abide at the intersection of characters and spectators, and personal and public history. The trauma they depict expresses and also hides the inevitable ambivalence of inheritance. This is not to say that in the future American land holdings cannot be more equitably distributed, but rather to say that the traumatic western embeds a narrativized version of history contextualized by familial and/or racial difference as its originary trauma. This is the blood-wet ground of history that seeps up through traumatic westerns, creating sodden patches for the spectator to traverse.

notes

Thanks are due to Edward Branigan and Chuck Wolfe for their insightful comments on this essay. I dedicate the essay to the memory of my inspiring teacher from many years ago, Andrew Britton.

1. Christopher Frayling, *Spaghetti Westerns: Cowboys and Europeans from Karl May to Sergio Leone* (New York: Routledge and Kegan Paul, 1981), 200, 203.
2. Neither is authentically historical. Moreover, films are much more emphatic than literary sources in presenting captivity as the white man's tale in that they foreground the thoughts and actions of the rescuer rather than the captive. If films were to show the position of the captive (and in those exceptional cases where they do [*Little Big Man*, for example]), then issues such as adaptation to Native-American life would come more to the fore and captivity wouldn't so thoroughly justify genocide. See Barbara Mortimer, "From Monument Valley to Vietnam: Revisions of the American Captivity Narrative in Hollywood Film," Ph.D. diss., Emory University, 1990 (Ann Arbor: U.M.I., 1991); the dissertation includes a historical discussion of American captivity narratives as well as chapters on *The Searchers, The Unforgiven, Two Rode Together,* and *Comanche Station.*
3. Maureen Turim, *Flashbacks in Film: Memory and History* (New York: Routledge, 1989).
4. I'm relying on Robert Burgoyne's discussion of "generic memory" in *Film Nation: Hollywood Looks at U.S. History* (Minneapolis: University of Minnesota Press, 1997), 7–8.
5. Ward Churchill, "Lawrence of South Dakota," in his *Fantasies of the Master Race: Literature, Cinema and the Colonization of American Indians* (Monroe, Maine: Common Courage Press, 1992), 245.
6. Steven Spielberg, quoted in Brian Henderson, "*The Searchers*: An American Dilemma," *Film Quarterly* 34, no. 2 (1980–81): 9, from an article by Stuart Byron, "*The Searchers*: Cult Movie of the New Hollywood," *New York*, March 5, 1979, 45–48.

janet walker

7. Janey Place, "*The Searchers*," in *The Western Films of John Ford* (Secaucus, N.J.: Citidel Press, 1974), 163.

8. See Peter Lehman's discussion of this look in relation to *The Searchers*' use of offscreen space in "An Absence Which Becomes a Legendary Presence: John Ford's Structured Use of Off-Screen Space," *Wide Angle* 2, no. 4 (1978): 36–42, and in "Texas 1868/American 1956: *The Searchers*," in *Close Viewings: An Anthology of New Film Criticism* (Tallahassee: The Florida State University Press, 1990). For recent discussions of the passage in terms of its use of a musical theme see Kathryn Kalinak, "Music and the West: John Ford, Max Steiner, and *The Searchers*," unpublished paper delivered at the Society for Cinema Studies Conference, San Diego, April 4–8, 1998, and Arthur M. Eckstein, "Darkening Ethan: John Ford's *The Searchers* (1956) from Novel to Screenplay to Screen," *Cinema Journal* 38, no. 1 (1998), 3–24. Both scholars identify the nondiegetic music we hear while we see Ethan looking back toward home as the Civil War song "Lorena."

9. John Ford reputedly said of John Wayne's performance in Howard Hawks's *Red River*, "I didn't know the sonofabitch could act."

10. Alan LeMay, *The Searchers* (Boston: Gregg Press, 1978; 1954), 21.

11. This poster may be found in a press book for *The Searchers* in the Warner Brothers Collection, Doheny Library, University of Southern California.

12. Mortimer, "Monument Valley," 38, also makes this point that the audience is not subjected to a view of Martha's body, nor of Lucy's.

13. The phrase is borrowed from Lawrence L. Langer, *Holocaust Testimonies: The Ruins of Memory* (New Haven, Conn.: Yale University Press, 1991).

14. LeMay, *The Searchers*, 13–14.

15. Ibid., 13.

16. Ibid., 6.

17. Ibid., 5–6.

18. Though not with specific regard to trauma, others before me have written about the importance in the western of real and imagined landscapes, and about the landscape as a projection for characters' thoughts. See, for example, Leonard Engel, ed., *The Big Empty: Essays on Western Landscapes as Narrative* (Albuquerque: University of New Mexico Press, 1994). The volume contains Richard Hutson's essay "Sermons in Stone: Monument Valley in *The Searchers*," in which he writes that "landscape projects the human drama as a silhouetting effect of its presence. But it is also true that Monument Valley is itself a silhouette produced by the human narrative" (188). Or, as Jim Kitses writes (in a subsection, "Landscape") about the shoot-out among the crags that ends *Winchester '73*, "The terrain is so coloured by the action that it finally seems an inner landscape, the unnatural world of a disturbed mind." Kitses, "Anthony Mann: The Overreacher," in *Horizons West* (Bloomington: Indiana University Press, 1969), 72.

19. Cathy Caruth, introduction to *Trauma: Explorations in Memory*, ed. Cathy Caruth (Baltimore: Johns Hopkins University Press, 1995), 4–5.

20. Entry on "Posttraumatic Stress Disorder," in *Diagnostic and Statistical Manual of Mental Disorders*, 4th ed. (*DSM-IV*) (Washington, D.C.: American Psychiatric Association, 1994), 428.

21. Judith Herman, M.D., "Crime and Memory," *Bulletin of the American Academy of Psychiatry Law*, 23, no. 1 (1995): 7. Thanks are due to Dr. Herman for answering my query about perpetrator narratives with a copy of her article.

22. Ibid., 7.

23. Ibid., 11.

24. Janet Walker, "The Traumatic Paradox: Documentary Films, Historical Fictions, and Cataclysmic Past Events," *Signs* 22, no. 4 (1997): 803–25.

25. See, for example, Lenore Terr, *Unchained Memories: The True Stories of*

Traumatic Memories, Lost and Found (New York: Basic Books, 1994); and Elizabeth Waites, *Trauma and Survival: Post-Traumatic and Dissociative Disorders in Women* (New York: W. W. Norton, 1993). Thanks are due to Dr. Terr for allowing me to consult with her by phone about perpetrator narratives.

26. For the sake of scholarship I should indicate that the research I'm describing is part of a polemic; other memory researchers including Elizabeth Loftus and Richard Ofshe believe that memories cannot be "lost and found" but that they can be "induced," and that incest memories are being induced in the minds of misused daughters.

27. Ian Hacking, *Rewriting the Soul: Multiple Personality and the Sciences of Memory* (Princeton, N.J.: Princeton University Press, 1995), 250.

28. Herman, "Crime and Memory," 13.

29. Previous authors have noted the doubling of hero and "savage" in the western. See, for example, Janey Place's identification, in the chapter cited above, of similarities in the portrayals of Ethan and Scar in *The Searchers.*

30. Hacking, *Rewriting the Soul,* 250.

31. Robert Burgoyne, "Native America, *Thunderheart,* and the National Imaginary," in his *Film Nation.*

32. Will Wright, *Sixguns and Society* (Berkeley and Los Angeles: University of California Press, 1975).

33. Virginia Wright Wexman, "Star and Genre: John Wayne, the Western, and the American Dream of the Family on the Land," in her *Creating the Couple: Love, Marriage, and Hollywood Performance* (Princeton, N.J.: Princeton University Press, 1993).

34. Ibid., 88

35. Ibid., especially 75–89.

36. Ibid., 75.

37. Ibid., 82.

38. Edward Shorter, *The Making of the Modern Family* (New York: Basic Books, 1975), 55. Quoted in Wexman, "Star and Genre," 76.

39. Ibid., 82–83.

40. Ibid., 108.

41. Ibid., 105. Wexman then proceeds with a psychoanalytically informed discussion of male and female bodies in the western landscape that includes a critical application of Klaus Theweleit's study of the fascist "soldier-male" figure (*Male Fantasies,* vol. 2: *Male Bodies: Psychoanalyzing the White Terror,* trans. Erica Carter et al. [Minneapolis: University of Minnesota Press, 1989]). Soldier-males, according to Wexman's account of Theweleit's ideas, are "not yet fully born" and they face as their "central psychic issue" "the necessity of separating from the mother and preserving their body integrity in the face of fears of dissolution" (105). This trauma is played out in the western, Wexman argues, by the male assumption of the western costume as body armor and of the gun as the perfect weapon because the gun "can discharge and still remain whole" (112, quoting Theweleit). The female and especially the mother, on the other hand, is embodied by the simultaneously seductive and inhospitable landscape of the west. Given this situation, the shoot-out "constitutes the most significant violent response to the frustration caused by the vision of the cold mother" and it "assuages" the male anxiety represented in the western without ever really transcending the trauma of male psychic life (111–12).

42. Paul Willeman, "The Fugitive Subject," in *Raoul Walsh,* ed. Phil Hardy (Edinburgh: Edinburgh Film Festival/Vineyard Press, 1974), 63–89; Andrew Britton, "*Pursued:* A Reply to Paul Willemen," *Framework* 11, no. 4 (1976), reprinted in *The Book of Westerns,* ed. Ian Cameron and Douglas Pye (New York: Continuum, 1996), 196–205.

43. Britton, "A Reply," 13.

44. Willemen discusses the gap that opens up between the film's omniscient narration and Jeb's supposed role as narrator as evidence that the film problematizes the ideal of the unified subject.

45. Willemen, "The Fugitive Subject," 68.

46. Ibid., 83; emphasis added.

47. Jean LaPlanche and J.-B. Pontalis (*The Language of Psychoanalysis*, trans. Donald Nicholson-Smith, New York: W. W. Norton, 1973). Quoted in Willemen, "The Fugitive Subject," 77.

48. Willemen, "The Fugitive Subject," 82.

49. Ibid., 78.

50. Ibid.

51. This lends credence to Britton's insight that Jeb is "predicting," since in the end Callum does indeed appear accompanied by a lynch mob in search of Jeb.

52. LaPlanche and Pontalis, *Language*, quoted in Willemen, "The Fugitive Subject," 77. With this quote and other passages Willemen provides evidence for the point he ends up disavowing.

53. Precisely because this is a limited Freudian reading, one could argue, as Britton does, that if the boy character can be shown *not* to desire the mother, then the psychoanalytic import is thereby nullified.

54. Caruth, introduction, 9.

55. Frayling, *Spaghetti Westerns*, 194.

56. Ibid., 153.

57. Frayling indicates that the scene is loosely based on an actual historical occurrence; ibid., 125–26.

58. If we were to psychologize a character, we might also say that Harmonica is dead in the sense that he is stuck on an incident from childhood and cannot, therefore, develop into a sexually mature man. He tells Jill McBain he might return "sometime," but this is an even more dubious promise than that which Wyatt Earp (Henry Fonda) makes to Clementine in *My Darling Clementine*.

59. Frayling, *Spaghetti Westerns*, 200.

60. Ibid., 202

61. When Britton denies any Oedipal undertones in the Ma Callum/Jeb Rand relationship, saying that the young Jeb pulls away when Ma goes to embrace him, he fails to consider the potential feelings from the parental side (the mother's desire for the son) as well as the role of fantasy structures in general. Does Ma Callum literally desire to have intercourse with Jeb? We have no reason to think so. Does the film interpose Thorley as an appropriate love object between Jeb and Ma's desire? I believe it does. When Ma carries Jeb off in place of her dead lover she plunks him down next to Thorley in Thorley's bed. And when Jeb is about to be hanged Ma shoots Grant Callum, thus simultaneously saving her daughter's lover and avenging the death of her lover.

62. Wexman, "Star and Genre," 70, 76.

63. Patricia Nelson Limerick, *A Legacy of Conquest: The Unbroken Past of the American West* (New York: W. W. Norton, 1988), 27, quoted in Wexman, "Star and Genre," 76.

64. Wexman, "Star and Genre," 91.

65. Buddy Deeds is "the man who shot [but didn't really] Charlie Wade." In the comparison between *Lone Star* and *The Man Who Shot Liberty Valance*, it is as if Ranse Stoddard had lived his whole life in Shinbone.

251

contributors

Peter J. Bloom is Assistant Professor of English in the Film Studies Program at Indiana University-Purdue University at Indianapolis. He has published in French and English on various aspects of French colonial cinema, early cinema, scientific colonialism, and postcolonial Francophone visual culture. He is currently working on a book entitled *Colonial Suture: The Cinema of French Hygienic Reform*.

Corey K. Creekmur is Associate Professor of English, Cinema, and Comparative Literature at the University of Iowa, where he is also the director of the Institute for Cinema and Culture. He is the coeditor of *Out in Culture: Gay, Lesbian, and Queer Essays on Popular Culture*, and the author of *Cattle Queens and Lonesome Cowboys: Gender and Sexuality in the Western* as well as a forthcoming study of the film musical.

Claudia Gorbman is Professor of Film Studies in the Interdisciplinary Arts and Sciences program at the University of Washington, Tacoma. She is the author of *Unheard Melodies: Narrative Film Music* (1987) and of numerous articles on film music and sound. She has translated three books by Michel Chion, most recently *A Cinema Odyssey: Kubrick's 2001* (2001).

Kathryn Kalinak is Professor of English and Film Studies at Rhode Island College. She is the author of *Settling the Score: Music and the Classical Hollywood Film* (1992), and has published widely in the field of film music. Her recent work has been devoted to the impact of race and ethnicity on the musical score. Her current project, a book-length study of music and the West, is entitled *How the West Was Sung*.

Joy S. Kasson is Bowman and Gordon Gray Professor of American Studies and English at the University of North Carolina at Chapel Hill. Her published works include *Artistic Voyagers: Europe and the American Imagination in the Works of Irving, Cooper, Hawthorne, and Cole* (1982), *Marble Queens and Captives: Women in Nineteenth-Century American Sculpture* (1990), and *Buffalo Bill's Wild West: Celebrity, Memory, and Popular History* (2000).

Alexandra Keller is Visiting Assistant Professor of Film Studies at Smith College. Her book, *Re-Imagining the Frontier: American Westerns since the Reagan Administration* is forthcoming.

Tomás F. Sandoval, Jr. is a Ph.D. candidate in history at the University of California, Berkeley. He is a native Californian and a Chicano. His dissertation is to be an oral history of Latinos in San Francisco, 1945 to 1970.

William G. Simon is Associate Professor of Cinema Studies at New York University. Author of *The Films of Jean Vigo* and a specialist on the work of Orson Welles, he has also contributed articles to journals, including the *Quarterly Review of Film and Video*, *Persistence of Vision*, and *Artforum*, and chapters to a number of anthologies, including the *Alfred Hitchcock Reader*.

Louise Spence is Associate Professor of Media Studies at Sacred Heart University, Connecticut. The coauthor (with Pearl Bowser) of *Writing Himself into History: Oscar Micheaux, His Silent Films, and His Audiences*, her work on film and television has appeared in *Screen*, *Critical Arts*, *Cinema Journal*, *Quarterly Review of Film and Video*, and the *Journal of Film and Video*, as well as several anthologies. Dr. Spence has received two National Endowment for the Humanities grants and a grant from the American Council of Learned Societies.

Melinda Szaloky is a Ph.D. candidate in the Department of Film and Television at UCLA. Her essay on sound theory recently won first prize in the Society for Cinema Studies Student Writing contest and is forthcoming from *Cinema Journal*.

Janet Walker is Professor of Film Studies at the University of California, Santa Barbara. Author of *Couching Resistance: Women, Film, and Psychoanalytic Psychiatry*, and coeditor with Diane Waldman of *Feminism and Documentary*, her current project is *Trauma Cinema*, a book about the representation of catastrophic past events in documentary and fiction film and video.

254

index

index

index

264